PURSUING MILITARY JUSTICE

USCAAF Courtroom, Washington, D.C., 1953–1989

PURSUING MILITARY JUSTICE

VOLUME 2

THE HISTORY OF THE UNITED STATES COURT OF APPEALS FOR THE ARMED FORCES, 1951–1980

Jonathan Lurie

PRINCETON UNIVERSITY PRESS PRINCETON, NEW JERSEY

Published by Princeton University Press, 41 William Street,
Princeton, New Jersey 08540
In the United Kingdom: Princeton University Press,
Chichester, West Sussex

Library of Congress Cataloging-in-Publication Data

Lurie, Jonathan, 1939–
Pursuing military justice : the history of the United States Court of Appeals
for the Armed Forces, 1951–1980 / Jonathan Lurie.
p. cm.
Continues: Arming military justice. c1992.
"Volume II."
Includes bibliographical references and index.
ISBN 0-691-06945-X (alk. paper)
1. United States. Court of Military Appeals—History. 2. Courts-martial
and courts of inquiry—United States—History. I. Title.
KF7667.L874 1997
343.73′0143—dc21 97-19771 CIP

This book has been composed in Times Roman

Princeton University Press books are printed on acid-free paper
and meet the guidelines for permanence and durability of the Committee
on Production Guidelines for Book Longevity of the Council on
Library Resources

http://pup.princeton.edu

Printed in the United States of America

1 3 5 7 9 10 8 6 4 2

For Mac and David,
Deborah and Daniel,
in Memory of Robert Wiss

I am old soldier enough to remember that a commander must run his own show. I am also constitutionalist enough to know that a citizen army without orderly justice will not work. You fellows in the C.M.A. are daily faced with wise decisions between these admirable objectives, and the people of these United States owe you a salute.

Arthur E. Sutherland
Late Bussey Professor of Law,
Harvard Law School (1969)

Contents

List of Illustrations

All illustrations are from the files of the United States Court of Appeals for the Armed Forces and are reproduced with its permission.

Preface

THE EVENTS leading to the enactment of the Uniform Code of Military Justice (UCMJ), which provided for a Court of Military Appeals, have been detailed in the first volume of this study, *Arming Military Justice: The Origins of the United States Court of Military Appeals, 1775–1950.* That book brought the story to May 1950, when legislative passage and presidential approval of the new statute were a certainty, in May 1950. The Code represented, as one of the original three judges aptly put it, "a triumph of diplomacy, parliamentary strategy, and plain horse trading as well as of superior professional competence."[1] One month after President Truman signed the bill, the Korean War began. Understandably preoccupied, he did not get around to appointing the three judges for the new court until May 1951. The Court began to accept petitions and cases in July; it has been functioning ever since.

Justifiably labeled an experiment by its creators, the United States Court of Military Appeals (now known as the U.S. Court of Appeals for the Armed Forces, or USCAAF) has been in existence for more than forty years.[2] Two generations of litigants have appeared before it. More than thirty-thousand lawyers are members of its bar. Its decisions fill over fifty volumes, and its interpretations of the UCMJ and the Manual for Courts-Martial (MCM) are for the most part definitive. This judicial experiment is now a permanent part of the judicial establishment.

Why did Congress establish this Court in 1950? Why not in 1919 or even 1865? What did the legislature intend as its mission? What tradition of military appellate procedure had developed in the armed services? What role did they play in the drafting and ultimate enactment of the statute? How did congressional preferences and the process of politics affect the new legislation?

The first volume furnished answers to these questions. This study focuses on additional issues: To what extent did the new tribunal change administration of military justice? How has it operated since 1951? How did the armed services react to the court? How have members of its bench been selected, and how have the choices reflected political considerations usual for such

Parts of this preface have been "borrowed" from my earlier volume, *Arming Military Justice: Origins of the United States Court of Military Appeals, 1775–1950* (1992).

[1] USCMA Speech File, hereafter cited as SF, August 28, 1951. The speaker was Judge Paul Brosman, who served on the Court from 1951 to 1955. See infra.

[2] In order to avoid confusion, throughout this volume the Court is labeled "The United States Court of Military Appeals," or USCMA—the term by which it was then known.

presidential appointments? What mandate have its judges exercised, and with what success or failure?

Responses to this second set of questions are contained in the following chapters. As with its predecessor, they reflect several themes that are independent yet interconnected.

First is the maturation of the Court as an institution with its own policies, procedures, and personality. Related to this theme is an issue of court identity, both from within and without. The way the judges saw themselves—especially in the Court's early years—differed from the perceptions of other agencies of government, including the military. As will be seen, nagging questions concerning the "extent" to which USCMA was supposed to be an actual Court—similar to other federal appellate tribunals—have troubled its judges. Did Congress intend the Court to be part of the federal judiciary? Or rather, was it a mere administrative agency within the executive branch? Answers to these questions invariably raised the fundamental problem of the Court's legitimacy—a matter about which its judges, at least, had no doubt whatsoever.

Directly related to this problem has been another matter of vital concern to the Court. Since 1951, its judges have made extraordinary efforts—thus far unsuccessful—to persuade Congress to grant them life tenure. For reasons to be explored in some detail, the jurists of USCMA concluded early on that such permanence was essential in order to function properly as an independent federal appellate tribunal. Why have they maintained this position with such consistency, and why has Congress been equally consistent in its refusal to depart from the 1951 decision to provide for specific judicial terms, even as the lawmakers reaffirmed the independence and standing of the Court, comparable in prestige and salary to any other federal appellate court?

An additional major theme in USCMA's history has been its relationship to the military, in particular the Judge Advocates General. There is no doubt that Congress was concerned about this issue. What did the lawmakers intend this relationship to be? While mandating cooperation between judges and JAGs, the UCMJ virtually guaranteed conflict as well. Although the code charged the JAGs with the task of making "frequent inspections in the field in supervision of the administration of military justice," it made no mention of any supervisory function for the Court.

Yet an appellate tribunal, described by its creators as the "Supreme Court of the military" would of necessity claim for itself ultimate supervisory jurisdiction of military justice. And in actual fact, the relationship between these two bodies of leadership in military justice has ranged from ill-concealed antagonism, to grudging acceptance, with an occasional spasm of approbation. It has always been guarded. One can argue that this unstable synthesis may indeed have been what Congress anticipated, if not intended. The important point, however, is less the intention than the result, which the following chapters explore in some detail.

Finally, there is the emergence over time of a substantial body of military appellate case law. And, although the above themes are all independent, they rest on this common base. For almost half a century, USCMA has been deciding cases—delineating the permissible limits of acceptable military judicial conduct. How the military and the Congress reacted to its key decisions sometimes affected their relationship to the Court. While of necessity a number of important cases have been discussed in this study, my focus is not legal doctrine as much as institutional evolution.

USCMA's formal decisions are readily available for all to study, but how the Court matured from a new experiment to an established civilian federal tribunal represents a more difficult historical challenge. Indeed, I hope that these volumes will lessen an unfortunate though understandable "impression that the system [of military justice] is fundamentally arcane and inaccessible." Perhaps, civilian accounts of its origins as well as greater civilian practitioner involvement in its procedures will "encourage the free flow" of ideas, analyses, and innovation between the military and civilian justice systems. Both "can benefit from such interaction."[3] In the long run, being subject to rigorous scholarly scrutiny may be of great significance in seeking that military justice attains the highest possible level of performance.

Because these chapters are based in large measure on sources not previously utilized, a few words about them may be appropriate. In the period of the Court's history discussed herein, eleven judges were appointed to its bench. One, Robert Quinn, served for almost twenty-five years (1951–75), including twenty as the Court's Chief Judge. His tenure both as judge and chief judge is the longest in the Court's history. In addition to the chronological files of most outgoing correspondence kept by the Court Clerk, Quinn preserved his own personal files, as well as some interoffice memoranda. Removed from the Court upon Quinn's death, these papers have been in the possession of his children, Robert C. Quinn and Norma Q. Richards, who kindly allowed me to examine and copy from them. They also have donated many of their father's papers to the Court for its own archive.

Although he never lived to see his recollections published, Judge George Latimer prepared and preserved lengthy autobiographical notes. His sons, Professor George Latimer, Jr., and Dr. Ronald Latimer, made them available to me and ultimately to the Court as part of its historical archive. The papers of Homer Ferguson, a former Michigan Senator, whose term on the bench

[3] Eugene R. Fidell, *Guide to the Rules of Practice and Procedure for the United States Court of Appeals for the Armed Forces*, 7th, ed., 1996, 5. Fidell further notes that "many in the civilian bench and bar remain unimpressed by the Court and the system over which it presides in inverse proportion to their knowledge of each." Ibid., 6.

extended from 1956 to 1971, are housed in the Bentley Historical Library at the University of Michigan—and include a number of boxes with material from these years. The papers of North Carolina Senator Sam Ervin, a key sponsor of the Military Justice Act of 1968, are available for study through the Southern Historical Collections at the University of North Carolina, Chapel Hill. With the exception of the Kennedy Library, the various Presidential repositories from Truman through Carter have been of great value.[4] Alfred Proulx, the first Clerk of the Court, kept detailed files on important topics such as the recurring efforts to gain life tenure, or proposed legislative changes to the UCMJ. The "chrono" files as well as these topical materials, and other papers retained by the Court, have been studied and cited for this volume.

Moreover, a number of individuals interested in the relationship between USCMA and military justice during 1975–80 made their own files available to me. I am indebted to Brigadier General D. Wayne Hansen, Asst. JAG, U.S. Army (ret.); Brigadier General John Cooke, JAG Corps, U.S. Army, who from 1975–84 meticulously tracked and analyzed USCMA decisions; Rear Admiral William Miller, TJAG, U.S. Navy (ret.); and Deanne C. Siemer, former General Counsel to the Defense Department. In addition to materials provided by these individuals, including some published items, I conducted a number of oral history interviews with persons involved in the Court's history.

During its almost fifty years of existence, this tribunal has engendered controversy. Thus it is not surprising that individuals saw the same event or interpreted the same decision very differently. Occasionally it has been necessary to rely on a recollection in the absence of written documentation. Rarely, my subjects requested that some of their comments not be recorded, or that other statements not be quoted. I have respected their wishes, but the transcripts themselves will become a part of the Court's history archive.

The following individuals permitted me to record discussions, sometimes extensive, with them concerning military justice and the Court between 1950 and 1980—the period covered in this second volume: William Cook, John Cooke, William Darden, Robert Duncan, Andrew Effron, Robinson Everett, Oliver Gasch, Francis Gindhart, Albert Fletcher, Jr., D. Wayne Hansen, Martin Hoffman, Royce Lamberth, Felix Larkin, George Latimer, George Latimer, Jr., Ronald Latimer, William Miller, Ward Mundy, Matthew Perry, Alfred Proulx, George Prugh, Deanne Siemer, and Darlene Yarborough.

To the extent that the United States Court of Appeals invited me to undertake this study, and that its judges and staff have consistently supported,

[4] I imply no criticism of the Kennedy Library staff who, like all their counterparts, went out of their way to be of assistance. See below, chapter 7, for possible explanations concerning the paucity of materials in the Kennedy Papers.

facilitated, and encouraged my work, this is an "official" history. When my research began on the project in 1987, neither I nor the Court had any idea of what materials were available or where the investigation might ultimately lead. I had no prior experience with the military of any kind, and what little I had heard or read about military justice left me with the commonly held viewpoint that it was a contradiction in terms. On more than one occasion, colleagues have responded to news that I was at work on this study with the comment that "it would have to be a very short one," and that "a pamphlet might be more appropriate." Freely admitting that inexplicable and inexcusable lapses in military justice have indeed occurred and doubtless will again, in no way diminishes the significance of impressive changes which have taken place since 1951.

The conclusions that I have reached will be obvious in the following chapters. Because I am sure that the Court may well not agree with all of them, it should be emphasized here that they are my responsibility. As with the first volume, I have tried to let the principals in the Court's history speak for themselves. Thus, there are many quotations, some of them extended, and numerous notes. I could have summarized much more than has been the case, but believe, however, that frequently the original often tells us more about context and sequence than a historian's summary many years later. The notes will indicate, I hope, the source of every quotation. They are also intended to provide some additional points and sources that may be of interest to the scholar in military justice, rather than the general reader.

The research and writing of USCMA's history to 1980 has taken nine years. It would have been impossible without support and cooperation from a number of individuals, whose efforts were gratefully acknowledged in my first volume. As this study concludes, I thank them once again, but additional expressions of gratitude are also very appropriate. I remain indebted, first of all, to the current members of the Court, Chief Judge Walter Cox, Jr., and his colleagues Judges Susan Crawford, Andrew Effron, H. "Sparky" Gierke, Eugene Sullivan, and Senior Judge Robinson Everett. At all times, they have been extremely supportive, while consistently distancing themselves from my efforts to chronicle their Court's history. With sorrow, I note that their "brother," the late Robert Wiss, did not live to see my study completed. This volume is dedicated to his memory. Parts of the final chapters were written while I served as the Visiting Professor of Law at the United States Military Academy at West Point, in 1994–95, and the enthusiastic support of Colonel Dennis Hunt, Professor and Head of the Department of Law is gratefully acknowledged.

For many years, the Research Council of Rutgers University has aided not only this project, but my long-term research in American legal history. Its continued support has been much appreciated, as was a grant from the Rutgers Newark Graduate School Research Fund. The staff of the Court have been unfailingly kind and generous from the outset of this undertaking. Indeed, the current Court Clerk, Mr. Thomas Granahan, uncovered some office files for the period 1970–80 that neither he nor I had thought existed. I am especially obligated to him, to his Deputy John Cutts, and to the following members of the Court staff: Sherry Arter, Shirley Bates, Robert Bieber, Gail Bissi, Barbara Burley, Kathy Cassady, Reggie Crowne, Francis Gilligan, Barbara Hemsley, Lydia Hoffman, Agnes Kiang, and Patricia Stethem. Two veteran members of the Court Central Legal Staff, Robert Miele and James Richardson, always remained willing to answer my many questions; while John Holt, Robert Mueller, and Chris Sterritt have provided both strong support and candid advice, for which I remain very grateful.

Outside the Court, my debts remain equally extensive. Eugene R. Fidell, a distinguished practitioner and scholar of military justice, took the time to read and critique every chapter. I am deeply indebted to him for his encouraging and sometimes critical insights. The Director of the Bentley Library, Dr. Francis X. Blouin, Jr., kindly authorized the copying of extensive excerpts from the Ferguson Papers, and presented them to the Court for its archive. Judge Samuel Ervin III granted me access to his father's senatorial files, housed at the University of North Carolina Library Department of Special Collections—where the staff, particularly Richard Shrader, went out of their way to offer assistance. I also acknowledge the valuable assistance of the following Presidential Library Staff members: Truman Library, Dennis Bilger; Eisenhower Library, Herbert Pankratz; Johnson Library, Linda Hanson and Claudia Anderson; Nixon Presidential Materials Project, Byron Parham; Ford Library, David Horocks and Jenny Sternaman; and Carter Library, Keith Shuler.

R. Stan Mortenson facilitated my access to the Nixon Project. Mary Kilday and Betty Ann Drogula, daughters of the late Judge Paul Kilday, granted me access to their father's papers, housed at the Barker Texas History Center, University of Texas. For assistance while researching there, I am grateful to Alison Beck. The aid of E. Raymond Lewis, Librarian, U.S. House of Representatives, and Ann Womeldorf from the U.S. Senate Library is much appreciated. For permission to copy materials retained by the Army Times Publishing Company, I thank Pat White-Williams. Again, the consistent guidance and encouragement of Princeton University Press is warmly acknowledged, in particular contributions from my editors, Brigitta Van Rheinberg and William Laznovsky.

I remain deeply indebted to all these individuals, and to others who asked not to be listed here. None of them, however, are responsible for the conclusions that follow. Again, I would appreciate being informed of any mistakes that might still be lurking in either text or notes.

Abbreviations Frequently Used

ARF	Annual Report File, USCMA, preceded by chronological number, followed by date and page
BF	Building File, USCMA
CCC	File, Civilian Court Committee, USCMA
CF	Chronological Files, USCMA Clerk's Office
CLF	Code Changes Legislative File, USCMA Clerks's Office
CM	John Cooke materials, in temporary possession of author
CP	Jimmy Carter Papers, Jimmy Carter Library
EP	Dwight D. Eisenhower Papers, Eisenhower Library
ERV	Samuel Ervin, Jr., Papers, University of North Carolina Library, Southern Historical Collections
FP	Homer Ferguson Papers, Bentley Library, University of Michigan
GF	Gerald Ford Papers, Gerald Ford Library
JFD	John Foster Dulles Papers, Eisenhower Library
JMP	John Macy Papers, Johnson Presidential Library
LATPAP	George Latimer Manuscripts, in temporary possession of author
LBJ	Lyndon Baines Johnson Papers, Johnson Presidential Library
LP	Papers of Felix Larkin, in temporary possession of author
LTF	Life Tenure Files, USCMA Clerk's Office
MP	Materials of William Miller, in temporary possession of author
MPVU	Edmund Morgan Papers, Vanderbilt University
NP	Richard Nixon Papers, Nixon Project, Washington, D.C.
QPGF	Quinn Papers General Files
QPPC	Quinn Papers Personal Correspondence
SF	USCMA Speech File, 1951–66
SMR	Materials of Deanne Siemer, in temporary possession of author
TP	Truman Papers, Truman Library
USCMAP	U.S. Court of Military Appeals Papers

PURSUING MILITARY JUSTICE

CHAPTER 1

Journeys to the Judgeships, 1950–1951

WHEN the Senate passed the UCMJ in February 1950, its modifications of the House version made a Conference necessary. The primary issue between the two bills was the length of time the new judges would serve.[1] In spite of this problem, all concerned agreed that final passage was inevitable; and even before the bill reached President Truman, interest had begun to focus on selection of the first three judges. Two names frequently mentioned were Felix Larkin and Edmund Morgan, although in fact neither man was a serious contender for appointment.[2]

EARLY COURT CONTENDERS

On February 9, an old friend of Larkin—New York attorney Richard Wels—wrote to him. Alluding to the continuing and mostly unsuccessful efforts by the various lawyers' associations to change the new code, nevertheless he felt that it "is going to be able to accomplish the objectives that we all have had in mind—despite the carpings of us perfectionists up here." More important, he added, "I hope that someone is going to see that you are one of the three judges . . . because the success of the Code is going to depend upon having someone like you on that initial court."[3] Larkin agreed that "a great deal will depend on the caliber of the three judges . . . . [but] I am sure no one is thinking of me in those terms, nor have I given any thought to whether I would want such a job if anybody was serious about it."[4]

It soon became clear that in spite of Wels's compliments to Larkin, the New York County Lawyers Association—for which he spoke—continued to criticize the UCMJ. In a statement prepared for release on April 17, the day

[1] The House bill provided for life tenure, while the Senate opted for eight-year terms. The compromise ultimately established fifteen-year terms, with the first three judges only being named for fifteen, ten, and five years. See the first volume of this study, *Arming Military Justice* (1992), 244, 253, 255, hereafter cited as AMJ, followed by appropriate page number(s).

[2] See AMJ, where the major contributions of both men to the drafting and enactment of the Uniform Code of Military Justice (UCMJ) are discussed in detail.

[3] LP, February 9, 1950.

[4] Ibid., February 13, 1950. Although his name was frequently mentioned as a possible candidate and, indeed, as a probable selection, Larkin appears never to have expressed any enthusiasm for such an appointment.

before the Conference Committee was to meet, the Association accused Congress of abandoning "the heart of the proposed reform, the elimination of the power of commanding officers to influence the decisions of court-martials." Equally undesirable was the Senate's decision to provide the judges with eight-year appointments. "We are of the view that the utmost support should be given to the House in its efforts to resist this Senate change." Finally, the lawyers were "disturbed that the court for administrative purposes should be placed in the Department of Defense rather than in the administrative office of the United States Courts."[5]

The not unreasonable fear that the new court could somehow be dominated by the military establishment led to lawyers' groups adopting a series of resolutions. The one drafted by Wels's colleagues was typical. The association was authorized to consult with the President, Secretary of Defense, and the Attorney General, to appear before the Congress in order to insure the nomination and confirmation of persons deemed "to be competent and specially qualified," and to oppose those candidates they "deem to be unfit or not sufficiently qualified."[6] Probably, what the lawyers actually sought was less the opportunity to testify for or against a candidate, and more the ability to screen individuals in advance of Senate consideration.

Thus I. Howard Lehman, President of the New York County Lawyers Association, wrote to President Truman that his group "is anxious to be of all possible service in connection with the nomination and confirmation of such persons as may be selected for this important court." Truman should consider "our" special committee on military justice or the panel on the judiciary "at your command in connection with any advices [*sic*] or suggestions with respect to the selection of the Judges. . . . May we hope that, before definite appointment is made, we be given an opportunity to be of possible assistance?"[7]

Although Lehman could not know it, more than a year would pass before Truman sent his three choices to the Senate. Numerous letters similar to Lehman's were sent to Truman, and the response through his secretary followed a predictable pattern. The offer of service "will be borne in mind, and

[5] National Archives, Records Group 330, "SD 250 Court of Military Appeals, (Misc)" Box 580, March 23, 1950, 1–2. "We would not tolerate such tampering with the integrity and independence of our judges in other Federal courts that deal with money, property, and the liberty of civilians." The points raised in this report signed by Wels, should be kept in mind as the history of the United States Court of Military Appeals is traced in these chapters. It might be noted here, however, that Larkin and Wels started from very different premises that were probably incompatible. Wels wondered why the court should be any different in its construction than other federal courts. Larkin accepted as given the special military background of the tribunal, but within these parameters he wanted to make it as much like a federal appeals court as possible.

[6] Ibid., March 23, 1950.

[7] TP, Box 991, File 303 Misc., April 18, 1950.

you may be sure that careful consideration will be given to any recommendations which you may care to make regarding the membership of the Court. . . ."[8] Conspicuous in the reply is the absence of any commitment to submit the names of possible nominees to Lehman's committee in advance of formal nomination.

In the meantime, with final passage of the UCMJ imminent, Larkin's office prepared the first draft of a comprehensive press release on its passage. "The most significant change, the most decisive reform . . . is the new appellate system." It was "streamlined and simple when compared to its predecessors [largely because of] its resemblance to a civilian appellate system." In addition to the new judges being civilians—"men of high caliber and judicial experience"—another change was significant. The accused could ask that he be furnished counsel to represent him in appeals under the new code. Traditionally, military review had involved only an examination of the record. Now, "the new provision for appellate counsel will assure that all aspects of a case are fully presented to the court in the same way they are to any civilian [tribunal]."[9]

After the Conference Report had been accepted by Congress, Larkin wrote Morgan that "we would try to arrange a signing ceremony at the White House, but the prospects are very dim." As an alternative, he hoped the President would sign the bill "with a few different pens" with one intended for Morgan.[10] The law professor, now in his final year of teaching at Harvard, replied that "by this time, of course, the comparative importance of the Uniform Code is doubtless so small, and the number of bills that the President has to sign is so great, that no one could reasonably expect a signing ceremony."[11] If anyone deserved a pen, he added, it was Larkin, rather than himself. Morgan's sentiments were echoed by Louis Johnson, the Secretary of Defense. He wrote Larkin that "by your tireless and effective labor to

[8] Ibid., May 12, 1950.

[9] USCMAP, "Uniform Code of Military Justice," March 6, 1950, 1–2. The revised and shortened draft was released on May 5, 1950. On the other hand, Arthur Keeffe found the Code as a whole unsatisfactory, and the fact that it would certainly become law did not prevent him from complaining to both Forrestal's successor and Senator Kefauver. "Isn't it time," he asked Kefauver, "we provided that the Supreme Court of the United States supervise court-martial procedure and inquire into the guilt or innocence of any American boy or girl convicted by a court-martial in the same manner it does with respect to any federal court conviction?" Kefauver Papers, February 20, 1949. Kefauver sent a short noncommittal response on March 4.

[10] LP, April 28, 1950.

[11] Ibid., May 1, 1950. Within a matter of days, Truman signed the UCMJ into law, and in due course Morgan received one of the pens used by the President. Morgan, who possessed a dry, occasionally caustic wit, was genuinely touched. "I can never be grateful enough to you and Felix," he wrote to Marx Leva, "for giving me the opportunity to work on the Uniform Code, and for seeing to it that I received much more credit for my part in it than I have deserved. Never have I got such official recognition for services, public or private, that I may have rendered." Ibid., June 7, 1950.

bring about a substantial improvement in military justice, you have earned the gratitude of all the civilian and military officials of the Department of Defense."[12]

Morgan did more than compliment Larkin. He also wrote a letter to Marx Leva, who had become Assistant Secretary of Defense. "It seems to me exceptionally important that the first court should be composed of highly competent men and that no 'deserving' politician be appointed. The best assurance I could have that the Court would get off to a good start would be to have Felix appointed for the 15-year term. Is there any way that this could be accomplished or that I can help?"[13]

Leva showed this letter to Larkin who promptly replied to Morgan. "I treasure that recommendation above any other I could ever get. While, naturally enough I have thought of the Court, I have not been a candidate. . . . [A]t the present moment I wonder if I should, at my age, try to commit myself to what would probably be the last job I would ever do."[14] Leva also wrote Morgan, expanding on what Larkin had intimated.

"My own reaction—and I think that Secretary Johnson feels about the same as I do on this score—is that everything you say about Felix is true—but that his appointment to the Court at this stage of his legal career, while it would be extremely beneficial to the Department of Defense, might not be equally beneficial to Felix himself. . . . I hope that I will have an opportunity to discuss this matter with you further before the names of the judges are finally decided upon."[15]

If Larkin had doubts about his own desire for judicial service, others did not. As will be seen, it remains unclear exactly how many individuals were seriously considered for the first appointments. Two days after the bill creating the Court became law, one candidate—George Latimer—wrote to Truman's Military Aide, expressing real interest in the position. Shortly thereafter, another prospect—Paul Brosman—emerged with the support of the Air Force Judge Advocate General, Reginald Harmon. Since both ultimately received appointments to the new Court, their early candidacy deserves some attention.

On May 8, 1950, Harry Vaughan received a letter from George Latimer. A native of Utah, Latimer had successfully combined a dual career as counsel and combatant. During World War II, as an officer in the Utah National Guard, he saw active duty in the Pacific, rising to the rank of full Colonel. In

[12] Ibid., May 5, 1950.

[13] MPVU, May 15, 1950.

[14] LP, May 17, 1950.

[15] MPVU, May 22, 1950. Morgan conceded that "you may be entirely right about the advisability of Felix's taking a position on the Court . . . or any other which has a limit to opportunity for general development. Perhaps I was thinking too much about security for him and the success of the Court." Ibid., May 29, 1950.

1947, after he returned to Utah and reestablished his law practice, Latimer was elected to the Utah Supreme Court. While in the Guard, he had become acquainted with Harry Vaughan, who became Truman's Military Aide.

In a draft of his unpublished memoirs written toward the end of his life, Latimer claimed that "I heard through the grapevine that my name had been suggested to President Truman as a possible appointee" to the new court. The "source of my recommendation," he added, "was and is unknown to me."[16] Recollections recede as the years pass, and Latimer can be forgiven for his lapse of memory. It may well be that Vaughan brought Latimer's name to the attention of Truman. If he did, however, it was at the behest of Latimer himself.

Noting that the President had just signed the bill creating the new tribunal, in a letter to "my dear Harry," Latimer told Vaughan that "I am very much interested in being considered for one of these appointments[,] but realize that being a member of the Republican Party makes it difficult to receive support from Democratic sources." He emphasized, however, that "if the appointment is not to be partisan[,] I believe I can recruit in my behalf the outstanding members of the President's party in this state and both Democratic and Republican members of the bar." Latimer understood that the new Court would not become effective until May 1951, "and it may be that efforts at this time are premature. However, I would rather be early than overlooked."[17]

Vaughan was surprised to receive Latimer's letter. "I would imagine that a State Supreme Court Justice is a much more important legal job than this Armed Forces Court Martials Appeals board; but maybe the latter is more interesting and exciting. I don't know about these things."[18] Latimer hastened to educate his friend. "To remove your wonderment and justify my claims to sanity," Latimer cited three reasons for his interest.

In the first place, "I have a very honorable, dignified and respected posi-

[16] Notes, Latimer manuscripts, hereafter cited as Latpap, 47. Later, the syndicated columnist Drew Pearson wrote that Latimer owed his appointment to his friendship with Vaughan. Pearson also had some comments about Truman's other choices for the Court. See below, n. 83.

[17] TP, Box 993, Folder "L," May 8, 1950. Latimer told Vaughan that he well understood "that your position might be such that embarrassment could result if you would offer me advice or give me assistance. If either of these contingencies is present please advise me and I will pursue a different course." Latimer was correct in his belief that influential Utah Democrats would support him. He later recalled that the two Republican Senators were "neutral" concerning his candidacy while, as will be seen, the Democratic Congresswoman from Salt Lake City strongly fought for his nomination. Once it became clear that President Truman was seriously considering Latimer, the entire Utah Congressional delegation supported him. Nevertheless, in Latimer's case, party labels do not appear to have been a prerequisite for endorsement from either party.

[18] Ibid. Vaughan, known more for his friendship with President Truman than for political insight or influence, assured Latimer that "I will put your name on the list of those to be considered."

tion, which suffers only from meager pay and emoluments." Moreover, the Utah governor had just vetoed a nonpartisan judiciary bill. Thus, "if I remain here, I shall be required to accomplish the almost impossible, namely, to convince the voters to elect a Republican Justice in a normally Democratic state." Finally, "I am still ambitious[,] and I would like to earn some kind of reputation nationally. . . . It may be that I have overestimated the importance of the proposed court, but I believe the opportunities there to formulate and build a system might be challenging."[19]

But Latimer was not without an immediate rival, even at this very early stage of the selection process. Not only was another Republican candidate, Franklin Riter, also from Utah—he too was an officer in the National Guard, and had previously testified before the House Committee that passed on the UCMJ.[20] Writing to Utah Senator Elbert Thomas (shortly to be defeated for reelection), Riter reminded the Senator that "improper influence upon Courts-Martial by any person should constitute, not only a military offense, but [one] indictable [and punishable in federal courts]. In other words, I would make it a civil offense for an appointing authority to coerce the verdict of a Courts-martial." Riter admitted, however, that both Morgan's Committee as well as Congress had rejected this suggestion.

Nevertheless, "I have never changed my opinion in this regard. . . . I am certain that, had Congress written such a provision into the new law, once and for all[,] Courts-Martial would have been freed from improper influence, which has, unfortunately, been asserted innumerable times by indiscreet officers who did not understand our military justice system." Riter was "most positively of the opinion that a commanding general, if he is worthy of his responsibility, does not need to subvert the process of justice in order to maintain discipline." He wanted to emphasize this point to Senator Thomas "in setting forth my qualifications." It was essential "to understand the necessity of maintaining the integrity of the judicial process, free from suspicion of ulterior pressure."[21]

Unlike Latimer and Riter who might draw on their National Guard contacts for endorsement, Paul Brosman enjoyed the active support of Reginald Harmon, the Judge Advocate General of the Air Force. A graduate of the University of Illinois Law School, Brosman was appointed to the faculty of Tulane University Law School in 1929. Four years later, he became its Dean, and retained that title until 1951—although his tenure was interrupted by World War II, during which Brosman served in the Army Air Corps. In

[19] Ibid., May 26, 1950.

[20] See AMJ, 217–19.

[21] TP, Box 993, Folder "R," May 16, 1950; also in USCMAP. "I trust," Riter concluded in his four-page letter to Thomas, "that you will give consideration to this frank expression of my qualifications and ambitions."

1950, at the request of the Judge Advocate General of the now independent Air Force—with the approval of his university, Brosman returned to active duty. Nine years later, Harmon—still Air Force Judge Advocate General—recalled that Brosman had expressed interest in the new Court during the Spring of 1950.[22] According to Harmon, he and the prospective candidate agreed that Harmon would gather support within the Defense Department, while Brosman would enlist the backing of key legislators from Louisiana.[23]

There seems no reason to doubt Harmon's recollections. By July 12, 1950, Truman's assistant for personnel, Donald Dawson, had already requested a "full field investigation" into Brosman's background from the FBI. Ten days later, Dawson indicated that Brosman "has already been mentioned to us for such an appointment and we have background information concerning him in our files."[24] Harmon later recalled receiving a phone call from Dawson: "I understand you're recommending a Paul Brosman for a court appointment." Harmon: "Yes, I am. He's a good officer, a scholar, and a fine gent." Dawson: "What do you really think of him?"[25]

MORGAN CONSIDERS

It is not clear to what extent Riter, Latimer, and Brosman actively pursued their candidacies during the remainder of 1950. The outbreak of the Korean War occupied both President Truman and his new Secretary of Defense, George Marshall. Morgan, now settled in at Vanderbilt Law School, received word from Larkin that "candidates continue to appear" for the new court, but "nothing more is being done, and I expect no decisions will be made until February. At this time, I have no idea of the preferences of Secretary Marshall. You, of course, remain my number 1 candidate, and I hope you will continue to consider the idea."[26]

[22] These paragraphs on Brosman are largely based on Benjamin Feld's unpublished Ph.D. dissertation "The United States Court of Military Appeals: A Study of the Origins and Early Development of the First Civilian Tribunal for Direct Review of Courts-Martial, 1951–1959." Submitted to Georgetown University in 1960 while Feld was a member of the Court's staff, the source for his background material on Brosman, who had suddenly died in December 1955, was a lengthy interview with Reginald Harmon. Regretably, Brosman appears to have left no private body of papers.

[23] Feld, 60–61.

[24] TP, Box 992, Folder "B-2," July 12, 22, 1950. Brosman received endorsements from key Congressional Democrats such as Hale Boggs, John McCormack, and Louisiana Senators Russell Long and Allen Ellender.

[25] Feld, 61.

[26] MPVU, September 28, 1950. In October 1950, John Kenney—having resigned his position as undersecretary of the Navy to enter private law practice—wrote to Larkin, "Inciden-

But Larkin had additional news for Morgan. Under pressure from George Spiegelberg, the American Bar Association proposed that all potential nominees for the new court "be submitted to the ABA for ratings as to qualifications. Within very specified limits, I don't think it is too bad." However, Larkin added, if ABA standards included "adherence to their ideas, I didn't think their judgments would be too useful." Aware that the lawyers' associations had already expressed interest in working with the Defense Department to adapt the Manual for Courts-Martial to the UCMJ, Larkin asked Morgan what he thought of ABA rating the candidates for the new court.[27]

Morgan promptly replied to Larkin's letter with some comments that indicated both a respect for the ABA evaluative procedure, and a concern for the independence of the new court. "I think it would be well to have the candidates handled by the ABA Committee. . . . But I think it would be unwise to have the matter in the hands of a committee of the J.A.G. Reserve Officers or any such bunch. They will think only of the Army and may have too many axes to grind." Morgan added another caveat. "If the ABA has a committee which would not rate experience in the field too highly, its opinion ought to be well worth considering[,] but it ought not to be decisive. On the other hand, if the ABA is not consulted, there will be some adverse publicity."[28]

Apparently the ABA did not wait to be consulted. On November 9, its president sent identical letters to President Truman, Defense Secretary Marshall, Attorney General J. Howard McGrath, and the chairmen of the Senate Armed Services and Judiciary Committees. Cody Fowler reminded Truman of the long-standing ABA goal: the requirement of "the effective elimination of command control of courts martial." Unfortunately, in its present form the UCMJ "does not insure the desired goal."[29] It was all the more important, therefore, that selections for the court should "in addition to the high charac-

---

tally, what has happened on our efforts to get Eddie Morgan on the final Appeal Board created under the [UCMJ]? I hope that with the change of personnel in the Office of the Secretary of Defense his name will not be forgotten." LP, October 4, 1950. The change mentioned by Kenney referred to Louis Johnson's ouster as Secretary of Defense, to be replaced by George Marshall.

[27] MPVU, September 23, 1950, 2. Concerning the Manual, on July 27, Louis Johnson had sent a letter drafted in Larkin's office to Arthur Farmer. He welcomed Farmer's offer "to advise and assist us just as you did with respect to the Code." LP, July 27, 1950. On the other hand, appreciating advice did not necessarily imply taking it.

[28] MPVU, October 2, 1950. As for the revision to the Manual for Courts-Martial [MCM], Morgan assured Larkin that "I will be glad to see the text . . . , for I think it important that the instructions therein shall strengthen instead of weaken the safeguards which the Code provides." Morgan's point was well taken. If the UCMJ was the "constitution" for the military, the MCM was the practical source of regulations, guidance, and instructions for its actual implementation by the military—often, inevitably, at the hands of non-lawyers. Morgan suspected, not unreasonably as it turned out, that the military would make strenuous efforts to have the MCM reflect more a service rather than a civilian viewpoint.

[29] TP, Official files, Box 995. File "End-Misc," November 9, 1950, 2.

ter and qualifications" needed for judicial appointment also "possess a real interest in the possibility of improving the basic legislation under which they act." Fowler detailed for Truman how closely his organization had worked in the past with the President, other administration officials, and the Senate Judiciary Committee in selecting federal judges.[30] Truman replied that "should the Association care to submit a list of those it considers eminently qualified for appointment to the Court, I shall be glad to give consideration to its suggestions, along with the many others which are coming to me."[31]

One day later, George Spiegelberg—still chairman of the ABA special committee on military justice—wrote a follow-up letter to his friend Robert Lovett, Under-Secretary of Defense. He hoped that Lovett "will exercise the power of your high office to insure the appointment of the most highly qualified individuals available to this important new Court."[32] Although Lovett's answer to Spiegelberg could not be located, two weeks later the Under Secretary responded to an inquiry from Senator Kenneth Wherry on the same subject. "The President has not yet indicated the selection procedures he intends to follow. In the anticipation that the Department of Defense will be called upon for recommendations, however, this office is maintaining a file of those persons who have expressed a desire to serve."[33]

As the year came to an end, it seems clear that several groups assumed that they would have significant input into Truman's appointments. The ABA and its committee, the Defense Department, as well as its Office of General Counsel—a position to which Felix Larkin had been appointed—all prepared to offer their suggestions. The only problem was that the administration appears to have had little more than polite interest in what they had to offer. Several lists of nominations were ultimately submitted to the President through Donald Dawson. But Dawson apparently went about the process of narrowing the list of candidates for Truman's consideration much the way he

[30] "The administrative office of United States Courts keeps [the ABA] committee advised of any vacancies or prospective vacancies in the Federal Courts. The committee then conducts an investigation as to the available candidates and makes a recommendation to the President through the Attorney General. . . ." When an appointment was made, "the committee is promptly advised by the White House and the opinion and recommendation of our committee is requested by the Senate Judiciary Committee." If a candidate other than one recommended by the ABA is appointed, "a new investigation is made on behalf of the [ABA] to the Senate Judiciary Committee." Ibid., 2–3.

[31] Ibid., November 11, 1950. Truman's letter was carefully worded. Although willing to accept suggestions for the new appointments, apparently he declined to submit any names to the ABA in advance of nomination—something Fowler clearly desired. He had offered the President ABA assistance "in any manner in which it can be deemed to be of service, in the selection or screening of members for appointment to the newly created court." Supra, nn. 29–30.

[32] National Archives, RG 330, Box 629, SD 250, November 10, 1950.

[33] Ibid., November 24, 1950. "The applications of each candidate are given the most careful consideration, for it is felt that the success of the new Code will depend to a very great extent upon the calibre of those men who first constitute its highest Court."

did with other intermediate presidential appointments.[34] In the meantime,barely five months before the new Code was to go into effect, Truman had given no indication as to his preferences.

With the outbreak of the Korean War, Morgan wrote to Larkin that "if the situation gets really bad, I do not want to sit on the sidelines if I can help it." Of course, he added, "my age is against me." [Morgan was now seventy-two.] As for becoming a judge, "The possibility of appointment to the new Court is, in my opinion, definitely out." The recent Congressional elections have "left too many prime candidates available—and some of them entirely competent."[35] Yet Morgan hoped he might still be of some service, and with an understandable pride of parentage—despite the realities of his age—service on the Court he had proposed continued to tempt him. Morgan revealed his true feelings to some of his former students, rather than to Felix Larkin.

Writing to Van Tanner, Morgan acknowledged that John Kenney had urged his selection, but "I told them immediately that my age made such an appointment not only unwise but practically impossible."[36] Morgan added that "the best man I know of is . . . Felix Larkin. He knows more about the Code and its background than any other living man." But it was to Marx Leva that Morgan most clearly indicated his ambivalence.

> As to the Court of Military Appeals, I am in a fog in my own thinking, except as to one thing. I am absolutely certain that if I were in the position of Secretary Marshall, I should not nominate anyone of my age; and if I were in the President's position, I should not appoint such a person if nominated by the Secretary. . . . I certainly am not a candidate for the position, for I could not say to the Secretary or to the President that my appointment would be evidence of good judgment on his part. I am not too modest to think that I could do a reasonably good job in spite of my age; but I am convinced that there are among the applicants younger men who could do quite as well or better and (an important consideration) who would prove worthy of reappointment at the end of five years.[37]

[34] This statement is merely an assumption, based on the very limited information contained in those relatively few files on the Court in the Truman Papers. Dawson declined to allow examination of his papers, and in a brief but amicable phone conversation with this author even refused to indicate what materials he might have retained on the appointment process as applied to the new court.

[35] MPVU, January 4, 1951. Although Morgan could not know it, in fact age would be a serious consideration in one instance of judicial appointment to the new Court. In 1966, Lyndon Johnson reappointed Robert Quinn as Chief Judge of USCMA to a second fifteen-year term, in spite of the fact that he was already seventy-two. See below, chapter 7.

[36] Ibid., January 31, 1951. "There is no dearth of candidates; a great many of them are excellently fitted for the job, and frankly, I hope it will not be offered to me."

[37] Ibid., February 8, 1951. "You and I both know," added Morgan, "that Felix is the ideal man for the chief position on the Court; but I have most reluctantly to agree that at his age, he should not take a position in such a limited specialty. He is bound to go places." Within a year, Larkin

Actually, regardless of his own ambivalence, Morgan was considered a leading candidate by Larkin's assistant Robert Haydock, who had been charged with compiling the list of recommended nominees for Defense Secretary George Marshall. On January 24, Haydock had submitted a list of eight names to Leva, ranked in order of preference. Morgan's was first, and according to Haydock "is the only Republican [on] this list. When I talked with him on the phone, he said he thought he was too old, but did not indicate that he would refuse the appointment." Larkin was second, but "Mr. Larkin told me recently that he is not a candidate."[38] The third choice was Robert Pasley, the Cornell Law Professor who had assisted Keeffe and Larkin in preparation of the Navy Report in 1947. In last place was Paul Brosman, of whom Haydock commented that "Professor Morgan knows of Brosman and thinks he would be all right."[39]

Morgan thought highly of Pasley, and so wrote to Haydock.[40] So did Arthur Keeffe, who had taught Pasley at Cornell and dispatched a vigorous letter affirming his support to President Truman. Keeffe's very positive endorsement was matched by his equally vigorous condemnation of the new UCMJ. "There are many things about the new uniform code which in my judgment are a national disgrace," essentially because they did not appear to carry out the specific reforms Keeffe had urged in his report. Hence, it was vital to have "able and informed lawyers such as Bob Pasley" named to the new tribunal. "Only in this way will there ever be any hope that these Judges will raise their voices for that complete reform that is so badly needed." The first way "to wreck any hope of reform," he added, "is to appoint lame duck Congressmen or Senators."[41] Keeffe also sent a copy of this letter to George Marshall.

Morgan was pleased that Pasley was on Haydock's "preferred list." As to his own name, which Haydock listed as number 1, Morgan wrote Marx Leva what "I have, I believe, already told you and Felix, that in my opinion the President would be unwise to appoint anybody of my age. Consequently . . . I am not a

---

would resign to join the W. R. Grace Company, for whom he ultimately functioned in a number of executive capacities—including that of President—until his retirement.

[38] National Archives, RG 330, Box 629, SD 250, January 24, 1951.

[39] Ibid., 2. Haydock added that he had prepared a notebook "on all fifty of the candidates." This means that at least fifty names were being considered by the Office of General Counsel within the Defense Department. This number may be contrasted with a figure contained in a statement from Harry Vaughan, five days later. Vaughan wrote "The remarkable thing about these three appointments is that there were almost four thousand applications for the three jobs and the amount of political pressure for some of the candidates is really remarkable." TP, Official File, Box 994, Folder "T-V," January 30, 1951.

[40] MPVU, February 5, 1951.

[41] TP, Official File, Box 994, Folder "N-P," February 6, 1951. "Nothing you can do, Mr. President, would do more to give public confidence in this rotten court-martial system than to appoint Robert Pasley. . . ."

candidate for the position." On the other hand, "this is not to say that I would positively refuse it if it were tendered to me, but I could not be an active candidate when I believe the President would be unwise to appoint me."[42]

Meanwhile, Marx Leva had written to Robert Lovett, the Deputy Secretary of Defense, that prompt steps should be taken concerning recommendations for the new judges. "Time is fast running out on this subject. . . . If we fail to take action, we may wake up some morning and read in the papers that the President has appointed three men all of whom will be unknown to us. I think that action on our part is imperative."[43]

Four days later, Marshall responded with a memorandum to Leva. Presumably, the Secretary had received the list generated by Haydock, with revisions possibly by Leva and Larkin.[44] Marshall advised Leva "that it would be best to submit six names in alphabetical order. . . ." Moreover, according to Lovett, "the American Bar Association is unwilling to submit names," but preferred "to screen the names of candidates." Truman, however "will not accept the screening process."[45] Marshall added that "some advice has been received from a leading member of the Bar Association."[46] For his part, Lovett was already well aware of the differing views concerning the way the new judges should be selected.

[42] MPVU, February 12, 1951. Four days later, Morgan reiterated these points for yet a third time in a letter to Larkin. "I could not tell the President that I believed it would be either wise or politic to appoint me." Again, he ruled out a flat rejection, "if it were offered to me, but I cannot help hoping that it will not be offered." Ibid., February 16, 1951. One can understand and sympathize with Morgan's ambivalence. He had just left Harvard Law School, not voluntarily but because of age. On the other hand, Leva, Haydock, and Larkin had all endorsed Morgan for the short five-year term on the new court, a period of time which, given Morgan's excellent health, did not seem unreasonable. It is interesting to note that at the age of seventy George Marshall had become Truman's Secretary of Defense, while Henry Stimson was almost seventy-eight when in 1945 he finally retired as Truman's Secretary of War. Ultimately Morgan found himself caught between the forces of reality and desire. Again, he wrote to Haydock. "We shall see what we shall see. Even if the appointment is tendered me, I may not get past the senate committee. Don't forget that Alger Hiss was a student of mine." Ibid., February 23, 1951.

[43] National Archives, RG 330, Box 629, File 250, February 9, 1951.

[44] On February 8, Haydock informed Morgan of his revised listing for six candidates. Morgan, Larkin, and Pasley were the first three, but Paul Brosman's name had been deleted, and while George Latimer was one of the fifty or so names culled by Haydock, his name was not on the short list submitted to Marshall. Haydock's second list was itself revised, but there is no indication who made the changes. However, the list of nine leading candidates ultimately forwarded to Truman by his Secretary of Defense apparently included Brosman. Moreover, as has been seen, Truman's assistant Donald Dawson was already well aware of Brosman's interest, and on January 10, 1951, Dawson had received word that an FBI background investigation had been initiated on George Latimer.

[45] Ibid, February 13, 1951.

[46] Marshall may have been referring to some discussions with Cody Fowler, President of the ABA. As it turned out, both he and Marshall wrote to President Truman on the same day, each recommending several individuals for the new tribunal. See below.

Barely a month before Marshall wrote to Leva, Lovett had received an angry letter from George Spiegelberg, still chairman of the ABA Special Committee on Military Justice. The committee had been informed that "the positions on the Court must be used to build politically for 1952," when presumably Truman would run for reelection. For Spiegelberg "it would be a shocking thing politically to prostitute the Court, the last judicial forum for millions of young men and women of this country." He reminded Lovett that the UCMJ "leaves much to be desired." If the new Court, obligated by statute to suggest reforms in military justice, "is made the depository of political hacks . . . [,] essential needed reforms will never be proposed. Further, the Court, "if political, will be subject, because of its limited tenure, to baneful influences which will require independent and fearless men to combat." Lovett should "interest yourself actively in preventing what appears to be inevitable unless someone makes the good fight."[47]

Even before his letter to Lovett, Spiegelberg had sought additional external pressure for what he considered appropriate nominations. In October 1950, he had written a friend and fellow New York attorney, Harrison Tweed. "I am reliably informed that the Secretary of Defense, and not the Attorney General, will make recommendations to the President; and in view of General Marshall's appointment to the former office, there is a chance that good men will be appointed."[48] Spiegelberg asked that Tweed contact John McCloy, currently serving as United States High Commissioner to Germany, urging that he in turn write to Marshall emphasizing the necessity for recommending "men of unquestioned ability."[49]

[47] National Archives, RG 330, Box 629, File SD 250, January 11, 1951. Spiegelberg had tried to persuade Larkin "to see whether your Department would be willing to utilize the [ABA] in screening candidates for the Court. . . . I have been informed by Mr. Larkin that the suggested plan would probably not be adopted." Lovett hastened to reassure Spiegelberg that he and Larkin were committed to "the absolute essentiality of appointing lawyers of outstanding ability and integrity to be judges of the new Court." Moreover, "every indication we have received has been to the effect that the ultimate recommendations of the Department of Defense, as to the composition of the Court, will be given great weight by the President." Ibid., January 16, 1951.

[48] In retrospect, Spiegelberg's informant was not that reliable. Truman chose not to follow either of Marshall's two specific recommendations for nomination to the Court. It is not clear how many names Dawson placed before Truman for final consideration, because he declined to permit any examination of his papers, in addition to what has been preserved at the Truman Library. However, a partial list of proposed [and ultimately unsuccessful] candidates filed by Dawson indicates that he appended to each candidate the name(s) of either sponsors or influential supporters. If he followed this practice with his final list, Truman would have been very aware of Marshall's preferences.

[49] LP, October 10, 1950. McCloy and Lovett had been assistants to Secretary of War Henry Stimson. Stimson, in turn, was a great admirer of General George Marshall, whom Truman had named as Secretary of Defense in 1950. See Godfrey Hodgson, *The Colonel: The Life and Wars of Henry Stimson 1867–1950*. (New York: Alfred A. Knopf, 1990), 232, 244–45. McCloy [at this time United States High Commissioner to Germany] responded with a short note to Lovett, rather

On February 16, Marshall sent a "personal and confidential" memorandum to Truman, and it differed from what he had proposed to Leva a few weeks before. He included two lists—one with nine names, and the other with the remaining additional candidates, numbering about fifty.[50] In his covering letter, however, Marshall specifically mentioned only two, Edmund Morgan and Benjamin Mathews.[51] The Secretary recommended Morgan for the five-year term, and Mathews for the ten-year period. He urged Truman to consider a younger man for the fifteen-year slot, but refused to suggest a single candidate, contenting himself instead with listing seven other highly recommended nominees in alphabetical order, among them Paul Brosman and Robert Pasley—while among the other remaining candidates were the names of George Latimer and Frank Riter. "It appears of the utmost importance," Marshall reminded Truman, "that men of clearly outstanding ability be named to this newly created Court. Your initial appointees to this Court will set [its] tone . . . for many years to come."[52]

Two separate lists—one prepared by Haydock for Marshall, the other by Fowler—had now been submitted for Truman's consideration. Even before their arrival, Donald Dawson had already received a set of suggested nominees from the chairman of the Democratic National Committee. It included a name conspicuous by its absence from Marshall's, and Fowler's choices. This individual would ultimately be Truman's preference both as Chief Judge and the holder of the fifteen-year term. Since Robert Quinn ultimately served on the new Court longer than any other judge in its history—for almost twenty-four years—the absence of his name from so many of the supposedly "inside" lists deserves some attention.

THE QUINTESSENTIAL QUINN

In 1950, Robert E. Quinn was quietly serving on the Rhode Island Superior Court. A 1918 graduate of Harvard Law School, Quinn had been attracted to

than a letter to Marshall, and stated, "I do believe it is extremely important that we get a good court, and [it] probably means more to the Army than to anybody else." LP, November 1, 1950.

[50] The list was not included in Marshall's letter as filed in the Truman Papers. However, the Secretary of Defense File in the Archives contains a list of nine candidates recommended for the Court, and since Marshall specifically refers to nine names, it is highly probable that the archive copy was the same.

[51] Mathews was a distinguished lawyer, strongly supported both by former Secretary of War Robert Patterson—who, incidentally had been Truman's first choice as the new Secretary of Defense, and Federal Judge Learned Hand, already known among legal scholars as the "Tenth Supreme Court Justice." Mathews had been on both lists generated by Haydock.

[52] Truman Library, Martin Friedman Files, Box 5, February 16, 1951. On the same day, Truman also received a letter from ABA President Cody Fowler submitting six names for his consideration—among them Benjamin Mathews and Felix Larkin. Unlike Marshall, Fowler did not suggest any particular term for a specific candidate.

Rhode Island politics soon after World War I. In 1924, following a term in the state Senate, he had unsuccessfully sought the Democratic nomination for Lieutenant Governor. If it is true that the smaller the state, the more labyrinthine its politics, Quinn's later career well illustrates the principle. He served another term in the state Senate, and in 1932 came to the attention of a wealthy Democratic political figure, Theodore Francis Green, a candidate for governor. The young Irish-Catholic lawyer with strong ties to urban democratic circles provided a valuable counterweight to Green, an older, Protestant patrician type. Nominated for Lieutenant Governor, Quinn and Green were elected in 1932 and reelected two years later.

Quinn presided over the state Senate during an era for which the word "turbulent" may seem an understatement. On January 1, 1935, his appointment of a new Senate committee to recount ballots in two disputed contests resulted in the first Democratic majority of the Rhode Island Legislature in over one hundred years. Before the day ended, Quinn orchestrated votes for "initial reorganization of state administration, swept away the [entire] Supreme Court, and eliminated" various state office positions that had long been Republican power bases.[53] In 1936, he succeeded Green as Governor, when Green won election to the United States Senate—where he would remain until 1960. Quinn served only one term as Governor, and his tenure was characterized by intensive "infighting" that helped contribute to his defeat for reelection in 1938.[54]

Two years later, the Democrats nominated as their gubernatorial candidate J. Howard McGrath, a lawyer and state Democratic Chairman with strong ties to the national Democratic Committee. Quinn actively sought the nomination, yet did not force a vote during the state convention. It is interesting to note that one of McGrath's first acts as Governor was to appoint Quinn to the Superior Court. "In political circles," according to the *Providence Daily Journal*, Quinn's acceptance of such a position "was interpreted as meaning his retirement from active politics." Well aware of this interpretation, the former

[53] Matthew Smith, "The Real McCoy in the Bloodless Revolution of 1935." *Rhode Island History* 32 (1973), 76.

[54] The most unusual episode in Quinn's term involved a feud with a fellow Rhode Island Democrat that rapidly escalated into a power struggle between the governor and yet another Democrat, who was also the owner of a Rhode Island horse racing track. Before it was all over, two State Supreme Court decisions had gone against Quinn; he had responded by proclaiming martial law, calling out the National Guard, forcibly closing the race track, and filing charges of libel against its owner. The best account of the entire incident, which seems as bizarre today as when it took place, is Zechariah Chafee, Jr., *State House versus Pent House* (1937). Chafee, a professor of law at Harvard, was sympathetic with Quinn's objections to the race track. Nevertheless, he severely criticized the governor for what he considered to be truly outrageous conduct by a public official. He ended his little book by asking, "Was it for this that Roger Williams struggled through the wilderness?" Chafee, 80. Later, the episode was the subject of a famous poetic parody by yet another Harvard Law professor, W. Barton Leach. See *Harvard Law School Bulletin*, March 1968, 12–13.

governor had made no secret of his ambition to become a United States Senator, "but observers believed that [McGrath] would not offer him the [judgeship] unless . . . Quinn would consider the appointment permanent."[55]

Quinn requested and received legislative permission to take a leave of absence for service in the Navy during World War II, and returned to the bench just in time to encourage his supporters to launch an attempt to gain the senatorial nomination in 1946. Declining to play an active role in these efforts because of a fear of judicial impropriety—Quinn coyly stated that "he would run if the people want me."[56] In the meantime, McGrath, completing three successful terms as Governor, had resigned to become President Truman's Solicitor General. For the second time (but not the last), the paths of Quinn and McGrath converged.

In 1972, Judge Quinn claimed that McGrath had promised him that he would not seek the Democratic Senatorial nomination in 1946.[57] Possibly McGrath attached the same importance to this "promise" as Quinn had to the assumption that his 1941 judicial appointment implied an end to what political aspirations he might still have. At any rate, McGrath resigned as Solicitor General on June 7, 1946, to begin his campaign for the Senate seat, with the strong support of Theodore Green, himself ensconced in that chamber, as well as Governor [and future Senator] John Pastore. Against such an effective alliance utilizing appeals to Catholic, Protestant, Irish, and Italian interests, Quinn's supporters had little chance. The Convention rejected his candidacy by a vote of 145–52, although Quinn himself was not present at the convention.[58] In November, McGrath was elected, but his tenure as Senator would be very short.[59]

Two years later, Quinn again seriously considered running in the Democratic primary for United States Senator against the incumbent, Theodore Francis Green. But on July 30, 1948, the *Providence Daily Journal* reported that Quinn had removed himself as a candidate "in the interests of party harmony."[60] In the meantime, McGrath resigned from the Senate to become

[55] *Providence Daily Journal*, April 25, 1941, p. 22. Quinn was barely confirmed by the Rhode Island State Senate, the final vote being 22–21—with the Lieutenant Governor voting to break a tie. One Republican partisan hoped that Quinn "will make a good judge and uphold the Constitution on the bench better than he did as presiding officer of the Senate." Ibid., April 26, 1941, p. 1.

[56] Ibid., June 4, 1946, p. 1. It remains unclear how Quinn proposed to ascertain "if the people want me" except through the political tactic of a campaign on his behalf, but supposedly without his participation.

[57] Robert Quinn, *Oral History*, August 7, 1972, part II, 8.

[58] *Providence Daily Journal*, September 12, 1946, 1.

[59] While a Senator, he also served as the Chairman of the Democratic National Committee.

[60] Ibid., July 30, 1948, 1. Quinn apparently included the words "this year" in his withdrawal statement, leading a reporter to ask if these words meant that he might well run another time. Quinn responded, "He would have to leave that to the reporter's own imagination."

Attorney General, succeeding Tom Clark whom Truman had appointed to the United States Supreme Court. Again, Quinn found his way to another chance at a Senate seat blocked, this time by the plans of Governor Pastore to run himself—with the support of both Green and McGrath. By 1950, it may well have been clear to the former Governor that a seat in the Senate was not to be his. And while Green, McGrath, and Pastore realized the same thing, they were also well aware that Quinn's nickname "Fighting Bob" had some basis in fact. Comfortable neither with Green's organization, nor with McGrath's supporters, Quinn's continuing availability as a "dark horse" candidate might explain why all three politicians were so quick to urge his name upon Truman for appointment to the new Court.

Indeed, Green had first written to Truman about Quinn on August 1, 1950, when the selection process had barely begun, of "my interest in having Judge Quinn appointed to this position." He also reminded Truman that Quinn had been named to the Superior Court by "the Governor of Rhode Island, now Attorney General of the United States, our friend, J. Howard McGrath." Both my colleague John Pastore and I, Green concluded, "wish to recommend Judge Quinn for this appointment and we trust, Mr. President, that he will receive your favorable consideration."[61]

By March 1951, Marshall was aware of Quinn's candidacy. On March 26, his aide informed a member of Truman's staff, presumably John Steelman, that the Secretary wanted the Rhode Island judge listed for the new court. In turn, Steelman told Truman's assistant Martin Friedman that the former Governor "has already been brought to our attention as a candidate for this Court, [and] you will no doubt want to show the Secretary's interest."[62] There is no doubt that Truman had great respect for Marshall. Certainly his endorsement of Quinn may well have bolstered a candidacy already assured, as has been shown, of strong support by important Rhode Island political figures—not least of whom was Truman's own Attorney General and former Chairman of the Democratic National Committee, J. Howard McGrath.

TRUMAN'S ULTIMATE CHOICES

Thus by the spring of 1951, Donald Dawson—the presidential assistant charged with maintaining files from which Truman made numerous appointments—knew that Brosman, Latimer, and Quinn all were important candidates for the new tribunal. Even as George Marshall endorsed Quinn, addi-

[61] TP, Box 994, Folder "Q-R," January 11, 1951. Five days later, the Chairman of the Democratic National Committee, William Boyle, Jr., wrote to Dawson urging that President Truman give "serious consideration" to four individuals. The first name on Boyle's list was Robert E. Quinn. Ibid., Box 995, Folder "End-Misc," January 16, 1951.

[62] Martin Friedman Papers, Truman Library, Box 5, March 26, 1951.

tional efforts were launched on behalf of Latimer, a Republican from Utah, by a Democratic Congresswoman—Reva Beck Bosone, the first woman ever sent to Congress from that state.[63] A strong Truman loyalist during the 1948 campaign, in 1951 Bosone took aim at Frank Riter, the other Utah Republican in the running for a seat on the Court. She advised the White House that "Riter is a vitriolic and venomous hater of the President, the Administration, [and] practically all Democrats, and she sincerely hopes that the President is not thinking of appointing him."[64] Dawson was promptly informed of Bosone's comments.[65]

Bosone was not the only Utah Democrat in favor of Latimer's appointment. Essentially uninterested in politics, the State Supreme Court Justice enjoyed bipartisan support. His candidacy, for example, was strongly endorsed by the Utah Secretary of State and the Chief Justice of its Supreme Court, both Democrats. Indeed, Chief Justice Wolfe emphasized to Truman that "in making this recommendation I have allowed nothing but my belief in Judge Latimer's fitness for the position to influence my recommendation."[66]

Although it seems likely that Dawson had narrowed the list of candidates to about a dozen by April 1951—it is far from clear how many applicants were known to the White House. On July 3, 1950, Vaughan wrote that there were about "six thousand applications for the three positions."[67] Three months later, Vaughan informed another correspondent that there had been 3,500 applications, including "several members of Congress and two State Supreme Court Judges."[68] By the end of January 1951, Vaughan observed that "there were almost four thousand applications for the three jobs[,] and the amount of political pressure for some of the candidates is really remark-

[63] She served from 1949 to 1953, being defeated for reelection during the Eisenhower landslide of 1952. An attempt at recapturing her seat in 1954 failed, and she never again sat in Congress.

[64] TP, Box 995, Folder "End-Misc," March 23, 1951. Although at first Bosone seemed content with her phone communication to the White House, later she decided to discuss Latimer's candidacy directly with the President—whom she saw on April 10, 1951. Ibid., Box 991, File "303 misc," April 5, 10, 1951.

[65] Bosone later recalled that "when it came time for President Truman to appoint the three judges, and I found out about it," Quinn and Brosman had apparently been selected. Truman "was then considering the Republican member[,]" for which there were numerous candidates, including Latimer. "When I heard this I dived in and did all I could to get the appointment for George. If the Democratic spots had gone, then I couldn't see why Utah couldn't get an appointment even though it was a Republican one. George Latimer was appointed and I am proud of him." Reva Beck Bosone Papers, University of Utah Library, Box 1, Folder 13. See also Beverly Clopton, *Her Honor the Judge*. (Ames: Iowa State University Press, 1980), 228–29.

[66] LATPAP, April 12, 1951.

[67] TP, Box 992, Folder "C," July 3, 1950. Vaughan added that "I can't see how the Department of Justice would have any influence in this choice as it is largely a military matter." Possibly unaware of the McGrath-Quinn connection, here Vaughan indicated yet again his failure to understand the nature of the politics involving presidential appointments.

[68] Ibid., Box 992, Folder "B," October 23, 1950.

able."[69] For his part, Truman stated on February 2, 1951, that "I have almost a thousand applications for these three jobs . . . and I am having a very difficult time in getting them sorted out."[70] In April, Donald Dawson remarked that "actually, it seems there are many people who feel qualified and want this particular appointment more than any other I have ever seen."[71]

With the new Court mandated by law to begin operations in June, by May 15 Felix Larkin became concerned about the delay in appointments. "We are at a loss," he wrote to Edmund Morgan, "to know what is going on in the White House. The time is now running so short that I am quite alarmed about the ability of any judges to be oriented in time to handle the problems that are going to start flooding in on June 1. There have been no announcements as to appointments, as you know. I expect that I will have to get busy in the next day or two and see if we can't get something done."[72]

On May 15, Connecticut Senator William Benton wrote to President Truman concerning segregation in the military. Evidence compiled by Thurgood Marshall, "special counsel for the NAACP . . . indicates a considerable degree of race prejudice in the administration of the court-martial machinery." The problem was worse in the Army than in the other services. Benton knew that "race problems in the administration of military justice cannot be eliminated merely by a Presidential directive or by a blanket amendment [to the UCMJ]. "Your appointment of a qualified Negro to the highest tribunal of military justice, however, would give dramatic emphasis to your policy and program of equality, and would have cumulative and incalculable effects on the administration . . . throughout the armed forces."[73]

According to Truman's secretary, Benton's letter was not received at the White House until May 23, one day after the President had sent the names of his three choices up to the Senate. He assured Benton that Truman's appointments, all of whom were white, "will constitute a Court eminently qualified to take fair and impartial action in all cases which come to it for review."[74] In fact, neither Presidents Truman, Eisenhower, Kennedy, nor Johnson appointed any blacks to the Court of Military Appeals.[75] That precedent fell first to Richard Nixon followed by Gerald Ford, as will be discussed in a later chapter.

Truman interviewed each of his ultimate choices before announcing their

[69] Ibid., Box 994, Folder "T–V," January 30, 1951.

[70] Ibid., Box 992, Folder "D–E," February 2, 1951.

[71] Ibid., Box 994, Folder "S," April 25, 1951.

[72] LP, May 15, 1951. What specific steps Larkin may have taken are not known, but within five days Truman announced his choices.

[73] TP, Box 995, Folder "End-Misc," May 15, 1951.

[74] Ibid., May 23, 1951.

[75] In his list of suggested names submitted to Dawson, the Chairman of the Democratic National Committee had specifically endorsed one black candidate, Roy Garvin.

appointment. Although he left no written evidence as to why he specifically selected Brosman, Latimer, and Quinn for the Court, besides the political connotations which have already been discussed—the President may well have been aware of some if not all of the following factors.

Each service was represented on the new bench: Quinn from the Navy, Latimer from the Army, and Brosman from the Air Force. Each had worked in military justice, although only Latimer appears to have had actual combat participation. They came from disparate sections of the country: Quinn from New England, Brosman from Louisiana, and Latimer from Utah. In terms of religious preference, the new judges included a Catholic, a Mormon, and an Episcopalian. Two of the three had prior judicial experience: Quinn at the trial level as a Rhode Island Superior Court Judge, and Latimer at the appellate level as a member of the Utah Supreme Court. While both Quinn and Latimer had long been away from the mainstream of major changes in legal education, Paul Brosman was currently Dean of Tulane University Law School.

It is not unreasonable to conclude that Truman chose carefully. Unlike any of his successors, Truman took the time to interview all three men before making his final selections. Politics, of course, was a factor. But such considerations may not have dominated his thinking. Thus, he could have named the Republican, Latimer, to the short five-year term. Instead, Latimer received the ten-year appointment.

On the other hand, the President appears to have been party to an arrangement unique in the history of the Court. When he named Quinn as Chief Judge with a fifteen-year term, Truman agreed that Quinn could maintain his chambers in Providence, commuting to Washington only when the Court was in session or conference. There were probably two reasons for Quinn's preferring such a policy. He would not have to uproot his family, which included five children. Also, while remaining in Rhode Island he might be better able to capitalize on an opportunity, should it arise, to run for the Senate.[76] It may well be that Quinn, who alone among the first three judges appears not to have solicited his appointment, insisted on such an arrange-

[76] Both Norma Q. Richards and Robert C. Quinn have indicated in several conversations with this author that even after he had joined the new Court, their father continued to hope that an opportunity for him to go to the Senate might yet materialize. In 1960, nine years after he assumed his USCMA post, and at the age of sixty-six, Quinn quietly encouraged a movement to nominate him as the Democratic candidate to succeed Senator Theodore Green. There was a small amount of solicitation on his behalf. Indeed, his old adversary J. Howard McGrath, recommended his selection. *Providence Daily Journal*, July 30, 1960, 1. Quinn drafted a statement. He was "not anxious to relinquish" his "very important job" as Chief Judge. "However, if after careful consideration, the responsible leaders of my party conclude that my energies and talents are of greater value to the state and nation in the United States Senate, I am ready and willing to stand for election. . . ." Quinn Papers Personal Correspondence, undated; hereafter cited as QPPC. The Quinn bubble soon burst, and neither he, McGrath, nor former Governor Dennis Roberts (who received the party's "official" endorsement) won the primary. Claiborne Pell captured both the nomination and election.

ment as a condition to accepting the new post. Whatever the reason for it, Truman's acquiescence in this arrangement has not been followed by any other president in appointing future judges to this tribunal. While it may have benefited Quinn, on the whole this practice was highly detrimental for the Court as an institution.[77]

With the three nominations pending before the Senate, George Spiegelberg wrote to his fellow members of the ABA Special Committee on Military Justice. He described Quinn as "almost surely a McGrath appointee," one who during his term as Rhode Island Governor "gave as fine a demonstration of command control as has ever been seen." The episode, according to Spiegelberg, "does not augur too well for the future of military justice." Latimer—while apparently well respected in Utah—"was a classmate of Gen. Harry H. Vaughan at one of the courses given by the Army, and there would seem to be little doubt as to the source of his backing." Brosman, on the other hand, "is universally respected." Spiegelberg concluded his letter with the accurate observation that "as you know, none of the [three] men were on the list sent the President by the [ABA] president."[78]

Truman sent the three names to the Senate on May 22, 1951. But the Armed Services Committee, absorbed in the MacArthur removal controversy, did not take up the nominations until June 16 and then with an interest that was desultory at best. At an unusual Saturday morning hearing, the Committee chairman, Georgia Democrat Senator Richard Russell, remarked that "this court is something new in anything I know of in the judicial system. . . . I personally had misgivings about the creation of this court." Conceding that there were cases within the military where individuals had not received even decent treatment, let alone justice, Russell still insisted that "any abuse of the powers of this court will be disastrous to this Nation. . . ." He further noted, "I am sure that you gentlemen will in your duties temper justice with that knowledge that this will indeed be a court of military justice[,] and will not be an agency that will be damaging to the observance of discipline in the armed services."[79]

Nevertheless, Russell recalled that members of his Committee "were so

[77] The arrangement frequently left Latimer acting as a quasi–chief Judge, with much of the responsibility but little authority. In a more subtle vein, Quinn's absence from the Court for weeks at a time inevitably meant a loss of collegiality. See below.

[78] Quinn Papers, hereafter cited as QPGF, May 31, 1951.

[79] Unpublished typescript of hearing (82) SArs-T. 34, Senate Armed Services Committee: Nominations to the Court of Military Appeals, 27–28 (June 16, 1951), on file in the United States Senate Library. From the Court's earliest history to the present, Russell's sentiments have been reiterated in different forums; insisting on the point that military justice was somehow subordinate to military discipline. Whether or not they cast a pall over the perceived independence of the new tribunal is unclear. However, their continued emphasis has probably been detrimental to rigorous civilian-judicial scrutiny concerning military justice. See Jonathan Lurie, "Military Justice 50 Years after Nuremberg: Some Reflections on Appearance v. Reality," *Military Law Review* 149 (1996), 178–86, 183.

impressed by the qualifications of the nominees that they took the unusual step of voting unanimous approval, with the appointees present in the committee room."[80] The full Senate concurred three days later. If the Armed Services Committee reflected little concern with the nominations, the Senate seemed more disinterested, if possible. The three judges were not even approved by voice vote, but merely with the presiding officer stating of each appointment that "without objection, the nomination is confirmed."[81] On June 20, the new judges were sworn into office by District Judge Matthew McGuire, whose criticism of military justice during World War II had preceded creation of the Code Committee.[82]

Its former chairman, Edmund Morgan, wrote to Felix Larkin that the columnist Drew Pearson had indicated "that I should have been named. This seems like high praise for the President's choice."[83] Morgan added that one reason he would probably have accepted the appointment, had it been offered, "was the chance to be where I could frequently see you and Marx (not Karl), and the chance to put our notions as to the Court in operation."[84] Larkin responded with "a keen disappointment that you were not nominated . . . , but I recognize that you are well out of it. Having met and talked with the Judges at some length, I feel fairly encouraged, and I think we can look forward to some fairly good operations."[85] The extent to which Larkin's optimism was justified is discussed in the following chapters.

[80] *New York Times*, June 17, 1951, 17. According to Spiegelberg, "I understand that Senator McCarran is going to make a fight as he believes that the judiciary committee should pass upon the candidates' qualifications." Supra, n. 78. As far as I can tell, McCarran made no such attempt. If he did, apparently it was not in the form of an official motion recorded in the Congressional Record.

[81] 97 *Congressional Record*, 82nd Cong., 1st sess., June 19, 1951, 6746–47. Senator Russell Long spoke briefly about Brosman. Utah Senators Watkins and Bennett paid tribute to Latimer, and no Senator commented about Quinn.

[82] See the first volume of this study, *Arming Military Justice*.

[83] According to Pearson, Robert Quinn "has some of the dictatorial brass hattedness that needs to be cured in the Army." Pearson's column, "The Washington Merry-Go-Round," appears in *The Washington Post*, June 19, 1951, 16. Harry Vaughan claimed that the column was "in line with Pearson's usual inaccuracies." He added, probably with some accuracy, that he "did not influence the final selections. . . . Pearson, as is characteristic of him, is more interested in writing an article that he considers will attract readers than he is in writing facts." TP, Official File, Box 991, File 303 Misc., June 28, 1951. According to Judge Latimer's son, George Latimer, Jr., Pearson later acknowledged that he had been wrong in attributing Latimer's appointment to Vaughan's influence. LATPAP, note 47, n.d., n.p., annotated by George Latimer, Jr. The recent biographers of James Forrestal described Pearson as "a muckraking journalist of demonic dimensions[,]. . . . endowed through a perversion of his Quaker origins with an invincible self-righteousness. . . . [H]e was, in fact, moved by his own ingrained prejudices. . . ." See Townsend Hoopes and Douglas Brinkley, *Driven Patriot: The Life and Times of James Forrestal* (1992), 432.

[84] LP, July 5, 1951. "Marx" was Morgan's former student Marx Leva, who had recently resigned as Assistant Secretary of Defense to enter private law practice. He wrote to Morgan that "the failure to appoint you [was] an error of monumental proportions." MPVU, July 9, 1951.

[85] LP, July 11, 1951.

1. Judges Latimer, Quinn, and Brosman

CHAPTER 2

Initial Court Organization and Operation, 1951–1955 An Overview

THE SELECTION and confirmation of Judges Quinn, Latimer, and Brosman represented the culmination of Felix Larkin's official involvement with the new Court—an association that began in 1948 with plans to enact a uniform code of military justice. Before 1951 ended, both Larkin and Marx Leva had left the Defense Department.[1] But while still serving as General Counsel, Larkin received the draft of tentative job descriptions for the various appointments of administrative positions within the Court of Military Appeals. It was one thing to appoint and confirm three judges. It was quite another to delineate the contours of a new judicial tribunal, with the special functions required by the UCMJ. Problems of appropriate quarters, initial court organization, and perceptions of the tribunal itself—all represented challenges apart from the business of adjudicating cases.

CONFIGURATION OF COMMISSIONERS AND CLERK

Although not dated, the memorandum submitted to Larkin was probably prepared in the spring of 1951, and may well have served as the basis for the initial organizational meetings held among the three judges during June and July. The document provided descriptions for proposed staff positions—such as librarian, reporter, and marshal. Of special interest, however, were the descriptions for the "Law Assistant" and clerk of the Court. John Henderson, the member of Larkin's staff who signed—if not wrote—the memorandum, noted the unusual importance of the law assistant.

This post should be held by a lawyer "of considerable maturity[,] with

[1] Larkin became an executive with the firm of W. R. Grace, and received a warm letter of congratulations from Edmund Morgan, teaching law at Vanderbilt University. "As someone remarked to a friend of mine who had taken a high executive position with a large baking company: 'You're in the big dough now.'" MPVU, September 13, 1951. Although Larkin did serve on the soon-to-be-constituted Court Committee, his active and effective role in developing a military justice appellate system ended with his resignation as General Counsel of the Department of Defense.

experience in the field of military justice."[2] His basic function "would be to provide continuity of legal assistance to the three judges." His responsibilities, in other words, were to be quite different from those of a law clerk to a specific judge. Here, Henderson could draw on the traditional law clerk responsibilities as developed in other appellate tribunals—functions that have remained remarkably constant over the years. The law clerk would summarize briefs, abstract cases, research points of law, develop a legal position on other issues that might not have been covered in submitted briefs or oral argument, and prepare rough drafts of opinions on pending cases for the judge. Henderson assumed, quite reasonably, that as with many appellate courts, the law clerk would be a recent law school graduate.[3]

On the other hand, since the court was a specialized tribunal, "the recent . . . graduates who will be the law clerks will have a greater problem training themselves to the point where they can be useful to the judges than do law clerks for circuit court [jurists]." Moreover, traditional appellate courts "operate in the broad spheres of constitutional, administrative, and private law for which law school training is peculiarly apt." But "the substantive problems of military justice . . . will have been considered little if at all in law school curricula." Henderson assumed, therefore, that the law assistant "will help indoctrinate each new law clerk, and will, at least for the first part of a law clerk's tenure, review the written material the law clerk prepares for his judge."[4]

There may well have been additional reasons, however, why this early draft for court structure called for a legal assistant or commissioner besides the factors just cited. Law clerks, often just beginning their legal careers, would understandably tend to reflect the nuances, style, and approach to issues demonstrated by the judge for whom they worked. The law assistant, and by implication the lawyers with whom he worked (now known as the central legal staff), would presumably have no such sense of juridical parochialism. Thus, at the outset the judges could receive an assessment of the case completely independent of chambers, and while their law clerks might later prepare their memorandum of the cases including recommendations, an additional independent opinion could be of great value. Moreover, there was an

[2] Quinn Papers, General Files, *QPGF*. Undated memorandum for the General Counsel. "Tentative Job Descriptions for the Various Staff Positions . . . ," 1.

[3] Ibid.

[4] Ibid. "The law assistant must [also] be an expert at researching with speed and accuracy all varieties of legal questions in the field of military justice. . . . It is to be expected that he will not only prepare legal memoranda for individual judges[,] but that he will also do intensive research on questions propounded by the Court as a whole." The question arises why such a memo came from the General Counsel's Office in the Defense Department, rather than from the judges themselves, and whether it indicated inappropriate intimacy between the military establishment and the new tribunal. As will be seen, Quinn and his brethren became much more sensitive to this issue.

important element of practicality. Time constraints indicated that it would be impossible for three judges to read every page of every record of every case submitted to them for possible review. Initial scrutiny from an experienced legal staff could only make the mandate of the new tribunal easier to fulfill.[5]

A final factor though not articulated, was probably assumed. While all three appointees to the Court were familiar with the military, none had had that extensive experience in working with military justice possessed by full-time attorneys specializing in this field. The new tribunal needed a specialist with hands-on expertise. Such a position might be unusual in a federal appellate court, but for jurists interpreting a new code within a new court of specialized jurisdiction, it was necessary—and the judges knew it. The candidate they selected, Richard Tedrow, possessed such qualifications; and in August 1951, Judge Paul Brosman explained with some candor the rationale for this new appointment to the Court staff.

Although ultimately the judges would decide for themselves whether or not to hear a case, "it is essential that first consideration and analysis be afforded by others, and that we enjoy the detailed guidance of mature, able, and experienced lawyers." It was to be expected that a law clerk "will be a bright but inexperienced young law school graduate, and ordinarily . . . there will be a good deal of turnover in the position." Seeking, on the other hand, "maturity and experience, as well as continuity, the Court provided for a functionary . . . [,] and arranged for him a position of relative dignity in the Government service, and a substantial compensation."[6] Viewed from the bottom, according to Brosman, "he might be regarded as a super law clerk. However, considered from the top, he might almost be characterized as an assistant judge."[7]

As Brosman indicated, the usual expectation in most federal tribunals is that the judges stay for many years, while their subordinates change on a regular basis. The Court of Military Appeals has not followed this pattern.

[5] As early as June 22, 1951, less than three weeks after he had formally applied for the post of law assistant [he ultimately received the appointment], Richard Tedrow made it clear that providing the initial examination of petitions for review could be a function of what would become the central legal staff. He wrote to Judge Brosman that "the proposition of an assistant legal advisor may be also open to question[. T]his depends on whether the court intends to vest any of the initial processing of applications in that particular office." QPGF, June 22, 1951. Tedrow had served in the Navy during World War II, but at the time of his appointment to the court staff was on active duty in the Air Force JAG Office. He had testified before the House Subcommittee that considered the UCMJ, and was well acquainted with both Quinn and Brosman. On June 4, when he formally applied for the job of "legal administrator" to the Court, Tedrow added a handwritten note to Quinn expressing "my sincerest thanks and gratitude for your kindness." Ibid., June 4, 1951.

[6] SF, August 28, 1951, 13. This "functionary," was briefly known as a law assistant, general counsel, and by July 16, 1951, as the chief commissioner: a title that remained constant for the next twenty years. Only the judges received a higher salary than the chief commissioner.

[7] Ibid.

Less than half of its members remained on the bench long enough to complete their terms. Thus far in the Court's history, only five judges out of sixteen have served more than ten years.[8] On the other hand, some lawyers originally described as law assistants or commissioners but now called the "central legal staff" have remained at the Court, while the judges have moved on. Even among counsel assigned to each Judge's chambers, there has been a tendency for these lawyers to continue on the court staff, often working first for one judge and then for the replacement.[9]

It seems clear from Henderson's draft that the chief law "commissioner" (now known as the director of the Central legal staff) was to receive a higher salary than the Clerk of the Court, who had to combine a "good legal background with a highly trained administrative ability."[10] The Clerk was responsible "for the general administrative supervision of Court proceedings." Legal training and experience was required "so that the clerk can draft orders of Court in accordance with opinions, present emergency matters to the Court, answer inquiries regarding court procedure[,] and in general function as an expert on the rules of Court and on the Federal Rules. . . ."[11] But from the early years of USCMA history to the present, the Court Clerk has had minimal involvement with the actual process of judging—examinations of petitions, assigning cases for review, decision preparation, etc.

With Henderson's draft as its basis, in September 1951 the Court submitted this description of the Clerk's duties to the Defense Department.

[8] Of this number, Robert Quinn served for almost twenty-five years, a record thus far unmatched in USCMA history. Homer Ferguson, who joined the Court in 1956, continued to sit as a Senior judge after the expiration of his fifteen-year term.

[9] Richard Tedrow, the first Chief Commissioner, served in this capacity for eighteen years, during which period six judges sat on the USCMA bench. There is no doubt that an appellate judge should be exposed to ongoing and changing developments in law—and new talent fresh out of law school can be very helpful in this sense. Nevertheless, it should be noted that lawyers who have worked for fifteen or twenty years on the staff of a specialized tribunal such as this one may well have developed expertise that an incoming judge will disregard to his or her detriment, as well as that of the overall quality of military justice. One solution, which USCMA has followed in recent years, is for a judge to have at least one position within chambers arranged so that there can be regular turnover, but not at the expense of continuity.

[10] Henderson listed the various proposed positions in a descending order of perceived importance, beginning with the law assistant, and ending with the marshal. A draft for court positions dated May 28, 1951, lists the law assistant with a proposed salary of $8,000, while the Clerk of the Court was to receive $7,600. An undated draft has the job listed as "Attorney-advisor," but both place the position at a civil service rank of GS 14, with that of the Clerk at GS 13. By July 1951, Tedrow had been formally appointed as the Chief Commissioner of the new Court, although newspaper clippings indicate that for a very short time, the post may have been called "general counsel" to the Court.

[11] Ibid. Henderson's job description for the Clerk remains valid. On the other hand, he did not anticipate the possibility of friction between the chief commissioner, now called the director of the central legal staff, and the Clerk—based not so much on personality as on differing perceptions of functions within the Court. Occasionally, such friction has been apparent in the Court's history. Interview, Alfred Proulx, July 26, 1988; Albert Fletcher, Jr., August 4, 1994.

> He will have full responsibility for establishing the office systems of the Court, including the procedures for the handling of all papers . . . , the organization and maintenance of files and filing procedures, the listing of all cases for hearing, the general administrative preparation for hearings, the maintenance of up-to-date dockets and court calendars, supervision of arrangements with the printer, preparation of budget estimates and/or fiscal procedures, recruitment and training of personnel other than the General Counsel and law clerks, and any other functions consistent with the business management of the court operations.[12]

For the post of Clerk, Quinn selected Alfred C. Proulx, a native of West Warwick, Rhode Island—the Chief Judge's hometown. As a young man, Proulx had played golf at Quinn's West Warwick Country Club, a course still operated by the Quinn family. Graduating from Holy Cross and Georgetown University Law School, by 1951 he was a captain in the Naval Reserve, and working for the Federal Register in Washington. Possessed of an ability to organize administrative procedures, comfortable in office management, and knowledgeable in the somewhat unusual nuances of governmental life in Washington—Proulx apparently was Quinn's first and only choice for the job. In addition to his long acquaintance with the former governor, Proulx shared his love of golf, lifelong identification with the Democratic party, and branch of military service.[13]

Like Proulx, Chief Commissioner Tedrow had also been in the Navy, and indeed had become acquainted with the new clerk during this period. But there the similarity between Tedrow and Proulx ended. Although he would work with Proulx and Chief Judge Quinn for almost twenty years, Tedrow seems never to have gained that close relationship that existed between the judge and the clerk of the court.[14] Intense in manner, and easily agitated, Tedrow combined ability with irascibility.[15] He also had marked appreciation

[12] Personnel File, Alfred Proulx, in USCMAP, September 6, 1951. Further examination of this job description reveals that potential for tension between the clerk and chief commissioner, previously noted. Thus the clerk's duties in addition to all those just cited, would also "include . . . the development, in conjunction with the judges, of what continuing procedures should be established which will develop a method of segregation of cases which should be heard by the Court[,] and those which should be returned without action due to the fact that they do not meet the legal requirements for [judicial] consideration." Ibid.

[13] Proulx later recalled that he found designing a new court administrative system an exciting prospect. When he reminded Quinn that he had no court experience, Quinn responded: "Don't worry about it. We'll start from scratch, and we'll work it out." Interview, Alfred Proulx, July 26, 1988, 9.

[14] Together with Richard Tedrow, the two men worked with Quinn for almost a generation, providing a link of continuity between the beginning and early maturation of the court as an institution. The link was unbroken until 1969, when after eighteen years of service Tedrow took early retirement on the grounds of ill health. Proulx would complete more than twenty years, not leaving until 1972 after Chief Judge Quinn had been summarily removed as Chief Judge by President Nixon. See below, chapter 9.

[15] Quinn undoubtedly appreciated Tedrow's legal acumen, but the relationship between the two never attained the level of confidence and trust that Quinn placed in Proulx.

for his own considerable proficiency as an expert in military justice.[16] Proulx, on the other hand, radiated charm blended with an easygoing efficiency, often disguised as informality.

As the new court recruited its staff, apparently the judges considered political endorsements as well as legal/military experience. In June 1951, the administrative assistant to Senator Green informed Chief Judge Quinn that "Major David F. Condon, a personal friend of mine . . . is definitely interested in being considered for appointment as a member of your staff. Between you and me, Bob, he is a darn good Democrat, got plenty on the ball, and a fellow that you would like to have working for you."[17] Other candidates employed different kinds of political contacts. When Navy JAG officer Francis Tappaan applied for a job as commissioner, letters on his behalf came in from the Chairman of the Atomic Energy Commission, Senators Richard Nixon and Harry Byrd, and Congressman Albert Gore—[father of the current United States Vice President]. Chief Judge Quinn not only acknowledged all the endorsements, but later wrote another series of letters confirming that Tappaan had indeed been appointed.[18] One individual, Charles Dickson—a former JAG officer—not only expressed interest in the new tribunal, but also claimed to have been one of its creators.[19] His almost proprietary concern for the Court was understandable, although ultimately unrewarding.

DICKSON DEMANDS NEW DEVELOPMENTS

In October 1951, Dickson addressed a handwritten card to the Secretary of Defense asking that his office determine "whether or not I possess the qualifications for appointment as a consultant of the Defense Department in military justice matters."[20] Upon receiving a polite letter of rejection, Dickson

[16] In 1957, for example, Tedrow informed an official of the Ford Foundation that "in connection with these matters[,] please allow me to say, without either vanity or false modesty, that it has been said, by others I assure you, that I know as much about the subject as any man alive." Declining to deny the statement, he added, "I can assure you that my knowledge is considerable." Homer Ferguson Papers, [hereafter cited as FP], June 7, 1957, 3. Box 17, Folder 3. Undoubtedly loyal to the Court he served for almost nineteen years, nevertheless Tedrow did not hesitate to criticize decisions with which he disagreed. As he wrote in a letter published in the *Judge Advocate Journal*, "nor do I by any means agree with all decisions by CMA [Court of Military Appeals], but you do not see my name on any of them." *Judge Advocate Journal* 20 (1955), 44.

[17] QPGF, June 11, 1951. Given Quinn's long association with Theodore Green, one might expect that an endorsement from his office would carry some weight. Condon was duly appointed commissioner to the Court.

[18] QPPC, May 2, 1952.

[19] For background on Dickson's earlier activities concerning USCMA, see AMJ, 150–52.

[20] 1 ARF, October 19, 1951. "I am certain," he added, that "early in 1952 the Congress should enact additional legislation relating to the Court of Military Appeals." In point of fact, Congress

responded with a longer letter, with copies sent to Truman's Military Aide Harry Vaughan, Senator Lyndon Johnson, and Congressman Paul Kilday, who ten years later would be appointed to the Court by President Kennedy. Replete with recollections of his personal efforts to see an appellate tribunal established, Dickson claimed that his original plan had called for a nine-member Court, serving with life tenure. "I am convinced," he wrote, that Congress would have created such a tribunal, "had it not been for the opposition from the Pentagon[;]" opposition personified by Kenneth Royall . . . "the most uncompromising antagonist of the idea of creating a Court of military Appeals."[21]

Based upon "personal knowledge from my personal contacts in the Pentagon," Dickson predicted that "no move to . . . amend the Military Justice Code will ever be initiated by the [JAG] Departments. . . . While I accuse no one of bad faith, I am certain that no tears would be shed in the Pentagon if the [USCMA] were abolished entirely." Emphasizing the need, as he saw it, to have more judges and staff named to the Court, Dickson concluded that he would "be glad to render any service I can" to the Department of Defense in the matter of military justice—"without any compensation in addition to my retired pay."[22] On behalf of the judges, Proulx wrote merely that they "were quite interested in your comments and recommendations[,] and have asked me to advise you of their appreciation of the same."[23]

Undaunted by the lack of interest generated by his offer, Dickson tried once more. He believed that USCMA "has made a good start[,] but I am convinced that unless a few of us 'civilians' get together and give this infant court some real help," its machinery "may break down of its own weight."[24] In 1953, he prepared a "Citizen's Petition" on the subject of military justice, and as he had done five years before, took care to see that it was widely distributed. Making due allowance for Dickson's myopia, his suggestion for changes in the Court remains a remarkable statement—especially in the light of future USCMA history.

In his mimeographed petition, the sixty-five-year-old retired army officer

made no major revisions to the UCMJ until 1968—although, as will be seen, this was not for want of interest on the part of the Court.

[21] Ibid., December 12, 1951. For information on Army Secretary Royall's opposition to the new civilian court that ultimately became USCMA, see AMJ, chapters 8–11.

[22] Dickson was wrong in his first prediction, but correct in the second. The military did indeed try to initiate changes to the Code, without approval of the Court members; and in 1990, Congress increased the size of the Court from three to five members. I have found nothing to substantiate his other claim that the military insisted on limiting the Court to three members. It would seem that Morgan had long supported a judicial council of "at least three three members." AMJ, 171–73. Who would appoint them and for how long were the main issues of concern.

[23] 1 ARF, January 25, 1952.

[24] 3 CF, but dated December 31, 1952.

called for an increase in the number of judges from three to seven. He urged that it be removed from administrative control of the Pentagon, and that it "function as an independent unit of the Judicial System of the U.S.A." Moreover, he proposed that the limit of its authority to matters of law be removed, that all intermediate Boards of Review be abolished, that USCMA appellate jurisdiction be expanded, that the Court, and not the JAG, should appoint appellate defense counsel, drawn from its own bar, and finally that the "orders, judgements and decrees of [USCMA] be enforceable by the Court's own process, with power to punish for contempt[,] for disobedience—as well as disorder in the Court's presence."[25]

Although Dickson failed to articulate his point clearly, the implication of his proposals was that as currently constituted the Court was not a real court, clothed with the authority common to most federal appellate tribunals. As will be seen, the judges of the Court of Military Appeals felt the same way, and while the name of Charles Dickson is not mentioned in any of the numerous memoranda that would flow from the court seeking such powers, they echoed his perceptions. Dickson concluded with a "statement which I am ready to prove to anyone who doubts its accuracy. If the suggestions I have made are adopted . . . the current cost to the Government of administering Military Justice will be cut to one-half of the present amount, and the quality of Justice dispensed will be greatly improved to the benefit of both morale and discipline in our Armed Forces."[26]

THE QUEST FOR QUARTERS

With three judges appointed and confirmed, with two senior administrative officers of the Court selected—the new tribunal was ready to begin receiving cases. But where would it hold court? While attention had been given to this question even before the judges were nominated, the actual process by which USCMA came to its present home remains an intriguing if unlikely tale. Quinn, it turns out, was quite right to rely on Proulx, who in this matter like so many others demonstrated discretion together with an adroit sense of timing.

From the Court's early years to the present, its relationship with the De-

[25] 1 ARF, March 5, 1953.

[26] 26. Ibid. Fiscal considerations aside, like Cassandra of ancient legend doomed to tell the truth but be ignored—Dickson seems to have been more right than wrong—even as those who reviewed his petition probably dismissed it as the work of a retired crank. Apparently oblivious to the requirements for political and practical compromise that had guided Morgan's committee as well as the Congress in enacting the UCMJ, nevertheless Dickson identified what UCMA's judges also felt was a weakness in their court's mandate. The extent to which it has affected the tribunal's ability to operate, and how the Court has acted to increase judicial authority where it is believed to be necessary remain matters of debate.

fense Department on occasion has been uneasy, although rarely hostile. There was no doubt that Morgan's committee intended the new tribunal to be judicially independent of the Pentagon. Yet, it is equally certain that the court was to be administered by that branch of government.[27] In retrospect, defense department officials have managed—for the most part—to respect this bifurcation, drawing a fine line between judicial interference and fiscal/administrative management. And indeed, while there have been instances where the line may have been obscured to some extent, it has yet to be obliterated.[28] Very early in USCMA history, the question about location of the Court indicated the difficulty in marking out the line's demarcation.

Even as President Truman sent the names of his three choices for USCMA to the Senate, Larkin's office was concerned about the possibility that the new tribunal might be assigned quarters outside of Washington, due to the shortage of available space. On May 23, 1951, Robert Haydock, a member of Larkin's staff (and, like his boss, soon to leave the Defense Department), drafted a letter to the functionary charged with space allocation. The new court "is conceived on a level with the United States Court of Appeals. It is a tribunal to which a significant share of public confidence in the administration of military justice will be attributable. For this reason it is appropriate that the Court should be located at the seat of government."[29]

Less than a month later, Deputy Secretary of Defense Robert Lovett addressed another letter to the Administrator of the General Services Administration. Again, he emphasized that the "success or failure of the Code [UCMJ] and its acceptance by the public depends to a large extent upon the distinction and influence of this court." Anticipating the point that the new court could have taken space in the Pentagon, Lovett emphasized that "this has been rejected as contrary to the wishes of Congress and the judicial character of the Court. While the Department of Defense is charged with performing certain administrative functions for the Court, these must not interfere or in any way appear to interfere with the independence of the

[27] The first and latest versions of the UCMJ reflect this tension. Morgan's draft as submitted to Congress in 1949 noted that the court, then called the judicial council, "is hereby established in the National Military Establishment." UCMJ, 1949, *Text, References and Commentary*, 94. The 1984 version of the UCMJ states that the court is "located for administrative purposes only in the Department of Defense." UCMJ, 1984, s. 867, Art. 67, (a) (1). Actually, this language long predates the 1983 amendments to the UCMJ.

[28] After a history of more than forty years, all parties involved in appellate military justice pay homage to the concept of an independent civilian appellate court. Much more difficult to assess is the effect of its very close relationship to the Pentagon in administrative areas. This author feels that rhetoric aside, the shadow of the Pentagon looms large over the Court; and while USCMA can be described as a sort of "judicial menace," looking, as it were, over the shoulders of the services, the same might be said of the awesome defense establishment in relation to the Court itself.

[29] National Archives, Records of the Secretary of Defense, SD 250, May 23, 1951; copy in USCMAP.

Court."[30] Apparently the plan to have the Court housed in the Pentagon went no further. But there remained a question of the court's actual location.

In the meantime, Proulx and his boss had not been idle. Originally, Chief Judge Quinn sought to get the old Supreme Court Chamber in the Capitol assigned as permanent quarters for the new Court of Military Appeals. He even spoke with the chairman of the Senate Rules Committee, only to learn that some senators were currently using adjoining rooms, and "he felt it would be impossible to move them."[31] Through a few of his contacts, Proulx negotiated an agreement to use the courtroom of the U.S. Court of Customs and Patents Appeals, then located in the Internal Revenue Service's building, on a temporary basis. In use only several days each month, it was readily available, all the more as the Court of Military Appeals planned—at least for the immediate future—to be in session for just two consecutive days each month.

At the same time, Quinn and his colleagues addressed a letter to Chief Judge Harold M. Stephens of the United States Circuit Court of Appeals for the District of Columbia. Knowing that this court would soon be moving into a large new building, and that Stephens would "have control of allocating space" in it, Quinn asked his help in providing appropriate accommodations for USCMA. The letter added that "during a recent conference with President Truman concerning the future of the court[,] Judge Quinn raised the pressing problem of the court's quarters. The President expressed interest and concern and indicated that he would consult you on our behalf. We have thought best that you should be advised by us of this conference."[32]

These sentences at first smack of candor. In reality, they were an excellent example of judicial disingenuousness. Quinn had indeed met with President Truman, and they had indeed talked about space. But there, the accuracy of

[30] Copy in BF, June 15, 1951. Larkin was so concerned about the space problem that he wrote a follow-up memorandum to Lovett that "it would help enormously if you could, personally, call Jess Larson [administrator of GSA] and tell him of our need for space for the Court[,] and ask him to take a personal look at the situation." Ibid., July 13, 1951. Proulx recalled that Quinn, supported by Latimer and Brosman, insisted from the outset that the Court's offices could not be in the Pentagon. "The military thought they would be housed under the same roof[,] and that wasn't consistent with . . . the spirit of the law. It was civilian control over the military. So you don't want them down the hall." Proulx, interview, 9. It is not clear if Lovett's letter had any direct results. As will be seen, temporary space was ultimately found for the Court, but more apparently at the behest of Proulx rather than of the Pentagon.

[31] Ibid., July 17, 1951. Quinn wrote to his old political acquaintance/rival J. Howard McGrath, asking his help in locating quarters. The assistant to whom McGrath assigned a response was less than impressed. "Looks like we are to be saddled with Bob Quinn's adm. [*sic*] problems—Shouldn't Pentagon front for him?" Ultimately McGrath himself replied to Quinn that the "best we can do" would be to have someone on his staff introduce Proulx or some other court functionary "to the people of the Public Buildings Division." Truman Library, McGrath Papers, File "Q," # 175. August 16, 1951.

[32] BF, July 26, 1951.

Quinn's account ended. The Clerk had previously learned that Stephens had an informal agreement with the Chief Judge of the Court of Customs and Patent Appeals (CCPA) to move his tribunal into the building soon to be vacated by Stephens's court. This explained, according to Proulx, why the CCPA judges were so willing to let USCMA share their courtroom. In consultation with Stephens, they had planned to move into the stately structure on E St., perfectly suited for a small appellate court—but now too cramped for the D.C. Court of Appeals, which had expanded in numbers and cases. In other words, they would invite USCMA to share their facilities, and would willingly let the new tribunal stay there, once the CCPA moved over to the old D.C. appellate court building. But the USCMA judges also coveted this judicial edifice.

Proulx discovered that upon becoming vacant, the old Court of Appeals building was to be placed under the jurisdiction of the Public Buildings Commissioner. He convinced Quinn to seek an appointment with President Truman in order to ask that he "write a chit out to the Public Buildings Commissioner that this is the building for [USCMA]"; to get a statement, in other words, that it was presidential preference that Quinn's Court move into the soon-to-be-empty building.[33] What Proulx, who probably drafted the judges' letter to Stephens, could not say was that Quinn had sought—successfully, it turned out—to undercut the earlier understanding through presidential intervention.[34]

Apparently, Proulx and Chief Judge Quinn kept their plans concerning the request to President Truman confidential. When Chief Commissioner Tedrow visited Judge Stephens in October, he seems to have been no more aware of Quinn's actions than was Stephens himself. "I did not get very far," he wrote. "Personally, I feel he favors the Customs Court getting that building. . . . As a matter of fact, I had trouble in getting any kind of answers out of him." What Tedrow sought was merely a statement that Stephens would write to the Public Buildings Service "advising that the building would be available." He suggested that Quinn should disregard Stephens, and use either the offices of the Attorney General or the Defense Department to press

[33] Proulx, interview, 11–13.

[34] Apparently Proulx and the Judges had their eyes on the old Court of Appeals building as early as July 1951. Proulx began his tenure as Clerk on July 24. The week before, Quinn informed McGrath that "it would be best for us to exert every effort to obtain the Court of Appeals building. . . . I have an appointment with the President[,] . . . and will request him to have this building set aside for us, and I will deeply appreciate anything you can do to help us along these lines." BF, July 17, 1951. One month later, Brosman stated, "It is certain that we shall remain in Internal Revenue until the completion . . . of the new Federal Courts Building. . . . At that time we shall move to the new building, or to the present Court of Appeals Building . . . or to other adequate quarters—outside the Pentagon. If I were to guess at this time in the bosom of the family, I would suppose that we will end up in the present Court of Appeals Building." SF, August 28, 1951, 11.

their cause. "Certainly we will get more cooperation from them than we have received from the present occupants."[35]

It is unclear when Stephens was informed, if indeed he ever was, of the ultimate decision to give his old building to USCMA. By November 27, Proulx had submitted space plans for the building to the space officer in the Pentagon, "who will immediately enter into formal negotiations with the [PBS] for the Circuit Court of Appeals Building."[36] On the same day, Stephens notified Judges Latimer and Brosman that there would be no space available for their Court in the new building, and that he would write PBS that the old building "will be declared surplus by him as soon as they move out."[37] The way was thus open for USCMA to get its chosen home.

Yet Proulx remained vigilant, fearing that some other governmental agency might covet the courthouse. In August 1952, a couple of months before the Court finally moved into the building, he wrote to Quinn that "in talking to a [newspaper] reporter . . . I mentioned to him that we had 50 employees on the staff[,] lest the actual number should give anyone the idea that the building would be too large for us."[38] As for the Judges of the Court of Customs and Patents upon discovering the presidential letter to the Public Buildings Commissioner and what apparently it had wrought, Proulx summed up the matter with characteristic candor—"they had a deal they were trying to work too, and in this town possession is 9⁄10ths of the law."[39]

A COURT IS A COURT IS A COURT? ROUND 1

All interested in the new tribunal conceded that it had been created by Congress, acting upon its constitutional authority to make rules and regulations for the governing of the armed services. In other words, USCMA was an

[35] QPGF, October 8, 1951. Actually, Quinn had already gone around Stephens, and with impressive results. Three weeks later, the commissioner of the Public Buildings Service informed the Defense Department that if the PBS "controls future assignment in the building now occupied by the Circuit Court of Appeals, the Department of Defense will be assigned sufficient space . . . to take care of the Military Court of Appeals." BF, October 29, 1951. On November 13, Proulx wrote to a staff member of John Fogarty, a Democratic Congressman from Rhode Island and a dear friend of Quinn. "We are setting our sights on the Circuit Court of Appeals . . . when it becomes vacated [*sic*] There are so many advantages of having a building of our own." 1 CF, November 13, 1951.

[36] Ibid., November 27, 1951.

[37] Ibid., November 28, 1951.

[38] 2 CF, August 7, 1952.

[39] Proulx, interview, 17. Although USCMA had planned to stay in the temporary quarters for only a few months, not until October 1952 did it finally move into the old Court of Appeals Building at 5th and E Streets. It has been the home of the U.S. Court of Military Appeals ever since, and on more than one occasion the judges have fought to keep their space from other hopeful federal occupants with a tenacity reminiscent of an earlier era.

"Article I court," in that the enacting power for Congress came from the first Article of the Constitution. Did it therefore follow that the Court was an agency of the executive branch of government rather than the judicial? Confusion and disagreement over this question and implications arising from the different ways it has been answered have dogged the Court since 1951. Supposedly settled, the issue remained unsettling.

A few months after USCMA began to function, the Court—through the Defense Department—stated to the Civil Service Commission that the new tribunal should be located within the judicial branch rather than the executive. Thus, as with most federal courts, appointment of court personnel would not come under the purview of the Civil Service Commission, and the judiciary "could make appointments as it saw fit."[40] If, however, USCMA was in reality a sort of judicial/administrative hybrid, rather than a real court, it would fall under the executive branch of government. Yet, language creating the Court "include[s] a mixture of the usual attributes of both courts and administrative agencies of a quasi-judicial nature. It is difficult to decide into which category the Court fits."[41] This conclusion, part of an internal memorandum from Daniel Walker—a newly appointed court commissioner—indicates that USCMA judges were aware that questions concerning their status and powers might have had some basis in fact. The memorandum, written by a court employee—one sympathetic to the Court's purposes—warrants some attention.[42]

Walker assumed, as did most scholarly opinion on the subject, that Congress had created USCMA by virtue of its legislative authority under Article I of the Constitution. Therefore, "even aside from the lack of life tenure by the judges, the Court may not be considered to be a constitutional court."[43]

[40] Civil Service Commission memorandum, September 25, 1951, 1, hereafter cited as memo; copy in 1 CF.

[41] LTF, memorandum "Status and Powers of the United States Court of Military Appeals," undated, but probably written during the fall of 1951. Its author, Daniel Walker, along with Tedrow and Condon, constituted the first group of commissioners appointed to the Court staff. Able, articulate, and ambitious, he later worked for Illinois Governor Adlai Stevenson. Indeed, in September 1952, Walker wrote to Chief Judge Quinn that "Stevenson has really caught the imagination of a lot of people—which is more than can be said for Eisenhower." QPPC, September 9, 1952. Eisenhower carried Illinois in both 1952 and 1956. Walker's future would include two very disparate terms of his own—one as governor of Illinois, the other a prison term as a convicted felon. See *Illinois State Journal-Register*, October 27, 1990, 24.

[42] The following paragraphs are based both upon Walker's memorandum, and the unsigned staff memo to the Civil Service Commission, calling for rejection of the Court's arguments—a step the commission took on October 4, 1951.

[43] Walker noted that the Supreme Court "has held that tenure is a basic consideration in deciding whether a court is created by the virtue of power granted by Article III." Since Congress clearly denied life tenure to its newest court, his conclusion was understandable. On the other hand, what was to prevent Congress from creating a court, clothing it in the raiment of courts, but providing terms for its judges, rather than life tenure?

Was it, therefore, a legislative tribunal? The answer to this question was complicated by the fact that Congress could also "create administrative agencies as well as courts to handle quasi-judicial or even fully judicial functions. The attributes of the tribunal created must be examined in order to determine into which category it fits."[44]

Walker found several factors to support the contention that USCMA belonged in the judicial, not the executive branch of government. Congress called its creation a court, and provided for three full-time judges. The legislators had clearly intended the jurists—regardless of their terms—to be on a par with other federal appellate court judges. Indeed, their salaries were to be identical, and ultimately judges of the Courts of Appeals could be designated to fill temporary vacancies on the USCMA bench. Moreover, the purpose and function of the tribunal was first and foremost that of judging. Hence it should be treated in the same manner as existing federal courts.

But Walker also found "several weighty factors" that in his judgment militated against USCMA status as a member of the federal judiciary. First was the life tenure issue. Salary similarity aside, much more important were the differences between USCMA judges and their federal counterparts. USCMA judges had fixed terms, and could be removed by the President. Federal district and appellate court judges served for life and could not be removed by the Chief executive.[45] Second was the placement of USCMA within the Department of Defense. This fact, "while certainly not by itself determinative, indicates a close relation[ship] to the executive department, as opposed to the judiciary."[46]

Most difficult for Walker was the fact that "review of military courts-martial has historically been entrusted by Congress to the Executive department, and the new code [the UCMJ] contains no clear intent to depart from that traditional procedure." Reviews of courts-martial from the convening authority up even to the Boards of Review established by the Judge Advocate General within *his* office—all pointed to the executive branch, to say nothing of presidential review of certain sentences.[47] Indirectly supporting Walker's contention, the Civil Service Commission [CSC] report had also focused on this point.

Its memorandum stated, correctly, that the President as Commander in

[44] Ibid., 2–3.

[45] The same point is found in the memorandum rejecting the Court's position, written for the Civil Service Commission. "If the Court were to be part of the judiciary system[,] it would be free of control of the President[,] and its judges would not be subject to removal by [him]. . . . " memo, 3.

[46] The Court may have had some difficulty rebutting this claim. The statement summarizing its position merely noted that the new tribunal was to be located "for administrative purposes" in the Pentagon meant only that a certain agency was "to handle the administrative work for the Court. It need be construed to do nothing more than this." Ibid., 3.

[47] Walker memorandum, 3–4.

Chief must approve certain court-martial verdicts. How then, could USCMA be located within the judicial branch of government? To so hold "would be to find that the decisions of a court in the judicial branch were subject to review by the Executive Department through the President. This would be an entirely new concept in the field of law," if only because the Constitution requires that the three branches of government operate "on a par with each other, the functions of one of which are not subject to control by the other two."[48] Moreover, because the military was part of the executive branch, and because courts-martial also came under the executive umbrella, "it does not appear that Congress intended to make any change in the basic concept that courts-martial are purely executive functions."[49]

Although he did not cite it, an additional point could have added support to Walker's position. The CSC Report observed that as early as 1939—more than ten years before USCMA was created—Congress had established the Administrative Office of the United States Courts, to do just what its title implied. By any reasonable rule of statutory interpretation, the fact that in 1950 the lawmakers had specifically designated the Defense Department to administer the new Court undercut its claim to parity with the other federal tribunals. USCMA judges when they retired, were to be covered by the Civil Service Retirement Act, while federal appellate jurists could retire with a different [and better] set of benefits.[50]

Walker emphasized what to him at least were the clear implications in his report, "[T]here is, at the least, considerable doubt as to the legal status of [USCMA]." But clarification of its status while important should yield to more pressing reasons for Congressional action. "Substantial question[s] may be raised as to whether the Court has the attributes of judicial power necessary to the exercise of its appellate and supervisory responsibilities. If [USCMA] is not a court in the true sense of the word, then it lacks several weapons of judicial action which may well . . . make the Court's jurisdiction advisable only."[51] Here, Walker meant the power to issue injunctions and other orders, to hold parties in contempt, to exercise subpoena powers, and to issue prerogative writs, such as writs of mandamus.

Walker's solution was "simple Congressional action." The appropriate provision of the U.S. Code included among the tribunals properly called a

[48] This contention had been raised not only during the Ansell-Crowder hearings, but later as the UCMJ was pending before Congress. See AMJ, 240–41. The author of the memorandum for the Civil Service Commission incorrectly assumed that appellate review was incompatible with presidential authority as commander in chief.

[49] Memo, 4. In the absence of any clear congressional intent to the contrary, the writer insisted that the Commission should not deviate from "the long adhered to [*sic*] rule that the military is part of the Executive branch." Ibid., 5.

[50] Ibid., 2–3. These points, although debatable, are tenable. They may have been sufficient for the Commission to decide against the Court, which it ultimately did.

[51] Walker memorandum, 6.

"Court of the United States" any "court created by Act of Congress[,] the judges of which are entitled to hold office during good behavior." Giving USCMA judges life tenure would therefore bring the Court to the status of a U.S. Court, and "would clearly make the Court a 'Court.'"[52]

Walker's arguments, similar to those that convinced the Civil Service Commission to find that the new tribunal came within the executive branch rather than the judiciary, were not tenable. They reflect more the tenacity of outdated conceptions than a clear understanding of the transformation of military justice by 1951. While Walker did not get into this point, it was far from accurate by this time to characterize courts-martial as "purely executive functions." As early as 1917–18, the Ansell-Crowder controversy explored in some detail the conflicting claims that courts-martial were strictly within the presidential prerogative. Ansell himself had vigorously rebutted this viewpoint.[53]

For the time being, however, the judges did not challenge the decision of the Commission. Instead, the Court set out to gain life tenure, a quest that remains unrealized to this day. In the meantime, the Court proceeded to judge cases—and possibly with Walker's comments in mind, adopted an unspoken strategy. Absent a specific enactment by Congress, or a definitive holding to the contrary by the United States Supreme Court—Judges Quinn, Latimer, and Brosman quietly assumed the applicability of all appropriate appellate judicial authority to their court, and acted accordingly.[54] But they remained dissatisfied with the Commission's conclusions, in part because they had implications that went far beyond the original contention that, as part of the judiciary, the judges could hire and fire without regard to Civil Service Commission requirements. There was, for example, the question of the new Court Reports.

Barely one month after the CSC released its findings, Proulx and his deputy met with James Ryder, a representative from West Publishing Company—then as now the dominant source for publication and distribution of

[52] Ibid., 7–8.

[53] See AMJ, 63–65, and passim.

[54] To some extent, subsequent USCMA history has vindicated this assumption. From time to time, its judges have not hesitated to claim authority to issue certain writs and orders. Invariably in such litigation, one party would argue that the Court was without authority in the matter—a position consistently rejected by a majority of its jurists. On the other hand, the judges have been hesitant to apply their supposed authority in specific instances, contenting themselves with vigorous expressions of its existence, if not its implementation. See this author's comments in *Military Justice Reporter* 30 (1990), ccxxxvii–ccxlix. See also below, chapters 10–11. On one occasion, the Court upon appropriate recommendation from a duly constituted special committee formally disbarred an attorney from practicing before it. However, the power to hold in contempt of court appears never to have been utilized by USCMA, and has never been challenged. The United States Supreme Court has thus far declined to consider the extent to which USCMA authority as an appellate tribunal may or may not differ from other Article III appellate courts. But see n. 4 in *Edmond v. U.S.* 117 S. Ct. 1573 (1997).

judicial reports—both state and federal. Realizing that the reputation of the new Court would depend on how its opinions were received, and eager for them to have as widespread a circulation as feasible, Proulx hoped that USCMA decisions could be reported in the West F. 2d (the second series of West's Federal Reporter, and one that included decisions of the Courts of Appeals for the various circuits). But Ryder "informed us that the Judicial Conference decides what shall or shall not go into the F. 2d reports. West . . . does exactly what the Judicial Conference tells it in regard to said reports."[55]

Ryder cautioned, however, that "inasmuch as USCMA is not under the Administrative Office of the United States Courts for housekeeping purposes, but is dependent on the office of the Secretary of Defense for such purposes, it might be difficult for USCMA to get its opinions reported in F. 2d."[56] Ultimately, Chief Judge Quinn met with Chief Justice Fred Vinson, seeking to enlist his support for using F. 2d. But the Chief Justice was noncommittal, and asked Quinn to have his request "incorporated in a letter marked to his attention."[57]

Quinn informed Vinson that "all the members of our Court feel very strongly that it would be of benefit both to the . . . armed services and the American Bar at large to have our opinions given the wide circulation [that] such a plan would provide." This is especially true today, he added, "in view of the fact that a large and increasing segment of the American people has come to be directly concerned with the course and conduct of military law administration." Like a good Rhode Island Yankee, Quinn could not resist reminding the Chief Justice that using the federal reporter "would also, of course, save the Government a very substantial amount of money."[58]

This writer could not locate any response from Chief Justice Vinson to Quinn's request. Nothing favorable, however, came of it. Decisions of the United States Court of Military Appeals have never been part of F. 2d. While it is true that since 1975 West has published the *Military Justice Reporter*, replete with its own digest, efforts to achieve total USCMA integration with a national state/federal appellate court system of digesting and citations have not been successful, and failure to attain it after more than forty years continues to disturb the Court.[59] Proulx went ahead with alternative plans to publish the

[55] 1 CF, December 3, 1951, reporting a meeting held November 20, 1951.

[56] Ibid.

[57] 1 CF, January 29, 1952.

[58] Ibid.

[59] At least one perceptive observer of USCMA has noted the very close relationship between the influence that an appellate court may have on other tribunals, and the way in which its decisions are or are not digested and distributed. See Eugene Fidell, "If a Tree Falls in the Forest . . . : Publication and Digesting Policies and the Potential Contribution of Military Courts to American Law." JAG Journal 32 (1982), 1–29. In recent years USCMA has made minor

decisions through the Lawyers Cooperative Publishing Company, the firm that ultimately produced the first twenty-three volumes of USCMA reports.

JUDGES AT WORK: THE SETTING

During the summer of 1951, the USCMA judges, Proulx, and Tedrow worked out basic procedures for the Court. The first set of Rules of Practice and Procedure were promulgated on July 11, and two weeks later the judges held their first session in the Court of Customs and Patents Appeals courtroom on the 7th floor of the Internal Revenue Building.[60] A number of lawyers were admitted to its bar, including the Judge Advocates General of the Air Force, Army, and Navy. Very quickly, the new court settled into the routine of receiving, hearing, and deciding the cases placed on its docket. The judges functioned well together, although they brought divergent experiences and philosophies to their work. On the other hand, operations of the Court—often without the presence of the Chief Judge—occasionally created tensions not only between the staff and other judges, but among the jurists themselves.

Quinn spent most of his time in Providence, usually coming to Washington only for the oral arguments and resulting judicial conferences—returning two or three days later. He maintained a prolific correspondence that included not only frequent letters from Proulx, who served as the main conduit between the Chief and the Court, but also a wide variety of contemporary political figures. Moreover, his files contain an unusual variety of requests for assistance, most of them from Rhode Island residents who may well have remembered Quinn as "Governor Fighting Bob."[61] The requests ranged from a patient in a state mental hospital, to anguished letters from parents concerning their children in the armed services, to people in trouble with the law, to persons seeking advancement in government, education, or some other career. Quinn apparently acknowledged the great majority of these re-

---

progress toward improving its "digesting" problem. In 1991, West agreed to include Military Justice cases in its ALLFEDS computer database, and in February 1992 the publishers took a further step toward integration of USCMA decisions within its famous Key citation system. They informed Chief Judge Eugene Sullivan that "we will now dual classify constitutional points of law made in [USCMA] decisions. . . . Most of these additional classifications will be to the topic of Constitutional Law." USCMAP, Files of the Chief Judge, February 10, 1992. Although this change has great potential, the actual process of USCMA decision reporting through West remains haphazard and inadequate.

[60] Although they did not anticipate it, the judges and staff of USCMA would spend more than one year in their "temporary" quarters.

[61] One anonymous correspondent wished "that you were still up in the County Court House so I could refresh my perspective a little every once in a while. This is a very unwholesome place politically. . . . They'd sell tickets to the Crucifixion!" QPPC, November 10, 1951.

quests, usually referring the matter to Proulx with a notation "can we do anything to help?"[62]

Because he functioned in two cities, Quinn operated with a split staff. His commissioners remained in Washington, but his law clerks worked in his Providence chambers. And, especially in the early years, there appears to have been some good-natured rivalry between them, aided by Chief Commissioner Tedrow. On one occasion, Tedrow forged a note to the Chief Judge, stating that the time sheets for the "Providence branch of USCMA" had not been received, resulting in "no checks for these people. However, I am sure that this little lesson will have a salutary effect in the long run. Such being the case, I know you will agree that the loss of a few hundred dollars is relatively unimportant."[63] Similarly, when the Providence staff sent down some newspaper articles about Quinn's early years in Rhode Island politics, including a famous fistfight with a fellow legislator, Tedrow noted "the extremely high level of the legislative proceedings of that sovereign State," while another commissioner added that "New Englanders are adept at any style of forensic argument."[64]

Quinn served as an USCMA judge for almost twenty-five years, longer than any other jurist in its history. Until 1971, he was also Chief Judge. He seems to have had little difficulty in arriving at his decisions, sometimes relying on instinct rather than intellectual persuasion. One observer described Quinn as a "hell yes, hell no," kind of judge.[65] He sometimes found it difficult to accept the fact that it might take his commissioners longer to draft an opinion than he took in reaching the verdict. "I am disappointed," he once wrote, "in not receiving more opinions from my learned associates

[62] Quinn never abandoned his conviction that the first rule of politics was to help people who seek and need it. He had developed this patristic tendency during his tumultuous years in Rhode Island politics. By the time he came to the court, he felt neither the inclination nor obligation to change his practices; and his attentions to the needs of others, often strangers, persisted to the end of his two dozen years on the federal bench. One observer wrote of Quinn in 1970 that "every day, in some way, he does something for someone." Excerpt from *Rhode Island Year Book, 1970* in QPPC.

[63] 1 QPPC, July 13, 1953. Tedrow signed Proulx's name to the letter. For his part, Quinn asked Tedrow when the chief commissioner underwent surgery, "Did they attempt to operate on your brain while they had you in the hospital? My associates here think it might have been a proper field for exploration." Ibid., April 14, 1954. Knowing that his remarks would be relayed to Quinn, Tedrow later reciprocated with a comment to Proulx upon looking at a new formal portrait of the Chief Judge that somehow the artist had "failed to capture your mean disposition." Ibid., November 19, 1954.

[64] Ibid., April 29, 1954.

[65] Interview, George Latimer, Jr., July 20, 1989, 14. Latimer recalls that his father used these words to describe Quinn's occasionally "instinctual" jurisprudence. Proulx stated that Quinn "never had second thoughts about decisions. In other words, when he decided a case and he made a decision, that case was closed as far as he was concerned. He didn't agonize about it. He went on to the next one." Proulx, 43.

[commissioners] Carney and Feld."[66] A few months later, he instructed Proulx to "speak to the boys on the third floor. The opinions are flowing in like molasses."[67]

Unlike Quinn and Brosman, George Latimer had commanded troops in combat. This fact, according to his son, gave him a different perspective from his brethren when it came to military justice. "My father fought at Guadalcanal. He commanded troops at Leyte. . . . So my father first of all was interested in the services doing justice in the broadest sense of that term. He was not so concerned with small details."[68] For different reasons, Latimer shared with Quinn an ability to decide the given issue with little difficulty. However, he was in no hurry to release a decision until it had been refined and polished to his satisfaction.

The only one of the original judges to have had both prior experience as an appellate judge and involvement in actual military combat, Latimer was not comfortable with Quinn's prolonged absences. They resulted in what he saw as a vacuum in leadership, all the more annoying to Latimer because he could not fill it. Although he functioned as senior judge in Quinn's absence, in fact the commissioners and Proulx looked to Providence for guidance and ultimate decisions. Much more reserved in manner than the gregarious former Governor, Latimer felt frustrated by the management style Quinn brought to the Court. He also had difficulties with the way the Commissioner system was evolving within the new tribunal.

Alone among his brethren, Paul Brosman came from an academic background, and he seems to have experienced the most difficulty in the actual process of judging. If Quinn and Latimer brought some sort of outlook to their judging, whatever might be its origin, Brosman approached military justice with intellectual curiosity rather than institutional consistency. Courtly and quiet in manner [Quinn affectionately referred to Brosman as "his Lordship"], the former dean bought a home directly across the street from Latimer.[69] Often they traveled to and from court together, and while they frequently disagreed as to results, each relished the opportunity to discuss and debate the legal issues presented by the cases.[70]

[66] Ibid., October 22, 1953.

[67] Ibid., January 27, 1954.

[68] George Latimer, Jr., 13.

[69] Because Brosman apparently left no papers, my comments about his court career are based upon the recollections of Latimer's two sons, the observations of Alfred Proulx, and the small collection of candid letters that Brosman exchanged with Edmund Morgan during the first two years of USCMA operations. These, together with Morgan's typed replies, have been preserved in Morgan's papers at Vanderbilt University.

[70] Proulx remembered Brosman as "very southern, [he] never carried a dime in his pocket . . . and he had a Packard Roadster," which apparently he did not like to drive—one reason why he may have driven so often with Judge Latimer. At any rate, added Proulx, Brosman used to say "Fred, there are only two happy days for a man who owns a Packard Roadster: the day he buys

With the judges, commissioners, clerks, and staff in place, all that was needed were the litigants. By June 1952, the new Court had docketed almost one thousand cases, releasing ninety-seven written opinions. One year later, between June 1952 and June 1953, more than two thousand cases were docketed. What types of issues did they raise? How did the judges respond, and with what results?

---

it and the day he sells it." Proulx, 46. George Latimer, Jr., 8; interview with Dr. Ronald Latimer, October 22, 1989, 23–24.

CHAPTER 3

The Court Commences, 1951–1955

ALTHOUGH the judges of the United States Court of Military Appeals faced the challenge of interpreting a new statute, in large measure the UCMJ itself was a synthesis of existing military law. Judges Quinn, Latimer, and Brosman assumed, not unreasonably, that Congress had not intended the Court to interpret military justice with a *tabula rasa*, with no regard for principles and policies articulated in an earlier era. On the other hand, they realized that the UCMJ mandated substantial improvements in military justice, especially in the area of due process. Through its decisions, beginning in the fall of 1951, USCMA sought to reconcile if not harmonize these two discordant themes.

On one level, this did not appear a difficult challenge. A new code of military justice was on the books, and the armed services were expected to follow the new law in its administration. Military justice was not to be dispensed in the same old way. Easy to propose, this precept proved much more difficult to ensure. In a real sense, the early years of USCMA's history can be seen as a determination by its judges that the revolution wrought by the UCMJ would not fall victim to a sort of silent "counterrevolution," nurtured by efforts of the military [often well intentioned] to conduct business as usual. The clash between a guilty plea and a superficially simple doctrine of harmless error illustrates the point.

EARLY CONSENSUS ON THE COURT

Using several cases decided in the fall of 1951, the judges unanimously agreed that in certain instances a guilty plea by the defendant obviated the necessity for a military court to comply with provisions set forth in Article 52 of the UCMJ.[1] "Cast in the background of a plea of guilty, we are convinced that the failure to vote did not prejudicially affect the accused."[2] These findings may have reflected a desire not to disturb the trial practices of

[1] It detailed procedures for the casting of votes by court members during the course of a court-martial, as well as listing the number of votes required for conviction.

[2] *United States v. Lucas*, 1 USCMA 19, 25 (1951). Speaking for the Court, Judge Latimer emphasized that failure to follow the Code's procedural requirements was error as a matter of law. But in the context of a guilty plea, such error did not materially prejudice "the substantial rights of the accused." In accord, see *United States v. Goodrich*, 1 USCMA 26 (1951); *United States v. O'Brassill*, 1 USCMA 27 (1951); *United States v. Bishop*, 1 USCMA 29 (1951).

the military justice system without clear evidence that the alleged error itself had a substantial influence on the trial's outcome. When the record of trial presented such evidence, however, the outcome on appeal might be very different.

Less than three weeks after deciding this series of cases, the Court decided *United States v. Clay*. The case was the first landmark opinion issued by the new tribunal. What distinguished it from the earlier holdings was that *Clay* involved two separate pleas, one guilty, the other not guilty. Again, the trial court had not followed required procedures. Judge Latimer had no trouble excusing this error in the guilty plea, in accord with the earlier decisions cited above. The accused's plea of not guilty to the other charge, however, was a more serious matter.

Latimer noted that a not guilty plea automatically "placed the burden upon the government to prove beyond a reasonable doubt all the essential elements of the offense." Moreover, unlike a guilty plea, "it permitted the assumption of innocence to weigh in his favor and required that any reasonable doubt must be resolved against his guilt."[3] Under these circumstances, to neglect instructing members of the court on issues such as the burden of proof and the presumption of innocence was unacceptable. Latimer could have ended the opinion at this point. Instead he went on to detail those rights for an accused that even, as he put it, "a cursory inspection" of the UCMJ would reveal:

> To be informed of the charges against him; to be confronted by witnesses testifying against him; to cross-examine witnesses for the government; to challenge members of the court for cause or peremptorily; to have a specific number of members compose general and special courts-martial; to be represented by counsel; not to be compelled to incriminate himself; to have involuntary confessions excluded from consideration; to have the court instructed on the elements of the offense, the presumption of innocence, and the burden of proof; to be found guilty of an offense only when a designated number of members concur in a finding to that effect; to be sentenced only when a certain number of members vote in the affirmative; and to have an appellate review.[4]

In identifying the source of these rights beyond the text of the UCMJ, however, Latimer hedged. "In keeping with the principles of military justice . . . we do not bottom those rights and privileges on the Constitution. We base them on the laws as enacted by Congress."[5] Later in the opinion he added, "We need not concern ourselves with the constitutional concepts." If a civilian court could find that denial of these benefits resulted in a loss of due process, "it should be apparent to a casual reader that denial of a similar

[3] *United States v. Clay*, 1 USCMA 74, 77 (1951).

[4] Ibid., 77–78.

[5] Ibid., 77.

right granted by Congress to an accused in the military service [violates] military due process."[6]

But Latimer was not content with his detailed delineation of due process doctrine. He wanted "to impress on courts-martial the undesirability of short-cutting the plain mandate of Congress."[7] In response to the government's claim that members of the court were Navy officers, familiar with the rules of law, Latimer—with more military experience than his two colleagues—observed, "We are not convinced that all members of courts-martial are sufficiently versed in law to know all the elements of all offenses." He concluded that "we find the trial of the accused far short of what is deemed essential to military justice."[8]

USCMA reiterated this concern with military due process in a different context. *United States v. DeCarlo* involved a soldier accused of unpremeditated murder in the shooting death of a young Korean boy. Shortly before the victim died, he stated that "it was an accident." Upon motion of the prosecution, this statement was stricken from the record, and DeCarlo was convicted. In an opinion by Chief Judge Quinn, the Court reversed. Drawing heavily upon civilian law precedents, he emphasized that the dying youth "would have no reason to tell an untruth. His testimony, although certainly not conclusive, should have been before the court to assist them in evaluating what was a difficult question of fact." Exclusion of the statement was prejudicial error.[9]

The Court tried to maintain a balance between zealous concern for the rights of an accused, and the realization that the administration of military justice had to be practical. *United States v. Monge* illustrates the difficulty of maintaining this balance. It involved an eighteen-year-old soldier, apparently with limited intellect, who had completed only the 9th grade in school.

[6] Ibid., 79. One can only speculate why in 1951 USCMA was unwilling to find a constitutional source for the due process safeguards it articulated so clearly—all the more as Latimer discussed a number of federal cases affirming them. The era of the Warren Court was still in the future. Later USCMA decisions reflected a preference to rest these rights on a constitutional basis rather than a statute.

[7] Congress "proclaimed that the giving of instructions was a valuable right, the court-martial crashed through that mandate, and now we are asked to say that right was unsubstantial. . . . A conviction supported by a proceeding which is so lacking in correct procedure should fall of its own weight." Ibid., 80–81.

[8] Ibid., 82. Although in this case Latimer vigorously defended the role of his court in military justice, his opinions suggest that in general he was much more sympathetic to the "military viewpoint" than his two brethren. See, for example, his dissent in *United States v. O'Neal*, 1 USCMA 138, where he emphasized USCMA's limited authority. "Courts-martial and boards of review are the fact-finding bodies of the military system[,] and they are free to determine questions of fact independently and without interference, control, or supervision by this Court." Ibid., 150. This tendency became even more pronounced after Homer Ferguson joined the Court for the last part of Latimer's term, 1956–61. See below.

[9] *United States v. DeCarlo*, 1 USCMA 91, 92–93, 94 (1951).

Suspecting him of burglary, at 4 in the morning two soldiers "pulled him from his bed, forced him to lie on the floor, held a bayonet at his back, and questioned him concerning the thefts." Shortly, defendant admitted stealing some money. Later, he made a second confession. But the accused was not informed that "any prior involuntary confession could not be used against him." Had he known this fact, "he would not have made the second."[10]

Speaking through Chief Judge Quinn, the Court unanimously affirmed the conviction. After emphasizing that especially in the military, confessions in the presence of superiors "gives cause for additional suspicion," nevertheless he declined "to conclude . . . that the effect of the prior abuse was so strong as to make unreasonable a conclusion that it did not dominate the mind to such an extent as to render the subsequent confessions involuntary."[11] Critical reaction to *Monge* came from an unexpected source—none other than Edmund Morgan.[12]

MORGAN AND BROSMAN—CONSTRUCTIVE COLLOQUIES

Monge was handed down on January 8, 1952. It took Morgan barely a week to react concerning "the perfectly outrageous conduct of the arresting officers, conduct which is rarely equalled in civilian cases." Even worse, he commented to Brosman, "When you take into account the inexperience and low-grade intelligence of the accused . . . , the result, and particularly the failure of the Chief Judge to denounce the original coercive conduct, will shock most laymen, and it will cause the critics of the services to insist that the Court has pointed out a way in which coerced confessions can be obtained and their results used in all contest cases."[13]

Brosman had concurred silently in *Monge*. He immediately sent Morgan's letter to Daniel Walker, the commissioner who had "worked with Chief Judge Quinn" on the decision.[14] Walker responded that the force used—"holding a bayonet at petitioner's back was applied to prevent escape and not to force a confession." Moreover, it was far from clear that military justice officials as opposed to army officers had participated in this episode. "Reversal under the facts in this case would practically compel the view that no good confession can ever follow a bad one. This, to my mind, would impose a serious burden on law

[10] *United States v. Monge*, 1 USCMA 95, 96 (1952).

[11] Ibid., 100. "We cannot hold either service personnel generally or criminal investigation agents particularly to a detailed knowledge of the judicial rules concerning the factors which would make a confession voluntary or involuntary."

[12] Several sections of this chapter draw heavily on an unusual collection of letters between Paul Brosman and Edmund Morgan, written between 1952 and 1953. Preserved in Morgan's papers, the letters are remarkable for the candor with which the older law professor and the former dean, now suddenly an appellate judge, exchanged views.

[13] MPVU, January 17, 1952.

[14] If Walker functioned as did Quinn's other commissioners, he probably drafted the opinion.

enforcement personnel."[15] But Brosman had much more to discuss with Morgan than just this case. Morgan had alluded to some talk at a recent bar association meeting about "the inadequacies of the Code and the noncivilian character and attitude of the Court."[16] His remark bothered Brosman.

"I earnestly invite," wrote the former law school dean, "any comment you may care to make at any time about the Court, any of our cases, or my own judicial conduct or ideas. As you know, I am rather new at this business and I am not too familiar with the amenities of my craft."[17] Morgan could only be aware "that appellate judicial administration is not without its compromises[,] and that every member of this Court can be expected to make some mistakes." The Court has to "take into account the realities of the military situation on the one hand and the demands of an enlightened approach to civilian criminal law on the other." Hence, "it is sheer nonsense to apply the term 'noncivilian' to the character and attitude of any of us. . . . [I]t is just plain silly for anybody to think of me as 'service minded'. . . . We are doing our level best, I promise you, to call them as we see them."[18]

In reply, Morgan emphasized that "I do not want any member of the Court to think that I imagine that my opinion will cut any more ice than that of any other lawyer." Of course he was anxious that the Court should stand "high with the Bar and be the instrument for deleting that much advertised command control and devious hidden exercise of it by camouflage in legal formulae." I may tell you confidentially, he added, that the civilian court "was my chief[,] personal contribution, the one feature that I was prepared to fight for even if the lid had to be blown off to accomplish it."[19]

[15] Ibid., January 21, 1952. Morgan was unimpressed with Walker's memo. "As to the law governing confessions, it leaves me cold." If Quinn was right, "The commissioner's suggestion that the bayonet was used to prevent escape . . . borders on the ridiculous. This accused, [was] pulled from his bed, and probably not dressed, with a corporal, a military policeman and another solider having him in custody—and they think that a bayonet at his back while he was on the floor [is] a proper safeguard to prevent escape!!" Ibid., February 4, 1952.

[16] Ibid., January 17, 1952.

[17] Ibid., January 22, 1952. Whatever the rule might be about a judge "explaining or defending his court's opinions . . . [it] does not apply to you. This is true not only because you have been a longtime friend and mentor of mine, but because no one stands in quite the same relation to the Court as you do."

[18] Ibid. As for the *Monge* case, "Maybe you should not put all the monkey on Judge Quinn's back. I participated fully in the discussions . . . and have no wish to avoid full responsibility." Brosman added, correctly, that Quinn's opinions "tend to be a little on the short side, just as mine are probably too long." The opinion here might have been "more acceptable" had Quinn "talked a little more . . . about the facts as developed in the testimony at the trial." Facts, he might have added, that, under the Code, were binding on his court.

[19] Ibid., February 4, 1952. In the same letter, Morgan returned to the *Monge* case. Without responding to Brosman's point that perhaps Quinn should have gone into greater detail in the decision, Morgan observed that "the securing and use of confessions in the services has been a source of violent criticism; and when a situation such as appears in this record is dealt with by the Court, its attitude should be made so clear that he who runs may read. 'Not while this Court sits' has lost much of its force since Holmes died."

When writing to Brosman, Morgan had not hesitated to voice his critical reaction to a particular decision—be it Brosman's or that of another judge. Brosman appreciated his candor. "A good job needs doing here and I want to do the very best I can. . . . I shall always be grateful for whatever criticism you are willing to pass on to me."[20] He further informed Morgan of his desire to establish as broad a base as possible for USCMA authority. After explaining his move toward this end in a series of cases dealing with prejudicial error, Brosman stated, "Anything you can say about this whole business—including my nefarious motives—will be greatly appreciated."[21]

As *Clay* and *Berry* indicated, USCMA demonstrated concern with the instructions to members of a court-martial that were to be given by the law officer—as mandated by the Code. Morgan shared this concern. The Code Committee realized, he wrote, that these instructions had to be given by a trained lawyer, in open court. Otherwise, "the instructions might come to be regarded as a mere ritual or formality." Morgan recalled that the men in the service who were assisting the Committee . . . thought it nigh impossible to have the law officer operate as a civilian judge."[22] Thus, he welcomed USCMA reversing some convictions because of incompetent or inappropriate instructions. The appointing authorities would learn therefrom "that the law officer's duties are not to be regarded as less important than any other lines of duty. . . ."[23]

In one of his letters to Morgan, Brosman included a copy of an Interim Report prepared by the judges summarizing USCMA activity through March 1, 1952. Barely eight pages in length, the report came only from the judges. Although the UCMJ required a joint committee of JAGs and Judges to report to Congress on an annual basis about the workings of the Code and military justice, the JAGs refused to participate in this first effort. After less than six months of activity by the Court, the decision of the Judge Advocates General not to join with the judges reflected a growing tension between judges and JAGs—one that warrants examination.

NOT SO CONSTRUCTIVE CRITICISM

An early sign of friction between practitioners and administrators of military justice came in a letter to Secretary of Defense Robert Lovett from Congressman Overton Brooks, one of the key members of the House Armed Services Committee and chairman of the subcommittee that had considered

[20] Ibid., February 27, 1952.

[21] Ibid. The three cases, all authored by Brosman, concerned conduct either preceding or during a court-martial that USCMA deemed prejudicial to the accused. See *United States v. Lee*, 1 USCMA 212; *United States v. Bound*, 1 USCMA 224; *United States v. Berry*, 1 USCMA 235.

[22] MPVU, April 3, 1952. See also AMJ, 164–70.

[23] Ibid.

and supported the UCMJ. He had spent, Brooks reminded Lovett, "four months almost uninterruptedly working on [this measure], and entertained the high hope that it would be the solution of our military judicial problems[,] and that it would work toward the elimination of the suspicion and mistrust which fills the mind of many in our civilian population regarding military justice." In recent months, however, "I am beginning to receive a good many complaints about the lack of proper administration of the act. . . . Perhaps it may be due in part to the failure of the Defense Department to immediately and energetically put into effect the provisions of the [UCMJ]."[24]

Lovett hastened to reply, and reminded Brooks of the requirement that Judges and JAGs "shall make a comprehensive survey of the operations of the Code every year," with submission of the same to Congress. He informed the Congressman that "this report will be submitted shortly," and sent copies of his letter to all the JAGs, as well as the USCMA judges.[25] It was this report that the JAGs declined to join. The judges felt it important to inform Congress that the Court was functioning, even though as Brosman wrote to Morgan, we "are only speaking for ourselves." However, he added, "between us girls, I am not sure how much joinder there can be between the JAGs and ourselves. Some fairly sharp differences are developing and—while they may be ironed out—it is entirely possible that no one of them will be willing to join fully in whatever report we send over later. Of course, these expressions must be strictly between ourselves. I certainly do not wish to prejudge the situation—but I have my fears."[26]

Morgan reiterated his point to Brosman that the requirement for a joint report was "considered one of the most important provisions of the [UCMJ]." The code was "to require the same sort of administration of justice in all the armed services[,] and to make it as nearly like the administration of justice in the federal civilian courts as possible." He recalled, quite accurately, that while the Navy and Air Force "approved this object," the Army resisted and "interposed one objection after another.[27] Morgan predicted, again with some accuracy, that the Court might encounter difficulty in getting the unified report.[28]

[24] 1 ARF, February 26, 1952.

[25] Ibid., March 13, 1952.

[26] MPVU, April 1, 1952.

[27] MPVU, April 4, 1952. Morgan added that Army JAG Thomas Green "did his best or worse to foul up the bill before the Committees of Congress by devious devices." The efforts of the Army to block key provisions of the UCMJ are discussed in detail in AMJ, chapters 8–11.

[28] In addition to the Interim Report, Brosman sent Morgan an autographed picture of the judges on the bench. "Quinn is not at all the sleepy solemn person he is made out to be. As for me, I don't quite know whether I look more like a poolroom bum or a reformed roue. In my defense let me say that I have never played pool at all well and have never been either a roue or reformed." Ibid., March 28, 1952.

The Interim Report identified key issues that had been confronted by the Court in the first six months of operation. Among them were: its own jurisdiction, due process of military law, trial and appellate procedure, sufficiency of the evidence as a matter of law, improper representation, insufficiency and inadequacy of instructions, and legality of sentences.[29] Unintentionally, this matter-of-fact list concealed the underlying causes for the friction between Judges and JAGs. To better understand these causes, some comments about the historic relationship between the Judge Advocates General and military justice may be appropriate.

As was discussed in the first volume of this study, while the views of the JAGs were certainly considered during the drafting of the UCMJ, they were not controlling. In several instances, their preferences had been rejected. Moreover, although few would admit it, members of the Judge Advocate General's Corps may well have seen USCMA as an institution that had been forced upon them by outsiders, not military officers.[30] Such resentment, though unfortunate, is understandable. In point of fact, with incredibly few changes the "modern" American military justice system had prevailed for over 150 years, long enough—among other things—for American armed forces to win two world wars. And from first to last, the entire system revolved around the JAGs. In 1991, the Judge Advocate General of the Army stated that "historically, securing the fairness of the justice system in the Army has been our principal reason for being."[31]

Indeed, for military justice the JAGs were the *sine qua non*, without which the military justice system could not operate. After World War I, a professor of law at the University of Wisconsin described the customary role of the JAG. "Technical and expert knowledge of the law," wrote William H. Page, "is supposed to be possessed by the judge-advocate." As with a civil jury, court-martial members "are not supposed to know the law as technical experts." Rather, they "should be guided by the opinion of the [JAG] on any questions of law or procedure that may arise during the trial," and they "must consider the grave consequences which may result from a disregard of legal advice given them by the [JAG]. It was not too much even to describe the JAG as "the oracle of the law."[32] According to Page, "The key to the development of military law is probably to be found in the position of the Judge Advocate General."[33]

And so it was until 1951. Thus one can understand why the JAGs would

[29] Interim Report for the Period May 31, 1951, to March 1, 1952, 4.

[30] These paragraphs are based on a lecture originally presented to the USCMA Judicial Conference in May 1992.

[31] Remarks by Major General John Fugh, reprinted in *The Army Lawyer*, June 1991, 3.

[32] William Herbert Page, "Military Law—A Study in Comparative Law," *Harvard Law Review* 32 (1919), 349–73.

[33] Ibid., 372. His role was all the more important because the members of courts-martial are neither "a permanent court," nor a "technically trained body organized primarily for the purpose

be less than comfortable with USCMA. A decision that found in favor of the defendant, whatever the specific grounds might be, could be seen as a condemnation of a JAG practice or procedure. The JAGs could conclude—with some justification—that the establishment of USCMA was, in reality, a reflection of their inability to provide what the civilian legal order deemed acceptable standards of military appellate review. This civilian court could be seen as a lasting acknowledgment of JAG failure to provide real justice, and they resented it.

On the other hand, even the JAGs recognized political reality. Indeed, it may not be unreasonable to observe that no one becomes a Judge Advocate General without a working sense of such conditions. The Code and Court were not going to go away. Cooperation if not consultation was not only mandated; it was an operational necessity. For better or worse, judges and JAGs were partners in the process. In one sense, the more effective and thorough were the JAGs, the less work of correction there would be for the Court. While the judges appreciated this relationship immediately, the JAGs took somewhat longer.

Understandably, as the decisions against long-accepted military justice practices came down, the JAGs sought somehow to confront the Court, rather than their own commanders. But the Judge Advocates General were also personally acquainted with the judges, and on paper at least, relations between them were cordial.[34] Hence, they distinguished between the Court and its judges—seeking to force changes in the former, without directly criticizing the latter. Their target, barely five months after USCMA issued its first decisions, was nothing less than control of the court's docket.

As enacted, the UCMJ provided three routes that could result in USCMA review of a case:

> **1.** All cases in which the sentence, as affirmed by a Board of Review, affects a general or flag officer[,] or extends to the death penalty;
>
> **2.** All cases reviewed by a Board of Review which the Judge Advocate General has certified to the Court of Military Appeals for review;
>
> **3.** All cases reviewed by a Board of Review in which, upon petition of the accused and on good cause shown, the Court of Military Appeals has granted a review.

The first two criteria for judicial review were mandatory upon USCMA. If the lower court's decision fell within either of these two categories, the judges had to review the case. Under the law, the Court exercised no discre-

of adjudicating cases." In reality, "the court does not know the law in theory, and frequently does not know it in fact." Ibid., 371–72.

[34] See below for several examples. Judge Brosman was a close friend of Reginald Harmon, the Air Force JAG who had strongly supported his selection as judge.

tion. The third criterion was very different. All a petitioner had to do upon receiving an unfavorable Board of Review verdict was *a*) file with the Court, and *b*) show good cause.[35] It was a matter of record, and the JAGs could only have been well aware of the fact, that even in its first year USCMA was very selective in accepting cases under # 3.[36] Nonetheless, it was the only category in which the judges could pick and choose the cases in accord with their own inclinations.

On March 14, 1952, the three Judge Advocates General submitted a proposed amendment for the UCMJ to Quinn, Latimer, and Brosman, and asked that it be included in the annual joint report for the period May 31, 1951, to May 31, 1952. It would have changed the third criterion as follows: "All other cases reviewed by a Board of Review in which, upon petition of the accused or his appellate counsel and on good cause shown, The Judge Advocate General, the Assistant Judge Advocate General in charge of a branch office, or the board of review that reviewed the record issues a certificate of probable cause. . . ."[37]

"In very strictest confidence," Brosman informed Morgan about the proposal. The judges had every intention of continuing their meetings with the JAGs. "I am, however, doubtful about very much accomplishment here." As to the proposed amendment, "I really regard the proposal as an insult to our intelligence. Of course, we shall have nothing whatever to do with it."[38]

[35] The term "good cause shown" is capable of widely differing interpretations. If the petition raised questions or issues that were interesting, timely, and important, review could well be granted. Also, under all three of these provisions, the judges were able to specify issues on their own that they wanted argued—possibly in order to build a foundation for a statement of judicial intent in future cases. Moreover, it made no difference if defendant's counsel had not raised these points on petition to the Court. Thus the Court could compensate for what it might consider poor judgment by an attorney. The practice of specifying issues continues to the present day, and remains controversial. The best critical analysis is the article by Eugene R. Fidell and Linda Greenhouse, "A Roving Commission: Specified Issues and the Function of the United States Court of Military Appeals," *Military Law Review* 122 (1988) 117–48. The authors conclude that specifying issues "represents a holdover from an earlier age when the military justice system was substantially less reliant on lawyers than it has been since the 1960s. . . . On balance, the arguments in favor of [it] are unpersuasive, while . . . the practice erodes the Court's institutional position by taking it out of the relatively passive role properly demanded of appellate tribunals in our adversarial system of justice." Ibid., 141. Justification for the Court's continued use of the practice can be found in Robinson O. Everett, "Specified Issues in the United States Court of Military Appeals: A Rationale," 123 *Military Law Review* 1 (1989). See also Eugene R. Fidell, *Guide to the Rules of Practice and Procedure for the United States Court of Appeals for the Armed Forces*, 7th ed., 27–30.

[36] According to its Interim Report, between May 1951 and March 1952 USCMA received 447 petitions, and granted 68—less than 20 percent of the total. Interim Report, 3.

[37] 1 ARF, March 14, 1952.

[38] MPVU, April 10, 1952. In this letter, Brosman refers to the memorandum "signed personally by Russell, Harmon, and Brannon [the JAGs of the Navy, Air Force, and Army, respectively]. The memorandum is preserved in the Court's first Annual Report file.

Shortly, Brosman wrote again to Morgan emphasizing the need for confidentiality. His letter indicates awareness on Brosman's part that there might be more behind the proposed amendment than just its words.

"We wish," he wrote, "to be entirely fair to the JAGs, and I for one do not wish to release their proposal so long as there is any chance of their withdrawing it. Although I have some doubt in the matter, they may ultimately come to do this." More important, "I may be able to break their ranks by talking Reg Harmon into withdrawing his approval." Finally, perhaps the proposed amendment "should be regarded as in the nature of a proposal made during the course of negotiations around a conference table, and should not at present be made public." In any event, "if it turns out that war must be declared, so be it."[39]

The judges had more to confront, however, than JAG criticism. Although they refused to admit it, these officers attacked the Court for what they saw as excessive interference in military justice. At the same time, however, other lawyers criticized the new tribunal for not taking sufficient steps to improve military justice. Typical of this group was Cornell Law Professor Arthur John Keeffe, who published an article in *Reader's Digest* with the less than objective title "Drumhead Justice: A Look at Our Military Courts."[40] Essentially a rehash of his earlier comments that military justice would be much improved if only the recommendations of *his* 1947 Committee Report on Navy courts-martial had been followed, Keeffe's article described the UCMJ as "a step in the right direction, but an unfortunately short one." He repeated his objections to USCMA as currently constituted, and concluded that "a drastic improvement in our system of military law is needed."[41]

Keeffe's strident spasms were, of course, nothing new. But previously they had been confined to law review articles which, in terms of public perception, were relatively insignificant. For better or worse, the same could not be said about the *Reader's Digest*. The USCMA judges received a nine-page memorandum from Chief Commissioner Tedrow, exposing Keeffe's article as riddled with inaccuracies and contradictions—including numerous and specific examples taken from Keeffe's earlier work. Probably assuming that the piece would fall of its own internal contradictions, Ted-

[39] MPVU, April 14, 1952. Ultimately, this specific proposal disappeared; although as will be seen, it reappeared in a different guise—one which the judges found as offensive as the first version. Exactly what the JAGs hoped to accomplish by their amendment remains unclear. But it may well be that they saw it as an effective source of pressure on the judges, a subtle suggestion of what might happen if USCMA went too far in "tampering" with the traditional tools and techniques of military justice. This type of intimidation by intention would again be used against USCMA in 1977–79. See below, chapters 10–11.

[40] For an account of Keeffe's earlier activities during the drafting of the UCMJ, see AMJ.

[41] Arthur John Keeffe, "Drumhead Justice: A Look at Our Military Courts." Copied from *Reader's Digest*, August 1951, 43, in FP, Box 20, File 5.

row believed that "any further action or investigation by the Court is not warranted."[42]

Keeffe may have suffered from a lingering resentment both because he was virtually ignored during the drafting of the UCMJ, and that apparently no serious consideration had been given to his possible candidacy for a seat on the Court. He visited USCMA in August 1952, and so impressed Daniel Walker with his "predetermined antagonism to the Code and the Court" that Walker dictated a memorandum for the Court directly after the interview. Concerning reform recommendations that could be made by the Court, Keeffe stated that the judges "would probably not fulfill this responsibility and, in fact, could not do so." He also "indicated his previous dissatisfaction with the three judges who were appointed."[43]

Keeffe's frustration about military justice seems to have been shared by the Special Committee of the Association of the Bar of the City of New York. It reported in October 1952 that the past year, "far from seeing further progress in the court-martial reform, has brought only regression from the advances that had been made in recent years."[44] Coming after the first year of USCMA, these comments irritated Frederick Bernays Wiener, the former JAG officer and a well-known scholar on military justice, who wrote to the new chairman of that committee.[45] "While your Committee is . . . frightening the bar with loose talk of regression," both JAGs and judges "are feeling their way through a new system, which has bad points as well as good."[46] Unless the committee "is prepared to look at facts . . . and to eschew loose talk, instead of spewing forth unfounded exaggeration and, generally, working off its members' wartime frustrations, I submit that it would best serve the interests of the legal profession and of the nation by quietly disbanding."[47]

[42] Tedrow's memorandum is undated and untitled. It apparently was not filed either in Quinn's papers or Proulx's chrono files. It was located, rather, in the papers of Homer Ferguson, who did not join the Court until 1956.

[43] QPPC. Walker's statement is untitled, and dated August 8, 1952. It was retained in Quinn's personal correspondence files, and appears not to have been preserved in Court records. It might be noted that within a year or two, Keeffe seems to have changed his mind about USCMA, perhaps because he came in contact with Alfred Proulx, a charming spokesman for the Court. Proulx wrote to Quinn about a friendly letter from Keeffe that "came as a surprise[,] for while I knew him I didn't realize we were so chummy." QPPC, August 6, 1953. Quinn replied, "I am glad to learn that you have converted Mr. O'Keefe [*sic*] into a close friend of the Court." Ibid., August 10, 1953.

[44] QPPC, excerpt from Record of the Association of the Bar of the City of New York, vol. 7, October 1952, 346.

[45] Wiener's numerous comments about the Code and new Court are discussed in AMJ, chapters 9–10.

[46] QPPC, November 28, 1952. "'Wait and see' at this juncture, when the Code has been in operation only about a year and a half, might be a good watchword even for a militant bar committee."

[47] Ibid. Proulx merely acknowledged receipt of Wiener's letter, noting that the correspondence

These examples of court criticism for doing either too much or not enough were reminiscent of earlier comments about the UCMJ. They served to remind the judges, if any such prodding was necessary, that public interest in military justice had not totally abated. Disagreement among the judges themselves over how far the Court should go in "overseeing" the system reflected this tension.

In the *Clay* case a unanimous Court had listed in unequivocal terms the due process rights held by members of the armed services. The extent to which such rights were self-defining increasingly became a source of disagreement between Brosman and Latimer. In a revealing letter to Ray Forrester, Dean of Vanderbilt Law School, Brosman observed that in several of the due process cases, he had sought to articulate a concept that he called "general prejudice." It applied "whenever I was able to find a departure from some important and basic notion derivable from all four corners of the Code[,] although not in specific violation of any express provision."[48] Brosman added that "Latimer and I simply differ in willingness to find prejudice. That is, I am more likely to find it than he, call it what you will." The same thing is true, he wrote, "with regard to our views concerning review . . . on questions of fact. That is, I am much more inclined to find a want of substantial evidence in the particular case than he—and this regardless of the yardstick either of us may verbalize."[49]

By early 1953, Brosman had concluded that Latimer was intent on undermining his earlier decision by insisting that in determining error during a court-martial, the Court also had to find prejudice rather than a purely unintentional mistake. "If *Clay* means no more than this," he wrote to Morgan, "it is reduced to the level of empty, pompous, almost spurious phrases." Even worse, "I think there has also been a recent tendency on the part of Bob Quinn to depart to some extent from the implications of *Clay*—not because of any fundamental change of heart but because I genuinely do not believe he realizes that some of George's opinions [which] he has been buying are really chipping away at *Clay*."[50]

Morgan advised Brosman that his dissents "exhibit too much emotion."

---

between him and the committee chair would be shared with the judges. "I am sure it will be of interest to them." Ibid., December 2, 1952. Later, Wiener changed his mind about USCMA and by 1956 was much more positive concerning its role. See below.

[48] MPVU, May 5, 1952. Brosman isolated four situations in which USCMA could set aside a court-martial conviction: *a*) deprivation of jurisdiction, *b*) a violation of military due process, *c*) general prejudice, and *d*) specific prejudice.

[49] Ibid. Brosman's point involved more than semantics. Finding a substantial lack of legal evidence as a basis for an error in fact-finding could bring the case within USCMA jurisdiction, limited by the UCMJ to matters of law. It might, in other words, dramatically expand the scope of court authority—something that Brosman favored, but Latimer feared.

[50] MPVU, April 21, 1953.

Referring to the Brosman rhetoric just quoted, that "one of the finest flowers of this Court's effort is reduced to the level of empty, pompous phrases," Morgan asked, "Does this add anything . . . except an implied accusation of insincerity in rendering the former opinion?" In his dissents, Brosman would benefit from brevity, "and a complete absence of adjectives and adverbs would make them much more effective as well as more dignified. It is needless to add that I should not have ventured these suggestions had you not invited them."[51]

Brosman moderated his tone, but not his basic disagreement with Latimer—which involved differences in perception both of judicial philosophy and jurisdiction. They are documented in his lengthy and heartfelt concurrence in *United States v. Woods and Duffer*.[52] Again, the judges struggled with both the "harmless error" doctrine and the concept of general prejudice. Again Brosman took issue with Latimer's "substantial and varied misconceptions and confusions."[53] On the basis of the record, "it is sadly clear that my brother is waging what is essentially a war of tags and labels—a really pointless debate in the sphere of semantics." Admittedly, Brosman's views according to Latimer's dissent, resulted in "an excess of administration . . . [,and] it must be confessed, indeed, that the majority of this Court . . . has been willing to engage more than he in the practice reprehended by Judge Latimer." But Brosman, possibly alluding to the fact that he and Latimer remained on friendly terms whatever their juridical discourses, added a graceful disclaimer. "This does not necessarily mean, however, that we have misconceived our office; it may, in fact, mean that he is doing the right thing at the wrong time. In this sense, therefore, it may be said that he is ahead of his era."[54]

Fearful that such judicial "flexibility" as exercised by Brosman might be seen as judicial aggrandizement, Latimer urged caution. His extended dissent built on the point that "unless opinions of this Court announce rules of law which can be applied practically by tribunals and other persons who are required to follow our decisions, its usefulness will be impaired." He objected to a rule of law "so incomprehensible and so lacking in identifiable standards that it can be measured only by the individual whims of appellate judges." The net result was that "a practical application of the principle is most difficult if not impossible."[55] Moreover, he insisted that "we should not

[51] Ibid., April 23, 1953. Brosman responded, "If you wish to help me[,] you can do so in a no more effective or appreciated manner than to write me, whenever you think I am off the beam in anything—content, style or what have you." As to "a longtime habit of overstatement. . . . I know what you mean and I promise to try to reform." Ibid., April 30, 1953.

[52] 2 USCMA 203 (1953).

[53] Ibid., 206.

[54] Ibid., 214.

[55] Ibid., 215.

reverse a conviction unless we could find in the record of that case some prejudice to the substantial rights of the accused."[56]

MORE CONFLICT BETWEEN JUDGES AND JAGS

In May 1952, Morgan received added evidence that the military—in this case the Army—was violating the spirit if not the letter of the UCMJ. A cordial letter from Felix Larkin commented on the operation of the UCMJ. "I gather it is going along pretty well even though I also understand that the JAGs are giving the Court a little trouble."[57] On the same day, Morgan heard from Robert Haydock, the young lawyer who had been Larkin's assistant in the Defense Department Office of General Counsel. Haydock wrote of a letter obtained from the ABA special committee on military justice to the effect that the "Army has sought to deprive accused personnel of their right to petition [USCMA] for review by inducing them to sign waivers of that right. Indeed, this latter practice is so common that mimeographed forms are now being used for that purpose."[58]

Morgan promptly replied to Haydock that discouraging petitions for review was "in my opinion, another indication of the interference and exercise of command control." If the petitions "are too numerous for the Court to sift . . . the solution certainly is not to cut down the right to petition or to put the sifting in the hands of the military."[59] He also sent a copy of this response to Larkin. "It seems apparent," he added, "that not only the JAGs, but the services also, are giving the Court considerable trouble and are attempting to preserve the kind of military control which we were all so anxious to prevent." The new code and court presented the services with "a fine opportunity to set themselves right with the Bar and the public with reference to the administration of military justice[,] and . . . those in control do not have

[56] Ibid., 217. Latimer's words may be contrasted with Brosman's concurrence in a different case. "Unless it is perfectly clear that the accused could not have been harmed, the present error should be regarded as reversible." *United States v. Young*, 2 USCMA 470, 477 (1953).

[57] MPVU, May 19, 1952.

[58] Ibid. Haydock was also concerned with the need to "prevent frivolous appeals to [USCMA—those] which are taken merely because they are free and the defendant has nothing to lose." Obviously, the method employed by the Army to discourage such appeals was unacceptable. But there was always the possibility that too much time would be taken by the need to consider all types of petitions duly filed. The issue of frivolous appeals troubled the judges, and indeed still does. But it also served in part as a sort of doctrinal litmus test for sensing the relationship between jurists and the military.

[59] Ibid., May 23, 1952. "We are certainly not going to sit idly by and see the Uniform Code emasculated . . . in the manner in which the Army weakened and to a large extent destroyed many of the reforms intended to be accomplished by the 1920 Act."

enough sense to realize it."[60] Even as Morgan wrote about waiver of the right of petition for review, however, so did the Court.

In an unsigned "per curiam" decision, the judges considered the validity of a waiver form prepared by the Navy. They did not mince words. "[T]his agreement between the accused and the [Navy] complete to the extent of purporting to provide a consideration to the accused is, for appellate purposes a legal nullity." Moreover, "the execution of similar documents—however imposing in appearance or verbiage—will not be considered by us as in any way affecting his right to petition this Court for relief. We are anxious to make this conception crystal clear to the services."[61] The Court reiterated the point that "the right of convicted persons freely and directly to petition this Court must be protected fully and in nowise abridged." Furthermore,

> It is distinctly arguable that without a full, complete, and careful explanation of the waiver and its legal effect, that its use is a legal trap for the uninformed. Despite the unenforceability of such a document, it is possible that an inadequately advised accused might attach legal validity or significance thereto and be misled as to his right to appeal. For these reasons[,] in any case coming before this Court which involves both a failure to petition timely and a waiver of the right, the surrounding facts and circumstances will be scrutinized by this Court with the greatest care to assure that the accused was fully advised of his rights, and was in no way misled into waiving them for the convenience of the Government.[62]

COPING WITH CRITICISM

The continued carping of the JAGs about the UCMJ and USCMA, as opposed to criticism of its three judges, troubled the Court—although worse was yet to come. Quinn and his brethren hesitated to respond directly to the complaints, if only because as appellate jurists, it would be inappropriate to engage in public colloquy with the JAGs. On the other hand, they could not afford to sit still while the senior legal officers within the services used political contacts and publicity to press for changes in the UCMJ—changes that might directly affect operation of the Court. In the fall of 1952, the three decided to select, as Quinn put it, "a number of distinguished lawyers . . . to serve as a committee to study certain questions" which might later to be

[60] Ibid., May 23, 1952.

[61] *United States v. Ponds*, 1 USCMA 385, 387 (1952).

[62] Ibid. A few months after this opinion was released, Alfred Proulx wrote of a lecture delivered by a Marine Corps general during his two weeks of training duty at the Naval School of Justice, to the effect that "there were just too many damn acquittals under the new Code. From conversations and other remarks I got the idea that the old-time Navy spares no love for the UCMJ." 2 CF, September 22, 1952.

referred to Congress. These included, among others, command control, and the problem of limiting appeals to the Court.[63]

The civilian "court committee" would be a consultive body separate from the Court, able to comment upon whatever it deemed appropriate, including—of course—JAG criticism. It would be composed of able and experienced civilian lawyers—all of whom strongly supported the concept of a civilian appellate court over the military. In a real sense, the committee was to run interference for the judges, to counter JAG comments with constructive proposals, to speak to the Court's concerns without appearing to speak for the judges.[64] It included individuals such as Felix Larkin; Harvard Law Professor Arthur Sutherland; Whitney North Seymour, former President of the Association of the Bar of the City of New York and chair of the committee; and Joseph McClain, Dean of the Duke University Law School. Quinn promptly asked advice from Morgan about the new committee, but the Vanderbilt Law Professor was less than enthusiastic about the proposal.

Concerning command control, "Is there," Morgan queried, "anything to be said now that wasn't said . . . before the committees of Congress and which was given full consideration? Are we to have rehashed the cases which occurred before the Code went into effect and new conclusions drawn as to the theoretical effectiveness or ineffectiveness of the Code provisions to cure the evil?" The possible limiting of appeals in wartime was "a proposal, I suppose, emanating from the services. It is the kind of thing that has a plausible appeal of practicability. In essence it is the first major attack on civilian control of military justice."[65]

Those who supported such a scheme confused symptoms with causes. Morgan reminded Quinn that calls for the reform of military justice invariably took place not so much in time of peace as during actual war. This period would be the least desirable interval in which to attempt to curtail the right of appeal. The remedy for excessive petitions, he repeated, "is certainly not to limit civilian review." The only proposal for Morgan that "is feasible at present in my opinion is one to make the tenure of the judges for life instead of for terms of years."[66] No response from Quinn to Morgan could be located, but Brosman did write a lengthy letter to his friend and mentor—one that

[63] CCC January 5, 1953.

[64] The second Annual Report, from May 31 1951, to May 31, 1952, stated that "the Court is genuinely concerned about the merits of most of the suggested improvements in the Code. In order to make a study of each as far reaching as practicable, a Committee of members of the bar representing the services and the public is being appointed to assist the Court in arriving at appropriate recommendations." 2 ARF, 11. It is not accurate to describe the committee as "representing the services." While members like Larkin and McClain were well acquainted with the service viewpoint, it was their ability to see beyond, if not through, such positions that probably led to their appointment.

[65] CCC, February 2, 1953.

[66] Ibid.

reveals much about the rationale for the civilian committee, and also the condition of USCMA in 1953.

Brosman first pointed to a problem possibly even more serious than he indicated. "We are really working under a good deal of pressure—indeed too much to permit a finished job in our opinions."[67] One could "hold up publication until a really thoughtful and careful product is produced. Latimer is much more likely to do this than Quinn and I." But the Chief Judge believes that in this early period of Court and Code operation, "it is extremely important that we act promptly—and I agree with him in the main."[68] Brosman felt "that we are just playing into the hands of those critics who charge that a civilian court is an incubus if we do not get our opinions out as soon as we possibly can."[69]

In retrospect, Brosman's position pointed to an extremely unfortunate situation. It can be argued that USCMA commits a real disservice if it hands down decisions that are not well conceived, structured, or articulated. In the peculiar context of this Court, however, the negative effects of such action can be still more destructive. Fairly isolated, as one distinguished scholar of military justice observed in 1982, from the civilian judicial system as well as the civilian bar, failing in general to attract sustained and thoughtful academic interest and critical scrutiny, limited in the extent to which its holdings are distributed, bound by the requirement for political balance in appointment to this bench—these conditions make premature dissemination of decisions such as those described by Brosman even more inopportune. Such considerations "serve to deprive the court of many of the sources of institutional strength that furnish the mortar for a sound appellate structure."[70]

Brosman went on to imply, accurately, that Morgan was "somewhat doubtful of the real utility" of the new committee. While the former chairman of the Code committee might indeed be correct, Brosman and his colleagues were simply too busy to give much consideration to the proposals for Code

[67] The Court's statistics support Brosman's statement. By December 1952, USCMA had delivered written opinions in 178 cases, with almost half of them (81) decided to the advantage of the accused. Proulx noted that more than two thousand cases had been filed. He expected a schedule with "an average of 24 cases heard per month, or 8 opinions for each judge. Add this to the passing on of an average of 200 petitions per month, I doubt if they can do more." 2 CF, November 17, 1952; 3 CF, February 11, 1953.

[68] CCC, March 20, 1953. "Latimer, on the other hand, is inclined to write more elaborate opinions and to hold up publication for a longer time. Actually, I suppose I am between the two, but I more nearly agree with Bob than with George."

[69] Ibid.

[70] Eugene R. Fidell, "'If a Tree Falls in the Forest . . . ': Publication and Digesting Policies and the Potential Contribution of Military Courts to American Law," *JAG Journal* 32, (1982) 1–29, n. 55. Brosman wrote in 1953, while Fidell published his essay twenty-nine years later. His points remain relevant, and I am very indebted to him for the many insights found in his perceptive criticisms of appellate military justice. Fidell, however, is in no way responsible for the conclusions or implications I have drawn from them.

changes that were now coming forward. These proposals, "as you would suspect, come from . . . the services and the old-line service point of view on the one hand, and from what at least some people regard as the lunatic fringe on the other. In terms of our statesmanship at least, I genuinely cannot believe that our Committee will not serve a very useful purpose." When, for example, the JAGs propose changes, "some . . . will doubtless be of a minor nature and at the same time both safe and desirable. On the other hand, some are likely to be major and out of keeping with the spirit of the Uniform Code. We will certainly wish the advice of the Committee as to all of these proposals. . . . I think you will have no difficulty in seeing what I am driving at."[71]

Suspecting that Morgan possibly had been disappointed not to be named himself to such a committee, Brosman wrote that "your name was the first one we thought of. . . . Ultimately we concluded that for a variety of practical reasons it would perhaps be best not to have you on the Committee's membership—and I know you will understand fully what I mean here. We did not regard the loss as irreparable, however, for we were assured that you would be willing to advise us personally—as you certainly will be asked to do."[72]

Finally, Brosman reassured Morgan that "although we tend to scrutinize service proposals carefully, we are doing our level best to maintain a cooperative attitude with the [JAGs]. Although there have been tough moments and there probably will be more of them, we have so far been able to maintain a sound working arrangement. Incidentally, the services do not at all like the appointment of our Advisory Committee."[73] Judicial awareness concerning the services' hostility to Morgan may explain the decision not to name him to the committee. A month later, Brosman told Morgan that the JAGs "appear to dislike us just about as much as they dislike you. I suppose the Services disapprove of Bob to the greatest extent; I come next; and George is most acceptable. However, he is merely an SOB and not a dirty one."[74]

The Court Committee, so called to distinguish it from the Code Committee mandated by the statute, set to work with results that will be discussed in the following chapter. In the meantime, the Court finally was able to move into its new home, the building at 450 E St. having been vacated with the relocation of the U.S. Court of Appeals.[75] By October 1952, the judges were hold-

[71] CCC, March 20, 1953, 3. "Let me say, of course, that in speaking thus, I am talking for myself alone. I cannot know of the purposes my brothers had in mind when we agreed on the desirability of setting up such an agency."

[72] Ibid. "Of course we deemed liaison with your committee important[,] and with this in mind we asked Felix [Larkin] to serve."

[73] Ibid.

[74] MPVU, April 21, 1953.

[75] For brief commentary on the USCMA building, see AMJ, xi–xii.

ing forth in their own courtroom, but Proulx's office and the rest of the Court staff did not move in until the end of the month. The move, Proulx observed, "is going to be chaotic enough without trying to get in before the painters and their scaffolding have pulled out. When they said we would move in October last summer, someone forgot to mention the year."[76] The problems associated with the move, although a bit bothersome, were solved much more easily than a question that had remained unsettled while the Court functioned in its old quarters. The question concerned the role of the Court's commissioners and their relationship to the judges.

CONTENTIOUS COMMISSIONERS

As Chief Commissioner, Richard Tedrow had been functioning as a sort of legal advisor to the judges. Indeed, for a short time the Court gave serious consideration to listing his job as "Chief Counsel."[77] By early 1952, apparently each judge had been assigned at least one commissioner, but they all reported to Tedrow. Their primary function was to screen the incoming petitions for review. This involved preparation of a memorandum for each case to be given to the judges. The memoranda not only summarized the relevant facts and issues, but also made an initial recommendation as to disposition. Further, they could suggest points not raised by counsel that might be considered by the Court. Thus, these reports could be pivotal in convincing the judges which cases should be granted plenary review. In addition, Tedrow decided what commissioner would work on which case, and reviewed the memo before forwarding it to the judges, sometimes adding his own comments.

Had the relationship between Tedrow and one of Chief Judge Quinn's commissioners, Daniel Walker, been amicable rather than antagonistic, the above pattern might have continued indefinitely. But as Proulx put it, "They couldn't consult with each other about a legal opinion or anything, so there was a complete split between these two."[78] It was in this context on February 27, 1953, that Walker proposed major alterations in the existing procedures. Tedrow immediately assumed that Walker's proposals were intended to strip him of major responsibilities.

Walker first listed no less than fourteen "major existing defects," and these criticisms, he emphasized, were directed not "at persons but at the system." The defects included contentions that 1) the processing of petitions for review took too much time, 2) commissioners worked in a vacuum, being too

[76] 2 CF, October 2, 1952.

[77] Alfred Proulx recalled that ultimately the judges rejected the title because they felt it inappropriate to have a "counsel to a court." Proulx, Interview 2, July 21, 1992, 10.

[78] Ibid., 14.

far removed from the current views and attitudes of the Judges, and 3) too many commissioners advised on petitions, and not enough assisted the judges in the preparation of opinions. In words that remind one of Brosman's comments to Morgan cited above, Walker argued that "the inevitable result of the present terrific pressure at the opinion stage is poorer opinions. Personally, I am frank to admit that I have turned out many that I felt should have had more work, more research, and more thought. Under the present system, giving the necessary attention to each case is largely impossible."[79]

Walker asserted, further, that the quality of the "advice" memos would be better "if performed by those working directly with another judge." He suggested that Tedrow be redesignated as "General Counsel," with largely clerical responsibilities. These would include, among others, checking opinions before publication, compilation of statistics, public relations, preparation of the annual reports, and preparation of *per curiam* decisions and hearing memoranda.[80] All the remaining legal work "should . . . be concentrated in the Judge's Chambers." Each judge would have several staff members. They would "review records, write petition memoranda, and assist on opinions. . . . These are the most important functions of the Court and should, in my opinion, be performed under the immediate supervision of the individual judges."[81]

Under Walker's plan, the Chief Commissioner would become essentially a traffic cop for the Court.[82] Proulx recalled that its net effect would be to "strip the Chief Commissioner's office and abolish it." On the other hand, Walker had clerked for Chief Justice Fred Vinson, and was familiar with the system at the Supreme Court, where each set of chambers and not a chief commissioner could vote on what was "a [justiciable] cause to be heard."[83] At any rate, Walker submitted his plan to Quinn and his colleagues, including Tedrow. The Chief Commissioner did not take long to react.

Tedrow conceded that Walker's proposal "contains some good, although not new, points." While it "appears to be of great benefit to me personally, I am forced to state that I am unable to find [how] it would necessarily benefit the Court to any similar extent."[84] Several of Walker's statements "at best are generalities, actually some of them are not well taken, if not in fact, misstate-

[79] QPCF, Daniel Walker, "Memorandum to the Court," February 27, 1953, 1–2.

[80] Ibid., 3–5.

[81] Ibid., 5.

[82] Walker insisted, on the other hand, that it "would give greater responsibility to the General Counsel, who would under this system be free to spend most time on important issues and projects." Ibid., 7. Probably well aware of how Tedrow would view the plan, he reiterated this point, emphasizing that his ideas would "produce more assistance for the judges and greater responsibility in the right areas for the present Chief Commissioner." Ibid., 8.

[83] Proulx, 14.

[84] USCMAP, Tedrow File, "Memorandum for the Court," 1. Undated, but probably submitted in February or March 1953.

ments."[85] Responding to Walker's criticism of *per curiam* opinions, Tedrow confessed that "I am in a rather difficult position . . . as far as any answer is concerned [if only because] the author of the memorandum was in charge of this type of opinion." Nor did he "advise me as to any specific items in regards to the 'poor handling' of those opinions."[86]

As to the hearing memorandum generated by the Judge's commissioner prior to oral argument, Tedrow insisted that "its basic purpose . . . should be to provide the Court with the greatest assistance in connection with the case involved, as prepared by a *disinterested reviewer*" [emphasis added]. Here, Tedrow might have been inferring that a commissioner could better demonstrate objectivity in the preliminary assessment of a case than might a judge's own clerk. Such an attribute could only help the USCMA judges who "have, as far as I know, a greater individual workload than any Judge of an appellate court in the country." Indeed, he added, "it is from my personal knowledge of this undesirable and unfair situation that I proceed from my basic premise that we should point our efforts towards relieving the Judges of as much work as possible."[87]

Finally, Tedrow dismissed Walker's memorandum as "a high-pressure rush job." The tone of immediacy and emphasis on the dangers of "further delay[,] plus the sugar-coated build-up . . . increase my buyer resistance. If our operations have reached such a critical state, assuming merit in the memorandum, I wonder how and when this emergency sneaked up on us. . . . I am a little confused as to why a system the author always favored while here, must be immediately replaced, now that he is gone, by a system [Walker] always opposed vigorously."[88]

Although the exact date is not clear, within a matter of weeks following receipt of Walker's proposals, the Court determined to give them a tryout. On March 27, Proulx wrote to Chief Judge Quinn "of Dick and his concern about the trial run of the new plan. I believe that he is slowly coming around to reconciling himself to the proposal. . . . I have talked with him and impressed upon him that . . . Judge Latimer is in no way seeking to ease him out of the picture." Proulx apparently believed that Tedrow "is wasting too much of his good talents on Petitions[,] and that he could render the Court a greater service by having an overall control of the opinions—maintaining

[85] Ibid., 3. "The use of terms such as 'tailored approach,' and 'capsule form,' etc., etc., etc., makes nice reading but adds nothing."

[86] Ibid., 5.

[87] Ibid., 4. Possibly with himself in mind, Tedrow added that this was the reason for hiring well-trained and competent commissioners in the first place. Salaries of the commissioners, according to Tedrow, are equal to or higher "than the comparable assistants in any court of which I have any knowledge. The grades are higher than those of the United States Supreme Court." Ibid., 9.

[88] Ibid., 9–10. Walker resigned as a commissioner soon after he submitted his reform proposal.

liaison with the services—manual and civilian committees—and continuing work on the annual report."[89] A month later, Proulx informed Quinn that Latimer "mentioned to Dick that, despite the change for the next sixty days, he wanted him to take a look at all Petitions as a precautionary measure before final action is taken. Needless to say, this was about the nicest thing that Judge Latimer could say to Dick, for since then, he has been in very good spirits."[90]

How the Walker plan appeared to work in actual practice will be discussed shortly. But the controversy arose during a difficult period for the new tribunal. By the middle of this first segment in its history, internal frictions were matched by external pressure initiated by the JAGs to change the Code—as a means of placing pressure on the Court. Creation of the civilian advisory committee, plus the first steps toward gaining life tenure represented the Court's initial response to JAG criticism. The JAG reaction and the results it produced was another matter.

[89] 3 CF, March 27, 1953.

[90] Ibid., April 27, 1953. Proulx's comments make it clear that Latimer was uncomfortable with the commissioner system. Two explanations come to mind. First, alone among his colleagues, Latimer came to the Court with almost half a dozen years of experience as an appellate judge. He was accustomed to preliminary examination of the record within his chambers and by his own clerks. Second, he was confident of his judicial abilities, and did not feel it necessary to rely on commissioners to help him make up his mind. Latimer's son recalled that "my father's position was that the commissioners were clerks." Interview with George Latimer, Jr., July 20, 1989, 5. Judge Latimer's later statements at a 1956 American Legion hearing on military justice support his son's recollections. See below.

CHAPTER 4

Judges v. JAGs, 1951–1955

DEVELOPMENTS in USCMA history that are traced in this chapter must be seen in the context of the themes that link this entire study. How did the Court define and attempt to carry out its role? How did the military react, and how in turn did the Court respond? How would external political currents, such as appointment of a new judge, affect the tribunal?

Thus far, the controversy between the JAGs and USCMA judges had been largely an internal matter. By 1954–55, it burst wide open—although the services were very careful to distinguish between the Code and the Court, criticizing the latter only by implication on the basis of "operational difficulties" with the former. Moreover, the JAGs sought to distinguish the Court as an institution from the judges as individuals—although their goal was obvious: to use criticism of the Code as an indirect means to control the Court's authority. While concerned about this development, the judges were also involved in the first of numerous efforts to gain life tenure—a subject on which the JAGs likewise held views, markedly different from those of the Court. Finally, Congressional interest in the UCMJ revived during this period. It reemerged as USCMA experienced its first change of judicial personnel, and was related to both issues—revision of the Code and life tenure.[1]

TRAVAIL OVER TENURE

From the Court's viewpoint, it was appropriate that the first external call for life tenure after its establishment should come from Edmund Morgan, architect of the new tribunal. In April 1952—less than a year after the Court commenced operations—he wrote to Carl Vinson, still chairman of the

[1] Although they could be considered as connected, these issues appear to have been treated separately. One reason for this may be that at first, the Court sought life tenure as a goal in itself, regardless of how the new Code would work. After several years of living with the UCMJ, the military determined to move ahead with its own proposals for change—amendments that did not include life tenure. Inability of the Court to agree with some of these changes probably left the judges disinclined to merge life tenure into the other suggested UCMJ alterations. On the other hand, the JAGs were never enthusiastic about life tenure. Their response to USCMA's repeated efforts ranged from strong opposition to disinterest—possibly because the method they proposed to limit the Court would have been effective regardless of tenure. See below.

House Armed Services Committee. Morgan reminded Vinson that (with Morgan's enthusiastic approval) his committee had stipulated life tenure for the Court, only to acquiesce in Senate substitution of limited terms. "If my memory is accurate, the sole reason for prescribing a limited term was the fear that the original appointees might be men poorly qualified for the position, whose selection might be dictated by considerations other than fitness for the office."[2] The chairman need have no such qualms. According to Morgan, the first three judges "have made inapplicable all the reasons which induced the Senate and its Committee to amend the provision for life tenure. . . ."[3]

Morgan received a reply not from Vinson, but rather from his chief counsel, Robert Smart. Diplomatic in tone, it quickly dampened any hope Morgan held that Congressional support for life tenure might be *easily* obtained. "I seriously doubt," Smart observed, "if you are aware of the current attitude of the Congress . . . with reference to giving anybody anything. In everyday vernacular, it's rough." The Court, after all, had been in existence "for less than one year . . . I think that it is premature at this time to propose any [congressional] action. . . ." Better "to let the dust settle and get a happier Congressional atmosphere in being before any proposal on this subject should be presented. . . ." Smart had not yet gained an opportunity to discuss his response with Vinson, but "I think I know him well enough to predict that he would concur with my opinion."[4]

There appears to have been more to Smart's view, however, than just consonance with his boss. Eager himself for a seat on the USCMA bench, the last thing Smart wanted was for the incumbent judges to become frozen in their positions, the inevitable consequence of life tenure.[5] This understand-

[2] MPVU, April 9, 1952. Morgan's memory was accurate as far as it went. However, the Senate Armed Services Committee appears to have been troubled with the concept of life tenure for this tribunal, no matter how well qualified were its first appointees. The three nominations, it might be noted, were approved without recorded opposition. Both Senators Kefauver and Saltonstall supported limited terms, at least until the Court had had an initial trial period. There may also have been a question whether or not there would be sufficient work for a tribunal with life tenure. Saltonstall and Kefauver had implied that the matter of life tenure could always be brought up later, after the Court had established itself. Of course, for Morgan this had already come to pass. See AMJ, chapters 10–11.

[3] Ibid. "They are impressing upon the military establishment the necessity of recognizing that a court-martial is not a mere agency to advise higher military authority, but is a real court. They are insisting that the accused be given the kind of fair trial that the Congress has prescribed. They are not overawed by . . . military men of high rank."

[4] Ibid., April 14, 1952.

[5] Smart was aware that the Senate Armed Services Committee was the confirming authority prior to Senate approval, and that its views were more likely to carry weight than those of the House Committee. Also, life tenure would likely shift confirmation to the Senate Judiciary Committee, or at least require that confirmation jurisdiction be shared. The issue of possible friction between the two committees over USCMA judges would surface later in the Court's history. See below.

able and unstated preference indirectly raised a secondary issue related to life tenure. It had to do with the current judges. Morgan believed that Quinn, Latimer, and Brosman all merited life tenure, but how might this be accomplished? Could they be reappointed after an appropriate statute had been passed? How could one insure that the President would reappoint these three individuals? Indeed, could the legislature compel the chief executive in the matter of a presidential appointment? Might, on the other hand, their current terms simply be extended to life by Congressional fiat, bypassing the executive entirely?

Morgan replied promptly to Smart, and he appears to have been concerned with these questions. "Of course," he wrote, "you know more about tactics in a minute than I should after years of study."[6] My interest is "in getting tenure, so as to keep a lot of lame ducks off the Court and keep politics out as much as possible." Alluding to Brosman's leak of the proposed JAG amendment, Morgan added, "I happen to know that some of the brass would like mightily to cut down the jurisdiction of the Court, and I think that every time a new appointment is to be made, there will be a lot of wire pulling to get a man selected who would favor the service point of view."[7] Indeed, Morgan sent Brosman a copy of Smart's letter. Brosman acknowledged that "Smart may be entirely correct." If Vinson "is against the measure it will have tough sledding. He may be, too, for certainly the Navy will be against it and, as you know, Mr. Vinson is very close to and interested in this service."[8]

Smart's implied negative advice to Morgan appears not to have dissuaded the judges from their goal. Less than two months later, and at Quinn's urging, Senator Green introduced a bill conferring life tenure on the USCMA judges.[9] It would have changed existing law in two ways: First, "the salary, retirement benefits, and other perquisites of the judges shall be the same as those provided by law for the judges of the United States Courts of Appeal," and second, "each [USCMA] judge . . . who holds office as such on the date of enactment of this Act shall continue to hold such office during good behavior."[10] Thus, with one short bill Green sought to resolve both the question of legitimacy for the Court and the need of life tenure for its members. But his measure had a very brief tenure of its own, and died in committee.

Undaunted, Quinn tried again during the next session. He may have realized, however, that there was little congressional interest in granting life

[6] Here Morgan demonstrated false modesty, given the skill he showed in guiding the committee that prepared the UCMJ. See AMJ, chapters 7–11.

[7] MPVU, April 17, 1952. Morgan believed that while it would be very appropriate for the JAGs to recommend life tenure, "I should think it unseemly for Court members to do so. But I do not expect the JAGs to urge anything favorable without the accompaniment of something detrimental. The Army is unhappy."

[8] Ibid., April 22, 1952.

[9] LTF, 82 Cong., 2d Sess., S 3309, June 10, 1952.

[10] Ibid., 2.

tenure to new judges on a tribunal that had been deciding cases for less than a year. This time, the former governor sought to utilize his considerable charm and extensive political contacts in seeking legislative action.

In March 1953, Quinn wrote to another old friend, Congressman Philip Philbin, a Massachusetts Democrat on the House Armed Services Committee. He enclosed a copy of the revised proposal, essentially the same as the 1952 version.[11] Given the magnitude of the Republican election victories in the fall of 1952, "we thought perhaps, that the chances of passage would be improved if it were introduced by . . . some other Republican member of the Committee." Quinn also enclosed a memorandum explaining why changes to the Court should be enacted. He had sent copies to all members of the Rhode Island delegation, including Congressman Fogarty as well as Senators Green and Pastore, "but in the meantime if you can do any missionary work on the matter, I will appreciate it."[12] This explanatory memorandum, drafted by a court commissioner and revised by Quinn, drew heavily on an earlier analysis prepared by Daniel Walker during the debate over the civil service status of court personnel. Quinn catalogued a number of reasons for life tenure.

> **1.** Congress had obviously created a court when USCMA was established, but Title 28 of the United States Code defines a "Court of the United States" as "any court created by act of Congress *the judges of which are entitled to hold office during good behavior*." [Emphasis in original draft.][13]
>
> **2.** Quinn observed that for managerial purposes, USCMA was administered by the Defense Department. Possibly because of this fact, the Civil Service Commission has "insisted on placing all personnel of the Court under its jurisdiction. . . . This not only wastes valuable time[,] but interferes with the proper operation of the Court."
>
> **3.** According to the existing statute, in case of sickness or a temporary vacancy on USCMA, the President could designate a member of the United States Court of Appeals to fill in on a temporary basis. "This plainly indicates that Congress intended to put the judges of both courts . . . on the same plane."[14]
>
> **4.** Whatever may have convinced the Senate to delete life tenure from the UCMJ, its action "casts serious doubt upon the judicial stature of the court. It is undoubtedly looked upon in some executive circles as a cross between an ad-

[11] The judges also prevailed upon Morgan to write again to Vinson.

[12] LTF, March 20, 1953.

[13] LTF, undated draft of memorandum, but sent to designated members of Congress on March 20, 1953. One might respond to the quotation from the U.S. Code by claiming that USCMA could not be called a federal court. Anxious to avoid the implications of this line of reasoning Quinn sought, rather, to bypass it simply by gaining life tenure for his tribunal. He ignored the fact that Congress could create a Court without granting its judges life tenure, as indeed it had done with his tribunal.

[14] Unfortunately for Quinn, it could be argued that this provision merely permitted the President to draw on available federal circuit court judges to fill in, as needed. It could also be claimed, however, that the provision offers at least some evidence that USCMA and the Circuit Courts were roughly comparable.

ministrative agency, and a judicial entity. This, naturally, creates doubt as to the court's power to:

a) punish for contempt;

b) issue subpoenas;

c) issue writs of mandamus, habeas corpus, and other prerogative writs."[15]

5. Unless USCMA "has complete independence and judicial integrity it is in danger of deteriorating into an executive instrumentality. It should be independent of both the military establishment and of all pressure groups. And this court, perhaps more than any other, is subject to both kinds of pressure."[16]

These points were all drawn from the draft memorandum as first submitted to Quinn. He appears to have added, however, a final summary paragraph. USCMA, he noted, heads a judicial system "which currently administers approximately one-ninth of the criminal trials of the entire nation." In time of war, about one-third of such trials would reach its judges. "The jurisdiction of [the Court] is concerned not with mere property rights, but with the lives and liberties of Americans from all walks of life, all segments of society, and all sections of the land. It was the clear intention of the Uniform Code to assimilate the administration of military justice as nearly as possible to that of the civilian community. All of these factors argue strongly for a Court of Military Appeals which is firmly integrated into the Federal judicial system."[17]

These arguments would be repeated with variations and changes in emphasis throughout USCMA's continuing history. Quinn died without obtaining life tenure for his court. As will be seen, Congress has consistently declined to grant this status to USCMA judges. Nor is there any reason to believe that the immediate future will see a change in congressional sentiment. What is striking about USCMA history, however, is the fact that absence of life tenure has not prevented the Court from exercising and augmenting its judicial authority. In other words, without life tenure, the judges have been able to accomplish some of what Quinn believed would be possible only *with* life tenure.[18] Moreover, the United States Supreme Court has

[15] In 1976, USCMA unanimously and unequivocally reaffirmed its authority to issue such writs in the famous decision of *McPhail v. U.S.*, 1 M.J. 457 (1976). Consistently, as Judge William Cook indicated, the Court has viewed its jurisdiction in "broader terms than [those] defined by the Government." See ibid., 460–63. Although Cook later disavowed his own holding, see *Stewart v. Stevens*, 5 M.J. 220 (1978), the case continues to have the support of a majority of USCMA judges—and in theory at least remains good law. It also provides an excellent summary of how the Court had dealt with the issuance of prerogative writs, without waiting for specific congressional action, prior to 1976. See below, chapter 10.

[16] In its sphere, added Quinn, as the highest tribunal in military judicial hierarchy USCMA "should have the power, dignity, and prestige of the United States Supreme Court."

[17] Memorandum, 2–3.

[18] On the other hand, the perimeters of USCMA authority remain somewhat vague. See Fidell, *Guide*, 12–24. Moreover, there is still no definitive USCMA ruling on its power to find individuals in contempt of court. And while its rhetoric points to judicial independence, its

shown little inclination to define the contours of USCMA power, in terms of its judicial authority as an appellate tribunal.[19]

As soon as Green introduced his bill, the new chairman of the Senate Judiciary Committee, William Langer, wrote to Leverett Saltonstall, a member of the Senate Armed Services Committee—to which the new bill had been referred. Langer bluntly articulated two assumptions that, taken together, might well have troubled Quinn. In the first place, he claimed, Green's bill "in effect creates three new lifetime Federal Judgeships on a par with an appointment to the Circuit Court of Appeals."[20] Quinn probably would not have used the frank language employed by Langer, especially during a time of political emphasis on retrenchment. Moreover, there could be some dispute as to the accuracy of Langer's point.[21] Yet, the new Judiciary Committee chairman went further.

He asserted that according to the language used in the UCMJ, USCMA "is not now actually a 'court' in the Constitutional sense at all, but is merely sort of a review board of last resort for the purpose of considering appeals from court-martial convictions." Because the judiciary committee "has primary jurisdiction with respect to the creation of new federal judgeships," Langer wished that the bill (assuming a favorable report from Saltonstall's committee) be referred to the Judiciary Committee.[22] He agreed to report it back to the full Senate within two weeks of receipt.[23] Speaking for the Court, Quinn informed Green that we "would certainly have no objection . . . in the

---

reality has always been to exist within the shadow of the huge federal defense establishment. Given this fact, there may well be some elusive aspects of judicial independence that do not apply to USCMA—possibly by congressional intent, as noted by Senator Russell (see above, chapter 1), possibly by judicial inclination.

[19] In recent years, the High Court has had opportunities to consider the question, if only because this trend of expanded judical authority—evident during the Quinn era—dramatically increased after 1975, the year of his death. There is a vast difference, however, between claiming judicial authority to act in general terms, and consistently declining to do so in specific instances. In cases where this has happened, of course a plaintiff gains no benefit from the vigor with which the Court discusses constitutional protections, only to find them inapplicable to plaintiff's case. See, for example, *Unger v. Ziemniak*, 27 M.J. 349 (1989); *United States Navy-Marine Corps Court of Military Review v. Carlucci*, 26 M.J. 328 (1988); *United States v. Graf*, 35 M.J. 450 (1992). See also this author's comments in 30 MJ, ccxxxvii–ccxlix (1990), chapter 10, below, and his article "Military Justice 50 Years After Nuremberg: Some Reflections on Appearance v. Reality," *Military Law Review*149 (1996) 178–86 (1996). Perhaps in its quest for life tenure, USCMA has become a victim of its own compromises.

[20] LTF, April 29, 1953.

[21] Quinn might have argued that—contrary to Langer's claim—the bill did not create new judgeships. It merely transformed three existing term appointments into nominations with life tenure.

[22] Exactly the same point for exactly the same reason had been offered by Senator Patrick McCarran during Senate debate over the UCMJ in 1950. See AMJ, chapter 11.

[23] Ibid.

event that the delay would not make it impossible to get action on the bill this year." But he rejected Langer's second assumption. "The power to create the Court undoubtedly arises out of that section of the Constitution [Article I, section 8] which gives Congress the power to make laws for the government of the [armed services]; so that the authority stems from the Constitution, although perhaps not directly from the judicial article."[24]

QUINN'S QUEST FOR CONSENSUS

In trying to build support for Green's proposal, Quinn drew on a variety of sources. Thus he sent the Rhode Island congressional delegation an excerpt from an article by New York University Law School Professor John V. Thornton, dealing with military justice under the new code and court. Thornton was impressed with "the combined scholarly and practical character of the Court's opinions. Their high caliber is particularly remarkable since the Court has only three members and disposes of a tremendous volume of litigation. In a little more than a year[,] this bench has demonstrated that it deserves to be ranked with the elite of federal and state appellate tribunals."[25]

Similar approbation came from a well-known Senator, Margaret Chase Smith (R-ME). Writing in the *Boston Globe* about a recent USCMA decision dealing with imposition of bread and water as punishment for certain military offenses, the Senator lauded the Court even as she excoriated naval officials.[26] This decision, according to Senator Smith, "surely gives real hope that this tribunal will not be the mere lackey of the naval and military brass." Further, she added, "there is considerable question in my mind whether [USCMA] should be placed in the Department of Defense where its members can feel even the slightest feeling of being beholden to the military and civilian chiefs of the department."[27] Immediately, Quinn sent excerpts to his Rhode Island congressional contacts. He emphasized that Smith's article "supports our bill for life tenure. She is a powerful member of the Armed Services Committee, and her help would undoubtedly be of great value."[28]

[24] Ibid., Mary 6, 1953. "However," Quinn added, "it would probably be a good thing for us to have the stamp of approval of the Judiciary Committee, as well as the Armed Forces Committee." As was seen in volume 1 of this study, such turf battles had been carefully and successfully avoided by Larkin as he navigated the UCMJ through Congress in 1949–50.

[25] LTF, June 1, 1953.

[26] Speaking for a unanimous Court, Judge Brosman upheld a provision of the UCMJ which expressly limited military officials to imposing such a penalty for a maximum of three days. Any practices to the contrary, even though they might be sanctioned by the MCM (Manual for Courts-Martial), would presumably be "in conflict with this construction of the Code," thus "they are without sanction of law and must fall." *United States v. Wappler*, 2 USCMA 393, 396 (1953).

[27] Smith's column appeared in the *Boston Globe* on June 8, 1953, Excerpt (unpaginated) is in LTF.

[28] Ibid., June 9, 1953.

Smith's support might indeed be helpful, but the key to congressional action would lie with the chairmen of the Armed Services and Judiciary committees. Thus, Quinn had met with Dewey Short, the new Republican chairman of the House Armed Services Committee, hoping for a firm committment to support the bill. The best Quinn could get, according to Proulx, was a sense that "Short seemed disposed to back the bill, but that he did not commit himself as to whether or not he would drop it in the hopper."[29] Short was more candid with a fellow Congressman, Aime Forand of Rhode Island. "Frankly, I don't know whether or not it will be feasible to entertain legislation for life tenure of these judges. The Committee has a very heavy workload[,] and in my best judgment we probably could not conduct hearings before the next session."[30]

The JAGs, of course, were fully aware that a bill to grant USCMA judges life tenure would be submitted to Congress. Brosman advised Morgan in April that "the Service people are planning to attack it on the ground that the provision freezing-in the three incumbents is unconstitutional as an unwarranted exercise of the appointive power by the legislature."[31] Such opposition from the armed services, although not unexpected, would be unfortunate. Even worse, however, might be objections by the General Counsel of the Defense Department, echoing the services' viewpoint. In July 1953, Brosman wrote Quinn that reservations—if not outright disapproval—from the Pentagon would be forthcoming. According to Brosman, there were several areas of difficulty.

"Actually," he wrote, "it appears that the comments of . . . Defense will not be nearly as favorable as we had been given to believe." The department would indeed reject the bills as submitted, offering instead "a substitute which omits the freezing-in provision."[32] Moreover, the department declined to hold "that the Air Force claim of unconstitutionality is without support." Instead, it would submit an alternative bill "without the naughty language." The only possible benefit that occurred to Brosman was that at least the Defense Department "favors life tenure as a matter of principle."[33]

Whatever enthusiasm the new Republican chair of the Armed Services Committee might have for USCMA, according to Brosman, appeared to be more than offset by his general ignorance of military justice. "Short obviously knows very little about either the bill or the Court. . . . Actually he

[29] 3 CF, May 28, 1953.

[30] LTF, June 10, 1953.

[31] MPVU, April 21, 1953. Brosman further remarked to Morgan that Quinn, "the judge they dislike most is untouched by any attack of theirs on a tenure bill. Given Bob's age, he has *de facto* life tenure now." Two days later, Proulx also noted the unfavorable attitude of the armed services in a letter to Quinn. 3 CF, April 27, 1953.

[32] It is unclear what role the JAGs played in persuading the General Counsel's Office to make these changes in the proposed legislation.

[33] LTF, July 15, 1953.

had so little background as not to know [that his own committee] had any finger in the confection [*sic*] and passage of the Uniform Code." Short—whom it is difficult to see as other than a lightweight—was even unaware that the House had originally provided life tenure for the judges.[34] Apparently, wrote Brosman, "he thought the Uniform Code was a product of the Judiciary Committee!"[35] Finally, there was the matter of Robert Smart, counsel to the House Committee, who "is still interested in membership on the Court." Smart could therefore be expected to "do whatever he can to stall passage of any life tenure bill which will close the door on him." All in all, Brosman suggested, "maybe we had better start thinking about a five-judge compromise."[36]

Quinn conceded that "your report . . . is far from encouraging. . . . It looks to me as if we better concentrate our energies on the Senate in the hope that we might be able to get a hearing there." It seemed to the Chief Judge that "Short knows more about the bill than he pretends to. . . ."[37] It "looks to me as though they may be playing tag with us[,] and that we have little or no hope of making any progress with them unless we could actually get some of our friends on the Armed Services Committee to put the pressure on."[38]

Within four days of Quinn's reply to Brosman, the Defense Department's General Counsel forwarded a letter to the Director of the Bureau of the Budget—one that confirmed Brosman's earlier conjecture. "[I]t would appear more appropriate to amend the bill to provide that the indefinite appointments . . . should be made upon the expiration of the term of each judge who holds office as such on the day of enactment in order to avoid any

[34] Aptly described by Forrestal's biographers as an "eloquent and bibulous congressman," at the conclusion of General MacArthur's speech to Congress in April 1951 Short had shouted that "we heard God speak here today, God in the flesh, the voice of God." His assessment may be contrasted with that of President Truman, who characterized the same speech as "a hundred percent bullshit." MacArthur's histrionics reminded Dean Acheson of "the father who had zealously guarded his daughter's chastity and who, when she announced that she was pregnant, threw up his hands and cried: 'Thank heaven, it's over!'" Townsend Hoopes and Douglas Brinkley, *Driven Patriot* (1992), 447; William Manchester, *American Caesar* (1978), 661–62.

[35] LTF, July 15, 1953, 2. To make matters worse, Short indicated that the Court "should shake down a little more" before consideration should be given to life tenure. Furthermore, due to the burdens of other legislative issues, his committee "could not possibly get around to any consideration of the bill this session."

[36] Ibid. Thirty-six years later, in 1989 Congress enacted legislation which expanded USCMA to five judges, its current size. But the lawmakers refused to provide life tenure.

[37] "I remember very distinctly," Quinn recalled, that Short "whispered to me that Bob Smart was really the father of the bill, and had engineered it through the [House] Armed Services Committee, and I am quite sure that he knew as reporte[d] originally it carried life tenure." As was seen in AMJ vol. 1, Smart served as an important contact for Larkin while his committee formulated the UCMJ. But it is an overstatement to describe him as "really the father of the bill." LTF. July 20, 1953.

[38] Ibid.

legal question as to the validity of legislatively appointing certain individuals to office[,] thereby infringing upon [presidential] power . . . to appoint by and with the consent of the Senate."[39] A revised draft listed the dates on which the three judges' terms were to expire, and provided that "all successors, including any judge who is appointed to succeed himself and any judge appointed to fill a vacancy, shall hold office during good behavior."[40]

The Defense Department, through its office of the General Counsel, also referred the revised version of Senator Green's bill to the Civil Service Commission. On September 15, Chairman Philip Young responded that the change of status for USCMA judges "is a matter of legislative discretion." Since they were presidential appointments, with Senate confirmation, "they are not subject to the Commission's jurisdiction[,] and we have no comment to make with respect to the proposed changes. . . ." He distinguished however, as had the Commission's 1951 memorandum, between the judges and the court itself. Recalling that the Commission had ruled that court employees were subject to laws, rules, and regulations applicable to federal employees of the executive branch, Young stated that "we see nothing in the . . . proposed legislation that would be a sufficient basis for a different conclusion."[41]

The action of the Defense Department in supporting life tenure, but possibly not for the incumbents, left the judges uncertain as to their future course. Defense officials assured them that the Court would have ample opportunity to comment on the proposed changes, prior to the next session of Congress scheduled to begin in January 1954. In the meantime, Richard Tedrow prepared a memo for the judges, explaining why the revised bill—even though it rejected life tenure for them but not for their successors—was so important.

The proposal "would resolve once and for all the confusion, at least in some quarters, as to our exact status." Its origins were less important than that such confusion "should be dispelled without delay." Moreover, without the finality of a legislative act, questions could "arise as to the Court not being completely independent of the military establishment and of pressure groups, or of its being merely an Executive instrumentality."[42] The great difficulty confronting USCMA was that in claiming to be a real court, it did not appear to fall within the various statutory provisions "affecting the Federal Judiciary generally."[43] Thus, corrective legislation was even more neces-

[39] LTF, July 24, 1953.

[40] Ibid.

[41] LTF, September 15, 1953.

[42] LTF, October 8, 1953. Tedrow's reference to the supposedly archaic notion of courts-martial being instruments of the executive had relevance, even as late as 1953. See below.

[43] Ibid., 2. Unfortunately, USCMA could not look to legislative intent as supporting its position. While the House had indeed provided for life tenure, the Senate had not, and the House

sary.[44] Replete with citations, Tedrow's points apparently failed to convince the Justice Department, the third agency whose views on the pending bill had also been requested by the Bureau of the Budget. Although William Rogers, the Deputy Attorney General, was sympathetic to the Court's position, Green's bill troubled him.

At the outset, Rogers claimed that the bill "appears to be designed to place the judges beyond the removal power by the President."[45] He based this contention on a portion of Article 67 of the UCMJ. As enacted, this section provided that USCMA judges could be removed by the President "upon notice and hearing, for neglect of duty or malfeasance in office, or upon the ground of mental or physical disability, but for no other cause." Because this provision obviously could not be reconciled with the principle of life tenure (that could end only by resignation, death, or impeachment), Green had deleted it from his bill. It was this deletion that bothered Rogers.

He summarized again the old controversy over the nature of a court-martial, and pointed to the creation of USCMA as a partial response to it. He also emphasized that the judges "are in large part free of command control."[46] Conceding that courts-martial might in their nature be judicial, Rogers denied that this concession changed the essential character of such a proceeding from "a method of discipline exercised by the Commander in Chief and his authorized representatives." Further, he noted the limited jurisdiction exercised by USCMA, when compared to Article III tribunals. Finally, he questioned the need to change again what had itself been so important an innovation.

Indeed, "not only is the Code an experiment, but so too is the establishment of the Court and the use of independent civilians as judges." The entire system "has been in operation for . . . only slightly over two years. This seems to be hardly enough time for an informed judgment to be made as to whether the experiment has been a success."[47] Rogers concluded that when all was said and done, because USCMA "is an instrument designed to carry

---

had accepted the Senate action. If anything, legislative intent indicated a clear preference against life tenure.

[44] See p. 3 of Tedrow's memorandum where he observes that unless USCMA's status is clarified—especially concerning issuance of prerogative writs—members of the armed forces serving abroad "could actually be deprived of all rights and liberties under both the Constitution and the [UCMJ], with no judicial forum available to them in which to obtain an appropriate remedy."

[45] LTF, November 20, 1953, 2.

[46] Ibid., 4. "The judges are independent of the military, and even the power of the President to remove them is substantially limited."

[47] Ibid., 5. "Unless some imminent threat to the independence of the judges or some other immediate need exists, it is believed that the experiment should be given a further chance to be observed in action before so substantial a change is made." Here Rogers hints at the point raised earlier in this chapter. The obvious success of the Court in its early years without what it considered vital to its function; i.e., life tenure—in one sense made such a change all the more difficult to justify.

out the President's . . . function as Commander in Chief, it would seem unwise to place any further restriction upon the power of the President to remove members of the Court." Accordingly he "is unable to recommend the enactment of the bill."[48] Although he probably had so concluded even before receiving Rogers's memorandum, Quinn realized that the bill was stalled at least until 1954. Meanwhile, the JAGs had not been idle.

CONTINUED CONTENTION BETWEEN JUDGES AND JAGS

In their disagreements with the judges, the JAGs had an important tactical advantage: flexibility. They could articulate, adjust, and alter their positions, while the judges had to consider their roles as appellate jurists. In a real sense, while Quinn and his brethren had to wait for trouble to reach the Court, the JAGs were under no such constraints. Their response to the Court's outrage over the proposed change in review discretion, discussed in the previous chapter, illustrates the point. Well aware of the hostile judicial reaction to their first proposal, the JAGs shifted ground. On March 30, 1953, they submitted a joint memorandum to Quinn, insisting that his court "should be protected against petitions for grants of review that are wholly lacking in legal merit. Under present law there is no means of regulating or eliminating these appeals, which may be initiated by the accused himself, who, though most frequently acting in entire good faith, generally has little or no knowledge of the points of law involved."[49] In some instances, "petitions have been filed primarily for dilatory purposes."[50] Finally, these undesirable conditions were exacerbated by the Code's provision that gave an accused thirty days to appeal to USCMA from an unfavorable decision by a Board of Review.[51]

This latter problem could be solved simply by reducing the time limit for such an appeal from thirty days to only ten.[52] As to the primary difficulty of

[48] Ibid. It seems incredible that the Deputy Attorney General could make such a fundamental error, especially in the light of more than two years of USCMA reports. It may well be that Rogers had not informed himself either of the earlier Ansell-Crowder controversy, the history of the UCMJ, or of the state of military justice even as he wrote.

[49] Copy of the memorandum signed by all the JAGs is in 3 CF, March 30, 1953.

[50] Ibid. Air Force JAG Reginald Harmon assumed that USCMA "must deal constantly with this problem." Of course the judges had been dealing with it since they started accepting petitions in 1951. In 1953, Harmon apparently concluded that the judges were incapable of doing this by themselves.

[51] In 1968, the name of the intermediate military appellate tribunals was changed to Courts of Military Review, and in 1994 to Courts of Criminal Appeals.

[52] The JAGs ultimately did so recommend. Commissioner David Condon "wholeheartedly condemn[ed]" this suggestion. "If the petition has to be filed within ten days, the accused may be deprived of adequate service prior to filing his petition and, as a result, may in fact decide

frivolous appeals, the JAGs offered a more subtle proposal than their first suggestion—which had been to condition an appeal to USCMA upon JAG certification that such a step was warranted. Now they proposed to restrict USCMA review to those cases where "counsel who represented the accused at trial . . . or appellate defense counsel appointed by the Judge Advocate General if the accused was not represented by [civilian] counsel before the Board of review, shall certify that in his opinion the errors of law relied upon materially prejudiced the substantial rights of the accused." The report accompanying this proposal noted that "this particular means of regulation was selected because the accused's counsel may be expected to be fully cognizant of the circumstances of the case[,] and because it does not permit arbitrary restriction of the right to petition in any case."[53]

In a memorandum to the Court, Tedrow assessed the value of the JAG suggestion as minimal. "These fellows," he noted, "keep on trying." Seeking to protect the Court from cases "lacking in legal merit," the JAGs failed to understand that "we are unable to find whether there is merit until *we* have reviewed the record"; exactly what the JAG revision would have restricted.[54] Tedrow commented further that "in 25% of our cases of substance, we decided issues that counsel never saw fit to raise." Given this "lack of legal ability[,] I fail to see how . . . we could place such extreme reliance on counsel."[55] Finally, "the requirement of such a certificate from one in the Service, to a greater or lesser degree makes the jurisdiction of this Court dependent upon the military."[56]

not to file." 2 ARF, Draft of comments by Tedrow and Condon (apparently in reaction to JAG proposed changes in UCMJ, August 1953), 5. If ten days was an unsatisfactory time frame, one wonders how Condon reacted to the Army JAG's original position on the time limitation. Major General Ernest Brannon had urged that the period in which an accused may petition USCMA for review "be five days from the time he is notified of the [Board of Review] decision. Such a period should be sufficient for the accused to determine his future course of action since counsel is furnished by the Government." Brannon did not trouble to explain how the government-appointed lawyer—in getting together the requisite materials for appeal—might solve the problem of distance when the accused was, for example, either on the west coast, or in Europe. USCMAP, "Action of the Appointing Authority on Recommendations for changing the [UCMJ]," May 28, 1953.

[53] Ibid., enclosures 3 and 4; USCMAP, Report of Proceedings by Board of Officers, June 3, 1953, Exhibit A, p. 8. This report was one of several efforts by the JAGs to coordinate their suggestions for changes in the UCMJ.

[54] USCMAP, "Memorandum to the Court," August 4, 1953, 2, emphasis added.

[55] Tedrow's point is of interest in a broader context. It indicates that early in its history when faced with what it considered poor lawyering, USCMA elected to study the record itself—instead of demanding a higher quality of work from its bar. Here, again, is the problem of specifying issues; and USCMA's choice—to which it has adhered continually—is fraught with implications that remain troubling. See above, chapter 3, n. 35.

[56] Ibid. Tedrow described other sections of the report as "anachronistic if not atavistic." The chairman of the Board, General J. L. Harbaugh, Jr., was one "whose progressive views are well known except they progress in the wrong direction." Ibid., 3.

Commissioner David Condon dismissed the proposal as "a snide attempt to retain control over lemons or clear busts such as we have had occasion to see on motions for a new trial." More important, "it is also an attempt to get around the decisions of our Court." Most important for Condon and Tedrow was that this blatant effort by the JAGs takes "away the right which Congress has given to a man to determine whether or not he should appeal[,] and places it in the hands of a lawyer who in most instances is a Government appointed man subject to control by his [military] superiors."[57]

The criticisms offered by Condon and Tedrow were perceptive, although two additional comments can be offered: *a*) Regardless of the confident contention by the JAGs to the contrary, in no way did their proposal insure against "arbitrary restriction of the right to petition." Indeed, the change would have left petitioners at the mercy of counsel, with no recourse to USCMA when counsel—for whatever reason—might decline to certify. *b*) It will be recalled that virtually all military appellate counsel were assigned to particular cases, as Condon stated, by their JAG. But this officer was responsible also for evaluating counsel's effectiveness and quality of performance. The potential for command influence was obvious, except apparently to the JAGs.

About two weeks after Tedrow presented his comments to the Court, the JAGs submitted their Report on recommended changes in the UCMJ. It included, among other suggested amendments, the provision for certification so soundly criticized by the Chief Commissioner. The language, however, indicated one intriguing change that may or may not have been another JAG adjustment to judicial hostility. The report stated that the Code should be amended to provide that USCMA "need only consider" petitions when certified by counsel.[58] In the context of a statute dealing with possible actions, the word "need," as opposed to the word "shall," carries very different legal implications. By the change, the JAGs may have intended to retain USCMA flexibility, while pointing toward a way to avoid its utilization. Whatever the intent, this change utterly failed to assuage the doubts of the judges, who awaited findings from their own civilian Court Committee as a suitable basis for responding to the JAGs. Chaired by New York City attorney Whitney North Seymour, the committee submitted its report to the Court late in December 1953.

CONCERNS OF COURT AND COMMITTEE

Creation of the Court Committee, as distinguished from the Code Committee, had resulted from judicial awareness that an external group of distin-

[57] 2 ARF, draft of comments by Tedrow and Condon on proposed changes to the UCMJ, 5–6.

[58] Ibid, August 20, 1953, 5. The earlier version sent to Quinn by Air Force JAG Reginald Harmon used the word "shall." See above, n. 49, March 30, 1953, enclosure 3.

guished lawyers, all selected because they were 1) knowledgeable in military law, and 2) sympathetic to enactment and implementation of the UCMJ, could be a useful counterpoise in dealing with the JAGs. Not restrained by the constraints applicable to sitting judges, the committee could also bring a sense of objectivity to its deliberations.[59] Quinn and his colleagues, on the other hand, were involved in the demanding routine of hearing, considering, and deciding cases; burdens that left them little time to evaluate—let alone confront—suggested changes in the UCMJ. All parties involved—judges, JAGs, and the committee—realized that the new Code needed some improvements and changes. No one urged that the document remain completely unchanged. The extent to which it should be modified, however, was a different matter.

The JAGs had already achieved unanimity on a number of proposed changes. These included, among others, providing expanded jurisdiction for military courts with a single law officer serving alone. Further, they sought greater flexibility for themselves when taking corrective action in a court-martial where there was clear evidence of error, without having to refer the case to the Board of Review. The committee endorsed these changes.[60] It declined, however, to support reducing the time available for petition to USCMA from thirty to ten days, as the JAGs had sought. Instead, they recommended a fifteen-day period.[61]

Moreover, as Quinn and his colleagues probably anticipated, it "definitely opposed" the JAG suggestion on limiting appeals to the Court.[62] Although the members revealed concern with the workload of the three jurists, the committee declined to recommend any changes whatsoever in jurisdiction over their docket, all the more as the judges had not sought any such modification. They pointed, rather, to the fact that "the Court has been able to function efficiently and justly under its present heavy workload."[63]

[59] The Code Committee was mandated by the UCMJ, and included the judges and JAGs. The Code required annual reports to Congress from both. The Court Committee, however, was strictly the creation and responsibility of the three judges to whom alone it reported.

[60] USCMAP, CCC Report, December 21, 1953, 5–7.

[61] This reduction of the time limit never became law. To the contrary, in 1981 Congress changed the UCMJ to provide for a 60-day period, and on occasion even this limitation has been extended—the Court striving to insure that an accused will have every reasonable opportunity to file an appeal.

[62] USCMAP, CCC December 21, 1953, 9.

[63] Ibid., 10. One suspects that the committee's purpose in raising this point was anything but subtle. The judges had not complained about the ease of appeals to their court. It was the JAGs who suddenly demonstrated a novel solicitude for the court in the wake of the allegedly excessive numbers of appeals that threatened to swamp the tribunal. From their perspective, Quinn and his brethren were wary of what they saw as the real motive for JAG concern—irritation over various USCMA decisions that mandated new standards for due process, and now involved civilian judges in areas that previously had been the exclusive domain of the JAGs—rather than aggravation over the supposedly high level of "frivolous" appeals. Speaking for the Committee,

Whether by accident or intent, the committee's recommendations reached the Court as Proulx was preparing the Annual Report, a document mandated by the Code. It included separate sections by each of the JAGs, a section for USCMA, and a joint report filed by JAGs and judges together. Drafted during the first part of 1954, this report indicated where consensus had been achieved and where conflict could be anticipated. The JAGs and judges unanimously recommended seventeen changes to the UCMJ, virtually all of which had already been endorsed by the Court Committee. Listed among them was, despite Condon's criticism, the proposal to reduce the time for appeal from thirty to fifteen days.[64] Conspicuous by its absence was the plan to limit the right of appeal.

The JAGs included as part of their report the August 1953 proposals which contained the ten-day limit, as well as the certification requirement for appeal to USCMA. More ominous, at least from the Court's viewpoint, was the statement by Ira Nunn, Judge Advocate General of the Navy. Although he had signed the joint report replete with the seventeen recommendations unanimously supported by all parties, Nunn noted that the JAGs endorsed the August suggestions as well. Indeed, "proposed legislation implementing [them] has been drafted and will be submitted to the Department of Defense for inclusion in the . . . Defense Legislative Program for 1954."[65]

Nunn's move cannot have pleased the judges. But their immediate concern lay less with Nunn than with the opposition of the Justice Department to Green's bill, still pending before the House Armed Services Committee. Quinn and his brethren had little doubt that continued opposition at this level would ultimately prevent its passage. In February 1954, therefore, Judge Latimer determined to speak with Deputy Attorney General Rogers "with the view of seeking to have the Department reverse its standing."[66] Rogers assured Latimer that "as a matter of policy, there was no consideration of the patronage feature involved in the bill."[67] Rather, Rogers apparently focused on the "newness" of the tribunal, and the corresponding lack of a critical

---

Seymour hoped that Quinn would find the report "satisfactory and useful. If for any reason you should desire it recast in form, please let me know and that can be done quite readily." CCC, December 21, 1953.

[64] It may well be that the Court viewed this specific proposal as one in which the judges could accept the underlying JAG objection to the current practice—that thirty days for appeal was too long—and compromise on the new time limit. No such compromise was possible in the question of USCMA control of its docket.

[65] 2 AR, 45. Although Nunn did not say so, the implication of his statement was that the JAGs were fully prepared to bypass both the Court and its committee, and go directly to Congress through the Department of Defense. This, in fact, is exactly what they did, and Nunn's comment can be considered an early published indication of JAG irritation with USCMA. Additional public examples of this displeasure would be forthcoming.

[66] 4 CF, February 17, 1954.

[67] Ibid., February 23, 1954.

need to make a fundamental change after such a short period of operation. He invited some Court staff members [Tedrow and Proulx] to meet with Justice officials to discuss changes in the department's position.[68]

Tedrow and Proulx urged that the emphasis on "newness" be discarded; "that we were merely interested in the bill insofar as it would remove all possible doubt that this Court was a Court of the United States; further, that the feature of freezing-in present incumbents was not a consideration at all."[69] As to the possible constitutional question raised first by the Air Force and later by the Defense Department, "we more or less agreed that perhaps it was valid."[70] By 1954, in other words, the USCMA judges seemed more concerned with the long-range goal of life tenure, than with the short-term objective of extending their own terms.

The position taken by Proulx and Tedrow received support from two independent and impressive sources. The first came in the form of a letter to Rogers from his old friend Felix Larkin. He explained the background of the Court's creation, as well as the Senate decision "that since this was a new Court of importance[,] it would be well not to provide life tenure for the Judges against the possibility that they might be poor political appointees. We felt this decision was debatable even at the time but could do nothing about it." Since then, Larkin added, "I detect a certain amount of difficulty on the part of the judges in resisting pressures from various quarters[,] and I think their work and the objectivity which they should bring to that work would be greatly enhanced if they had the protection of life tenure."[71]

The second source was the District of Columbia Circuit Court of Appeals, which ruled in January 1954 that USCMA, "is a court and not an administrative agency." In any view, "the Court of Military Appeals appears to us to be a court in every significant respect, rather than an administrative agency. Certainly Congress intended that in its dignity and in its standards of administering justice[, USCMA] should be assimilated to and equated with the established courts of the Federal system."[72] While at least one positive result later came from this holding, apparently Rogers remained unconvinced, even

[68] Ibid., February 25, 1954.

[69] Later, in a letter to Quinn, Proulx expanded on his comments about the meeting. The Court Clerk believed that "we were able to convince them that their position on the newness feature of the Court was very arbitrary, since a Court should have all the attributes of a Court, if it was to function on par with the Court of Appeals and as the Supreme Court of all military convictions." Ibid., March 1, 1954.

[70] Ibid., February 26, 1954.

[71] LTF, March 11, 1954.

[72] *Shaw v. United States*, 209 F2nd 811 (D.C. Cir., 1954). The case involved several members of the Navy who after conviction by court-martial sought review from USCMA, without success. They then turned to the Circuit Court of Appeals, arguing that USCMA "is an administrative agency[,] and [thus] its orders were subject to review by the Circuit Court"; a contention summarily rejected by the Court. See also *Judge Advocate Journal* 16 (March 1954), 25.

after Larkin's letter.[73] On March 17, Proulx received word that Rogers's "original comments would stand without amendment."[74] Although the Clerk did not know it, additional support for Rogers's position was circulating within the White House.

Given the facts that the Defense Department supported the bill if the provision for automatic tenure was deleted, that the Civil Service Commission raised no objection to the measure, but that the Justice department opposed the enactment—the Bureau of the Budget appears to have been uncertain as to its recommendation, and asked the White House for "guidance on the advice we should give Defense."[75] The "Assistant Director for Legislative Reference," Roger Jones, referred to the alternatives "of advising Defense that we concur . . . , or that we concur in the unfavorable Justice views, or we merely have no objection to the submission of both. . . ."[76] With this less-than-enthusiastic response, Eisenhower's Special Counsel Bernard Shanley wrote to an old friend, Arthur Vanderbilt, Chief Justice of the New Jersey Supreme Court asking "your views on the advisability of this Bill."[77]

Vanderbilt replied with a confidential letter to "Bern." He had known one member of the Court—Paul Brosman—for the last fifteen years, "and have the highest regard for him." Further, Vanderbilt had read some of the Court's opinions, "which impressed me favorably." Indeed, "I am told by some of my friends among the judges in the District of Columbia that the new tribunal has made a splendid record."[78] Nevertheless, Vanderbilt was far from ready to advise that USCMA "be transformed into a court with judges having life tenure."

He reminded Shanley that the tribunal "is still in an experimental stage." Moreover, "a very considerable proportion of the cases . . . involve offenses of a purely military character and breaches of military discipline, such as desertion, absence without leave, disobedience of orders, etc." Vanderbilt's point became clear after he recalled that shortly after World War II, he had

[73] Early in May, USCMA was informed that "henceforth the U.S. Law Week will carry the decisions of [USCMA] under "Courts" and no longer under "Executive Agencies and Boards." 4 CF, May 3, 1954.

[74] 4 CF, March 17, 1954.

[75] Eisenhower Papers (hereafter cited as EP), Official Files, 100 D, Box 376, April 13, 1954.

[76] Ibid., 2. Jones added that some White House Staff members felt "that there are no compelling reasons why, on the one hand, the present status of the judges should not be continued or, on the other hand, why they should not be given life tenure. . . . [P]ut another way, they do not think that, in the light of all the relevant factors, the precise nature of the judges' tenure is of any great significance as long as the appointive power of the President is preserved."

[77] Ibid., May 1, 1954. "I wonder if the tenure of the judges . . . should be placed beyond the President's power of removal. The answer, of course, I think pretty much depends upon what one considers to be the true function of this Court. If it is to be considered as an aid to the President in administering military justice and not an independent court, I don't believe the judges thereof should have life tenure. Was it ever intended that they should?"

[78] Ibid., May 13, 1954.

chaired a committee to examine army military justice. "We considered the suggestion that there be created a court composed of civilians . . . but we rejected it and made no recommendation on the subject, because we felt that administration of military justice should remain within the Army, even though it should be independent of the Commanding Officer." Because he may have been unconvinced that it was fully appropriate for civilian judges to decide military cases, Vanderbilt "would not be in favor at this time of changing the tenure of members of the Court."[79]

Shanley sent Vanderbilt's response to the Bureau of the Budget, and Jones was quick to note the similarity between his views and those of the Justice Department that had been articulated by Rogers "that the Court is still in the experimental stage and sufficient experience has not yet been gained to make an informed judgment." Jones advised Shanley that given the caution reflected in the consonance of these views, the Bureau of the Budget concluded that enactment of life tenure "would not be in accord with the program of the President."[80] Even as Shanley pondered this question, the JAGs offered their own assessment of military justice.

GOING PUBLIC

Late in 1953, the Navy released an assessment of military justice under the UCMJ, and claimed that adoption of the Code, "with its unwieldy legal procedure, has made the effective administration of military justice within the Armed Forces more difficult."[81] The point was not lost on some of Quinn's friends in Congress. Representative John Fogarty spoke to his colleagues, and lauded the work of the Court. He referred to an editorial in the *Navy Times*, which included the excerpt from the report just quoted. But it also contained an excerpt from a September 1953 speech delivered by the "able" Chief Judge. If the JAGs wanted to pick up the gauntlet, perhaps it was because the Court was willing to throw it down.

> We have not lost sight of the necessity for discipline in military law. We will not lose sight of the fact that the first obligation of armies and navies is to fight and win wars. We will never do anything to improperly interfere with the efficient operation of our military forces. But consistent with these objectives, we will do everything in our power to see that every member of the military forces accused of crime gets a fair and speedy trial, and an absolutely square deal.[82]

[79] Ibid., 2. The findings and recommendations of the Vanderbilt Committee Report (1946) are discussed in AMJ, chapter 6.

[80] Ibid., June 2, 1954.

[81] LTF, QPPC, clipping from *Congressional Record—Appendix*, February 16, 1954, A1265.

[82] Ibid. See also SF, September 24, 1953, 4, from which the excerpt is quoted. Quinn's remarks, incidentally, were delivered to an audience that included the three JAGs.

The American Bar Association also contributed to public support for USCMA, and the quest for life tenure in particular. Its standing committee on judicial selection, tenure, and compensation listed several reasons why the ABA should approve a recommendation for such a change. First, life tenure would insure that "the Court's powers will be more clearly delineated." Further, "the dignity of the Court will be enhanced." Because the Civil Service Commission apparently had jurisdiction over the Court staff, "there is danger that the Court will become an executive instrumentality." Finally, life tenure would protect USCMA judges "from political pressure, . . . an important consideration in view of the nature of the cases handled by this Court."[83]

Unfortunately, when ABA approval came almost four months later, the tenure bill was moribund. In May, Proulx reported to former Court Commissioner Daniel Walker that "the life tenure bill is still stymied at the Bureau of the Budget. We have not given up hope of getting favorable action. However, as time rolls on and adjournment moves closer and closer, the prospects of favorable action . . . become dimmer and dimmer."[84] Proulx's pessimism was not misplaced. Within three weeks of his letter, the Bureau of the Budget informed the Secretary of Defense that it "recommends against favorable [congressional] consideration." In a somewhat surprising letter, the budget director called attention to the unsettled question concerning USCMA's authority to issue writs, and urged that the code committee "explore in detail[,] and make recommendations with respect to the particular writs the Court should be empowered to issue in order to discharge properly its special functions."[85] Quinn immediately understood the negative implication of the letter.

Less than one week after receiving a copy of this unfavorable recommendation, Alfred Proulx informed Senator Green's office that "the judges agreed to let the bill ride until the next session of Congress. . . ."[86] They would try again in 1955, but in the meantime other issues claimed their attention. Although the life tenure bill might be moribund, JAG efforts to effect other changes in the UCMJ were not. In part, this was due to the fact that the Defense Department had incorporated JAG recommendations into its 1954 legislative program, in the form of "Military Justice Omnibus Amendments to Uniform Code."[87] Furthermore, the JAGs decided to go public with their comments about both the Code and the Court.

[83] LTF, May 27, 1954. At its annual meeting in September, the ABA approved the committee resolution.

[84] 4 CF, May 27, 1954.

[85] Ibid., June 18, 1954. The draft of these comments was sent to Shanley on June 2. See EP, Official Files, 100D, Box 376.

[86] Ibid., July 23, 1954. The other bill to which Admiral Nunn had referred, however, was alive and well. Its proposed changes in the UCMJ did not include life tenure.

[87] USCMAP, 2 ARF for copy of proposed amendments dated May 28, 1954. See also *New York Times*, June 13, 1954, 1.

Thus, on August 14, 1954, Air Force JAG Reginald Harmon addressed the Annual Meeting of the Judge Advocates Association. Entitled "Progress Under the Uniform Code," his speech implied that little, if any, had resulted from its enactment. Harmon railed against three weaknesses inherent in its operation. First, the cost of administering military justice under one year of the Code, he claimed, was "over a quarter of a million dollars, or approximately ten times the cost of operation under the Elston Act [the legislation superseded by the UCMJ in 1951]."[88] Further, the Air Force JAG described the UCMJ as "unnecessarily laden with built-in delays." There are, he complained, "too many reviews on reviews indiscriminately granted to all offenders."[89] Worst of all is the Code's "tendency to destroy what once was the principal asset of the military justice system, that is, the swift and certain punishment of the guilty man." Now, Harmon lamented, "the certainty of punishment and the promptness of prosecution seem to be becoming a matter of historical interest." Without once mentioning the Court or its judges, Harmon in effect blamed both for the current condition of military justice.[90]

When administering the UCMJ, "in many instances," claimed Harmon, "form has been elevated over substance. In case after case, convictions have been set aside for reasons that do not seem to the ordinary man to have the slightest bearing upon either the fairness of the trial or the fundamental rights of the accused."[91] Yet, "when faced with . . . some really fundamental rights of the accused, like that of unreasonable search and seizure, the safe-

[88] 2 ARF, August 18, 1954, 5. In a memorandum to Quinn, Tedrow denounced Harmon's statistics as "so grossly unrealistic" that they were "deliberately misleading." His "jumbling of figures is either grossly inept[,] or deliberately intended not to give a correct picture." Ibid., January 10, 1955.

[89] Harmon, 7. Tedrow replied that USCMA review time "will be found far superior to that of any function of the Services," including Harmon's own JAG department. As to the excessive number of reviews of a guilty plea, the Chief Commissioner observed that correction of this flaw had been urged by both JAGs and Judges. Tedrow, 2.

[90] Shortly after Harmon's speech, a close friend of Quinn and Proulx, William Mott—later to become the Navy JAG—wrote a confidential letter to the Chief Judge. He reported that some members of the Air Force Reserve JAG Association supported Harmon's position, and had begun to write to certain members of Congress, including Robert Smart, counsel to the House Armed Services Committee. "I also saw Mr. Smart's reply, which I did not like very much because it tended to agree with the Air Force writer that the Court is too expensive to justify. Of course, . . . Smart may have been making a mere political acknowledgment. . . . Rumor is rife, for instance, that the Department of Defense intends to sponsor legislation abolishing the Court." QPPC, December 2, 1954.

[91] While Harmon offered no examples, he may well have had in mind the case of *United States v. Crunk*, 4 USCMA 290, decided a few months before he delivered his remarks. The Court unanimously reversed a conviction in which the law officer during the court-martial later participated in the Staff JAG review. Latimer wrote that when the JAG officer concurred in a guilty finding based upon a recommendation signed by the law officer, such "was the handicraft of a disqualified person, and a mere concurrence by the Staff Judge Advocate would not remove the vice which Congress sought to eliminate when it provided for a review by an impartial examiner." (P. 293.) See also *United States v. Coulter*, 3 USCMA 657, 659 (1954).

guards which the services have set up and carefully maintained under the earlier laws are struck down."[92]

Previously scheduled to report to the JAG conference about the Court, Judge Latimer responded indirectly to Harmon's comments. He reminded his audience that congressional debate over the "present system of military justice as compared with its predecessor systems" had been lengthy; with the outcome that military justice—on the appellate level, at least—would "be governed to some extent by civilians."[93] Possibly with Harmon in mind, Latimer observed that his Court "needs the support of all military and civilian lawyers and that that [*sic*] support has been forthcoming from most quarters."[94] Speaking also for his colleagues, Latimer concluded "he is satisfied that the Court has a place in our judicial system, and is here to stay."[95]

The next entrant into the public commentary by the JAGs against the UCMJ was Admiral Ira Nunn. In 1953, he had sent Quinn an inscribed photograph as "an expression of my highest respect and esteem."[96] Now, he reiterated Harmon's claims. Nunn predicted that the UCMJ "is bound to fall flat on its face in the event of mobilization. . . . Moreover, we think it is harmful and burdensome, even in times of peace, as at the present time."[97] As for USCMA, it is "in no way protected from frivolous appeals. . . . The result is our appellate bodies are badly crowded. The thing is badly bogged down, even now."[98]

[92] Harmon, 7. "May we join together," he concluded, "in an effort to devise a safe, yet simple, system of military justice which provides prompt and efficient justice at a reasonable cost to the American people[,] and which will work in a global war." Ibid., 9. Clearly for the Air Force JAG, the UCMJ did not fit the bill.

[93] *Judge Advocate Journal* 18 (1954), 3.

[94] Ibid., 5.

[95] Ibid. Shortly after Harmon's and Latimer's comments were published in the *Judge Advocate Journal*, Proulx commented to a friend that "there has been a great deal of scuttlebutt that the services are opposed to the Code more and more." 4 CF, November 15, 1954. The Chairman of the Federal Bar Association Committee on Military Law and Justice noted that Harmon "did not want to enter into a personal fight with the Court[,]" nor at this time did he favor eliminating the tribunal. Harmon "desired by his remarks in Chicago to merely raise a question of this nature so that persons concerned would give thought to it. . . . [If] this has been accomplished, as he feels it has, he prefers to sit on the sidelines until some real suggestion is put forward." QPPC, November 23, 1954.

[96] QPPC, April 13, 1953.

[97] 2 ARF, text of remarks by Rear Admiral Nunn, November 30, 1954. Nunn reminded his audience that the military justice system was unlike its civilian counterparts in that "we exist for other purposes . . . which are more fundamental, namely the protection of this country and the imposition of its will on other nations."

[98] Ibid., 4. Along the same lines, see also manuscript draft of an article by Major George Prugh, Jr., [later to become JAG of the Army]. "Some Observations on the Uniform Code of Military Justice," written for publication in *The Brief*, Fall 1954; QPGF. In August 1955, with the comments of the new Army JAG Major General Eugene Caffey, the JAGs attained unanimity in their public critique of the Code. Caffey essentially echoed the complaints raised by

As the JAGs intensified their attacks, USCMA continued to decide cases and issue opinions. If, by their tactics, the JAGs sought to intimidate the judges, they seemed not to have succeeded. On the other hand, the judges continued to strive for balance between due process and the needs of the military. One example illustrates how difficult this challenge could be.

COURT AND CONSTITUTION

The question in *United States v. Sutton* was whether written depositions could be used in evidence against an accused, not present when they were taken, if the accused had not waived the right to be present. It was not unreasonable to assume that the unanimous holding in *United States v. Clay* (1951) was dispositive. The Navy Board of Review so concluded, and reversed Sutton's conviction. In *Clay*, Judge Latimer had noted that among the rights Congress granted the accused in the UCMJ was the right "to be confronted by witnesses testifying against him."[99] Admiral Nunn certified the case to USCMA, where it was argued in the spring of 1954.

A split tribunal reversed the Board of Review. Three years after *Clay*, Latimer now insisted that the Code specifically sanctioned what Sutton sought to have proscribed. He argued that examination of earlier versions of American military law showed that—except in capital cases—where notice has been given to the other side in the litigation, a deposition "may be read in evidence."[100] This well-established acceptance carried over into the UCMJ which reiterated the same provision.[101] Latimer held that due process privileges granted by Congress "had to be consider[ed] . . . in the light of any limitations set out in the Code. Surely we are seeking to place military justice on the same plane as civilian justice[,] but we are powerless to do that in those instances where Congress has set out legally, clearly, and specifically a different level."

The judge noted further that the particular witness was in Korea, with the trial being held in California. To insist that the witness be returned in order to testify "might elevate the role of a witness to one of being a commercial

---

Harmon and Nunn. "Maybe," he concluded, "the time has come for a new look [,] . . . to work over this system of military justice and try to speed it up some, try to cut out the useless parts of it, give the accused the protections they are entitled to, but work out a system that will be effective, which of course this one is not now. . . . The system we have now is very, very expensive, and time consuming, and about 95% of it accomplishes nothing." SF, unpaginated text of Caffey's address before the ABA Annual Meeting, Criminal Law Section, August 24, 1955.

[99] 1 USCMA 74 (1951).

[100] *United States v. Sutton*, 3 USCMA 220, 222 (1954).

[101] Ibid., 223–24.

tourist."[102] Further, Latimer turned to the famous scholar on evidence, and a former member of the JAG Corps, John H. Wigmore. Cross-examination, Wigmore had written, is certainly a help to the tribunal hearing the case "if only it is available. But it is merely desirable. Where it cannot be obtained, the requirement ceases."[103]

Finally, Latimer turned to the fact that "the right of an accused in all instances to be confronted by witnesses[,] and the right of the Government to take depositions by written interrogatories are inconsistent." But rather than attempting to explore whether or not the Court could reconcile them under the Code, he retreated into a dogmatic defense of the military viewpoint. "What may be desirable must give way to the absolute necessities of the services."[104]

Early in June, Quinn wrote to his commissioner that Brosman "has serious doubts about the interrogatories." If so, Latimer must have convinced him otherwise. Of Latimer's opinion Brosman wrote that while it "uses somewhat broader language than I would have selected, I concur generally in its terms, and warmly approve the result it reaches. . . ."[105] It is possible that by 1954, given the JAG unrest about Court and Code, Brosman and Latimer may have wanted to avoid finding a conflict between the Code and the Sixth Amendment's confrontation clause. It was one thing to hold a military practice unconstitutional under the UCMJ. It was quite another to hold a portion of the Code itself unconstitutional, and this from a new court that in some circles was not even considered to be a bona fide federal appellate tribunal.

Quinn, however, had no such hesitation. "I would be very reluctant," he wrote to his Commissioner, "to indicate that we feel that men in the military service are deprived of the constitutional protections set forth in the 5th and 6th amendments, except in cases where the amendment itself excludes the protection. . . ."[106] Sutton's conviction would have to be reversed, "unless we admit the deposition. My view is that we should . . . forcibly assert the right of men in the military service to all constitutional guarantees not specifically excepted. . . ." If Brosman declined to accept this viewpoint, "then I desire to dissent and will proceed to prepare a dissent."[107] And he did.

Quinn's position may be an example of his "hell yes, hell no" viewpoint discussed earlier in chapter 2.[108] He concluded that his brethren "would deny the accused the full measure of his constitutional right because of the mo-

[102] Ibid., 225.

[103] Ibid., 226.

[104] Ibid.

[105] Ibid., 227.

[106] QPCF, June 5, 1953.

[107] Ibid., 2.

[108] "I have absolutely no doubt in my mind that accused persons in the military service of the Nation are entitled to rights and privileges secured to all under the Constitution . . . unless excluded directly or by necessary implication. . . . " *Sutton*, 228.

bility of potential witnesses in the military service. However, I cannot disregard a constitutional safeguard for reasons of expediency."[109] Brosman appears to have been uncomfortable with his chief's claim of constitutional absolutism. Quinn "has assumed the power to hold an act of Congress unconstitutional—at least in part. I say he has assumed this power, because he has not undertaken to demonstrate that we possess it. Perhaps he believes that the existence of such authority in the judges of this Court to be so evident as to dispense with exposition." The Chief Judge, complained Brosman, "is viewing the present problem with an eye single to one pan of the scales. Rather, I would urge a binocular approach here. . . . I find it genuinely difficult to understand why he will allow no place whatever to the claims of necessity, however pressing and however respectable."[110]

In 1975, an anonymous writer of the official Army JAG Corps history observed that USCMA "has felt its way carefully and, due to its small membership, the attitudes of individual judges have particularly affected its willingness to expand due process rights and grant relief."[111] *Sutton* may well prove the point. The certainty of Latimer's conclusion was matched by Quinn's emphatic dissent. Brosman cast the deciding vote, and his term would expire in one year. Even though Quinn apparently supported Brosman's reappointment—with more than ten years left to serve, the former governor probably assumed that he would have another opportunity to reiterate his constitutional philosophy. He was correct.

COMMISSIONER'S CONCERNS REVISITED

It will be recalled that USCMA, in spite of Tedrow's opposition, decided to try the so-called Walker plan, under which the initial examination of petitions for review was shifted to chambers, rather than through a central staff of commissioners. In June 1953—just before the trial period expired—Tedrow reaffirmed his conviction that a "first view" by such legal experts was essential. He wrote to the chairman of the court committee that "a statutory commissioner system, modelled after that provided for on the Court of Claims, would certainly attract and retain able lawyers."[112] Moreover, in time

[109] Ibid., 228–31.

[110] Ibid., 227, 228.

[111] *The Army Lawyer: A History of the Judge Advocate General's Corps, 1775–1975* (1975), 208; hereafter cited as *History*.

[112] Although the function of the commissioners, now known as the Central Legal Staff, is appropriate and, as will be seen, probably beneficial to the Court, the title has been a source of confusion. It is possible that after 1951, with employees of the new Court under Civil Service jurisdiction, the judges felt that the fancier title might insure a higher grade of salary for their staff attorneys. However, the USCMA commissioners did not carry out the functions required of

of war with an expected increase in cases they could be of great assistance to the judges. "The naming of these commissioners would be within the sole discretion of the Court[,] and thereby should insure that [it] would obtain qualified people." If additional personnel would be needed to handle the vast increase in cases to be expected during wartime, Tedrow much preferred that commissioners be selected, rather than judges, and that they be appointed by the Court, rather than the President.[113]

Holding this somewhat egotistical view of the commissioners' function, Tedrow apparently saw no need to be tentative in his assessment of the Walker proposal. It had proven to be "economically, procedurally, and administratively inefficient, unsound, and indefensible."[114] In particular, he objected to examining petitions after they had been acted upon in chambers.[115] "This has resulted in the return of at least one case a day to a Judge and his legal assistants for further consideration and additional views. There have been probably fifteen cases of this type where the originating judge has specifically reversed his first action."[116] With characteristic candor, Tedrow insisted that "the inadequacy of reviews is depriving accused of their day in court."[117]

Although he did not articulate them, the implications of his comments were very clear. The judicial process was best served if commissioners, competent in military justice and beholden to the Court rather than an individual judge, first examined the record in a case and suggested a course of action for the Court; it being understood, of course, that each judge could work out his own approach to review once the initial recommendation had been circulated. Apparently, Tedrow's points were persuasive. The Walker plan was discarded, and with minor modifications, USCMA has followed Tedrow's recommended procedure to the present day. Incoming petitions are first routed to a member of the Central Legal Staff, whose suggested disposition of the case is submitted along with the record to the judges. While the need for new legal talent to assist both commissioners and chambers cannot be denied, the availability of experienced lawyers who know the case law is certainly of great value to the judges—if only to provide a foundation on which each judge can further consider the case.

---

other federal commissioners, and it may be that the discrepancy over title as opposed to function led the Court in the mid 1970s to abandon it in place of the generic description of the "Central Legal Staff."

113 CCC, June 23, 1953, 4. "There is, of course, no guarantee that in time of war the President would appoint unqualified or inept politicians, nor is there any guarantee that he would appoint able lawyers with experience in military law. Such being the situation, I see no reason to leave the matter open to chance."

114 QPGF, June 25, 1953.

115 It would be of greater benefit to all parties, Tedrow implied, if the commissioner[s] saw the petition first.

116 Ibid., 3.

117 Ibid., 4.

CONTROVERSY OVER CHANGE

With the life tenure bill in legislative limbo, attention now focused on the omnibus amendments to the UCMJ that had been proposed by the Pentagon. The Judges were offered an opportunity to comment on the suggestions which included more than the original seventeen amendments acceptable to both JAGs and judges. Although, for example, all had agreed on the compromise fifteen-day appeal limitation recommended by the Court Committee, the new bill cut it to ten. "It seems inconsistent," fumed Proulx to the Chief Judge, "to have the JAGs go along on the fifteen-day compromise[,] and turn around and plug for their original recommendation of 10 days." Moreover, the impression gained from the new bill was that USCMA had done "much to slow down the administration of military justice."[118] On behalf of the Court, Proulx later reminded the Bureau of the Budget that some suggested changes were at variance with those unanimously endorsed in the 1953 joint report. "The Judges believe that only those amendments . . . wherein unanimity has been reached, should be the subject of legislation at this time."[119]

In yet another memorandum for yet another of Eisenhower's assistants, the Budget Director declined to "concur in the philosophy behind the foregoing statement" by the USCMA Judges. "While we think that substantial weight should be given to the recommendations of the Code Committee as well as the civilian Court Committee, we do not think these should be conclusive. Otherwise those who have fundamental responsibilities with respect to the Code and its operation would be subject to a veto by groups whose responsibilities are clearly secondary in character."[120] As to the two changes of special interest to the Court, the Budget Bureau offered its own suggestions.

It agreed with the Court that a reduction of the time period for filing an appeal from thirty days to fifteen was preferable to the military's proposal of ten. But it concurred with the JAGs that counsel for the accused should be required to file a certificate as a prerequisite for appeal to USCMA. The idea of a certificate "appears reasonable, especially since counsel will resolve any doubts in favor of the accused."[121] In the margin at this point in the memorandum appears the handwritten comment, "will they?"[122] Another comment

[118] QPCF, June 16, 1954. Even in the face of a difficult situation, Proulx kept his sense of humor. He advised Quinn that "I am now being approached to work out a plan as to where the Court will sit in the event a H-bomb drops on Washington. . . . I see no better place than Providence at the present time!!" Ibid., June 11, 1954.

[119] 4 CF, September 24, 1954. It is indicative of the unusual authority that Proulx exercised on behalf of the frequently absent Chief Judge, that as Clerk he could virtually negotiate with the Bureau of the Budget.

[120] EP, Official File, 3-M, Box 101, February 26, 1955.

[121] Ibid., 3.

[122] Ibid., 4.

in the middle of this paragraph indicates that the White House wanted "something less strong."

And indeed, when the Bureau sent its formal letter to the Secretary of Defense clearing the bill for submission to Congress, the changes in the certificate section reflected these earlier comments. "It is considered, under all the circumstances, that the terms of such a certificate should be less stringent than those contained in the proposal. . . . It is believed that it would be sufficient to require that counsel certify that a substantial question of law is presented and that the appeal is made in good faith."[123]

As 1954 passed into 1955, the future of the life tenure bill as well as the other suggested amendments to the UCMJ remained doubtful—as was, still, USCMA stature in the federal court hierarchy, and this in the third year of its history.[124] The one constant was JAG negativism toward the Code and, by implication, the Court itself. Writing to Representative Philbin, Quinn insisted that "there would seem to be no good reason for refusing life tenure any longer. The resistance, if any, would undoubtedly come from the military establishment, which probably still resents the general idea of a *civilian* court acting as the court of last resort for the court-martial system."[125] A meeting between JAGs and Judges only two days later illustrates the point.

The Army JAG, Major General Eugene Caffey, called for expanding discretionary authority under nonjudicial punishment, to allow commanders to award more than two weeks of confinement. He favored use of bread and water as punishment. He recommended that military justice should be decentralized. "Do away with automatic review of death sentences." Rather, "power [should] be given to the convening authority in the field to carry out a death sentence without review at headquarters." Indeed, "speedy justice of this kind would prove to be an example to others." The "times have changed," noted Caffey, "and Congress may be receptive to his suggested amendments—in any event he feels it his duty to so advise . . . Congress."[126]

For the Air Force, Harmon insisted that the JAG and not appellate counsel should certify petitions to the Court. He "realizes that this suggestion would meet with criticism and also appreciates the Court's reluctance to accept it." He "guarantees, however, . . . that it would still have a workload[,] but that [his plan] would afford [the Court] more time to devote to the more impor-

[123] Ibid., 2. Originally the Bureau had supported the JAG version which required that "there must be material prejudice to the substantial rights of the accused."

[124] When Proulx asked why the listing of the Court in the Congressional Directory had been shifted, he was informed that Chief Judge Bolitha Laws of the U.S. District Court had asked that his tribunal be listed "immediately following that of the U.S. Court of Appeals for the District of Columbia." Never mentioning USCMA, Laws emphasized that "the line-up should be made on the basis of constitutional courts. . . . Thus . . . our Court suffered by being placed at the tail end, just ahead of the [U.S.] Tax Court." 4 CF, December 1, 1954.

[125] LTF, December 11, 1954.

[126] 4 CF, Minutes of Code Committee Meeting, December 13, 1954, 2.

tant problems." Moreover, "if the [JAG] abused their power, they would be subject to removal."[127]

Latimer reiterated his opposition to any change in Court control of its docket. "He could not in good conscience appear before the Congress and support this provision which would, in effect, be an admission that the Court could not handle the job it had been assigned." Judges and JAGs should "build constructively within the existing framework of the Code rather than junking it as an unworkable law."[128] Similarly, Brosman "could not see how the code committee could go to the Congress and suggest that we return to the old system within [only] three years after the enactment of the Code."[129] As if to emphasize their differences, JAGs and Judges agreed that like the 1953 version, the 1954 Report would have separate sections—"Joint Report-Court Report-individual service reports."[130]

Again, at the behest of Quinn, early in 1955 specific proposals for life tenure—and also for expanding USCMA to five judges—were introduced in Congress. Again, he communicated with various friends in Congress, while Proulx labored to insure that publicity favorable to his Court would be forthcoming.[131] Again, the Court put forward the same arguments it had previously employed, often with only the date changed. And again, this time for Judge Brosman, Richard Tedrow prepared a comprehensive memorandum on the subject of life tenure. He concluded that "the military opposition to the Court, with or without life tenure, has been continuous." Whether such opposition to this latest measure "will be active or passive or indirect is not now

[127] Ibid., 3, 4. On the other hand, Harmon "would not oppose bread and water punishment, if Army and Navy wanted it, but the Air Force would never need or use such punishment."

[128] Ibid., 4.

[129] Ibid., 5.

[130] The chairman of the Court Committee alerted Quinn about "a recent letter from Paul Brosman [indicating] that there would be some attempt to restrict the activities of the Court by legislation." CCC, December 20, 1954. Three days later, Seymour informed the entire committee that Quinn wanted to meet with them. "There may be some movement to abolish or limit the Court[,] and I think that this may be the topic for discussion." Ibid., December 23, 1954. Early in January, Proulx reported that the JAGs had declined to offer additional suggestions to the Code Committee, because the prospects for approval by the entire group were so slight. Rather, each JAG would use his individual report to specify any further proposed changes in military justice. 5 CF, January 5, 1955.

[131] Thus Proulx went out of his way to assist a writer, Irwin Ross, who planned to prepare a story on the Court for *Reader's Digest*. Ross, reported Proulx to Quinn, "has been assigned a desk and given all available facilities here at the Court. . . . I feel sure that the article he writes will be complimentary to the Court—at least everything that he has been told so far could only lead to that conclusion." 5 CF, February 1, 1955. Ross's piece, very favorable to the Court, was indeed published—not in the *Digest*, but rather in a now defunct magazine called *Pageant*, vol. 11, August 1955, 156–61. Thirty-seven years later, while taking the Washington–New York train home from a research trip to the Court, an elderly man sat down next to this author. Seeing my collection of USCMA manuscript copies, he told me that he had once written a piece on the Court. To my amazement, this person later identified himself as Irwin Ross.

known." The indirect approach, i.e., "we do not oppose it, but" was, he recalled, used effectively against the 1953 proposal.[132]

Proulx was also aware "that the latest attacks on the Code from various military quarters can cause a friend thereof to be concerned." He believed, however, that Congress would not restore the old system. "The point of no return was reached in 1950," with the passage of a comprehensive code.[133] On the other hand, he wrote to a friend in the Navy, "I know you will appreciate that the members of the Court will not engage in debate on this matter—but silence here is no indication of nonactivity."[134] Moreover, "the attacks have gone so far as to be looked upon as the best ammunition for the continuation of the Court and the Code. The sharper the criticism in some instances, the stronger the need for the Code."[135]

By March 1955, the Air Force had become well versed in what Tedrow described as the "indirect approach" for opposition to life tenure. Its spokesman reiterated the point that "substantial doubt exists as to whether the Court accomplishes . . . the most effective appellate system possible in the administration of military justice. Until, therefore, "amendments are adopted, observed in action[,] and informed judgment made that the procedures as amended will function effectively in time of war and mobilization—only then can a determination on the life tenure feature be formulated."[136] While waiting for responses from the Army and Navy, a delegation from the Court's civilian committee met with Deputy Attorney General Rogers, who had rejected the life tenure proposal in 1954. Proulx reported that this time, Rogers would not object to the bill "should it be passed (this is very fine but it is the cart before the horse—actually we want the Department of Justice's approval prior to passage)."[137]

[132] LTF, March 10, 1955.

[133] Proulx might have had in mind the comments by Congressman Paul Kilday, a member of the House Armed Services Committee, during an address on February 24, 1955, to the National War College. "I am fully aware of the view of some officers of our Armed Forces that this code has constituted a severe handicap in performing their duties. . . . On the other hand, I know of many criticisms leveled at the code which should be pointed elsewhere. . . . Likewise, it may be that the code is an easy scapegoat for some deficiencies of command. I make you a fair proposition: While Congress is reappraising the code and its work in formulating the same, you reevaluate the criticisms you have made of it, and determine how many thereof should be directed elsewhere." Excerpt, February 24, 1955, in LTF. Later, Proulx wrote to Quinn that "there were rumors of a thorough investigation of the UCMJ by Congressman Kilday. . . . Judge [Latimer] seemed a bit concerned about it." 5 CF, March 29, 1955. Although Kilday could not know it at the time, his future was intimately connected with USCMA, to whose bench he would be appointed by President John F. Kennedy in 1961.

[134] 5 CF, February 21, 1955.

[135] Ibid., 2.

[136] LTF, March 17, 1955, extract of comments submitted by the Air Force office of legislative liaison to the Secretary of Defense.

[137] LTF, Memorandum, May 20, 1955.

Early in June, Proulx received word that "now the Navy has no objection on the five-man court or life tenure." The Army, however, objected to USCMA expansion. It also rejected life tenure if it was connected to "the freezing-in of the present incumbents."[138] Like the Navy, it did not object in principle to life tenure, leading Proulx to comment that "on the basis of present-day affairs, I would peg this report as most favorable to the Court."[139] For its part, the Defense Department saw no need for increasing the Court to five members, and restated its support for life tenure "without infringing upon the power of the President to appoint by and with the advice of the Senate."[140] Again, Quinn sensed the portent for postponement.

He informed Proulx that "I talked with Sen. Pastore and he is apparently waiting for Green to move. I told him time was running out. . . . He will go to [Senator Richard] Russell [chairman of the Senate Armed Services Committee], with Green if Green asks him to."[141] Whether or not Pastore and Green visited with Russell is not clear. On June 21, Pastore talked with Majority Leader Lyndon Johnson, and later the same day sent him a letter along with a court-produced memorandum on the need for life tenure.

Aware of Johnson's influence, Pastore reminded the majority leader that Quinn, Latimer, and Brosman "have started from scratch. From the creation of the Court to the present time, they have decided well over six thousand cases . . . a phenomenal amount of work when you realize that these cases are indeed the precedents to be followed in the future." More important, "the present calibre of this Court is undisputed and I dare say unmatched. They have acted in a nonpartisan fashion in the determination of all their cases." Even assuming that President Eisenhower would reappoint all three incumbents, "it is a matter of common principle . . . that this important judicial tribunal should have all the characteristics of our other important courts, namely, life tenure during good behavior."[142] All during the summer, the bill awaited review by the Bureau of the Budget. Finally in November, word came to Proulx that the Bureau had reported unfavorably on the bill.[143] By

[138] LTF, Memorandum, June 6, 1955.

[139] 5 CF, April 12, 1955.

[140] LTF, June 13, 1955.

[141] LTF, June 3, 1955. Like most of his notes to Proulx, Quinn signed this one "The Gov."

[142] LTF, June 21, 1955. At this point, Pastore got down to the real reason for his letter. "I renew my appeal to you to urge our distinguished mutual friend, Dick Russell, to look favorably upon this legislation. . . ." Ibid., 2. Pastore admitted what Quinn had acknowledged, that unless and until Russell was willing to move, the bill would not. Neither did.

[143] LTF, November 15, 1955. On November 3, the White House had informed Jones that "since the circumstances have not changed, this office is of the same opinion that it expressed last year. . . . It is, therefore, suggested that the Department of Defense be advised that favorable consideration of the bill is not recommended for the reasons expressed last year." EP, Official Files, 100 D, Box 376, November 3, 1955.

this time, the Judges were concerned with another challenge that was indirectly linked to the matter of life terms—Paul Brosman's tenure.

EXIT BROSMAN

The judge with the shortest term (ending on May 1, 1956), and holding a Democratic "slot," Brosman obviously understood what having a Republican president in office could mean. Very anxious for reappointment, Brosman apparently had the firm support of his brethren.[144] One might expect a Republican to name one of his own party to Brosman's seat, giving the Republicans two of the three seats. Thus Quinn and Brosman, the two Democrats on the Court, were encouraged when Proulx reported on his meeting with Rogers, noted above. "Brosman's reappointment came up in the conversation[,] and Mr. Rogers pointed out that the present administration has not allowed politics to enter into the judicial appointment picture in those cases where Democratic Judges have done a good job."[145] Similarly, Senator Pastore also assumed in the event that life tenure was enacted, "that in all probability the present judges will be reappointed. . . ."[146]

While the written record is scant, it is not unreasonable to assume that during the summer and fall of 1955 Brosman tried to gain support for his reappointment. Within the limits of his own keen sense of what was politically possible, Quinn helped where he could.[147] Further, Brosman had the support of the Civilian Court Committee. Indeed, on December 20, he and Proulx traveled to New York to discuss the reappointment with some lawyers, possibly Whitney Seymour, the Committee chairman. On December 21, Seymour wrote to Eisenhower's Attorney General, Herbert Brownell, Jr. By coincidence, most of the committee members were Republicans, "but we are unanimous in the view that Judge Brosman should be reappointed and that political considerations should not interfere with the continued service of the present Court team which has been so notable."[148] Seymour reminded Brownell that in the earlier meeting with Rogers, "we emphasized the importance of Judge Brosman's reappointment, along with the desirability of ultimate life tenure for members of this Court."[149]

We will never know whether Brosman would have been reappointed. Be-

[144] George Latimer, Jr., interview, July 20, 1989, 15; Alfred Proulx, interview, July 21, 1992, 26.

[145] LTF, May 20, 1955.

[146] Ibid., June 21, 1955, 2.

[147] Proulx recalled that Quinn "was hoping against hope that [Brosman] was going to get it. I think [Quinn] was interceding on his behalf." Proulx, ibid.

[148] CCC, December 21, 1955.

[149] Ibid., 2.

cause his term did not expire until May 1, 1956, it is possible that no decision had been reached when Seymour drafted his endorsement. But his letter did Brosman no good. On December 21 (the day Seymour wrote), shortly after lunching with two of his staff, the judge "complained of a pain near his heart and in his arm." A physician was summoned immediately from a nearby government building, but "before the doctor arrived[,] within a few minutes, he was beyond medical attention."[150]

Arthur Sutherland, professor of law at Harvard and a member of the Court Committee, well expressed the sense of shock that engulfed the Court community. He wrote to Quinn that if Brosman "had been twenty years older, such a sudden and easy end would not be so bad. But it is hard to see a man with whom we all spent such a happy day last week, suddenly laid low, comparatively young, with years of great usefulness ahead."[151] Quinn in a note to Seymour added that Brosman "had the affection and esteem of everyone attached to this Court."[152] Writing an official letter to the President, the Chief Judge called his late colleague "a fine man. He discharged his judicial obligations with unremitting energy, with dignity, and with fairness and devotion to the cause of justice."[153]

His Court honored Paul Brosman during a brief but poignant memorial tribute on February 15, 1956. Brosman, recalled his chief, "was loved by every man and woman connected with this Court. He loved people, and was loved, and respected in return. He was a happy soul. He enjoyed life. He radiated cheerfulness, and he generated affection."[154] The three JAGs also spoke briefly. But rereading the tributes in the light of almost forty years, the words of Frederick Wiener, speaking for the Judge Advocates Association, remain especially apt.

As a member of the association, Wiener remembered, "we felt the glow of his outgoing personality; and we grieve now that his zest and sparkle are gone, leaving so much the losers those of us who remain." Brosman had consistently insisted that "the service lawyer's obligation is quite as rigid as that of his civilian brother." In his quest for the synthesis between "the lawyer's reason and the soldier's faith," Brosman's efforts were "unexpectedly cut short. Yet who, when the end comes, would not wish to be taken otherwise—without pain, without lingering, and at the height of one's powers? And so, in [Justice] Holmes' fine phrase, 'we end not with sorrow at the

[150] 5 CF, December 31, 1955.

[151] CCC, December 22, 1955. Proulx responded that Brosman "thought very highly of you[,] and was most appreciative of all the efforts being made on his behalf for reappointment." 5 CF, December 30, 1955.

[152] Ibid., December 28, 1955.

[153] 5 CF, December 27, 1955.

[154] 6 USCMA, v. "He was no respecter of rank. He was just as gracious to the most inconsequential shavetail as he would be to the most famous lawyer in the nation. He loved justice and struggled hard to attain it with both word and pen."

inevitable loss, but with the contagion of his courage, and with a kind of desperate joy we go back to the fight.' "[155]

Paul Brosman's unexpected death came at an important time in USCMA history. There was the obvious sense of loss, heightened by the suddeness of his passing. But his demise also created a sort of juridical void in that Brosman had tended to function as a pivot between Quinn and Latimer—both of whom on occasion took opposite sides of a judicial issue with an identical sense of certainty. More often than they, Brosman seems to have pondered—perhap even struggled—to reach an outcome he felt warranted by the record. Finally, his death took from the Court a jurist who possessed personal charm and grace, also the ability to remain on friendly terms with the JAGs even as they battled over divisive issues.[156] With life tenure still only a dream, with Congress about to consider UCMJ revisions some of which the Judges believed were quite harmful to their Court, with JAG criticism increasing in pitch, with uncertainty regarding the new appointment to the Court—Proulx was not guilty of understatement when he wrote of Brosman that "we certainly are going to miss him around here."[157]

[155] Ibid., x–xi.

[156] In the annual report for 1954, the Court did not feel it necessary "to set out in this report our reasons for not joining those members of the Code Committee who seek substantive changes which we believe to be unnecessarily hostile to the purposes and intent of the Uniform Code. However, if Congress concludes to proceed with hearings on the proposed changes, the Judges stand willing to, and request the privilege of, presenting their individual views." 4 ARF, 1954, 14.

[157] 6 CF, January 5, 1956.

2. Judges Latimer, Quinn, and Ferguson

CHAPTER 5

New Judge, Old Issues, Same Forum, 1955–1956

THE EXTENT of the disagreements between USCMA and the Judge Advocates General became even more evident with publication of the annual report for 1954, not distributed until May 1955. Judges and JAGs could only agree to join in a very brief report of less than two pages acknowledging that because "reconciliation of the different concepts has not been attained, the respective military departments have proposed their individually desired recommendations. . . ."[1] The rest of the report consisted of a number of disparate sections, including not only the original seventeen recommendations, but also drafts of two sets of UCMJ amendments separately urged by the Navy and the Air Force. Although both retained the certification requirement for USCMA review, there were substantial differences between the two versions.

The Navy would have required defense counsel rather than the JAG himself to certify justification for USCMA appeal. Moreover, it proposed reduction of the time limit for appeal from thirty days to ten.[2] The Air Force pointed to what it claimed was a need to "lighten the workload of [USCMA] and to eliminate excessive and frivolous appeals. . . . [which result in] unnecessary waste of time, money, and manpower with no benefit to an accused's substantial rights."[3] Its version restored JAG authority to certify for a review, but added an interesting twist, possibly as a result of USCMA opposition already known to Air Force JAG Reginald Harmon.

Harmon called for creation of a Judicial Appeals Board to be set up within the JAG office, to consist of at least three officers above the rank of lieutenant colonel or commander, who have "at least ten years' legal experience, and who are members of the bar of a Federal Court or of the highest court of a State."[4] This panel would first consider all appeals for USCMA review. If it unanimously agreed that the accused had not shown good cause for appeal

[1] 3 ARF, 3. Quinn, Latimer, and Brosman contented themselves with a terse statement. They "do not favorably recommend any of the additional [JAG] proposals . . . because of a belief that either the need for them has not been demonstrated or they turn back the wheels of progress and destroy some of the substantial rights granted by Congress to members of the Armed Forces." Ibid., 14.

[2] Ibid., 39, 46.

[3] Except, of course, the right to appeal to a civilian appellate Court created by Congress!

[4] 3 ARF, 54. These requirements in terms of legal training went beyond those mandated by USCMA for admission to its bar.

from a Board of Review decision, no appeal would be allowed. If, however, there was no unanimity—even if a majority found no justification—the JAG was required to issue the certificate of cause, and forward the case to USCMA, which in turn would decide whether or not to grant review.[5]

In that it apparently modified the JAG's absolute right to grant or not grant certification for USCMA review that he had first proposed, Harmon's proposal had a superficial plausibility about it. On the other hand, it kept the appeals process insulated within the JAG office, contained no provision for civilians on his new Judicial Appeals Board, and in no way guaranteed a defendant's right of appeal to the civilian court created by Congress. Harmon insisted that it would eliminate all those frivolous appeals, apparently so troublesome to the JAGs if not the Judges, but at the same time would also "still guarantee an accused the right to appeal from the decision of the Board of Review.[6]

The separate reports of Judges and JAGs prompted a number of newspaper articles and comments. The *Washington Post* pointed to the "wide disagreement over some fundamental concepts of the present court-martial system."[7] Later, the same reporter criticized Harmon's certification proposal. "No doubt some of the cases referred to [USCMA] are frivolous; this is one of the prices of a legal system that seeks to provide an accused with every feasible safeguard. To permit the services themselves to decide whether cases could be appealed, even though the petitions might have the most high-minded consideration, would be to revert to a situation in which the military acted as jury, judge, and jailer."[8] Even a service-oriented publication, the *Navy Times*, described the certification clause as "objectionable," although it joined the USCMA Judges in urging swift Congressional approval for the seventeen proposals that all parties had supported.[9]

Release of the Service Reports was followed by an announcement that the Defense Department would soon submit a bill embodying the changes sought by the JAGs. Proulx informed Quinn, however, that the Department "subscribes to only those changes which have met the approval of the Court."[10] A former Navy Chaplain and longtime advocate of reform in military justice, Robert White, concluded a few weeks later that "at this late date the whole situation has become confused by the great additional numbers of

[5] Ibid., 55, 61–62.

[6] Ibid., 35. Despite Harmon's insistence, his proposal can accurately be described as a transparent attempt to undercut civilian review.

[7] *Washington Post*, June 3, 1955 1, 15; clipping in USCAMAP, ARF.

[8] Ibid.; clipping from the *Washington Post*, June 5, 1955.

[9] Ibid., June 11, 1955. See also clippings from *Navy Times*, June 11; *St. Louis Post-Dispatch*, June 12; *Washington Post*, May 26; all in 3 ARF.

[10] 5 CF, May 26, 1955. Proulx's information was wrong, as he immediately discovered when the text of the DOD bill was released, complete with the certification requirement given to counsel rather than the JAGs. Ibid., May 27, 1955.

proposals to change the Code as well as the development of acute personal feelings" regarding it. White predicted to Proulx that "I would think . . . Congress would not go into the matter at all."[11] He was correct. The legislative session ended with the UCMJ unchanged.

By January 1956, with a new session of Congress underway, USCMA had been informed that hearings on the proposed amendments to the UCMJ—first submitted by the Defense Department almost two years before—were to be scheduled. Seven years had passed since the House Armed Services Committee considered the new code. In those first hearings, the Department had spoken on behalf of the military establishment. The fact that the armed services were less than enthusiastic about a uniform code had concerned but not controlled Larkin's efforts. This sense of single-minded purpose obvious in 1949 seems to have been lacking in 1956. Quinn and Latimer were justifiably concerned about what the hearings might produce.

The JAGs and the Judges were not in full agreement, and the bill reflected this. The Court believed that some of the suggested changes went too far, while the JAGs desired to go further. Alfred Proulx observed that while all parties had agreed to support the original seventeen recommendations, "each JAG reserv[ed] the right to plug for his individual amendments, if called upon to testify." But Proulx could not believe "that the uniformity of the Code would be sacrificed by allowing each JAG to pull away separately." Because they were not united, "their individual efforts will not succeed."[12] On the other hand, the JAGs *were* united in their support of the proposed bill.

Their endorsement together with another factor contributed to USCMA uneasiness. In its earlier efforts to gain life tenure as well as legislative enactment of the original seventeen amendments to the Code, the judges had felt in control of their causes. *They* had drafted the tenure bill and lobbied for its passage; *they* had convened a committee which had considered and—in concert if not total harmony with the JAGs—recommended the new changes. But the legislation soon to be examined by the House Armed Services Committee came from the Defense Department at the behest of the Navy, with the judges relegated to the position of any interested party—merely afforded the right to appear and be heard.

Writing to Judge Latimer as the hearings were about to begin, Tedrow was both perceptive and candid. He reminded Latimer that the UCMJ required not only regular consultation between Judges and JAGs in the form of the Code Committee on the state of military justice, but also a written annual report to Congress. And indeed, this Code Committee had reached consensus on seventeen proposed changes. But the legislation as submitted contained

[11] Ibid., July 11, 1955.
[12] 6 CF, January 5, 1956.

amendments, added with neither Court input or endorsement. Thus, the judges were "forced to question that the present unilateral . . . Defense Bill can be construed" as a product of such consultation.[13] Moreover, the bill itself "was never referred to the Court by the Department of Defense." Possibly with intentional understatement, Tedrow observed that "the Court has some difficulty with the positions of the Judge Advocates General who have apparently favored conflicting recommendations as appear from a comparison of the present Bill with the . . . Annual Report[s]."[14] Unlike the earlier era of Felix Larkin, it seemed that USCMA could no longer count, as it were, on having a friend at court.

A third reason for the Court's concern lay in the fact that its newest member was scheduled to take his seat on the bench even as the hearings commenced. Although Homer Ferguson chose not to testify before the Committee, his appointment to the Court had the potential for a dramatic change in its future direction. Who was Homer Ferguson, and how had he come to USCMA?

FERGUSON AND THE FRUITS OF DEFEAT

In 1954 Homer Ferguson, Republican Senator from Michigan, was nearing the end of his second term. As a young lawyer, Ferguson gained public attention when he functioned as a one-man grand jury, investigating local corruption. While Senator, he had served on the committee investigating the Japanese attack on Pearl Harbor—an experience, according to one correspondent, that left him "unawed by the military."[15] During his second term, his Senatorial career had been characterized by consistent support for President Eisenhower's domestic programs. Conservative and capable, if undistinguished, Homer Ferguson had played a dominant role in amending the pledge of allegiance to include the words "under God."[16] Such was the man who ran for a third term in November 1954.

As early as April 1953, Eisenhower was aware that Ferguson faced an

[13] USCMAP, "Memorandum to Judge Latimer, March 13, 1956," 2.

[14] Ibid. Tedrow also was concerned that in his testimony to the Committee, Latimer emphasize that some of the Defense proposals went far beyond the intentions of Congress as embodied in the UCMJ.

[15] Homer Ferguson Papers, hereafter cited as FP, May 8, 1955, Box 17, Folder 2. Ferguson later commented that "as a rule, the military does resent civilians interfering in their command. I discovered this early in my service in Washington in the Senate. . . ." Ibid., October 20, 1964. Box 17, Folder 8.

[16] He also supported Eisenhower in a protracted battle with another Republican Senator, John Bricker, who sponsored a proposal that would have placed major limitations on the President's treaty making authority. It sought "to enhance Congressional control of the conduct of foreign affairs, [so] that it would have virtually stripped the President of authority to make even routine executive agreements." The Bricker Amendment divided the Republican Party, and was narrowly defeated—with Ferguson casting a vote against it. Hughes, *Ordeal of Power*, 143–45.

extremely difficult campaign. During a cabinet meeting, the Postmaster General warned that "we've simply got to be thinking of ways to help Ferguson. Give him a good bill to carry in the Senate. Or something."[17] On September 9, 1954, the President was urged to visit Michigan during the campaign "to insure Sen. Ferguson's victory." Eisenhower's key aide, Sherman Adams, responded that "the President is well advised of the situation in Michigan . . . and will do all he possibly can within the limitations of time and energy to insure Homer's election."[18] Eisenhower did visit Michigan, but to no avail. The result, although close, revealed the author of the patriotic "under-God" to have been a political underdog.

A few days after the election, Secretary of State John Foster Dulles reported to Eisenhower that Ferguson "had been in."[19] Dulles and the defeated Senator "agreed that he would like a diplomatic appointment. The Pres. is looking for a judicial post. The Sec. said F. would like a Circuit Court of Appeals, but not a district." Dulles "suggested sending him to Belgium," and observed that the current ambassador—a Michigan native—"has not worked out too well." Eisenhower responded that Dulles "should do as he pleases."[20]

A month later, Dulles and Sherman Adams discussed Ferguson's career alternatives.[21] Adams indicated that the former Senator could accept an appointment on the CAB [Civil Aeronautics Board]. "A. suggested that he take the CAB for a couple of years and he would try to get him on the Court of Appeals." Dulles again referred to the possibility of sending Ferguson to Belgium. He then "asked if A. thought F. would take a post like the Philippines. A. said he might as this is just a stopgap. He [Ferguson] is calling the turn pretty arbitrarily. He wants this post but wants the Court of Appeals when there is a vacancy. A. thinks he should stay here and we should stand up to him to get him to take the CAB. A. has told the Pres. about this. The Sec. said that he wouldn't mind offering him the Philippines."[22]

Early in January, Dulles informed Adams that there is "nothing new on Ferguson. Adams said we should just sit quiet and let him come around."[23] Later that month, Dulles informed Adams that Eisenhower approved Fer-

[17] Ibid., 118.

[18] Eisenhower Papers, hereafter cited as EP, Central Files, Alphabetical File, September 13, 18, and 21, 1954, Box 1018.

[19] John Foster Dulles Papers, hereafter cited as JFD, Telephone Call Series, Box 10, November 6, 1954. The original abbreviations have been retained.

[20] Ibid.

[21] A former governor of New Hampshire, Adams functioned as Eisenhower's Chief of Staff, although that title apparently had not yet come into vogue within the White House.

[22] JFD, Telephone Calls Series, Box 10, December 7, 1954. A few days later, Adams and Dulles talked about a number of candidates for positions within the Foreign Service. Ferguson's name was on the list left with the Secretary. Dulles's assistant promised Adams that "we will insure that every person on this list is given the fullest consideration." Ibid., Special Assistant Chrono Files, Box 7, File December 1954 (3).

[23] JFD, Telephone Calls Series, Box 10, January 4, 1955.

guson's posting to the Philippines. However, since then Dulles "heard [that Secretary of Commerce Sinclair] Weeks is planning to ask him to be Under Secretary of Commerce for transportation. The Sec. would prefer that."[24] Within twenty-four hours, however, Adams told Dulles that he was prepared "to sign off on Ferguson," who "wants to go to the Philippines. The Sec. thinks Mrs. F is [in] back of it."[25] On March 11, Ferguson's ambassadorial appointment was announced.

Thus, at least four different posts for the defeated Senator had been discussed within Eisenhower's administration, and while a federal appeals court position had been mentioned for Ferguson, it apparently was not the Court of Military Appeals.[26] On the other hand, Eisenhower's administration was well aware that Brosman's term was to expire on May 1, 1956. As early as June 30, 1955, one presidential assistant—Bryce Harlow—noted that Democratic Senator Walter George "is very desirous" that Brosman "be reappointed."[27] A few weeks later, Edward Tait, Special Assistant to the President, wrote to Judge John Minor Wisdom acknowledging Wisdom's enthusiastic endorsement of Brosman for reappointment.[28]

Finally, Tait's office informed yet another of Eisenhower's assistants that "there have been no appointments made to the U.S. Court of Military Appeals by this Administration. The office of the General Counsel of the Department of Defense is primarily interested in any appointment to this Court. Recommendations should be submitted to the Secretary of Defense who then refers them to the office of the General Counsel."[29] This undeniable evidence of awareness concerning the USCMA vacancy is noteworthy because at the time of his senatorial defeat, Ferguson received no apparent consideration within Eisenhower's inner circle as a possible successor to Brosman. In the meantime, Ferguson headed for Manila, USCMA continued to function, and Brosman sought his renomination even as others saw themselves as his replacement.[30]

[24] Ibid., January 24, 1955.

[25] Ibid., January 25, 1955.

[26] Eisenhower had received numerous letters urging that something be done for Ferguson in the wake of his defeat. Besides the suggestions already noted, other writers proposed his appointment either as Attorney General, or a member of the United States Supreme Court. As a matter of fact, Eisenhower had already decided to name John Marshall Harlan to the High Court, even as Ferguson faced defeat in the November 1954 elections. Although the President made three more appointments to this Court, [he had five in all], there is no indication that Ferguson was seriously considered for any of them.

[27] EP, General Files, Box 95, June 30, 1955.

[28] Ibid., August 26, 1955.

[29] Ibid., Official Files, Box 376, September 14, 1955. Throughout USCMA's history, this "procedure" for filling Court vacancies has never been consistently followed. Occasionally the General Counsel's Office has been involved in selecting the judges. On numerous occasions, it has not.

[30] There are approximately thirty-one files in the Eisenhower Papers, containing endorsements for candidates seeking appointment to USCMA in place of Brosman, many submitted during the

Brosman's unexpected death removed whatever advantage the incumbent might have had, and probably caused many more applicants to seek the post. Less than two weeks after the judge's death, Proulx wrote to a friend that "there are many rumors flying as to who will be nominated. . . . [W]e do know that the number of candidates for the position is increasing daily." A former commissioner was an applicant, and also "Dick Tedrow is in there pitching. . . . Bob Smart is an avowed candidate and apparently he has very good backing."[31]

One of Tedrow's pitches went to Maryland Governor Theodore McKeldin, to whom he wrote one week after Brosman's death. "I am, of course, a Republican," he emphasized, and "I believe I am considered somewhat of an authority on military law." Tedrow further noted that "Chief Judge Quinn . . . will also recommend me for the vacancy insofar as he can do so with propriety."[32] He "did not know when the vacancy will be filled but I understand it is a matter of some urgency due to the fact that the two existing Members of the Court will have some difficulty in operating without a full bench"[33] McKeldin promptly forwarded Tedrow's letter to Sherman Adams without his specific endorsement—stating merely, "I am sure that Mr. Tedrow . . . would be most appreciative of any consideration given him for such a position."[34]

Meanwhile, members of the White House staff assembled basic information about the various candidates for appointment. A January 5 memorandum listed about a dozen names including the former Court Commissioner Francis Tappaan, the current Chief Commissioner Richard Tedrow, and Robert Smart, still with the House Armed Services Committee. Smart apparently was supported by one of its Republican members, Dewey Short. One name, however, was not on the list—and its omission is noteworthy. Writing to Quinn a day later, Proulx reported that "for some reason Judge Latimer feels

---

summer and fall of 1955. At least two came from aspirants who had applied in 1951 for the first three seats. In December, Florida lawyer Miles Draper wrote to Eisenhower's assistant Bernard Shanley that he had been on Truman's list of ten finalists. "Then General Harry Vaughan got into the act and some cronies of his were appointed." EP, General Files, Box 95, December 9, 1955. Draper appears to have been as accurate in his conclusions as he was successful in his efforts at appointment. See above, chapter 1.

[31] 6 CF, January 5, 1956.

[32] EP, General Files, Box 95, December 28, 1955. I could find no evidence to confirm that Quinn supported Tedrow, but this in no way proves that Tedrow was inaccurate in his claim. Since Eisenhower would almost certainly name a Republican, and since Quinn was the ranking Democrat on the Court, one wonders, however, how much "propriety" he could have exercised in recommending his chief commissioner. On the other hand, one wonders if a sitting judge can ever properly be an advocate for an aspiring office seeker.

[33] Ibid., 2. Here Tedrow hinted at what was common knowledge within the Court, that Quinn and Latimer tended to differ on their philosophical approach to military justice. Latimer was much more sympathetic to the military viewpoint than his colleague. Thus the third member of the Court was necessary to avoid deadlock in those cases where Latimer and Quinn disagreed.

[34] EP, General Files, Box 95, December 30, 1955.

that Senator Ferguson is the strongest candidate."[35] It remains unclear what information contributed to Latimer's conclusion, but he was correct.

The day before Proulx wrote to Quinn, Charles Wilson, Eisenhower's Secretary of Defense and an old acquaintance of Ferguson, spoke with Dulles. "Homer Ferguson would make a good judge. W. wondered how the Sec. thought he was getting on where he is and whether it would be good to consider him for the appointment." Dulles replied that the move "might be worth thinking about. The Sec. does not think he is terribly happy there, and his wife has not been well." Dulles recalled that Ferguson had "wanted a judicial appt. at the time but nothing [was] vacant. W. thought he could put his name in the hat if the Sec. thought it all right."[36]

On the following day, Dulles conferred with both Wilson and Adams. He told Wilson that "he thinks well of the suggestion about Ferguson. He is doing well . . . and the Sec. thinks that he would probably like it and be good at it."[37] A few hours later, Dulles called Sherman Adams about the Ferguson appointment. He had "checked with his people and as far as we are concerned, we would be happy to see him take it. He is doing all right but is not exactly a star of the first magnitude yet[,] and his wife has been sick most of the time."[38] Adams responded that "they will support it if that is what the Sec. wants."[39] Wilson called Dulles again on January 10. "Has the Sec. found out if [Ferguson] wants it? The Sec. thinks he would. He talked with Adams and the Pres. and the Pres. thought it a good move. W. said the thing to do is to contact Ferguson," and asked Dulles "to sound him out."[40]

Whereupon Dulles wrote an "eyes only" letter to Ferguson. "Charlie Wilson . . . is anxious to have you appointed to this Court. . . . I told Charlie that I would, of course, pass this information on to you right away. I do so

[35] 6 CF, January 6, 1956, 3.

[36] JFD, Telephone Calls Series, Box 5, January 5, 1956.

[37] Ibid., Box 5, January 6, 1956.

[38] Early in December, Dulles had written to one of Eisenhower's aides who had commented favorably on two foreign service appointees, one of whom was Ferguson. "I appreciate having this confirmation of the good work that they are both doing at their posts." EP, General Files, Box 176, December 6, 1955.

[39] JFD, Telephone Calls Series, Box 11, January 6, 1956. On January 10, Dulles reported to Eisenhower about the proposed Ferguson appointment. "The President authorized me to proceed." Ibid., White House Memoranda Series, Box 4, January 10, 1956, 4. On the same day, Proulx relayed a message to Quinn from Tedrow if the Chief Judge would "request [Rhode Island] Senators Green and Pastore and [Representative] John Fogarty to also write to Wilson endorsing him." 6 CF, January 10, 1956. In the meantime, of course, additional names were coming into the White House. For example, Senator Everett McKinley Dirksen—Republican from Illinois, and accurately but affectionately described as "the wizard of ooze"—endorsed three candidates. He further observed that with a Roman Catholic and a Protestant already on the Court of Appeals, "it may be that you would want to give serious thought to Colonel [Edward] Chayes as a member of the Jewish faith." EP, General Files, Box 95, January 7, 1956. A Deputy Assistant assured "Dear Ev" that "the biographical data on Colonel Chayes . . . will be most helpful." Ibid., January 10, 1956.

[40] JFD, Telephone Calls Series, Box 5, January 10, 1956.

with very mixed feelings. On the one hand, I am pleased (but not surprised) that such a possibility is available to you. On the other . . . I would be distressed to lose you from this post." Dulles realized that "because of the nature and importance of this Judgeship . . . you may wish to consider this matter rather carefully before giving us a reply." Asking that Ferguson give him and Wilson "an indication of your thinking in this matter" as soon as possible, Dulles commented of his cabinet colleague that "I need hardly add that our community of interests stops here. He shall be hoping for one reply and I another."[41]

Ferguson cannot have deliberated very long. On January 18, he called Dulles at 6:30 in the morning "to say he would be glad to accept the judicial appointment but he didn't want to do it until April. . . ." Ferguson was concerned, however, "that he might not be confirmed for the full fifteen-year term, as the Democrats would be able to block the confirmation and stall for the remainder of the year in the hopes that next year they would be able to fill the job with a Democrat."[42] The following day, Ferguson received a telegram that the matter of "clearing confirmation with Congressional leaders" was underway.[43] Wilson sent the formal nomination to the White House on January 23, and noted that it had been cleared with several key Republican Senators including William Knowland, Styles Bridges, and Leverett Saltonstall.[44]

By this date, the inevitable rumors were beginning to circulate within Washington. On January 24, Proulx wrote to a member of the Court Committee that "the list of candidates is growing daily with the latest rumor . . . to the effect that the White House has made a commitment and that . . . Ferguson . . . [is] the man selected."[45] Two days later he could not be much more specific on the subject to the Chief Judge. I had thought, he wrote to Quinn, that by this date "there would be definite word on the appointment emerging from this mass of rumors and counter rumors." Latimer "is now convinced that Ferguson is the man. . . . [and] for the sake of betting, I accepted one from Judge Latimer—a luncheon at the new Courthouse—he says Senator Ferguson, and I have the field." Proulx added that "I did learn that Senator Ferguson was Secretary Wilson's idea—he, I am told, made the offer in all probability to offset" some incident which may have contributed to Ferguson's defeat.[46]

[41] Ibid., Chrono Series, Box 13, January 11, 1956.

[42] Ibid., Telephone Calls Series, Box 5, January 18, 1956. Ferguson's fears turned out to be groundless in part because of traditional Senatorial support for one of their own (the Senate Committee did not even request Ferguson to appear before it) to say nothing of Eisenhower's triumphant reelection in November 1956.

[43] Ibid., Chrono Series, Box 13, January 19, 1956.

[44] EP, Official Files, Box 376, January 23, 1956.

[45] CCC, January 24, 1956.

[46] 6 CF, January 26, 1956. While Proulx did not provide any details about the nature of

If Drew Pearson claimed to have uncovered the "inside scoop" about Truman's three choices for the USCMA bench, Westbrook Pegler made the same assertion for Eisenhower's lone appointment.[47] Noting correctly that Ferguson had provided essential support for the President in issues involving Senator Joseph McCarthy, as well as the Bricker Amendment, Pegler insisted that when Ferguson lost his Senate seat "if there was any gratitude in Ike and the eastern claque which belittles the sovereignty of the United States and berates McCarthy for his 'methods,' he had little to worry about." The ambassadorship was "a stopgap measure." Such positions usually "cost the occupant more than they pay and it was obvious that Ferguson couldn't last long." Instead, Eisenhower named him to USCMA, "a soft spot for $25,000 a year. . . . The Court sits in Washington where Ferguson is really at home and Mrs. Ferguson knows her way to the supermarket, the movies, and church."[48]

Quinn and Proulx were both acquainted with the new Judge, although Ferguson's personal experience with the Court may have been based on a very brief appearance by Quinn before the Senate Appropriations subcommittee in June 1953. Ferguson had chaired the hearing, and his few questions were succinct, if not superficial.[49] Proulx assured his chief that he would try "to learn how the Senator operated while he was on the Hill."[50] In the meantime, the chairman of the Court Committee wrote that "Ferguson will be a valuable addition to the Court, particularly in its relations to Congress. . . ."[51]

But his value would be based on his presence, and the new judge seemed in no hurry to return to Washington. Although unanimously confirmed on February 17, Ferguson indicated that he would not be available until the latter part of March because he wished to remain in the Philippines until after Dulles's long scheduled visit. Finally, the State Department informed Proulx that Ferguson "expects to arrive in Washington during the fourth week of March. . . . Judge Latimer had been on edge until this call came in[,] for he was contemplating

---

Wilson's role, either for good or ill, in Ferguson's campaign, material in the Eisenhower and Dulles Papers support his conclusion. The incident appears to have been based upon some offhanded remarks that Wilson apparently made during the course of Ferguson's campaign for reelection. On January 26, the *Washington Post* reported that Ferguson's appointment was imminent. Four days later, Eisenhower sent the nomination to the Senate.

[47] See above, chapter 1.

[48] USCMAP. This typed copy of Pegler's column states that it "appeared in the Shreveport, Louisiana newspaper during the month of February, 1956."

[49] See *Hearings Before the Subcommittee of the Committee on Appropriations on H.R. 5969*, 83rd Cong., 1st sess., part 1, 651–54.

[50] QPPC, January 31, 1956.

[51] CCC, February 9, 1956. A lawyer who had served with Ferguson on the Hoover Commission was also enthusiastic about the appointment. Henry Shine, Jr., wrote to Proulx that "I personally believe that [Ferguson] will be a great help to the Court in preventing continuing sniping by the various [JAGs] of the Services." QPPC, February 10, 1956. In retrospect, Shine appears to have been mistaken. See below.

wiring him asking when he would be on the scene—he thinks the Senator is displaying very little interest in his new position."[52]

Latimer and Ferguson would serve together for the next five years [all that remained of Latimer's term], and as will be seen, Latimer occasionally found himself at odds with Ferguson's interpretation both of the UCMJ and the role of the Court in its administration. Before his appointment expired, Latimer's dissents increased in number as well as stridency of tone. There may well have been another aspect to their relationship, however, besides doctrinal divergence. Latimer's son recalls that his father believed Ferguson to have been a "political hack," and as such, "a dismal choice for the position."[53]

Quinn, on the other hand, enjoyed his new colleague. More than Latimer, Ferguson shared Quinn's conviction that involvement by officers of high military rank in no way implied superior military justice. Both men were "old-time" politicians, and both had held important elected office. Possibly because both had suffered from the exigencies of the electorate—Ferguson and Quinn remained very sympathetic whenever possible to the numerous requests for nonjudicial assistance they received as judges. Even before he arrived, Ferguson's past experiences indicated that he had more in common with Quinn than with Latimer.[54]

A CONGRESSIONAL COMMITTEE REVISITS THE CODE

Although the primary purpose of the hearings before the House Armed Services Subcommittee was to consider the Defense Department Omnibus bill,

[52] 6 CF, February 28, 1956. Actually, Ferguson did not resign until March 22. According to Proulx, "he had to resign in Manila if he wanted Mrs. Ferguson to get Government paid transportation back to the States—A State Department regulation." Ferguson, he added, "is attending a conference in Tokyo . . . (a Japanese-Irish conclave, no doubt)." Ibid., March 2, 1956.

[53] Interview, George Latimer, Jr., July 20, 1989, 15. Given Latimer's extensive military experience, and Ferguson's complete lack of it, as well as the former Senator's limited legal career—one can understand why Latimer might be critical of Ferguson's appointment. But with two Republicans now on the Court and a Republican President in office, Latimer never suggested that Eisenhower elevate him to be Chief Judge, although Congressman William Dawson, Republican from Utah, had so requested of Eisenhower as early as the spring of 1953—something Eisenhower could have done. The presidential prerogative to appoint or remove an USCMA judge from the post of Chief Judge was not eliminated until 1992. See below, chapter 9. It may be, as George Latimer, Jr., recalls, that Latimer and Quinn worked out an "understanding" to the effect that Latimer would make certain administrative decisions for the Court during Quinn's absences. Ibid., 7. There is no reference to this matter in Quinn's papers. On the other hand, Quinn remained as Chief Judge until the Nixon Administration, and Dawson made it clear that Latimer had not asked him to urge the change in his status upon Eisenhower.

[54] In 1951, the first three judges of USCMA had been sworn in at the Pentagon. Probably working through the office of Senator William Knowland, Ferguson made arrangements to have Chief Justice Earl Warren administer the oath of office in the Supreme Court Building on April 9. 6 CF, March 21, 22, 1956.

other interests lurked beneath the stated agenda. Judges Quinn and Latimer continued to push their life tenure proposal either as part of the omnibus bill or as a separate statute. While the proposed DOD legislation included the seventeen recommendations for changes that had been suggested three years before, Alfred Proulx observed that "each JAG has been plugging for individual items and the hearings might spill over into their respective areas."[55] Realizing that the UCMJ would not be subject to extensive congressional revision, the service representatives instead elected to accentuate the positive about its effect—to offer constructive legislation that would make the overall statute even better.[56] This strategy also included avoiding direct criticism of USCMA, while at the same time attacking specific provisions under which the Court operated.

Thus the first witness to appear before the Committee, Albert Pratt—Assistant Secretary of the Navy—argued that while the Code provisions "to safeguard the individual are, for the most part, entirely proper and fine . . . . [t]he complications of review have slowed the process of justice, which is always a disadvantage, and they have increased the administrative burdens in the number of people who are, in a sense, not productively employed. That has to be balanced against all the greater rights given to the individual."[57] Vice Admiral J. L. Holloway specified what Pratt had suggested. The UCMJ "has not only hamstrung the commanding officer with administrative minutiae, but it has weakened his historic role . . . that of a wise, just, fatherly mentor, quick to punish the sinners and equally quick to help a man redeem himself and start afresh."[58] Procedures mandated by the Code have been carried out, "but with excessive delay and at a great unnecessary cost in man-hours."

Holloway reminded the Subcommittee that his service was neither a judi-

[55] Ibid., March 13, 1956. Two days later, thé Subcommittee Chair, Representative Overton Brooks, noted that "it might be well to go a little bit afield in the course of these hearings to see how the whole program of military justice in the armed services is working. We have never had such a hearing." The UCMJ was adopted, "and we have never had a hearing to see how it has been working." 84th Cong., 1st sess., House, Armed Serices Subcommittee Hearings on H.R. 6583, March 13, 1956, 8422; hereafter cited as Hearings, followed by appropriate page number.

[56] In addition, spokesmen for the Navy emphasized the importance of Congress in reforming military justice. Sometimes, this tendency toward flattery verged on fawning. Thus, Vice Admiral J. L. Holloway said to one subcommittee member that "of course, . . . there is no one who leans more heavily upon the counsel of the Congress and the law than I do." The UCMJ "as it stands is a fine piece of legislation. It represents the synthesis and thinking of very devoted people." *Hearings*, March 15, 1956, 8443, 8445. Holloway, it might be noted, was not even a member of the Navy JAG Department. He served as Chief of Naval Personnel.

[57] Ibid., 8425. Pratt added, "I think it is quite remarkable that a code of this nature should have as few bugs in it as have been developed. It is a very comprehensive job that was done; you were plowing new ground, and I think it is greatly to the credit of the people who originally drafted this legislation that there has not been more bad trouble with it." Ibid., 8426.

[58] Ibid., 8436. It would seem, given his rhetoric, that Holloway was not familiar with the celebrated 1842 incident involving Alexander MacKenzie, commander of the U.S. Navy Brig *Somers*. While at sea, MacKenzie ordered the summary execution of three young officers, including the son of the Secretary of War, for allegedly plotting a mutiny. See AMJ, 21–29.

cial nor law enforcement agency. It, like the other branches of the Armed Services, existed "solely to provide an adequate national defense." And, "when the procedures of courts-martial and other related legal matters become so cumbersome that officers must neglect . . . primary duties . . . then it is time that we take action to change the system." Such was the purpose of the measure under consideration, one drafted "without reducing in the smallest amount the features of the [UCMJ] that protect the rights of individuals."[59]

Navy JAG Admiral Ira Nunn, possibly regarded by Quinn as the nemesis of his premises, reminded the Subcommittee that—unlike a civilian criminal code—the UCMJ "must not only maintain a good social order but we must foster and produce a dedicated fighting spirit."[60] Like Holloway before him, Nunn insisted that "not many of these proposed changes have great significance. In fact, they are very mild, it seems to me."[61] Nunn then summarized the key amendments, but omitted any mention or description of the proposed requirement of certification by counsel as a condition for appeal to USCMA. After two days of hearings, Tedrow reported to Latimer that "no witness has as yet criticized the Court in any way. Once or twice they were cornered and had to praise the Code and the Court." The attitude of the Subcommittee, he felt, "continues to be pro-accused, pro-Code, and suspicious of the military."[62]

The awareness by military witnesses of this tendency may explain why they sought to minimize their differences with the Judges. Thus, General Albert Kuhfeld, the Air Force Deputy JAG, told the Subcommittee "this entire bill was worked out during conferences with [the Code] committee[,] and practically all of the provisions, all of the changes suggested, were approved by the three Judge Advocates General and the members of the Court. . . ."[63] Here, Kuhfeld was disingenuous if not actually dishonest.[64] In no way did the USCMA judges accept, let alone approve, any version of the certificate requirement even though it had been modified in a vain attempt to mitigate their opposition. Both Quinn and Latimer were prepared to make their views very clear, but the Subcommittee recessed the hearings for nearly

[59] Ibid. Holloway added that "the discipline of the present day does not appear to me to be as good as it was before the war." Ibid., 8437. Of the proposed changes in the UCMJ, "all we want and recommend is some modifications that would appear to me to be comparatively mild. . . ." Ibid., 8442.

[60] Ibid., 8446. Nunn claimed that the proposed bill had the support of all the armed services, as well as the departments of Defense, and the Bureau of the Budget. He failed to mention either the U.S. Court of Military Appeals, the Code Committee, or the Civilian Court Committee.

[61] Ibid., 8449.

[62] USCMAP, March 16, 1956. The Subcommittee hearing record confirms Tedrow's conclusions.

[63] Hearings, 8486–87.

[64] Tedrow reported that Kuhfeld "with great emphasis said that practically all of the amendments . . . had been approved by the Judges, that the Bill came out of the study made by the Judges and JAGs. My impression was that he was conveying that [*sic*] the Court just about approved this Bill in toto. For some reason none of the members asked him any questions regarding this." USCMAP, March 19, 1956.

a month; and not until April 16 did they resume. Quinn and Latimer testified on April 18, with Ferguson in attendance as an interested observer.

The Chief Judge did not mince words in his condemnation of the proposed legislation, submitted by the Defense Department at the behest of the Navy. "It contains provisions which cannot be justified by experience, reason, or logic[,]" including "some proposed amendments which were either rejected by the Court members of the [Code] committee" or were not even presented to it for consideration.[65] On the other hand, Quinn endorsed the seventeen proposed changes that had first been submitted in 1953, and urged that any legislative changes to the UCMJ "should not, at this time, go beyond the recommendations unanimously agreed upon by the Code Committee."[66] The worst of those that did, of course, was the certification requirement.

"This proposed change is so hostile to the spirit and intent of the code that I most earnestly oppose its adoption. It reads innocuously but it requires that an accused obtain a certificate of probable cause from counsel before the Court must consider his petition for a grant of review."[67] The result of this amendment "is to return control of military justice to the armed services[,] for under its provisions they can prevent the flow of all but a relatively few cases to the court. . . ." Quinn reminded the Subcommittee that 97 percent of the appeals coming to USCMA were handled by military lawyers assigned by the JAGs. "If appellate processes can be controlled by the military, a good deal of the Court's influence can be eliminated." Lurking in the innocent words of the section "is the possibility that the services will choose the cases they desire to be heard."[68]

Judge Latimer echoed the views of his colleague. The certification proposal represented the area where the two judges "clash head-on with the services." Indeed, "if you want to render us impotent, and deny us the right to hear cases, that is the area in which you can do it. If the services can tell us what cases we can hear, those they do not want us to hear are not going to get to us."[69] Latimer did "not know of any reason in the world why any man in the service should be denied the right to reach our court." As to the

[65] Hearings, 8554–55.

[66] Ibid., 8556. As early as 1954, when the first version of the Defense Department bill had been introduced, Quinn had taken the position that "only those amendments proposed by the Code Committee . . . wherein unanimity has been reached should be the subject of legislation at this time." In 1955, the Bureau of the Budget rejected his position. "While we think that substantial weight should be given to the recommendations of the Code Committee as well as the civilian Court Committee, we do not think these should be conclusive. Otherwise those who have fundamental responsibilities with respect to the Code and its operation would be subject to a veto by groups whose responsibilities are clearly secondary in character." EP, Official Files, 3-M, Box 101, February 26, 1955, 1–2.

[67] Hearings, 8557.

[68] Ibid., 8558.

[69] Ibid., 8589.

military's claim that USCMA had to be protected from frivolous appeals, "let me worry about our workload."[70]

As was noted in earlier chapters of this study, the JAGs had modified the language of their certificate proposal, ostensibly to meet judicial objections. Nevertheless, every civilian who testified during the hearings condemned the certification proposal. The question can be raised as to exactly what the 1956 draft stated, and whether or not the censure visited upon it by the USCMA Judges in particular was still warranted. The suggested amendment would have changed one category of USCMA review as follows:

> All cases reviewed by a board of review in which upon petition of the accused and on good cause shown, the Court of Military Appeals has granted a review: but the Court must consider a petition for a grant of review only if (A) counsel who represented the accused at his trial or before the board of review, (B) appellate defense counsel appointed by the Judge Advocate General if the accused was not represented by counsel before the board of review, or (C) civilian counsel retained by the accused, certifies that in his opinion a substantial question of law is presented and that the appeal is made in good faith.[71]

It would seem from an examination of this language that USCMA *must* [emphasis added] review a case only under condition set forth above as A, B, and C. However, the provision does not appear to alter the Court's ability to choose what it *may* hear as apart from what it *must* hear. If so, one wonders why Quinn and Latimer were so perturbed. Indeed, a spokesman for the Navy JAG department emphasized this point in a statement delivered to the Subcommittee after the hearings had ended. It really was a rebuttal to all the negative comments, submitted by the Service that was the moving force behind the proposed legislation.

> There was no attempt to vitiate and circumscribe the present power of the Court . . . and the proposal as drafted in fact would not permit such a result. The right

[70] Ibid. In addition to his statement recorded in the hearings, Latimer had prepared a commentary on each of the changes in the proposed legislation. He referred to it several times in his testimony, but it does not appear in the printed record, and it is probable that he did not leave it with the Subcommittee. In these comments on the certification issue, the Judge's candor is noteworthy. It may explain why Latimer apparently decided against submitting them. "We are trying to improve the system without changing the relationship between the military and civilian community. Unfortunately, the same general comment cannot be applied if the [JAGs] seek to restrict the Court and return the control of appellate processes to the Services. Considered in that light, the recommendation embodies the age-old fight of the military to avoid any interference by civilians." The JAGs, Latimer added, "seem to take a deep interest in our postulated inability to perform. In my judgement . . . if the system fails to function properly in a future emergency, it will be because of difficulties encountered at the trial level or within the Services, not at the level of this Court." USCMAP, undated, "Comments on Proposed Amendments to the Uniform Code," 16–17.

[71] Hearings, 8415.

> of the accused to petition remains unchanged and the Court may consider any petition. [The amendment provides] that only in those cases wherein counsel certifies that a substantial question of law is presented and that the appeal is made in good faith is the consideration by the court mandatory. There is nothing in the language to prevent the court from reviewing every petition of an accused . . . should it determine to do so. Under these circumstances, it is difficult to see how this proposal can be characterized as an attempt to vitiate the present power of the court . . . . No such limitation on the present power of the Court was intended or in fact provided[,] but this point could easily be clarified by the addition of any language which is considered necessary.[72]

Whatever the JAGs' original intent in submitting this amendment, however they may have sought to explain if not justify their proposal—the Judges would have none of it. On this issue, JAGs and Judges appeared to be talking past each other.[73] But Quinn had other matters on his mind besides certification. One was the issue of civil service classification for the Court, a matter that had festered since its establishment.

The Chief Judge noted that the Civil Service Commission "naturally, I presume, take jurisdiction of everything that they possibly can include within their limits." And, indeed, members of its staff had investigated the various court positions. "They take up our time, they take up the clerk's time, they interfere with our business and progress." In truth, "these people . . . are not lawyers, they are not jurists, they don't know anything about the running of a court and they simply get in our way. I think it is very unfortunate."[74] Moreover, Quinn could easily identify the source for the Commission's claim of authority.

"[W]e did not have life tenure. . . . we were not judges of the United States in accordance with [the statute,] and therefore we were a part of the executive branch of the Government, rather than the judicial, and, therefore, they had a right to reach in and supervise us." Whatever the Civil Service Commission might claim to the contrary, argued Chief Judge Quinn, "this court has been a court in every sense of the word. It acts like a court, it looks

[72] Hearings, 8652–53.

[73] The Bureau of the Budget had also supported the certification requirement, noting that the "certificate required appears reasonable, especially since counsel will resolve any doubts in favor of accused." EP, Official Files, 3-M Box 101, February 25, 1955.

[74] Hearings, 8569. One suspects that Quinn's views typified the USCMA judges' attitudes since 1951 toward Civil Service classification for the Court staff. Over the years, however, staff members have taken a different position toward it, and for very understandable reasons. Quinn alluded indirectly to their concerns when he claimed that "no other body of men in the world can determine as well as the judges of this court how our commissioners, and law secretaries and clerks should be graded and what they should be paid. . . ." Ibid. One can easily understand why staff members might well disagree; and as will be seen, USCMA's history is replete with examples of friction between Court and Staff concerning the scope and extent of Civil Service authority over its personnel.

like a court. . . . and [it] certainly seems to me that we should have all the attributes of a court."[75]

Quinn also had some comments concerning the matter of frivolous appeals, apparently of great concern to the JAGs. "We can," he insisted, "very easily take care of them under our rules." When one considered that some 33 percent of the cases involving errors which were the basis for a grant of relief or reversal, "were errors never found by the services or by counsel for the Government or the defense, but were picked up by our law secretaries and commissioners, [it] seems to me that the court has nothing to worry about as far as frivolous appeals are concerned."[76]

Assisted by Tedrow, Quinn was prepared to submit three additional UCMJ amendments to the Subcommittee. As he wrote to Proulx, "The three recommendations are confined to court procedure and require no consideration by the JAGs."[77] The first would have redefined USCMA authority. Remaining in the Defense Department "for the purposes of administration only," the Court would consist of three judges appointed for fifteen-year terms. However, "the Judges of said Court shall be judges of the United States and shall have all the powers, prerogatives, and perquisites, including compensation and rights of retirement, of Judges of the United States Circuit Courts of Appeal."[78] Moreover, the amendment eliminated the political party requirement mandated when the UCMJ was adopted, namely, that no more than two of the three judges could be from the same party.

Tedrow commented to Quinn that the proposed change made no attempt to grant "life tenure either for the incumbents or their successors." The issue was "whether the present Democratic majority would wish to blanket two Republicans [Latimer and Ferguson] in office." Of course, "it is clear that the Services would vigorously oppose any provision for life tenure."[79] Quinn reluctantly agreed with Tedrow's points. "We still should emphasize and fight for life tenure. But if this can't be obtained I believe it wise to take the next best thing to wit, 15 y[ea]rs and the other federal prerogatives."[80]

The second amendment would have resolved the controversy between the Court and the Civil Service Commission, at least as concerned future court

[75] Hearings, 8572. When asked by Congressman Brooks if Congress should change the definition of courts-martial as a means toward clarifying USCMA authority, Quinn responded: "No; I think it would be more preferable if you enacted the life tenure bill." Of course, both men were well aware that numerous attempts toward this goal since 1951 had been futile. Brooks reminded Quinn that "perhaps from your viewpoint, it is a simple thing to do, but from the viewpoint of passing good legislation, we have to decide what we can get." Ibid., 8573. Congress has yet to grant USCMA judges life tenure.

[76] Ibid., 8575.

[77] USCMAP, undated, handwritten note to Proulx from Quinn.

[78] USCMAP, February 26, 1956.

[79] Ibid.

[80] Supra., n. 78.

employees. "The Court is authorized to appoint and fix compensation of such additional officers and employees as may be necessary to discharge its responsibilities without regard to Civil Service Laws or regulations."[81] The final change represented the Court's answer to the JAG claims that too many frivolous appeals were filed, and that the entire appellate system would break down in a wartime situation. It provided that the Court could appoint nine commissioners, all of whom could be removed by the Court, and who "would devote all of their time to the duties of the office." In time of war or national emergency, the Judges could select up to ten additional commissioners to serve for one year, and to be eligible for reappointment.[82]

One of the witnesses before the Subcommittee was John Finn, a lawyer and former Navy JAG officer, who had previously testified in 1949 on behalf of the American Legion. He did so again seven years later, and strongly urged that Congress postpone action on the UCMJ, because as he put it, "there are, frankly, many amendments to the code which we believe this committee should consider before it takes up a bill of this kind."[83] Finn further informed Congressman Brooks that the American Legion itself was about to hold hearings on the state of military justice and the UCMJ, and to hear from a large number of witnesses whom it had invited to appear—including the three service JAGs and the USCMA Judges. He asked that the Legion be given an opportunity to appear again before the subcommittee after its own hearings, which were scheduled for the first week in May.

Finn also observed that the UCMJ had not been "in operation [for] a sufficient length of time to be the subject of amendment at this juncture."[84] Moreover, it was not the Code, but rather the Manual for Courts-Martial [MCM], drafted by the military, that represented "the real difficulty."[85] Whether, Finn noted, "it was the product of deliberation or of ignorance, is

[81] USCMAP, February 29, 1956.

[82] Ibid. The JAGs would have limited access of appeal, while the Judges would have provided more quasi-judicial manpower to handle the petitions. The different approaches underlined the disagreement between the two groups. For reasons that remain unclear, however, neither Quinn nor Latimer presented these amendments when they appeared before the Subcommittee. As will be seen, Quinn had by no means abandoned his efforts to gain life tenure for his court.

[83] Hearings, 8597.

[84] Ibid., 8598.

[85] Ibid. The MCM stood in relation to the Code much as statutes stand in relation to the federal Constitution. It was (and still is) supposed to provide the specific rules and regulations under which the general precepts of the Code are to be carried out. From a fairly concise volume rewritten in 1951, the MCM has expanded into what the late Frederick Wiener aptly described as "a literally monstrous book," that was three inches thick and weighed some five pounds. For Wiener—its "bulk and complexity" typified the "labyrinthine quagmire" in which he believed operation of the UCMJ is "currently entangled." Frederick B. Wiener, "American Military Law in the Light of the First Mutiny Act's Tricentennial," *Military Law Review* 126 (1989) 76–77, 86–87 (1989). Without accepting his conclusion, this author readily agrees with Wiener's description of the MCM.

difficult to state; but if one were trying to sabotage the [UCMJ], one could not have devised a more artful or better means for so doing than is provided by the manual." It needed "amendment at this time far more than does the Code."[86]

Although Brooks assured him that there would be no objection to "carrying the bill over" until after the Legion's hearing, in fact the Subcommittee adjourned on April 20, and apparently did not reconvene to hear from the Legion.[87] Understandably disappointed, Proulx still remained optimistic. He wrote to Robert White that while "the outlook for any legislation this year on the Code appears dim[,]" he had "hopes of divorcing from the overall bill the life tenure provision."[88] But in August Proulx wrote that Congress had "adjourned without taking any action on the . . . Code." Indeed, "as a matter of fact, the House . . . Subcommittee never reported out the bill."[89] With national elections imminent, adjournment not amendment took priority.

The American Legion, however, did hold its hearings in May 1956. A number of witnesses including Judges Quinn and Latimer, as well as Tedrow, appeared before it. Although all three JAGs were invited, only Air Force JAG Reginald Harmon and his assistant accepted the invitation. Some of the testimony offered, as well as the recommendations ultimately adopted by the American Legion, warrant further discussion.

THE AMERICAN LEGION AND ITS PROPOSED REFORMS

In terms of political issues, it is an understatement to note that the American Legion is not regarded as liberal in outlook. Thus it is noteworthy that in support for expansion of the UCMJ and the role of USCMA in military justice, the Legion was in the forefront of those groups that sought greater protection for members of the military in military justice matters, usually at the expense of its commanders' authority. Nor was this "progressive" outlook new. During the 1949 hearings that led to the code's adoption, Franklin

[86] Hearings, 8599. Finn went on to denounce many of the changes proposed by the Navy in the DOD draft. The certification requirement, for example, "is quite definitely an attempt on the part of the proponents of the bill to vitiate and circumscribe the present power of the Court." Ibid., 8603. USCMA jurisdiction should be increased, not curtailed. Ibid., 8606. As to reducing the time frame for an appeal, "the delays thus far have been demonstrated to be entirely within the military, and why cut down a measly 15-day period at the end of the line for the poor person who is the accused . . . when you are giving the military no cutdown on the time that they have allowable to them?" Ibid., 8610.

[87] Ibid., 8598. Nor, apparently, did the Subcommittee issue any sort of formal report to its parent body; and indeed, no major changes to the UCMJ would be enacted for another twelve years, until 1968. See below.

[88] 6 CF, June 7, 1956.

[89] Ibid., August 7, 1956.

Riter had testified on behalf of the Legion, and suggested among other things that command influence be listed as a federal crime, punishable in federal courts.[90] In 1956, Riter was the chairman of the Legion committee to consider the current condition of military justice.[91]

Some witnesses who had not appeared before the House Subcommittee contributed to the hearings chaired by Riter.[92] Judges Quinn and Latimer essentially reiterated what they had previously presented. Possibly because of the congressional reaction to their earlier testimony, both men were very confident that the certificate requirement would never be approved. Quinn asserted that "I would say that there is no possibility whatsoever that Congress will buy that feature; no, not a chance in a million."[93] Latimer boasted: "I believe I can fairly state [that] when I finished up that subject before the Committee in Congress, there isn't any member in the Congress who would go for that."[94]

[90] See AMJ, chapter 9. In its 1956 recommendations the Legion repeated Riter's proposal. Congress, however, has yet to make command influence a federal offense, and the provision dealing with it that appears in the UCMJ has been ineffective. See Francis A. Gilligan and Frederic I. Lederer, *Court-Martial Procedure* (1991), 639. Justifiably concerned with the detrimental results that command influence has on military justice, with some regularity USCMA has railed against it. On the other hand, as an appellate tribunal USCMA is ill-equipped to go after commanders who are guilty of the practice. While it sometimes does mitigate the results, the Judges can do little to punish its perpetrators.

[91] As was discussed in the first chapter of this volume, Riter had been a candidate for appointment to USCMA and, being a Republican from Salt Lake City, had in a real sense competed with Latimer for the post.

[92] Discussion of some proposals that they supported, such as an independent JAG Corps for the Navy, is beyond the scope of this study. However, one witness—a former member of the Hoover Commission, Henry Shine, Jr.—indirectly pointed to *the* critical problem in military justice. He spoke in terms of the Navy, but his point applies to the entire military system, and it may well be as valid today as more than forty years ago. Commanders, he observed, find it difficult to accept the fact that a JAG officer has a dual responsibility, one side of which may be incompatible with the other. He must be a good officer under the chain of command with all that the term implies, but at the same time must be professionally responsible as an attorney to be sure that the best possible justice and legal service is accorded the accused in military justice affairs. Easier to articulate than assimilate, Shine's views raise a crucial issue. To the extent that military justice is scarred by the corrosive forces of rank and accompanying privilege, it has a built-in potential for failure. On the other hand, the military world cannot function without the dual forces of rank and discipline. Another witness, Ralph Boyd, who had been a member of the first civilian Court Committee appointed by Quinn, stated that the biggest problem in the Services is "the ability to recognize where discipline leaves off and where justice should step in." Legion Hearings, April 30, 1956, 41, 684.

[93] Ibid., 238.

[94] Ibid., 277. When compared with the House hearings, the Riter Committee seems to have been more informal in tone. In general, the witnesses appear to have been more candid in their comments. One witness, a member of the Reserve Officer's Association, described certain military commanders as so narrow minded that "a mosquito could land on their nose and pick out both eyeballs without moving." Ibid., 91.

Both judges also agreed with Riter in his opposition to another provision in the DOD bill that concerned the role of the law officer. Morgan's Committee had provided for the Law Officer not to vote as a member of the court-martial, nor indeed to participate in its deliberations. The JAGs wanted the UCMJ amended so that the law officer would be able to consult with the members of the Court on the penalty that would follow a guilty verdict. Quinn observed, "As a matter of fact, in my opinion, it would be preferable if he didn't go in at all."[95] Latimer agreed. "It would be ever so much easier to administer if the law officer didn't go into the secret deliberations at all."[96]

Latimer also indicated that the commissioner system in effect in his Court "is absolutely worthless to me."[97] He believed that his own examination of the record after his clerks had studied it was more than sufficient. Although he did not say so directly, Latimer further implied that he had opposed the commissioner system from the beginning. "[A]re you going to build an empire of one million employees[,] or are you going to build a court? I have fought from the beginning to that end and for a court, and that is why I am going to continue to fight." On the other hand, judges do "need some help[,] and we have all the help we need."[98]

Air Force JAG Harmon described the certification proposal as "the only method we could find to solve this problem [of frivolous petitions], and I am frank to confess to you that it is fraught with some dangers."[99] Assistant Air Force JAG Kuhfeld mentioned the short-lived Air Force proposal for a judicial appeals board. Confident that it could work in the Air Force, it apparently might not work "across the board." Whereupon the Air Force JAGs withdrew their suggestion, submitting instead "a very innocuous substitute."[100] As one justification for it, Kuhfeld and Harmon also emphasized the independence supposedly afforded Air Force appellate lawyers—who, after all, would sign the certificates.[101]

[95] Ibid., 232. For his part, Riter also believed that it might be better for a court-martial if the role of the president of the court was eliminated entirely. Quinn, however, was unwilling to go that far. All he would say was that "I think in the long run it would be desirable to decrease the powers of the president of the court, and to increase the functions of the law officer." Ibid., 233.

[96] Ibid., 326.

[97] Legion hearings, 265.

[98] Ibid., 265, 272.

[99] Ibid., 512.

[100] Ibid., 514–15. One suspects from Kuhfeld's comment that the panel proposition was not acceptable to the other services, who prevailed in their efforts to have the bill that ultimately went to Congress reflect the Navy preference. *If* one accepted the basic premise that there were a lot of frivolous appeals submitted to USCMA, the certification plan had some merit. But the JAGs' arrogant assumption that they and *not* the judges were best equipped to decide if such was the case was probably the fatal flaw that doomed their proposal.

[101] On the other hand, Harmon did not specify what criteria he used to evaluate Air Force JAG officers. One cannot help but be curious to see if his evaluations of successful defense lawyers were different from those of their counterparts, representing the Government. More-

Another witness was the former JAG officer Frederick Wiener. Almost six years after USCMA had started operations, Wiener had changed his mind on some issues about which he had spoken during the 1949 hearings on the UCMJ. Originally, he had strongly condemned removing the law officer as a member of the Court. Now, "I have completely changed my mind on that. I think the law officer should stay outside the courtroom."[102] Like Riter, he felt that the role of the Court President had become obsolete. While Wiener still had "grave doubts about the Court," he concluded that USCMA "has been a salutary influence," and that it "must be retained."[103]

The committee appointed by the American Legion to study military justice, the UCMJ, and USCMA submitted its report in September 1956. The Court had already received a sort of preview, possibly prepared by Tedrow. According to the memorandum, "needless to say, the military is and has been determinedly opposed to the Code, and particularly to the Court of Military Appeals. . . ." The JAGs had joined the Court "in approving a lesser number of suggested changes. But when the judges rejected other amendments, the military "in effect abrogated its agreement with the Court, and proceeded independently to sponsor the bill" through the DOD.[104] Yet this conduct represented only a symptom of the underlying issues.

> The attacks on the Code, but actually it is the Court, have been continuous and are now increasing in tempo. All the Services are parties to this. When I say Services, I generally mean the Judge Advocates General as almost all attacks are made by them or inspired by them. . . . [T]he real object of the criticism, although they will not say so, is the civilian court that acts as a watchdog over the military and has the final say in exercising the control that formerly was the personal possession of the Judge Advocates General, and often abused by them. The JAGs resent the loss of this power. By way of substitute they make two basic claims: (1) that the Code is too expensive (meaning the Court); and (2) that it involves too much delay.[105]

The Legion Committee report covered more than fifty pages, with one section devoted to USCMA. "The movement to take the Court out of exis-

---

over, he did not discuss the problem of having anyone in uniform—including defense counsel—in a position to bar the door to civilian review.

[102] Hearings, 735. Indeed, Wiener urged that the law officer have some sort of greater dignity added to his post, to reflect the importance of his judicial functions. Here, Wiener anticipated the Military Justice Act of 1968. See below.

[103] Ibid., 728. Wiener's reaction to the certification proposal was typical of the man: unhesitating and forceful. The amendment was "vicious. I am unalterably opposed to it." Ibid., 732. For Wiener's earlier comments to the House Subcommittee in 1949, see AMJ, 220–22, and passim.

[104] USCMAP. "The procedure the military now follows certainly violates the spirit of [the UCMJ provision] wherein the Congress provided that the Court and the Services would make joint recommendations."

[105] Ibid.

tence or to emasculate the Code to the extent that it would no longer be workable is probably much more deeply rooted in certain branches of the Armed Forces, than was realized by this Committee. . . ." Further, "We conclude . . . that the Armed Forces have definitely determined to abolish the Court of Military Appeals, or to so minimize its effectiveness that it would merely be a rubber stamp for the Military."[106] On the other hand, the Committee had received what it considered justifiable criticism of the tribunal. Thus it detailed a number of areas and cases wherein USCMA decisions had been analyzed as inconsistent, inappropriate, or erroneous."[107] Nevertheless, given the comments of its own witnesses like Finn, as well as those who later appeared before the Legion committee, its positive conclusions about the Court come as no surprise. "It is the most salutary advancement ever made in the field of military law, [and] nothing which we have said herein should be construed by any person as being anything but the highest endorsement of its continuance."[108]

The Report mentioned that "there has been a recent addition to the Court," because of the death of one of its three original members. Homer Ferguson had observed the House Subcommittee hearings, but participated neither in them nor in the sessions held by the Legion. He cannot, however, have been unaware of the comments offered concerning the tribunal he had now joined. His presence, according to the Legion, led to the hope that "time will congeal the legal rationale of the Judges . . . and that further years of experience with the Code will furnish decisions which are less likely to raise objections. . . ."[109] The accuracy of this prediction remained to be seen.

[106] Legion Report, 35.

[107] Ibid., 35–36.

[108] Ibid., 37. Indeed, the Legion proposed that contrary to the preference of its judges, USCMA should be given the added authority to weigh evidence, rule on matters of fact, and judge the credibility of witnesses, as could the lower Boards (now Courts) of Military Review. Furthermore, jurisdiction over these tribunals should be taken from the JAGs, and relocated in the office of the Secretary of Defense. Another recommendation provided that the JAGs should "be removed forever from the chain of command and no longer be subject to the influence of any officer, superior or otherwise." Ibid., 54–55.

[109] Ibid., 37.

3. Judges Ferguson, Quinn, and Kilday

CHAPTER 6

Congress Delays, Jurists Disagree, Judge Departs 1957–1961

THE PERIOD of Court history discussed in this chapter reveals several developments that often occurred simultaneously. An obvious realignment of judges took place, with significant results for military appellate justice. Examination of numerous USCMA decisions during the first five years of the Court's history indicates a sense of common purpose among its first three Judges. Perhaps because they had been together from the earliest beginnings of the Court, and possibly because they tended to seek consensus as they interpreted the UCMJ, for the most part disagreements between Brosman, Quinn, and Latimer were couched in relatively cool language. Dissents were concerned more with specific means to reach the goals mandated by the UCMJ, rather than with the end results. Further, while uncomfortable with Quinn's frequent absences from Washington, Latimer had accustomed himself to them—possibly because of his very frequent contacts with Brosman, his neighbor as well as colleague.

All this shifted with Brosman's unexpected death in December 1955, and the appointment of a new judge. Homer Ferguson's arrival brought subtle but profound changes to the pattern of decision-making, as well as the interrelationship among the three jurists; a transition not made any easier by Quinn's illness for about four months during the fall and winter of 1956–57.[1] More frequently than in the Brosman era, the Chief Judge provided the pivotal vote in a number of cases—choosing between the conflicting views of Ferguson and Latimer. On some occasions he sided with Latimer, leaving Ferguson to dissent—a practice the new judge apparently exercised more often than had Brosman. Infrequently he dissented, in disagreement with both Ferguson and Latimer. More often, however, Quinn joined with his new colleague, leaving Latimer alone.

By 1960, Latimer's dissents had sharpened in tone, reflecting an increased sense of judicial isolation and frustration. These feelings may well have been

[1] Early in 1957, Proulx stated that medication prescribed for Quinn's high blood pressure had affected him adversely, bringing on "an anxiety state, which will take time for him to shake off." Later, he added that the Chief Judge had not been able "to shake off his depressive state during the past four months." Finally, in March 1957, Proulx was able to inform Mrs. Paul Brosman that after shock therapy, Quinn had "completely snapped out of his anxiety state. . . . [B]elieve me, he is the Governor of old. . . ." 7 CF, January 10, 25; March 6, 19, 1957.

exacerbated by Latimer's inability both to become Chief Judge after Eisenhower's reelection in 1956, and to gain reappointment in 1961. Also, apparently Latimer found it difficult to accept Ferguson as a colleague, possibly because of the latter's utter lack of exposure to a military environment.[2]

The year 1956 had ended with continued uncertainty in the face of congressional inaction on two matters of concern to the Court—proposed changes to the UCMJ, and the question of life tenure for the USCMA judges. Finally, the tensions between judges and JAGs that had appeared to lessen during 1956–58, increased again in 1960—resulting in yet another effort by the military to alter the Court's jurisdiction. JAG irritation over several USCMA decisions contributed to this development, and while unhappy with it, at the same time Latimer found himself joining them in vigorous criticism of an expanded activism for the Court as charted by his colleagues—one that was, in Latimer's view, way off course.

CONGRESSIONAL INACTION

In 1956, Quinn and Latimer had been optimistic that the House Armed Services Subcommittee would support their efforts to block some of the proposed amendments to the UCMJ, despite the fact that these changes had the backing of the Defense Department as well as all the Service JAGs. Apart from the JAGs themselves, there appeared little enthusiasm to curb access to the Court. Even the *Navy Times* observed that one so inclined "must be suspected of being less interested in workable justice than in a return to unbridled authority and its too-frequent injustices."[3] As for life tenure, while the Defense Department bill did not address this issue, Quinn had spoken to the Subcommittee chairman, Congressman Overton Brooks, and "received assurances that everything will be done to include the life tenure provision."[4]

But the Subcommittee—and ultimately Congress—had adjourned without any consideration of life tenure, let alone reporting out the proposed amendments. The fact that 1956 was an election year with the resulting congressional desire to leave Washington for campaigning, plus the public interest occasioned by the accidental drowning of six young marine recruits at Parris Island, may have lessened the subcommittee's concern with disagreements

[2] One of Latimer's sons recalled that his father felt that Ferguson "was neither a qualified jurist, nor one with military experience." Latimer believed that Ferguson failed on both counts. Interview, George Latimer, Jr., July 20, 1989, 15.

[3] *Navy Times* editorial, April 21, 1956, in USCMAP, CCF.

[4] Ibid., March 19, 1956. On the other hand, less than one week later, Proulx noted for the record that Carl Vinson, the chairman of the full Committee, would not commit himself to support life tenure, saying merely that it could be discussed after the Subcommittee had reported on the bill. Ibid., March 24, 1956.

over suggested changes to the Code.[5] Despite this setback, Proulx believed that "the foundation has been laid and I feel sure that results will be had in the forthcoming session of Congress."[6]

One reason for Proulx's optimism was an informal understanding between JAGs and Judges that "everything should be done to eliminate the normal procedure of having a proposed bill go through the channels of the Bureau of the Budget and the Department of Justice for their comments."[7] More important, both parties now agreed that the new draft would be one from which "all controversial items have been eliminated, including those items which went beyond the 17 [original] recommendations."[8] On the other hand, the JAGs were not inclined to mention life tenure in the new bill. Because it had not been in the version considered in April 1956, they feared that its inclusion "would probably cause the Committee to refer the bill to the Bureau of the Budget and [Department of] Justice for views thereon." Before agreeing to support any of these changes, the judges decided that Tedrow would be asked "to analyze the proposed draft."[9]

Tedrow concluded that the new bill "seems to have omitted most of the things we found objectionable."[10] He took issue, however, with a proposed expansion of JAG authority to bypass Boards of Review in cases where the accused pleaded guilty. "There will be tremendous opposition to this both in and out of Congress." The lawmakers were not worried about the fact "that it may take time for a BR to review these cases." Rather, "they are only concerned with getting a thorough review for these draftees and inductees, [and] in any event they know what a time waster the military is." The Judges should realize, Tedrow concluded, that "as a practical matter [such a change] is a step backward toward centralized control by the JAG, one of the conditions that gave rise to the Uniform Code."[11]

Although, according to Proulx, the JAGs were "still insistent on removing the automatic review feature for guilty pleas," ultimately they accepted an-

[5] Ibid., excerpt from the Washington *Evening Star*, April 13, 1956. "The chances of amending the [UCMJ] on Capitol Hill also may be affected by the case. . . ."

[6] 6 CF, August 7, 1956. The *Navy Times* was concerned that delay in making Code changes that all sides had endorsed would play into the hands of those critics who sought more radical alteration. "The longer Congress puts off moderate changes needed to make the Code more workable, the more the enemies of the Code can denounce its shortcomings. Improving it with procedural changes might make it work so well [that] the opposition wouldn't have any ammunition left!" Excerpt in USCMAP, June 23, 1956.

[7] Ibid., January 17, 1957.

[8] Ibid., February 12, 1957. Indeed, it may have seemed to Proulx that the JAGs were sincere in their desire not to antagonize the judges. Besides deleting the noxious certification requirement, they also proposed restoration of the thirty-day period instead of their suggested reduction to fifteen days, in which to seek a grant of review from USCMA.

[9] Ibid. See also Proulx's letter to Chief Judge Quinn, 7 CF, February 14, 1957.

[10] USCMAP, Re: OSD Bill to Amend Code (1957), 1.

[11] Ibid., 3, 4.

alternative proposed by Judge Ferguson during a meeting on March 11, 1957. A review of a guilty plea by a BR would still be automatic "unless the accused states in writing that he does not wish to have his case reviewed by a Board of Review." Proulx added that "it was thought best to leave the automatic feature in instead of having the accused indicate in writing that he wanted a review."[12] As if to indicate their agreement, JAGs and Judges decided to include the text of the proposed "new" Code changes as part of their joint annual report for 1956.

Promptly reintroduced into Congress, the amendments languished. "My optimism for hearings this year," claimed Proulx, "is waning—it looks more and more now that the . . . Committee will not tackle the changes until the next session of Congress."[13] He predicted that Congress would not act on the amendments until 1958. In February 1958, Proulx had to admit that "with other defense legislation of priority nature under consideration, the prospects of action on our recommendations do not appear too bright, particularly in view of the fact that early adjournment customarily occurs in an election year."[14] Although the annual reports for 1956 through 1959 included drafts of the proposed legislation, in fact no major action by the lawmakers on military justice was enacted until after 1961. Proulx may have misjudged the episodic nature of the legislative process. Compared with 1949–50, there was no great consensus that changes in the UCMJ—only six years old—were urgent. Moreover, unified leadership concerning changes to the existing code proved to be a much more elusive goal than had been the case while preparing the UCMJ in the first place.

Further, examination of the separate JAG reports that were part of the annual military justice summary indicate that while the JAGs and judges had reached agreement on the Code amendments, the extent of agreement was somewhat less than Proulx had indicated earlier. The Army, for example, remained unhappy with the role of USCMA in military appellate justice. Judges and JAGs had urged adoption of the changes because they would be "beneficial to the sound administration and effectiveness" of the UCMJ. Yet the outgoing JAG of the Army, Major General Eugene Caffey, seemed more concerned with what the changes failed to address rather than with what they would accomplish.[15]

According to Caffey, some sections of the UCMJ "while burdensome in peacetime, could seriously impair the effective administration of military justice in time of war." Moreover, they "result in an excessive expenditure of

[12] 7 CF, March 11, 1957.

[13] Ibid., March 27, 1957. "I may be wrong but, as I said, hope is dwindling fast."

[14] 8 CF, February 28, 1958.

[15] In a letter to Proulx acknowledging receipt of the proposed amendments unanimously accepted by the Code Committee, Caffey commented that "the changes look good . . . as far as they go." 5 ARF, March 21, 1957.

time to process cases involving no substantial legal issues." Finally, commanders should be able to punish promptly, by ordering into execution sentences approved by Boards of Review, which in turn would be decentralized and relocated in Army areas throughout the United States, and other theaters of operations. Caffey envisaged a plan whereby death sentences that had been approved by a Board of Review "could be ordered into execution" by the appropriate commander. Under Caffey's proposals, there appeared to be no role for USCMA in this process except when the JAG might ask the Court to consider a case where Boards of Review disagreed over a matter of law.[16]

Although it was not mentioned in the 1956 Annual Report, another area of unresolved friction between USCMA and the Army concerned the offering of negotiated guilty pleas, a policy quite popular with this branch of the military. Judges and JAGs held a special meeting in May 1957 to discuss this issue—one that apparently split both groups. Strongly condemning the practice, Air Force JAG Reginald Harmon believed that "all hell will break loose if the program of negotiated pleas is continued, as it is now done in the Army."[17] He received support from Ferguson, while Latimer, along with the Army JAG, endorsed its use.

Trying to take a middle position, Quinn recognized that negotiated pleas were a part of civilian trial procedure, and thought the practice could be used within the military. However, he emphasized that the Court had a special obligation to see that the "system followed in the military is as fair as that in civilian life." Quinn added that this was a realm where his Court "probably may have fallen down on the job in the last two or three years." In a remark that may have sounded like bravado at the time, but which turned out to be prophetic, the Chief Judge warned the JAGs that USCMA "will reserve the right to take any remedial action if it turns out that evils are creeping into this area."[18]

LINGERING LONGING FOR LIFE TENURE

By 1957–58, Quinn had realized that while life tenure apparently was not a feasible objective, other changes in the law governing his Court might be more palatable to Congress.[19] Thus he wrote to Senator Pastore enclosing a proposed statute that did not give the judges life tenure. If, he noted, that

[16] Ibid., 5th Annual Report, 33–34.

[17] 7 CF, May 6, 1957, 2.

[18] Ibid., 2–4. For his part, Ferguson described negotiated pleas as "a very serious matter," and one with which he "was very much concerned." Ibid., 3.

[19] The earlier efforts to gain life tenure have been discussed supra, chapter 4. There seems little doubt that the judges, aided by Tedrow, had explored virtually every argument that could be advanced to justify this change. They saw no legal barrier to making USCMA an Article III

goal "seems impracticable now, the proposed amendment would help considerably."[20] Quinn's draft had three important provisions, and if life tenure could not be obtained, they would at least underscore the legitimacy of USCMA as a federal tribunal.

The proposal listed USCMA as a "court of record," and stipulated that its judges "shall be judges of the United States and shall be entitled to the same pay and shall have the same rights, powers, privileges, perquisites, and retirement benefits as judges of the United States Courts of Appeals." Quinn's draft also deleted the requirements that no more than two of the judges be from the same political party, and that each judge had to be either a member of the bar of a Federal Court or of the highest state court. Finally, USCMA "is authorized to appoint and fix compensation of such officers and employees as may be necessary to discharge its responsibilities without regard to Civil Service laws and regulations."[21]

Short and seemingly uncomplicated in scope, after April 1958, the draft was seen by the judges as a feasible alternative to life tenure. At a meeting with several Congressional staff members, the administrative assistant to Senator Richard Russell, longtime Chairman of the Armed Services Com-

---

tribunal, rather than its current status as an Article I court, a "legislative" tribunal. There was nothing sacrosanct in this designation. Tedrow informed Judge Ferguson that Congress had reestablished the Court of Claims under Article III, in response to a Supreme Court decision that this court was an Article I legislative Court—an action later affirmed by the High Court. See *Glidden Co., v. Zdanok*, 370 U.S. 530 (1962). If Congress could do this once, it could certainly do it again. Tedrow cited an additional reason for this conclusion. Article III courts exercise federal judicial authority as "to all controversies in which the United States shall be a party." In the Court of Claims, he added, "the United States is a party to all suits. . . . as a practical matter we can advance the same argument because the United States is a party to every case in this Court." LTF, December 18, 1957, 1.

[20] Ibid., January 28, 1968.

[21] Ibid. Quinn enclosed a copy of a memorandum he had prepared several years earlier on the same subject. He repeated his contention, for example, that the Court "is undoubtedly looked upon in some executive circles as a cross between an administrative agency, and a judicial entity," thereby raising doubts as to its authority to issue various writs common to the judicial function. In March 1958, however, Tedrow concluded that although life tenure might be highly desirable, it was not required in order for the Court to function as an independent judicial tribunal. He cited the United States Supreme Court decision in *United States v. Morgan*, which included a reference to Section 1651 of Title 28, USC; the "All Writs Act." That section provided that the High Court "and all courts established by Act of Congress may issue all writs necessary or appropriate in aid of their respective jurisdictions and agreeable to the usages and principles of law." 326 U.S. 502, 506 (1954). USCMA has not hesitated to issue extraordinary writs when deemed to be appropriate. See, for example, *Gale v. United States*, 17 USCMA 40 (1967); *United States v. Bevilacqua*, 18 USCMA 10 (1968); *McPhail v. United States*, 1 MJ 457 (1976); and cases cited in Fidell, *GUIDE*, 12–24. Moreover, thus far in USCMA history the Supreme Court apparently has not seen fit to differentiate USCMA authority in this regard from any other federal court, even though it has had several opportunities to do so.

mittee, indicated that this powerful Senator "was opposed to life tenure for any [federal] judge."[22] In view of "this opposition, which would be practically insurmountable," Quinn's bill seemed more feasible.[23] Working with David Martin, the legislative assistant to Massachusetts Senator Leverett Saltonstall, Quinn, Proulx, and Tedrow agreed that the bill would be presented to the Senate on a bipartisan basis.

Less than a week after this meeting with David Martin, Tedrow sent him a memorandum, explaining and clarifying some of the provisions in the proposed statute. Among other points he noted, correctly, that the political party provision was inappropriate for a federal court. Such a requirement "has always been limited to the administrative board or commission set-up." Similarly, the proviso concerning state or federal bar membership was also foreign, according to Tedrow, to federal courts—none of which had "any such comparable requirement."[24] Further, the bill would have eliminated existing presidential authority to remove a sitting USCMA judge. Tedrow observed, again correctly, that "elimination of this provision would put the Court in exactly the same situation as the Federal Circuit Courts."[25] Finally, Tedrow turned to the old issue of Civil Service coverage for Court employees.

He explained to Martin that one section of the bill did indeed authorize USCMA to "handle its personnel problems without regard to Civil Service." Tedrow added, however, that "no other Federal Court is subject to the requirements of Civil Service," a position that the Court had long maintained. "The present addition is to avoid all possible claims to the contrary."[26] Even as Tedrow wrote these words, this issue—unresolved since the Court's creation—was again provoking controversy.

On March 28, Judge Homer Ferguson asked the Attorney General about his court's "status under Civil Service," a question of "great interest to the Court in its judicial function."[27] We would appreciate it, he conconcluded, "if your Department would make a search of the law as to whether or not we are in fact under Civil Service." Ferguson's letter resulted in a fifteen-page memorandum to the Attorney General from Malcolm Wilkey, in the Justice Department's Office of Legal Counsel. Coming at a time when USCMA

[22] LTF, April 21, 1958. Russell's opposition was apparently based on his very critical reaction to recent decisions by Federal District Judges regarding school integration in the South, following the 1954 Supreme Court decision in *Brown v. Board of Education.*

[23] In 1958, Richard Russell's assistant was a young lawyer named William Darden. Ten years later, with Russell's enthusiastic endorsement, Lyndon Johnson appointed him to USCMA—not, it might be noted, with life tenure. See below, chapter 7.

[24] LTF, May 2, 1958.

[25] Ibid., 2.

[26] Ibid.

[27] Ibid., March 28, 1958. "I am sure it is the purpose of the Court to function as a court and not merely as a Department of the Services."

prepared to seek legislation on exactly this issue, Wilkey's missive—which resulted in no less than four responses from Tedrow, plus one from Ferguson on behalf of the Court—requires some analysis.

USCMA AND CIVIL SERVICE—ENVELOPING DARKNESS UNOBSCURED

Wilkey observed at the outset that the Court in his opinion "is subject to Civil Service," as it is in the executive rather than the judicial branch of government—a conclusion he assured his chief that "is certain to be controversial and subject to doubt." He added that "it may be preferable to consider the Court's request as a matter for legislative consideration, rather than a matter for authoritative determination by the Attorney General."[28] Wilkey next explored the legislative history of USCMA, being very selective in his choice of citation. His conclusion "that the Court is within the Executive Branch is based on the view that the Court is part of the system of courts-martial, which traditionally is an instrument for aiding the executive properly to command the armed forces."[29]

Wilkey went on to discuss a 1954 decision of the U.S. Court of Appeals for the District of Columbia Circuit, *Shaw v. United States*.[30] It involved a defendant in a court-martial who, upon being denied relief by USCMA, argued that the Federal Appeals Court was required by law to hear his case because USCMA was merely an administrative agency, whose rulings were inherently subject to federal appellate review. Since 1954, the unanimous decision in *Shaw* rejecting this argument had been widely cited by USCMA judges and staff as vindication of its claim to be a legitimate appellate tribunal. Nevertheless, Wilkey found the holding unpersuasive. The *Shaw* decision stated that USCMA

> with the entire hierarchy of tribunals which it heads, may perhaps be considered as being within the military establishment; perhaps, whether or not that is so, it is properly to be viewed as a specialized legislative court, comparable to the United States Court of Customs and Patent Appeals. But, in any view, [USCMA] appears to us to be a court in every significant respect, rather than an administrative agency. Certainly Congress intended that in its dignity and standards of administering justice the Court . . . should be assimilated to and equated with the established courts of the federal system.[31]

[28] USCMAP, Memorandum for the Attorney General, May 1958, 1. One wonders why after making this very valid point, Wilkey did not do what he considered "preferable," and just leave the question for congressional solution.

[29] Ibid.

[30] 209 F. 2d 311 (1954).

[31] Ibid., 313.

Although wrong to dismiss these words as "dictum," Wilkey had a point in claiming that they did not definitively resolve the question whether or not USCMA was within the military establishment. Certainly the words used by the Court indicated some doubt in the matter. For Wilkey, absent concrete proof to the contrary, the premise that the Court could be considered within the military led to the conclusion that because of the Executive's role as Commander in Chief, the Court was within the Executive branch—and thus subject to Civil Service.

Pointing to several examples of misquotation, Tedrow denounced Wilkey's statement as one that "contains so many inaccuracies, [and] misstatements," a document "apparently based on a basic misconception of our entire Constitution." He would be ashamed, Tedrow added, "to have my name on the [Justice] Department memo."[32] Within a week Tedrow had calmed down sufficiently to submit a revised version of his comments, one that in fact became the basis for a formal response by Ferguson on behalf of his colleagues to the Attorney General. As a practical matter, he wrote, "I consider the Justice memo over Wilkey's name as about as strong an argument as we could present to the Congress in support of any desired legislation."[33]

More important, Tedrow emphasized, it would seem correctly, that while Wilkey's memo was based on the traditional view of courts-martial, in fact "there is *no* legal basis for such view."[34] Unless the Court was prepared to demonstrate this fact, Tedrow feared that "any memo will degenerate into a mere 'it is, it is not' argument."[35] Apparently the judges agreed, because a letter to the Attorney General written by Ferguson utilized Tedrow's arguments, although they were couched in a much less confrontational tone.[36] In July, Quinn addressed a letter to the Chairman of the Civil Service Commission in which he asked him "to either rescind or reverse what we consider a rather hasty and erroneous holding."[37] But the Chief Judge was not very

[32] USCMAP, LTF, Memorandum to Ferguson from Tedrow, May 8, 1958, 1, 5. Tedrow submitted another memo four days later, and apparently he was still very angry. He detailed Wilkey's misstatements, particularly an unfortunate twisting of the words of Edmund Morgan about the evils of the "traditional view" of courts-martial. He rebutted comments made by Wilkey concerning the *Shaw* decision. "These things," he fumed, "make a memo that is merely bad become ridiculous. If Wilkey's shoestrings ever break during office hours, he will fall four floors." Memorandum, May 12, 1958, 2, 4.

[33] USCMAP, Memorandum to the Court, May 16, 1958.

[34] Ibid., emphasis in original.

[35] Ibid.

[36] Ibid., Memorandum for the Attorney General, May 20, 1958. The Judges may have found it disquieting that so many years after Samuel Ansell had, or so he thought, effectively rebutted any claim to validity for the "traditional" view of courts-martial, this view still attracted support from officials such as Wilkey. See AMJ, chapters 3–5.

[37] 8 CF, July 30, 1958. Quinn added that the Commission's ruling concerning USCMA "was ex parte in nature, the Commission apparently making the determination in a closed hearing without notice to the Court." One possible reason for the Court's vigor in pushing the Civil

optimistic, for most of the letter focused on the heavy burdens carried by Tedrow and Proulx, and urged that these two employees be given a very high Civil Service rating.[38]

In the meantime, the bill drafted by Quinn remained stuck in Senator Saltonstall's office, with Tedrow getting more and more restless. He saw David Martin rather than the Senator as the main stumbling block. With Saltonstall in the picture," Tedrow warned Ferguson, "we will have to forget about either Martin or the bill." He accused the assistant of "raising all kinds of objections (quibbles) [*sic*] about it."[39] When Martin finally sent a "revised" draft of the proposed legislation, the Chief Commissioner concluded that most of "this suggested Bill is either unnecessary or undesirable."[40] However, by the middle of July Tedrow came to believe that the problem might be less the assistant and more Senator Saltonstall himself.

He reminded Ferguson that Saltonstall had been the prime mover in the Senate Subcommittee to eliminate life tenure from the UCMJ chapter creating USCMA. The Massachusetts Republican had also supported very short terms of three, five, and seven years for the judges. Tedrow claimed that Saltonstall's overall attitude was "pro-military." Indeed, he concluded, "we may have placed ourselves in the hands of the enemy, or at least in the hands of one who is not completely in sympathy with the provisions and purposes of the [UCMJ].[41]

FERGUSON v. LATIMER

Of course, the main purpose and responsibility of USCMA was to review and decide cases raising serious issues of military justice. Even as it maneu-

---

Service issue may have been its sense that—as with the life tenure controversy—the tribunal was not being treated like other federal appellate courts.

[38] The Chief Judge may have been inconsistent here. In the same letter Quinn argued first that the CSC had made a mistake in claiming jurisdiction over the Court, and second that it should give Proulx and Tedrow extremely high Civil Service ratings—a position that may have reflected his assumption that ultimately the Commission would not retreat from its position. He was right.

[39] USCMAP, LTF, May 23, 1958. Tedrow urged Ferguson to take up the matter with Saltonstall personally, a suggestion he reiterated a month later when he reported "it hardly appears that the Bill is getting routine, let alone preferred, treatment." Ibid., June 19, 1958. Proulx had also commented that "knowing that Martin would not move on his own, Judge Ferguson was urged to contact Senator Saltonstall . . . The whole project sure calls for perseverance." 8 CF, May 1, 1958.

[40] Ibid., July 11, 1958. "We have now wasted about four months or more fooling with Martin."

[41] Ibid., July 15, 1958. Even when one makes proper allowance for Tedrow's attraction to conspiracy theories, his comments about Saltonstall merit some attention. There is no doubt that he was unenthusiastic about life tenure, and his attitude may have been more the norm rather than the exception. There is some doubt, moreover, as to how strongly Quinn's senatorial friends such as Green and Pastore actively pushed for any significant change in the status of USCMA beyond verbal assurances of support. To the present day, the Senate has yet to approve life tenure for this Court, to say nothing of the language Quinn had sought concerning the "rights, powers, privileges [and] perquisites" of its judges.

vered for the objectives discussed above, the Court exercised these functions. By 1958–59, it was clear that Ferguson's appointment had contributed to a significant expansion of judicial authority. There is no way to ascertain if its new activism specifically affected the chances for life tenure. There is no doubt, however, that this change split the Court and contributed to a new level of tension between Ferguson and Latimer, as well as between Judges and JAGs.

According to USCMA Reports, Homer Ferguson first participated in deciding USCMA cases on June 1, 1956. At the outset, it may have seemed to Latimer that the new judge would support him rather than Quinn in key interpretations of the Code. Thus in a case decided on August 31, Ferguson joined Latimer in reiterating the holding that certain due process provisions in the Bill of Rights did not apply to the military. Latimer announced that Ferguson had chosen to follow the precedent set down by Latimer and Brosman in the *Sutton* case, decided in 1953.[42] Any expectation, however, that Latimer could count on Ferguson for consistent support was very premature.

On the same day, for example, the Court reversed a conviction because the trial counsel (prosecutor) had referred to an instruction issued by the Secretary of the Navy. "Reasonable men," ruled Ferguson, must "conclude that once the Secretary of a service enters the restricted arena of the courtroom, whether the members of the court are conscious thereof or not, he is bound to exert some influence over them."[43] Although he concurred in this specific case, Latimer strongly rejected the idea that policy statements could not be called to the attention of court members "at the time they should be considered."[44]

Early in January 1957, Ferguson and Quinn again joined together to reverse a conviction for drug use based in part upon evidence that the commander had ordered the defendant to provide a urinalysis—something he had refused to do. The Court held that such an order was illegal under the Code, thus vitiating the resulting prosecution.[45] Latimer dissented, and warned that "if the sweep of the concurring opinion is as broad as it appears to me, then crime detection in the Services will be unnecessarily stifled."[46] The concurring opinion was written by Ferguson.

Another area of judicial change effected by a Ferguson-Quinn vote concerned adequate client representation by defense counsel. In *United States v.*

[42] *United States v. Parrish*, 7 USCMA 337, 342 (1956), reaffirming *United States v. Sutton*, 3 USCMA 220 (1953).

[43] *United States v. Fowle*, 7 USCMA 349 (1956).

[44] Ibid., 353. On the same issue, see also *United States v. Estrada*, 7 USCMA 635 (1957). Latimer again dissented, noting that "from this time on, policy letters on military justice have little, if any, value to the service. Perhaps the best solution would be to discontinue their promulgation." Ibid., 641.

[45] *United States v. Jordan*, 7 USCMA 452 (1957).

[46] Ibid., 460. See also *United States v. Butts*, 7 USCMA 472, 475 (1957), where Latimer accused the majority of erecting "a complex and confused legal structure out of a very simple issue."

Thornton, the accused was represented by a lawyer who had previously represented a key witness in this case—an individual who earlier had pleaded guilty during his own court-martial. Thornton argued on appeal that this "dual representation" deprived him of "the effective assistance of counsel."[47] Ferguson agreed. The legal "tightrope between safeguarding the interests of the accused . . . and retaining the prior confidences of [the witness] Field" was unacceptable. "Such a rope is too narrow. Such a walk is too long. The possibility of falling is too real. The probability of prejudicing the accused is too great."[48]

Latimer denounced his colleague's conclusion as one that "is, without doubt, based on the sheerest conjecture and speculation imaginable, for there is not the slightest shred of evidence in the record to support it."[49] As for Ferguson's comments on tightrope walking, "they are merely diversionary arguments." The position of counsel, added Latimer, "must be on a rope and not on the Chesapeake Bay Bridge. Here there is nothing to show any reasonable probability that the boundaries between the interests of the accused and retaining the confidence of Fields had narrowed to the thickness of hemp."[50]

Almost a decade before the United States Supreme Court had established rules of conduct to be followed when interrogating suspects in custody, Quinn and Ferguson had explored similar terrain. Another 1957 decision involved the refusal of the staff Judge Advocate to give any legal advice to the accused, as well as his orders that the staff decline "to advise the accused on pain of having their 'heads roll.'" Consequently, the defendant was not informed "of his right to have a lawyer of his own selection present to aid him during the questioning. . . ."[51] Latimer found the opinion inexplicable if not inexcusable.[52]

An issue closely related to this case involved the right to counsel during an Article 32 pretrial investigation, the military justice equivalent to a civilian grand jury. The UCMJ had provided safeguards for an accused that went beyond those normally found in grand juries. These included the right to be present during testimony, and to have counsel available to assist in cross

[47] 8 USCMA 57, 59 (1957).

[48] Ibid.

[49] Ibid., 62.

[50] Ibid., 65. An earlier indication of the Ferguson/Quinn position on effective representation by counsel is in *United States v. Lovett*, 7 USCMA 704 (1957).

[51] *United States v. Gunnels*, 8 USCMA 130, 135 (1957).

[52] "I can only hope this is an ad hoc decision, for it contains a number of principles which make for bad law and difficult administration." See ibid., 136, where Latimer listed at least seven errors in the majority's opinion. He concluded by referring to the Board of Review decision, "a fully and carefully developed opinion. . . . It is unmentioned and not followed by the Court, but I commend it to those readers who may be interested in determining its logic." Ibid., 137.

examination. The question raised in the case of *United States v. Tomaszewski* concerned the qualifications of counsel in this pretrial procedure. Quinn and Ferguson concluded that counsel in an Article 32 investigation had to have the same qualifications as those set forth for counsel in a general court-martial—that is, be a graduate of a law school and a practicing member of a state or federal bar.[53] It would defeat the purposes of such an investigation, in reality a sort of discovery process for the accused, "if a person unskilled in the requirements of proof, or knowledge of legal defenses, represents the accused."[54]

Latimer rejected this latest example of what seemed to be rampant judicial activism. Echoing a treasured theme in American constitutional interpretation, he insisted that had Congress wished to require the same qualifications for counsel in an Article 32 matter as in a general court-martial, the preference would be found in the words employed, and they were not there. Not only had Congress remained silent on this issue, but "the history of military law argues to the contrary."[55] Moreover, the majority failed to consider the implications of this new requirement in terms of costs to the military, and "we should not impose [it] in the absence of specific legislation."[56]

Given the Ferguson-Quinn objection to the introduction at trial of policy statements from a service official such as the Secretary of the Navy, a logical corollary would be their hostility to examination by the court members of the Manual for Courts-Martial for use in closed sessions deliberation. The judges struck down this practice in *United States v. Boswell.*[57] Ferguson noted an earlier holding that these individuals might not understand cases cited in the Manual, "and may well be confused by additional matter appearing in the text, not applicable to the case before them." In another previous decision, USCMA had held that it was "error for the court members to consult cases" mentioned by the law officer "for the purpose of determining for themselves what law should be applied to the case." Court members, emphasized Ferguson, should not "consult 'outside sources' for information on the law."[58]

[53] 8 USCMA 266 (1957). "The connection between the investigation and the trial itself is so close that we are of the opinion that Congress did not intend to differentiate between the two in regard to the qualifications of counsel appointed for the accused." The fact that the phrase "legally trained" or "legally competent" is found in one provision of the Code, but not in the section dealing with Article 32, made no difference. There was no evidence that Congress intended to let the word "counsel" apply to "a competent officer," rather than an attorney. Ibid., 268.

[54] Ibid., 268.

[55] Ibid., 270. "Our function is to interpret the law as Congress passed it, not to construe it to our own liking."

[56] Ibid., 272–73.

[57] 8 USCMA 145 (1957).

[58] Ibid., 148. "In that respect the Manual is no different from other legal authorities. It, too, has no place in the closed-session deliberations of the court-martial."

To an observer familiar with modern standards of due process, Ferguson's conclusions do not seem unusual. One would not expect a jury to be given cases to read and examine as they consider their verdict, comparing and contrasting these decisions with the instant dispute. Latimer's vehement reaction to this holding is startling, even decades later.[59] A majority of his Court, he wrote, "seizes upon this case as a foot-in-the-door method of laying down a far-reaching and devastating principle whereby it overturns the procedure used by all courts-martial since the adoption of the Code."[60]

If Latimer was correct in referring to one foot, Ferguson and Quinn positioned the other in the famous case of *United States v. Rinehart.* Here, Ferguson ruled that use of the MCM by members of a court-martial "during the course of the trial or while deliberating on findings and sentence [must] be completely discontinued. . . ."[61] We "cannot sanction," he emphasized, "a practice which permits members to rummage through a treatise on military law . . . indiscriminately rejecting and applying a myriad of principles—judicial and otherwise—contained therein. . . . All the law a court-martial need know in order to properly perform its functions must come from the law officer and nowhere else."[62] Ferguson made no bones about what this implied.

He traced the evolution of the Law Officer under the UCMJ. This individual had been fashioned "in the image of a civilian judge. . . . In a word, he was made a fountainhead of the law in the court-martial scheme of things." The various changes mandated by Code [and Court] were intended "to bring court-martial procedure, wherever possible, into conformity with that prevailing in civilian criminal courts. We believe that military justice under the Code has come of age and the time has come when the use of the Manual by the court-martial must end."[63]

[59] Latimer may well have feared that, given the usual absence of legal training among court-martial members, the majority's ruling would deprive them of a valuable and necessary tool—an assumption possibly based on his perception of basic differences between civilian and military justice systems. While he emphasized the differences, Quinn and Ferguson accentuated the similarities of the two. In general, USCMA history has followed Quinn and Ferguson, rather than Latimer.

[60] Ibid., 150. "It is hard to conjure up a comparable instance where such a well-established custom is buried with so little justification." See also pp. 152–53, where Latimer argues that his colleagues elevated form over substance, leading to "an acquittal clearly not intended by the court-martial."

[61] 8 USCMA 402, 410 (1957).

[62] Ibid., 406, 408.

[63] Ibid. The MCM was a product not of the Court but of the military, issued on behalf of the services by the President. The 1951 revision apparently included sections drafted in an effort to circumvent some of the new requirements set forth by the UCMJ, and by 1957–58, a number of its provisions had been declared unconstitutional. This fact may be one explanation in USCMA's unwillingness to permit continued use of the Manual. See the cases cited by Ferguson on p. 406. Proulx acknowledged that while the judges did not like having to choose

By late 1957, Latimer must have been well aware of the judicial currents being stirred by his brethren. He seems to have sensed also that *Rinehart* represented a watershed in military justice since the introduction of the UCMJ, and he deplored not only the results of the decision but the reasons that had produced them. Latimer objected to "trying to force military law into the exact image of civilian law, [and] this case is a good vehicle to illustrate the folly of disregarding all differences between the military and civilian practices."[64] Latimer saw no advantage in "forcing members of military courts to operate in darkness in areas where they must rule if we deny them access to the law that should guide them."[65] He concluded with what had become a familiar theme in his numerous dissents. "Whether we like the law or not, until it is changed by Congress, it should not be emasculated by us."[66] Latimer's increasing bitterness was reflected in his comment late in 1957 that while his associates considered *Rinehart* "as a worthy contribution to military law, I assert quite to the contrary. All I can say about [it] is that it fairly well establishes that the Court took an unnecessarily drastic measure when it threw away the Manual. . . ."[67]

The response by the JAGs to these decisions was more subtle and varied, especially when contrasted with the 1952–53 controversies discussed in a previous chapter. Late in 1957, some members of the Army JAG Government Appellate Division asked Proulx "if the Judges would object to the installation of a tape recorder during the course of their arguments. . . ." Proulx informed Chief Judge Quinn of the request adding that "I smell a rat and my guess is that they are seeking a recording of the questions from the bench. I feel sure that you will not approve. . . ."[68] The JAG of the Navy in

---

between the Code and the MCM, when they did the choice was not difficult. "The terms of the law cannot be defeated by the terms engrafted thereon by an Executive Order and, if the two are inconsistent, the statute must stand alone." 7 CF, November 26, 1957. *Rinehart* was handed down on November 15, 1957.

[64] 8 USCMA 402, 414.

[65] Ibid.

[66] Ibid., 415. For other cases reiterating *Rinehart*, see *United States v. Shaughnessy*, 8 USCMA 416, 420. Here, "we have the anomalous situation of a law officer instructing a court to disregard and ignore something it shouldn't see in the first place. We need scarcely say that such a practice is strikingly unsatisfactory." See also *United States v. Davis*, 8 USCMA 425; *United States v. Starnes*, 8 USCMA 427; and *United States v. McGirk*, 8 USCMA 429.

[67] *United States v. Elliott*, 8 USCMA 548, 550 (1957). Well aware that Ferguson had articulated the rationale for *Rinehart* and its progeny, Latimer seems to have become less than impressed with his colleague's approach toward military justice. Early in 1958, he wrote of a Ferguson opinion that it "graphically demonstrates that absurd results are obtained when the Court adheres to a rule which is unsupported by reason or logic. . . . Here we have a more useless application—if that is possible." *United States v. Gittens*, 8 USCMA 673, 674 (1958). The fact that Latimer apparently found his earlier objections to Ferguson's appointment justified may explain the harshness of his criticisms.

[68] 7 CF, November 26, 1957. Proulx may well have suspected that the tapes would be used

his annual report for 1957 cited several "landmark decisions" from USCMA. "While undoubtedly these decisions are a necessary implementation and interpretation of the law . . . they represent drastic departures from former thinking and doing."[69]

During the last meeting of the Code Committee in 1957, Army JAG Major General George Hickman, Jr., "suggested that a critical examination of the Code be conducted. . . ." He added that USCMA decisions have resulted in "sweeping changes in some areas beyond the intent the drafters of the Code had in mind." Hickman hastened to emphasize that "he was not criticizing the recent [*Rinehart*] decision of the Court." He noted further "that he will continue to be zealous of the rights of the accused." He proposed that a working subcommittee composed of representatives from all the services and the Court be created. It would function much as the original working group had operated in 1948–49 with Edmund Morgan's original code committee.[70] The judges agreed, the committee was formed, and its report essentially repeated what had already been recommended.

In the meantime, the Ferguson-Quinn "entente" showed little sign of weakening. Early in 1958, the Court reversed several decisions on the grounds of improper instructions given court members by the law officer, as well as inappropriate advice offered by the staff JAG to the Commander—who would normally place heavy reliance on it when approving or rejecting a court-martial verdict. In each case, Latimer dissented.[71] In one, he accused his brethren "of veering away from a very substantial body of law. . . . We have written a series of cases dealing with this subject which may be swept away without mention by this holding."[72] In the other, Latimer reiterated his objection to the sudden judicial condemnation of language employed by staff Judge Advocates "where the terms used had been in vogue for many years and we had affirmed hundreds of cases employing the same expressions. The language was stereotyped and the reviews just did not become misleading, confusing, or erroneous overnight."[73]

---

either to try to anticipate future rulings, or as "evidence" to show what the JAGs possibly viewed as inappropriate and unnecessary judicial extremes clearly demonstrated in some of the 1957 holdings. I could find no follow-up to Proulx's comments. However, for some years it has been routine to record all USCMA hearings. See also Fidell, *Guide*, 167–69.

[69] 6 ARF, Annual Report for 1957, 49.

[70] Ibid., December 11, 1957, 3.

[71] See *United States v. Morris*, 9 USCMA 37, and *United States v. Fields*, 9 USCMA 70.

[72] *Morris*, 38–39.

[73] *Fields*, 77. For other examples of Latimer's continuing disagreements with Ferguson and Quinn during the remainder of his term, see *United States v. Nowling*, 9 USCMA 100, 104 (1958); *United States v. Smith*, 9 USCMA 236, 239–40 (1958); *United States v. Minnifield*, 9 USCMA 373, 379–80 (1958)—"Zeal for liberalism should not be the vehicle by which the meaning of a word or phrase . . . is stretched beyond recognition." *United States v. Horne*, 9 USCMA 601, 606 (1958)—"This is simply a case of this Court . . . substituting its judgment of

Ascertaining the proper relationship between law and change represents an age-old judicial dilemma. How USCMA viewed its connection to the military environment, and how the judges viewed their role vis-à-vis JAG and Congress may well have affected their approach to these cases. With no military experience to draw upon, Ferguson brought a very different perspective than Latimer who had served in combat. On the other hand, when the bottom line is reached, neither logic, consistency, nor continued reliance on precedent determine the outcome as much as votes. Depending on the way one viewed USCMA's functions, one could support or reject Latimer's position. From a perspective of almost fifty years, the changes ratified by Ferguson and Quinn were appropriate.[74]

Latimer may have hoped that these decisions, rendered between 1957 and 1959, represented the limits to his colleagues' judicial changes. If so, he was sorely disappointed with two decisions that were handed down within his last year on the Court. In *United States v. Russo*, Ferguson ruled that both the convening authority and the Board of Review could mitigate the severity of a death penalty sentence, thereby overruling an earlier decision by Brosman and Latimer—"a result," Latimer wrote, "that I am constrained to decry. . . ."[75]

> I was hopeful that, in a field as critical as this, we would respect consistency, leave the law fixed, and rely on Congress to effectuate a change if it subsequently concluded that our construction was inappropriate. I was too credulous, for today's opinion sweeps the past aside, overturns a principle which has long been firmly imbedded in military law, refuses to follow prior decisions of this Court, and clothes two appellate agencies with power to impose an original sentence. . . . [T]he law is being changed because of Judge Ferguson's interpretation. No doubt he believes that he should undo the handicraft of Judge Brosman and the writer, but that position undercuts stability and offers comfort

trial tactics for those of defense counsel." *United States v. Kraskouskas*, 9 USCMA 607, 611 (1958), *United States v. Albright*, 9 USCMA 628, 635 (1958)—"It seems to me to be paradoxical for us to hold that [a staff JAG] forfeits his right to wear his judicial robe merely because he has previously worn the gown of an advisor. Certainly it remains for us to deal practically with the peculiarities of the military service and to cut our coat from the cloth furnished by Congress." *United States v. Haynes*, 9 USCMA 792, 797 (1958)—". . . it must be conceded that I am losing the battle on many fronts. . . ." *United States v. White*, 10 USCMA 63, 65–67 (1958); *United States v. Simpson*, 10 USCMA 229, 233–41 (1959); *United States v. Jobe*, 10 USCMA 276, 280 (1959); *United States v. Keeler*, 10 USCMA 319, 321–23 (1959); *United States v. May*, 10 USCMA 358, 366–71 (1959)—"By some method of reasoning, my associates reach a result which is contrary to the Code, the Manual . . . and other cases. . . ." *United States v. Sessions*, 10 USCMA 383, 389–97 (1959); *United States v. Brown*, 10 USCMA 482, 489–95 (1959).

[74] On the other hand, result oriented jurisprudence can always seem more palatable if one agrees with the results!

[75] *United States v. Russo*, 11 USCMA 352, 359 (1960).

> to those who assert that we are a court of men and not law. Certainly, if there is any merit to the doctrine of *stare decisis* and the argument that if Congress believes we misinterpret its enactment, the remedy is by corrective legislation, then this case is one of the best examples I can cite as a violation of those principles.[76]

Ferguson indirectly replied to Latimer in what may still be described as one of the "great" cases handed down during the Quinn era. It will be recalled that in *Sutton*, Quinn had insisted that all provisions in the Bill of Rights applied to members of the Armed Services unless excluded expressly or by necessary implication. It will further be recalled that shortly after Ferguson joined the bench, he had concurred with Latimer rejecting the Chief Judge's position.[77] By 1958, however, Ferguson had changed his mind.[78] He waited until 1960 to join Quinn in scuttling *Sutton*.

Ferguson conceded that in the *Parrish* case, he had accepted Latimer's viewpoint "out of respect to the former holdings of this Court." Now, "critical reexamination . . . in the light of the Constitution convinces me that we erred in so giving effect to the doctrine of *stare decisis*."[79] The doctrine might have its uses, but "it should never be applied in order to perpetuate a mistaken view."[80] He concluded that in a court-martial an accused had the right to be present along with counsel at the taking of written depositions concerning the case.[81]

In a dissent that is almost twice as long as Ferguson's opinion, Latimer rejected the reasoning, rationale, and results reached by his associate. While many of his points had already been made in previous dissents, Latimer implied that Ferguson either was unable or unwilling "to follow recognized and fundamental principles of constitutional law."[82] More important, "in this instance, not unlike some others, my associates warp the Code to make mili-

[76] Ibid., 359.

[77] See 3 USCMA 220, and 7 USCMA 337.

[78] *United States v. Ivory*, 9 USCMA 516 (1958). "[I]t cannot be contended that a man who joins our armed forces and offers his person to fight for the Constitution and the institutions predicated thereon forfeits the fundamental guarantees granted to citizens generally, except those excluded by the Constitution expressly or by necessary implication. . . ." Ibid., 523.

[79] *United States v. Jacoby*, 11 USCMA 428, 430 (1960).

[80] Ibid. Ferguson could have stopped there. Instead, and possibly to make the point very clear to Latimer, he added: "Indeed, it is our duty to overrule and modify decisions which are erroneous, although there has been no legislative change in the law as originally construed." In other words, changes in the statute were unnecessary to justify USCMA's new holding, because Latimer had been wrong.

[81] Ibid., 433.

[82] Ibid., 434. Latimer's dissents reveal a thoroughness in exploration of doctrine and case law that one sometimes finds lacking in Ferguson and Quinn. Given this predilection, he may have found their apparent ability to reach a desired judicial result by ignoring other factors—such as precedent—as offensive as their ultimate conclusions.

tary law on all fours with civilian law. It is impossible to take the military out of military law, and . . . there is a fundamental distinction between the two[,] and recognition ought to be given by this Court to the differences." Ferguson and Quinn "should recognize that we are faced with issues which must be measured with regard to the necessities of the services and that a yardstick of civilian standards will lead us to false conclusions." Depending on one's viewpoint, Latimer may have had logic on his side but not the votes.[83]

Implicit in Latimer's words, of course, is the crux of the challenge facing a civilian court and code operating in a military environment. How the Court responded to it during the three decades since he left the bench is a matter of debate. This author believes that for all of Latimer's concerns—which any appellate tribunal ought to keep in mind—USCMA has unquestionably helped rather than hindered military justice. While Latimer feared it was doing too much, the point can be raised with at least equal vigor that it was not doing enough.

MORE CONGRESSIONAL CONVOLUTIONS

By 1959, changes to the UCMJ had yet to materilize, even though nine years had passed since the statute had been enacted. The JAGs and Judges still supported the original seventeen recommendations. Two outside groups, the American Legion and the District of Columbia Bar Association Committee on Military law, now added their views in the form of proposed amendments to the Code. Finally, Chief Judge Quinn apparently abandoning efforts to work with Saltonstall's office, turned to his old friend Congressman Philip Philbin, who agreed to submit the draft as originally prepared by Quinn and Tedrow. Both the Legion's reforms and Philbin's bill were introduced into Congress early in 1959, along with the latest version of the Defense Department draft.[84]

The Legion bill reflected some concerns raised during its hearings three years before. Two provisions are of special interest concerning appellate military justice. The Legion proposed that board of reviews be established by the Secretary of Defense, rather than the service JAGs. Further, USCMA could "affirm such findings . . . as it finds correct in law and fact. . . . In considering the record, it may weigh the evidence, judge the credibility of witnesses, and determine controverted questions of fact, recognizing that the trial court saw and heard the witnesses."[85]

[83] Ibid., 441–42.

[84] The details of Quinn's measure, reiterated in Philbin's draft, HR 4040, have been discussed above. On the similarities between Philbin's draft and the stalled Saltonstall measure, see Tedrow's Memorandum to Ferguson in USCMAP, June 26, 1959.

[85] USCMAP, 86th Cong., 1st sess., HR 3455, 9–10.

Although sympathetic in principle to many of the goals sought by the Legion legislation, Richard Tedrow objected to giving his court fact-finding power. Not only would it create "a tremendous and unnecessary workload[, but] if a BR [Board of Review] is a true independent fact-finding body this item is unnecessary."[86] Possibly aware of the reasons why BRs rather than USCMA originally had been given fact-finding authority, Quinn had opposed it for his court as early as 1952.[87]

A former USCMA commissioner writing to Tedrow also had reservations about the Legion's amendments for boards of review. Zeigel Neff urged that BRs should be composed of civilian lawyers, rather than military officers as had been predominantly the case. Under the UCMJ, JAGs could appoint civilians to BRs but rarely did so. Moreover, Neff urged that BRs should be known as "Courts of Review."[88] This "would emphasize the judicial character of the position and enable the board members to mentally separate themselves from the military. It would encourage them to become judges first, officers second."[89]

The D.C. Bar Association's revisions for the UCMJ were the work of Father Joseph Snee, a faculty member at the Georgetown University School of Law. Obviously influenced by USCMA history during its first decade, Snee proposed that the court be expanded to five judges, with life tenure and all the usual perquisites, powers, etc., common to federal appellate judges. They could also hire and establish salaries for their employees, including commissioners. Moreover, the USCMA Chief Judge would join his federal counterparts as a member of the Judicial Conference of the United States, an

[86] USCMAP, CLF, November 14, 1958. Tedrow reminded Quinn that the move to place appointment of BRs within the Secretary of Defense's Office "is highly controversial and will be bitterly opposed by the military . . . I am for anything that will strengthen the independence of BRs, if this is what is required I am for it." He further blasted the military for the time and effort "spent in attacking and circumventing the Code and trying to nullify it by amendments and otherwise. Their attitude denotes bad faith. It also indicates a little bit of stupidity because every Congressional pronouncement on the subject . . . show[s] that they do not have a prayer to repeal the Code or even modify it in any substantial extent." Ibid., 2. Tedrow proved to be a good prophet. With the exception of a limited increase in an officer's authority to impose nonjudicial punishment, no major changes in the UCMJ were adopted for another ten years.

[87] See AMJ, chapters 8–9. The Defense Department, as might be expected, opposed the Legion Bill, claiming that it would not "in any material respect, add to the safeguards presently available to accused persons under the Uniform Code. . . ." See memorandum to the Chairman of the House Armed Services Committee, April 11, 1959, in Kilday Papers [hereafter cited as KP], 2E 420; File P. J. Kilday, Chairman.

[88] USCMAP, undated memorandum from Neff to Tedrow. In 1968, the name was changed to the Court of Military Review, and currently they are called the Court of Criminal Appeals.

[89] Anxious to be named to the Court he had once served, in 1961 Neff apparently received serious consideration from the Kennedy administration. In fact, only once has a former USCMA commissioner become one of its judges. See below, chapter 11, where the appointment of Robinson O. Everett to the Court in 1980 is discussed in detail.

indication that USCMA was like any other federal appellate tribunal. Snee did not propose to enlarge the Court's jurisdiction beyond matters of law, but added that USCMA "may for good cause and on its own motion consider any issue of law raised by the record."[90]

Quinn sent copies of Snee's draft both to Edmund Morgan, teaching law at Vanderbilt University, and New York attorney Whitney North Seymour—still the chairman of Quinn's civilian Court committee, quiescent since the mid-1950s. Morgan endorsed Snee's revisions, although he told Quinn that "I haven't been following the work of the Court closely."[91] In response to Quinn's request that Seymour convene his committee to discuss and presumably endorse the amendments, Seymour reported "the general impression [is] that it is not very likely that anything will be done in the near future."[92] A month later, after the American Bar Association meeting, Seymour wrote again to Quinn that "there is little, if any, chance of Congress giving serious attention to Father Snee's proposed redraft. . . ."[93] Seymour might have also included the American Legion bill, the Department of Defense resubmission of the old amendments, and Philbin's draft. All suffered the same fate, and this in spite of rumors to the effect that major congressional review of the UCMJ was imminent.

On February 7, 1959, the *Navy Times* had reported that "action is promised" on Code amendments. The writer, however, may have hit upon the reason for the total lack of change thus far. It "is probably evidence of the basic soundness of the Code. For, if there were fundamental defects, the pressure on Congress to act long before this would have been irresistible."[94] On the other hand, within a few weeks Proulx noted that a new House Armed Services Subcommittee had been established to hold hearings on the UCMJ, to be chaired by Paul J. Kilday, Democratic Congressman from Texas.[95]

[90] USCMAP, Proposed Revision UCMJ and Rules of Military Criminal Procedure (1960), 33, 36. Snee provided a brief description of his changes in a letter to Paul Kilday. See KP, November 23, 1959.

[91] CCF, January 7, 8, 1960.

[92] CCC, February 11, 1960.

[93] Ibid., March 14, 1960. Under these circumstances, Quinn decided to postpone any reconvening of the court committee.

[94] USCMAP, editorial, *Navy Times*, February 7, 1959. The editorial further noted that there are those who would tighten the Code "mainly by curbing the power of [USCMA]." Ferguson's arrival may be what the writer had in mind when he added that "the Court has embarked on a program of making military justice more and more like civilian justice." The solution, however, was not to curb the Court, but "rather for Congress to spell out more clearly the differences there should be between military and civilian trial processes. . . ."

[95] 9 CF, February 24, 1959. In June, Proulx wrote that the Kilday subcommittee had put off hearings until "next session." Ibid., June 8, 1959. A member of Congress since 1939, Kilday had looked forward to becoming reacquainted with military justice. "I have become very rusty," he wrote to an official of the American legion. "Because this is a large undertaking, I felt it to be necessary that I refresh myself as to the provisions of the Code. . . . It is customary for me to

JAGS v. JUDGES

The JAGs had observed the Ferguson-Quinn "revolution" with concern if not anger. In his report for 1958, the Army JAG briefly described eleven recent USCMA decisions. "In many instances, these sharp departures from previous military practice have created difficult problems for military law enforcement authorities. In order to correct some of these deficiencies, proposed remedial legislation is under study."[96] What that service had in mind became clear in the Army JAG's 1959 Report.

Major General Hickman noted "an increasing lack of confidence in the present system of military justice because of its growing complexity and difficulty of administration." Complaints from the field, he added, "indicate a growing concern over lack of stability in the law. . . ."[97] Hickman reported that the Secretary of the Army had appointed a board of general officers "to study the present system of military justice and its impact on the administration of discipline in the Army as well as the essential fairness of the [UCMJ] both to the accused and to the Government."[98] He cited eight additional USCMA decisions, and quoted from two of Latimer's dissents.[99]

The Powell Report, named for the board's chairman, General Herbert Powell, managed to be perceptive, partisan, provocative, and in two instances prophetic. Its recommendations that a court-martial could be conducted by a law officer sitting alone, and that the court be expanded to a five-member tribunal ultimately became law.[100] But the suggestion was couched in such terms as to ill-conceal the Army's animus toward the Court.

---

prepare for hearings on important legislation." KP, September 28, 1959. Early in 1960, Quinn wrote to Seymour that Kilday had scheduled the hearings for March. "Of course it's possible that, with [an] election year approaching, the Committee won't be able to take up the matter until 1961. You know what Congressional Committees are." 10 CF, February 18, 1960. Actually, Kilday never presided over hearings on the UCMJ, but his involvement with military justice was far from over.

[96] ARF 1958, 45. Of the eleven cases cited, Latimer dissented in all but one. There, he concurred only because the law had become fixed, in spite of his dissents.

[97] 1960 ARF, 43.

[98] Ibid. Hickman anticipated that the findings of this board "should be of considerable value in determining the need for remedial legislation in addition to the proposed changes. . . ." On the other hand, Hickman was not alone in calling for additional changes. The USCMA judges in their section of the 1959 Report proposed that BRs should be consolidated under the Secretary of Defense and termed Military Courts of Review. Ibid., 35. They also accused the Civil Service Commission of interfering in USCMA matters. "We . . . are not subject to them in any way, and . . . no court can be a court in the full sense of the word if any Executive Agency can interfere in its affairs." Ibid., 36.

[99] Of the eight new cases cited in the 1959 report, Latimer had dissented in all but one.

[100] USCAMAP, Powell Report, January 18, 1960. See also Frederick Bernays Wiener, "American Military Law in the Light of the First Mutiny Act's Tricentennial," *Military Law Review* 126 (1989) 1–88, 44.

The Report claimed that a three-judge court "is not sufficiently conducive to stable procedures and consistent administration of justice." Moreover, the replacement of Brosman by Ferguson "has caused a dramatic reversal in the law. A five-judge court would be much less susceptible to fluctuation."[101] The two additional judges, however, would not be civilians, but rather would be selected from a pool of military officers with at least fifteen consecutive years on duty in a JAG division. They would serve four-year terms and, unlike their three civilian counterparts, would not be eligible for reappointment. The intent was that "there would always be one judge not more than two years removed from military experience."[102]

In his 1960 report, General Hickman noted "some twenty-five or thirty judicial decisions that . . . Army lawyers believe substantially hamper the operation of the Army."[103] He also reverted to earlier complaints, claiming that the 1960 *Jacoby* case "has resulted in time-consuming delays in trials, undue expense to the government, as well as dismissal of charges for economic reasons." General Hickman, who had been a member of the Powell Board, urged that the Defense Department bill be withdrawn, and that the Powell Report's legislative proposals be adopted.[104]

The USCMA Judges refused to join a joint report with the Service JAGs, and denounced some Powell suggestions. "The Court is appalled by the proposals contained therein." To adopt them would be to return military justice to the conditions that had spawned both the UCMJ and the Court itself. In fact, the "difficulties experienced by the military . . . since the inception of the Code have resulted from their own attempts to revert to 'the old system' through manipulations of the [MCM], and departmental regulations." Close "scrutiny of all practices thereby introduced must be maintained."[105]

Wiener aptly described the Powell proposed USCMA expansion as "a court-packing plan more crass and more blatant" than the one urged upon the country by President Roosevelt in 1937. It is a pity, he added, that no member of the committee "possessed a sufficient sense of history to be aware of that damning analogy."[106] If the Army had hoped to bring about any

[101] Powell Report, 194. Notoriously absent were the references to numerous delays in appellate justice, the expense of the system, etc., so typical of earlier JAG attacks on USCMA. Of course, it is hard to complain about expense when one proposes to add two new judges to an existing court.

[102] Ibid., 194, 198.

[103] 1960 ARF, Army JAG Report, 4.

[104] Ibid., 6–7. Significantly, in their 1960 Reports none of the other services endorsed the Powell proposals.

[105] 1960 ARF, USCMA Judges Report, 4, 10. Probably inspired by the Powell Report, the 1960 summary by the USCMA Judges was the longest thus far in the Court's history, and contains a useful summary of major cases decided between 1951 and 1960—as well as a cogent and at times eloquent justification for the Court's existence.

[106] Wiener, 46.

changes in the UCMJ as a result of the Powell Report, "approved glowingly" by Army Secretary Wilbur Brucker, it was disappointed.[107] Moreover, it was about to lose its staunchest supporter among the USCMA Judges.

"SENATOR" QUINN AND "CITIZEN" LATIMER

It will be recalled that one of the reasons Quinn had insisted that he remain in Providence was his hope that he might yet be able to win election as a Senator from Rhode Island. Senator Pastore showed no inclination to retire, but in 1960, Senator Green decided to step down. After some consideration, Quinn's close friend Congressman John Fogarty determined to seek an 11th term in Congress. Thus in April 1960—even as USCMA was dealing with the Powell Report—a senate race appeared wide open, and a number of potential senatorial candidates were identified by the Rhode Island press. One of them was, of course, Chief Judge Quinn. Now sixty-six years old, the former governor responded to a request that he comment on his political plans. "I am not a candidate . . . but I am available if the party is interested in me. I am at the command of the Democratic Party."[108]

Old political operative that he was, Quinn did more than just respond to the newspapers. He prepared a short statement to be available to the forthcoming meeting of the state Democratic Committee. For nine years he had served as Chief Judge, protecting "the rights, the liberties and the honor" of members of the Armed Forces, "the guardians of our liberties and our first line of defense against a ruthless and implacable foe—the Communist Conspiracy." Again, Quinn denied that he was anxious to relinquish "that very important job." In truth, Quinn had been prepared to relinquish it ever since he took the post, were an opportunity to run proffered him. Now, "if after careful consideration," party leaders concluded that "my energies and talents are of greater value to the State and Nation in the . . . Senate, I am ready and willing to stand for election in November."[109]

The Quinn candidacy, observed Proulx, would go forward only if the Judge was endorsed by the state Democratic committee. "Otherwise, I do not believe he will enter the primary contest. No one to date has ever been able to beat an endorsed candidate, largely due to the manner in which the names

[107] USCMAP, 1960 ARF, excerpt from *Washington Post*, May 18, 1961. The annual reports normally appeared in the early spring of the following year. Hence the 1960 report was not distributed until May 1961.

[108] QPPC, clipping from *Providence Journal*, April 10, 1960. Another potential candidate was Quinn's old rival and benefactor, J. Howard McGrath, who had been dismissed as Attorney General by President Truman in 1952.

[109] Ibid. On July 26, 1960, the *Woonsocket Call* reported that Quinn had filed a formal declaration of candidacy.

of the candidates appear on the primary ballot."[110] Proulx was both right and wrong. Denied the endorsement, Quinn declined to run. But the winner of the primary and later the election, Claiborne Pell, had also failed to gain endorsement.

While Quinn was willing to leave, Latimer was eager to stay. By December 1960, he began a belated effort to gain reappointment. There is little doubt that of all the USCMA judges thus far, Latimer was the least political. He had little interest in politics, and assumed that if he was performing appropriately, he would be reappointed. In retrospect, this may have been very poor judgment on Latimer's part, given his aggressive candidacy for the post in 1950. Also, as of 1960 no USCMA Judge had ever been reappointed. On the other hand, he had served with devotion and dedication. Moreover, his opinions reflected a thoughtfulness and depth sometimes lacking in decisions handed down by his brethren. Nevertheless, by December 1960 Latimer appeared to be from the wrong party, seeking a choice appointment at the wrong time from the wrong administration.

He sought support from Felix Larkin, former General Counsel of the Defense Department, "without knowledge of your political affiliation."[111] Larkin responded favorably with a comment "that your services to the Court have been in the finest tradition of the American judiciary." Although himself a Democrat, "I would certainly hope that the political requirements of the [UCMJ] would not prevent your reappointment."[112] Despite this hope, with a Democrat and a Republican already on the Court and with a new Democratic administration taking office, Latimer had little chance. When his term expired on May 1, he still had heard nothing concerning either his replacement or reappointment. "The lapse of time," he wrote to Larkin, "leads me to believe that my chances are remote."[113] And so they were.

Latimer was the first USCMA judge to go into retirement, in his case involuntarily. His record seems to have been a mixed one. Especially in his early years, he contributed to important doctrinal interpretations of the UCMJ. His last three years on the bench, however, found Latimer more and more unhappy not only at the pace of change from his colleagues, but with some of the changes themselves. The debate over the relative importance of *stare decisis* in appellate jurisprudence will never be settled. It is true, however, that the holdings that so disturbed him remain good law, and while Congress would in the future overrule USCMA decisions by statute, it would not be based on those decisions that he decried.[114] As Latimer prepared to

[110] 10 CF, July 26, 1960.

[111] LP, December 14, 1960.

[112] Ibid., March 1, 1961. Larkin wrote letters of endorsement to Robert Kennedy, as well as Robert McNamara.

[113] Ibid., May 13, 1961.

[114] See below, chapters 10–11. Latimer has one other claim to distinction. Among all the

return to Salt Lake City, interest centered less on his accomplishments than on his successor. By early June, Quinn and Ferguson were still waiting.

---

former USCMA judges, he is the only one who returned as attorney of record, and argued several cases before his old Court, where Robert Quinn still sat. Latimer's most famous case was probably that of Lieutenant William Calley, who was held responsible for the My Lai "massacre" of civilians during the Vietnam War. See below.

CHAPTER 7

Assessing Military Justice, Attempting Life Tenure, Attaining Reappointment, 1961–1966

DURING the spring of 1961, Quinn renewed his efforts to gain life tenure for members of his court. By now, the arguments for such a change repeatedly had been presented and explained to his friends in Congress, with concise regularity but no concrete results. Apparently his latest efforts were complicated by the delay in selecting Latimer's replacement, the issue of possible conflicts between life tenure and presidential appointment power, and the fate of the incumbents. On March 9, Proulx had observed that the Court "regardless of the incumbents, should have life tenure as a matter of prestige and to remove any and all doubt as to its status as a full-fledged Federal Court."[1] Here, Proulx recognized that ten years after the Court began to operate, this issue was separate from the fate of the incumbent judges, and that gaining the one without the other might be a realistic alternative. He had already received what he took to be a definitive indication that Latimer would not be reappointed, and promptly notified Quinn.

A NEW JUDGE

Proulx had learned "that Judge Latimer had seen the President . . . regarding his reappointment." Such news surprised neither Proulx nor Quinn, who knew that Latimer had been increasingly active in his efforts to retain his seat. More important was Proulx's discovery that Texas Congressman Paul J. Kilday "was [also] seeking the appointment and had Congressman Vinson [chairman of the House Armed Services Committee] personally see the President on his behalf." Quinn immediately urged Proulx to contact Rhode Island Congressman John Fogarty, asking that he speak to Vinson not only to express Fogarty's continued support for life tenure, but also because Quinn had his own candidate to replace Latimer.[2] But, according to Proulx, Vinson

[1] 11 CF, March 9, 1961. Lurking behind these two problems was also the potential for legislative interference with the appointment authority of the chief executive. As will be seen shortly, Chief Judge Quinn saw little difficulty here.

[2] Ibid. As early as November 1960, Quinn had indicated his strong support for former Court Commissioner Zeigel Neff as Latimer's replacement. See QPC, November 16, 1960, where Neff wrote to Quinn "I appreciate your encouragement more than words can tell."

had made it clear to Fogarty that "he had a candidate much closer to him." This was the number two member of his own committee, Paul Kilday.[3]

By May 1, Latimer's term had officially ended, thus temporarily reducing USCMA to a two-member Court. While, according to Proulx, Latimer "has not given up hope[,] the realities of politics being what they are, the fact that word was not received before the expiration of his term, I would have to say that his chances grow dimmer every day."[4] When Kilday's appointment was finally announced in June, it came more as a finale to what had become a foregone conclusion.[5] In his quest for reappointment, Latimer was supported by the armed services but not his two colleagues.[6] Yet, as he himself realized, given the time and political context, reappointment was too much to expect.

Kilday informed the Court that he did not plan to join his new brethren until the fall. Whether or not Quinn realized that lobbying for life tenure with a congressman soon to be a judge on the very court to which this change would apply might be questionable, he did not hesitate. Very shortly after Kilday's appointment was announced, Quinn and Proulx visited the

[3] Ibid., March 14, April 12, 1961. First elected to Congress in 1938, Kilday had continuously served on the House Armed Services Committee since 1939. Although deeply interested and involved in military affairs, he had not been part of the subcommittee that drafted the UCMJ, and had no direct experience with the administration of military justice. On the other hand, he consistently supported both Court and Code, and over the years Kilday had apparently gained the confidence of senior military officials. After his appointment to the Court was announced, an Air Force general wrote, "I know that we have never had, and never will have, a better representative on [USCMA,]" while a Navy JAG noted "your demonstrated ability to hold the services 'at bay' in their repeated efforts to amend the code virtually out of existence and into the limbo of the last century." Kilday Papers, June 23, 26, 1961.

[4] 11 CF, May 5, 1961. While Proulx had to have been aware of Kilday's interest in the new appointment, he still believed that Neff "has the inside track." Ten days later, he informed Quinn that "Ziggy tells me . . . " *any* announcement will bring relief to his mind." Ibid., May 15, 1961.

[5] President Kennedy nominated Kilday on June 28, 1961, and the Senate unanimously confirmed the appointment on July 17. Thus far in its history, all five nominations to USCMA had received unanimous approval from the Senate. As had been true of Homer Ferguson, so in Kilday's case, the Senate Armed Services Committee did not even trouble to ask him to appear at the "pro forma" confirmation hearing.

[6] Proulx remarked to Quinn that "I understand that Judge Ferguson hit the ceiling when he read [the editorial in the Navy Times] favoring Judge Latimer's reappointment." Ibid., June 12, 1961. Normally, the presidential appointment files carry some indication of the selection process by which judges were appointed to USCMA. Diligent research by the Kennedy Library staff in the 1960–61 files failed to locate any such papers on Kilday's appointment, indicating that the nomination was probably decided by informal agreement between Kennedy's staff and Kilday. Kilday not only had the support of Vinson but also that of his old Texas colleagues Vice President Lyndon Johnson and House Speaker Sam Rayburn. With such backing, documentation on the appointment process was hardly necessary and its absence is not surprising. On June 5, Kilday had written to Lyndon Johnson "to express my very sincere thanks for the recommendation you gave me and for the very material assistance you have rendered me in this connection." LBJ, Vice Presidential Papers, Box 265, 1961 Congressional File K, June 5, 1961.

new nominee. Kilday mentioned to the Chief Judge that a constitutional question about life tenure had already been raised. Quinn replied that "this obstacle if it did exist could easily be overcome," and promised to send Kilday a memorandum on the subject within three days.[7] He did.

Quinn conceded that opposition to life tenure for his court rested on the ground that the modification, as applied to the incumbent judges, "would usurp or contravene the President's right to nominate the Judges of the Court, with the advice and consent of the Senate." This objection, he insisted, "is contrary to established practice and law. Tenure of office is a matter separate and apart from the right to appoint and the manner of appointment."[8] Quinn emphasized that "there is a genuine need to assure the Court's independence as a judicial tribunal and to eliminate the possibility of interference by administrative agencies with the full discharge of its judicial obligations."[9]

Although Quinn was saying nothing new, the issues to which he referred were still current. During the summer of 1961, the Bureau of the Budget again received one of the congressional proposals for USCMA life tenure. So did the Chairman of the Senate Armed Services Committee, Richard Russell, who sought the reaction of the Defense Department. Again—this time speaking through the Air Force—the Department objected. Neither its rationale nor the rhetoric on this subject had changed. It was as if everything the Court had presented on the need for life tenure during the last decade had been ignored.

It is "well settled," according to the Air Force Department Memorandum, "that courts-martial are instrumentalities of the executive power provided by Congress for the President in his capacity as Commander in Chief, to aid him in properly commanding the armed forces and enforcing discipline therein."[10] Conceding that USCMA "is considered to be a court in every

[7] 11 CF, June 23, 1961. Quinn also visited Congressman John McCormack who assured Quinn that "if Mr. Vinson reports the life tenure bill out of committee as he promised Congressman Fogarty he would, Mr. McCormack would see to it that it would pass the House without delay." Ibid. The problem for proponents of life tenure however, was not in the House, but rather in the Senate. Ultimately, Vinson and McCormack kept their promises, but to no avail.

[8] Ibid., June 26, 1951. Quinn urged Kilday to consider the development of tenure for the judges on the United States Customs Court, the Court of Customs and Patent Appeals, as well as the Court of Claims. All three were specialized federal tribunals, created—as was USCMA—under Article I of the Constitution. More important, Congress had changed the terms of Customs and Patent Appeals judges from fixed years to life tenure, and with no discernible constitutional objection.

[9] Ibid.

[10] All quotations from the undated Defense Department memorandum to Russell, as well as Quinn's rebuttal, are taken from the copy found in Homer Ferguson's papers. Out of fairness to the Defense Department, as Tedrow observed, "it is only the military, and not the civilian office of Defense, that makes such claims." FP, "Memo Re OSD [office of the secretary of defense] (AF) Reply on USCMA Bill," August 23, 1961, 1. On the other hand, OSD apparently accepted the Air Force argument without question.

significant respect, not merely an administrative agency," the Department "is opposed to any legislation which would make the court part of the judicial branch, since the court, by virtue of its functions, should remain part of the executive branch." Further claiming that the proposed bill "contains a number of provisions which might be interpreted as tending to convert the Court into an Article III court," the memorandum argued that such action "could create an anomaly without precedent, possibly producing problems of greater moment than the benefits it purports to bestow."[11] Concealed in this verbiage was exactly the point to which Kilday had already been alerted.

If USCMA became a United States Court, could it still remain under the jurisdiction of the Defense Department? More important, what about presidential power to remove judges from this tribunal? Would not such a change infringe "upon the President's authority to remove members of a court that is part of the executive branch?" Flying in the face of federal judicial history since 1789, the memorandum insisted that this authority "should not be deleted; otherwise, the judges could only be removed by impeachment."[12] On the other hand, the memorandum utterly failed to consider whether Congress could grant life tenure to the judges of an Article I Court that it had created. One might have expected the Department to offer some new arguments in rebuttal to the claims made by proponents of extended terms for USCMA. But merely to repeat and rehash past assertions put forth by the armed services, reflected a "knee-jerk" reaction, rather than reasoned reflection.

Quinn wasted little time in replying to the Defense Department memorandum. Again he had a draft from Tedrow, which he may well have used in its preparation.[13] He cited federal judicial precedents, one of which had been noted more than forty years before by Samuel Ansell.[14] The "fallacy of the Air Force Report's basic premise is established by the foregoing authoritative pronouncements." Nevertheless, added Quinn,

> the theme of "instrumentality of command" is constantly reiterated by those charged with enforcing the law and professing to supervise discipline within the Armed Services! It was just such declarations that led to the abuses which caused the repudiation by the Congress of the administration of military justice under the Articles of War and the [regulations to govern] the Navy. It was just such spurious reasoning which created the need for the establishment of this Court as the civilian overseers of the system of military justice contemplated by

[11] Russell Memorandum, 1–2.

[12] Ibid. However, "the Department of Defense would not oppose legislation designed to enhance the dignity and prestige of the Court of Military Appeals." It proposed no such legislation in this memorandum. Nor, of course, did this glib reassurance solve the questions which had troubled the Court from its inception.

[13] "It is suggested," Tedrow had concluded, "that the military approach shown by the Air Force in the letter [report] in question is a further cogent argument for passage of this legislation."

[14] See AMJ, 78–80.

the Uniform Code. Are we to regard the reiteration of the oft-rejected premise [as] a precursor of further attempts to restore a repudiated system?[15]

For his part, Quinn reiterated the arguments in favor of life tenure. But his response also reflected some deeper issues that went beyond the usual comments about the need to be protected from undue political influence. "If this Court," he wrote, "is to secure for the future personnel equal in professional capacity and standing to that from which other Federal Judges are recruited, it is essential that the members of its bench enjoy similar treatment in this particular."[16] Quinn concluded that both premises and conclusions of the Air Force position were erroneous, "and approval should be withheld."[17]

Within a matter of months, Kilday resigned from Congress, and joined the Court. Meanwhile, the question of life tenure lingered, and indeed seemed to have gained a sort of tenure of its own—for not until 1962–63 would the House act upon the measure. Congress, however, was far from uninterested in military justice. Representative Kilday, it will be recalled, had planned to hold investigatory hearings in 1960–61. Instead, he joined USCMA, leaving two congressional subcommittees to consider key aspects of military justice. North Carolina Senator Sam Ervin, Jr., presided over hearings before a special panel of the Judiciary Committee to consider the constitutional rights of members of the Armed Services. Members of the House Armed Services Committee focused yet again on the question of life tenure for USCMA judges. Although more personally concerned with the latter, the three USCMA jurists participated only in the Ervin hearings.[18] Both, however, warrant some discussion.

THE SENATE, THE CODE, AND THE COURT

Even as the House Subcommittee prepared to consider life tenure for USCMA judges, and the related problems of pension and retirement benefits, a joint Senate Armed Services–Judiciary Subcommittee on Constitutional

[15] FP, August 31, 1961.

[16] Ibid., 4. Precisely the same point had been raised by former Army JAG officer and Washington attorney Frederick B. Wiener testifying about the proposed UCMJ in 1949. "I think we should face it frankly—the appointments to the specialized courts of our judicial system haven't attracted the same sort of talent that the courts of general jurisdiction have attracted." AMJ, 220–21. While it remains true that the quality of federal judges depends in large measure upon the care and importance that the president attaches to their selection, it may also be true that the prospect of life tenure as a federal judge might well attract better qualified candidates than an offer for a fixed number of years. The quality of the available pool may affect what is drawn from it.

[17] FP, August 31, 1961, 5.

[18] See, for example, Quinn's letter to Senator Ervin, 11 CF, September 25, 1961. Early in 1962, Quinn told Ervin that he would be pleased to present "my personal views on some aspects of the subjects under inquiry and to appear as a witness." 12 CF, January 9, 1962.

Rights scheduled hearings between February and March 1962, and focused in particular on the rights of personnel in the Armed Services. Unlike the 1956 hearings, Ervin's group had no specific bill under consideration. Rather, the panel as well as those who appeared before it probably saw the sessions as an opportunity for a general assessment of military justice, after eleven years of operation under the UCMJ. The judges welcomed the hearings as a friendly forum in which to push for life tenure, if only because a former commissioner to USCMA, Robinson Everett, also served as counsel to this subcommittee.[19]

One of the first witnesses before Ervin's subcommittee was Reginald Harmon, recently retired after a record number of years [12] as the Air Force JAG. In an earlier appearance during hearings held in 1956, he had argued essentially that both court and code were unnecessary. Six years later, recalling his old description of the UCMJ and the system of military justice it mandated as "unwieldy and cumbersome in peacetime, and . . . probably unworkable in the event of a major large-scale war," Harmon stated that "I have not been presented with any new evidence which would change that opinion."[20] He added that the "greatest single objection to the [UCMJ] is its tendency to destroy what was once the principal asset of the military justice system: that is the swift and certain punishment of the guilty man." Indeed, the "certainty of punishment and the promptness of prosecution seem now to be only a matter of historical interest."[21]

This was so because the UCMJ is "unnecessarily laden with built-in delays." Even worse, "in many instances, form has been elevated over substance in the administration of the code." Comparing the old Articles of War, the short-lived Elston Act, and the UCMJ which had superseded both of them—Harmon called the UCMJ "the most expensive, the least efficient and the most ineffective system of the three. . . ." The solution to this undesirable situation was simple. "I recommend the repeal of the [UCMJ] in its entirety."[22]

[19] A 1950 graduate of Harvard Law School, Everett had been a commissioner to Judge Brosman. He has maintained a professional interest in military justice throughout his later career, both as a law professor at Duke University Law School, and in his law practice. Everett is the only former USCMA commissioner in Court history to return to his old tribunal as a member of the Court. In 1980, President Jimmy Carter nominated him as USCMA Chief Judge, a position he filled until 1990. Everett's appointment, through a procedure unique to USCMA history, is discussed in some detail in chapter 11.

[20] "Constitutional Rights of Military Personnel." Hearings before the Subcommittee on Constitutional Rights of the Committee on the Judiciary, U.S. Senate, 87th Cong., 2nd sess. (1962), 165; hereafter cited as Rights, followed by appropriate page number.

[21] Ibid., 166.

[22] Ibid., 167–68. See AMJ for information concerning the passage in 1948 of the Elston Act, and Harmon's initial views of the UCMJ. In 1962, Harmon claimed that instead of making the Elston Act applicable to the Navy as should have been done, "we got into the field of statutory

The witnesses who immediately followed Harmon were the three USCMA Judges. Not unreasonably, they could have pointed to the first decade of the Court's history as a fitting rebuttal to Harmon.[23] Instead, they made some specific suggestions for future changes in the military justice system, beyond the obvious need for life tenure. Indeed, Quinn urged that the Boards of Review also "should have tenure, and perhaps greater stature."[24] More important, "the law officer should become a judge in the full sense of the word, with all the attributes that go with a trial judge."[25] Judge Ferguson agreed. "I think you would speed up justice . . . if Congress did try to give him more authority and have him feel that he was a real judge, and that the members of the jury would look on him as a judge and take the law from him rather than what they may think is the law."[26]

---

reform, and we went to a new one that, in my opinion, is much worse." Ibid., 178. Harmon demonstrated marked consistency in his opinions. In 1987, thirty-six years after the Court's establishment, he recalled about USCMA that "I had some strong feelings about that development and still do. I don't think we needed it, and I don't think we need it now." As for the UCMJ, "I was not for [it], and I am not for it now." AMJ, 181, n. 32.

[23] Referring to the old JAG "judicial councils" established by the Elston Act, Quinn observed that "they have superior officers. They have men who mark their fitness reports. They are indebted to certain members of their own organization. They have not the complete freedom of movement that a court of last resort should have." USCMA, on the other hand, "is completely independent in every sense of the word. No power on earth can influence our decisions. We decide according to the law and according to the facts." Rights, 181. Quinn was accurate, even though by statute USCMA is authorized to consider only matters of law in its appellate jurisdiction. A later witness, Frederick Bernays Wiener, noted that "any appellate court is going to look at facts regardless of what the book says on what their jurisdiction is. Facts influence them." Ibid., 794.

[24] Ibid., 183. Later Quinn hedged a bit. "I think perhaps that, to some extent, the boards of review should be made into intermediate appellate courts with a substantial tenure." Ibid., 186. The judges of these courts, now known as "Courts of Criminal Appeals," are appointed by the respective JAG of each service, and serve for a number of years at that official's pleasure. There are no fixed terms of office, nor is Senate confirmation required. In 1994, the United States Supreme Court unanimously rejected a constitutional challenge to both of these practices. See *Weiss and Hernandez v. United States*, 510 U.S. 163 (1994). For some comments concerning the apparent trend of the High Court toward marked disinterest in military justice, reflected anew in this decision, see Lurie, "The Role of the Federal Judiciary in the Governance of the American Military," in Richard Kohn, ed., *The United States Military Under the Constitution of the United States, 1789–1989* (1991), 405–30; and Lurie, "Military Justice 50 Years After Nuremberg: Some Reflections on Appearance v. Reality," *Military Law Review* 178 (1996) 178–86 (1996).

[25] Rights, 186. Quinn's comments should be kept in mind when the legislative result of Ervin's interest in military justice, the Military Justice Act of 1968, is discussed. See below.

[26] Ibid., 196. Kilday, fresh from more than twenty years in Congress, recalled Harmon's good reputation even as he dismissed his recommendations. "We have progressed further than that in modern times. . . . I think under the code you have come a whole lot nearer the Anglo-Saxon concept of justice and there has been great progress made." Ibid., 202. All three judges expressed concern with the proclivity within the military to use administrative discharges rather than the military justice system to separate individuals from the armed services. Kilday reminded the panel that "when you subject administrative action to review you get a whole lot

Although a number of additional witnesses appeared before Ervin's panel, the comments of two lawyers merit particular discussion. Both were experts and experienced practitioners in military justice. Frederick Wiener's credentials have already been noted. In 1962, Kenneth Pye was Associate Dean at Georgetown University Law School.[27] Both were critical of the existing boards of review.

Pye urged that these boards be combined into judicial panels. "What you need on an appellate bench of this nature are trained lawyers with a certain degree of independence, [and] that intimate knowledge of the military is not a particularly great asset."[28] Moreover, he added, protection in the UCMJ against command influence in military justice, Article 98, was less than effective. "I doubt from a realistic point of view whether it is ever going to be more effective."[29] Finally, Pye argued that "as a matter of constitutional law, it is questionable whether courts-martial should . . . try civilian type offenses and as a matter of desirability it is also questionable whether they should have this power." Indeed, he argued that some current problems in military jurisdiction "could be solved if [such] jurisdiction was limited to military-type offenses—offenses against the person or property of the military or offenses committed on a military reservation."[30]

---

better administrative action than when no review is necessary, even though it may not be a review within the department." Ibid., 205.

[27] Later, as will be noted, both men received White House consideration as possible USCMA judges. Pye went on to become president of Southern Methodist University.

[28] Ibid., 551. Pye was not concerned that the JAG reviews the performance of the judicial panels. He was more troubled by the fact that the panel might be "reviewing the work of their close friends in the field, including men whom they may serve under for their next assignment." Wiener went so far as to note that "the existence of the Board of Review does not help an accused substantially. . . . I no longer take retainers before Boards of Review because it is a waste of my time and my client's money. . . . I think if you get rid of Boards of Review you will considerably speed up the process, and you are not taking away anything from the accused by way of protection. . . ." Ibid., 782, 791.

[29] Ibid., 559–60. As had several witnesses in 1950, Pye urged that prosecutions against senior officers for violation of a serviceman's rights "be placed under the jurisdiction of a federal district court, in a proceeding by the U.S. attorney because [these witnesses] predicted there never would be a conviction of a senior officer. Their predictions have proved true." Ibid., 560. See AMJ, 199, n. 18. Pye's observation remains accurate. But so does Quinn's earlier comment to the same panel: "I think the very existence of the civilian court itself is a definite detriment to command control. . . ." Rights, 181.

[30] Ibid., 553. The statement on which Pye based his presentation before the Senate panel is on pp. 566–74. He noted that he was greatly concerned with the question "whether it is constitutional for courts-martial to try in time of peace, an offense committed by a serviceman within the United States where the nature of the offense is exclusively civil in the sense that it is not committed on a military installation, against military property or military personnel, and does not involve any matter affecting the maintenance of military discipline." No Supreme Court, he added, "has ever faced squarely the issue of whether the grant of jurisdiction to try servicemen

No stranger to congressional hearings involving the UCMJ or USCMA (he had already appeared at three of them), Wiener supported USCMA. He was less enthusiastic about the UCMJ. He observed that "the matter of military justice is a dilemma. . . . that arises out of the need for reconciling essentially irreconcilable concepts." A military organization "is and must be an authoritarian organization because its job is to send men obediently to death if need be."[31] Punishment in the military, he added, "is primarily deterrent. Punishment in the civil courts is, of course, primarily reformatory." And, "an army is not a deliberative body."[32]

Thus "military justice should be limited "to situations where the standards and techniques and procedures of military justice are necessary, and it shouldn't attempt to parallel civilian justice. . . ."[33] Here, Wiener took issue with those—among them the USCMA judges—who argued that military justice wherever possible ought to be identical with its civilian counterpart. Indeed, the UCMJ "introduces what I think are unsuitable civil concepts, civilian concepts [*sic*]." Even worse "is that the uniform code divorces the administration of military justice from the consciousness of the services. Instead of the services disciplining themselves and taking a precise interest in seeing that the guilty are convicted and the innocent go free, the whole thing is turned over to the cops and the lawyers. . . ."[34]

On the other hand, Wiener endorsed USCMA because "it is impossible to expect the services without [its supervision] to stamp out the endemic existence of command influence. . . ." Moreover, the court was necessary "to look over the shoulders of those people who just can't be relied upon to do a completely decent job by themselves."[35] Finally, Wiener echoed the opinion of Kenneth Pye, noting "I think that the civil courts should have primary jurisdiction over civilian offenses committed by military personnel off the post."[36]

---

for capital and non-capital civilian type cases in time of peace is constitutional." Pye doubted that it was. "My preliminary research indicates no historical precedent which would justify the conclusion that the Founding Fathers intended that anything other than disciplinary punishment should be exerted by the Armed Forces in time of peace within the United States." Pye's comments should be kept in mind when seven years later in 1969, the Supreme Court decided the question he had discussed. See below.

[31] Ibid., 776.

[32] Ibid., 777. The "need for military discipline enforced by prompt and certain sanctions does not meet what are publicly acceptable standards of criminal justice."

[33] Ibid., 778.

[34] Ibid., 780. "Don't let military justice be a thing apart as now." Ibid., 784.

[35] Ibid., 780–81. Wiener even cited a "list of the horribles[,] . . . shocking cases that weren't caught by the Board of Review." Here, Wiener seems to be endorsing a separate component of appellate military justice, something he had criticized moments before, because it was divorcing "the administration of military justice from the consciousness of the services."

[36] Ibid., 786.

Ervin's hearings failed to produce any immediate legislation, although he did propose a number of bills to address some of the issues raised in the hearings. His subcommittee did not resume the hearings until 1966, when they considered no less than eighteen bills, including those drafted in 1962.[37] Some of them were directly concerned with the issues raised by these earlier witnesses. In the meantime, the House Armed Services Subcommittee turned to the issue of life tenure for Quinn and his colleagues. Eleven years after USCMA's establishment, Quinn felt he had reason to be optimistic.

THE HOUSE, THE CODE, AND THE COURT

It will be recalled that spokesmen for the Defense establishment as well as the Executive branch had opposed previous life tenure proposals, essentially because they believed them to be incompatible with the power of presidential removal—a UCMJ provision in effect since the original enactment of this legislation in 1950. And indeed, under Article III auspices, federal judges can be removed *only* by impeachment. The 1962–63 House hearings centered on an attempt to provide life tenure for USCMA judges, while at the same time keeping the presidential removal power intact.[38]

Only one witness, Air Force JAG Albert Kuhfeld, appeared before the subcommittee on July 26, 1962, and he spoke for the Department of Defense. This time, Kuhfeld emphasized, "the status of the Court as an Article I, or a legislative court, would be clearly retained. . . . " Its judges, moreover, would not be "judges of the United States," because that term applied to Article III courts, created under federal judicial authority.[39] They would have life tenure, although they would remain subject to presidential removal. This provision, which apparently was sacrosanct to the Defense Department, could not be applied to an Article III court because "one of the very basic characteristics of an Article III court is that a judge can only be removed by impeachment."[40] Nevertheless, as the Committee counsel put it, "we are try-

[37] See below, chapter 8.

[38] *Hearings before Subcommittee No. 1 on H.R. 3179*, 88th Cong., 1st sess., June 4, 1963, 3189—hereafter cited as Hearings. For reasons that are not clear, the 1962 hearings were not published, but were included in the printed record of the 1963 session held one year later by the same subcommittee on the same subject.

[39] Ibid., 3190. The counsel to the Armed Services Committee, Russell Blandford, added that linking USCMA to an Article III tribunal might "conceivably raise the problem of bringing the entire Federal judicial system into the administration of military justice, and that, of course, is something we are trying to stay away from." Ibid., 3191.

[40] Ibid. It can be argued, however, that if the President has the power to remove USCMA judges "upon notice and hearing for neglect of duty or malfeasance in office, but for no other cause," the principle behind life tenure is diminished if not destroyed. To be sure, the President's options were very limited by the language employed, but to the extent that they existed at all—they lessened exactly what life tenure was intended to insure, the highest possible level of

ing to give all the elements of a U.S. judge, without making it an Article III court."[41]

The subcommittee also wrestled with the problem of mandatory retirement for the judges, something that Kuhfeld quickly reminded its members "is not done in any of the other [federal, Article III] courts." L. Mendel Rivers, subcommittee chair, replied, "The other courts do not compare with this. We want to get away from that." To which his own counsel responded, "No, Mr. Chairman, we do not want to get away from it. We are trying to get away from it as little as we can. That is the whole point." Of course, Russell Blandford added, with a legislative court, the Congress "can do about whatever you want to do. But every time that you make this court different with regard to its privileges, its rights of resignation, and its rights of retirement, then you detract from its dignity."[42]

Because of some questions concerning retirement pensions, the subcommittee put off final action on the life tenure bill question until June 1963. Reintroduced by Congressman John Fogarty, this bill reiterated essentially what the Armed Services Committee had decided one year before—life tenure subject to presidential removal, with the incumbent judges also eligible for reappointment. In addition, USCMA judges would be entitled "to the same salary, allowances, perquisites, retirement, and survivor benefits as judges of the U.S. court of appeals."[43] Again, General Kuhfeld stated that the Defense department supported the bill, and again Russell Blandford emphasized that USCMA was "a legislative court, as opposed to a constitutional court." Moreover, under this bill, "the jurisdiction of [USCMA] is not intended to be enlarged. . . . It is not intended to set up a new court of the

---

judicial independence. The bill as drafted by the judges did not include this provision, while the House Subcommittee draft of July 26, 1962, did. The distinction was very important. What Kuhfeld supported, and what the House would ultimately adopt, was in reality a grant of life tenure as long as the President made no effort to end it.

[41] Ibid., 3193. The subcommittee chair, South Carolina Democrat L. Mendel Rivers, noted another reason for making USCMA "permanent." It "will let you gentlemen in the Department of Defense and in the services know that this court is here to stay." Kuhfeld replied that "we haven't any problem with that." Rivers rejoined, "You don't know, because we will let you know that. We did have a little problem some time in the past." Ibid., 3192.

[42] Ibid., 3199. As Rivers put it, the subcommittee had difficulty "in trying our best to get away from Article III and carry on the philosophy of Article III," at the same time. Ibid., 3200. Possibly with the views of Senator Richard Russell in mind, Rivers noted further that "if there is a fallacy in the Constitution, it is to let the Federal judges sit during good behavior. I see a lot of good fellows turn from gentlemen to tyrants overnight, when they put on that shroud." Ibid., 3203. Even so, the future Chairman of the House Armed Services Committee supported life tenure for USCMA judges along the lines discussed above. Like many of his southern colleagues, Rivers was uncomfortable with both civil rights legislation and the expanded role for federal judges regarding integration cases in the years since *Brown v. Board of Education* (1954).

[43] Ibid., 3237.

United States as a result of the enactment of this legislation."[44] Without even a voice vote, the panel reported the bill favorably to the full committee.[45]

During a session on July 16, 1963, the House Armed Services Committee considered a number of pending measures, including H. R. 3179, the USCMA tenure bill. Speaking for the subcommittee, Mendel Rivers emphasized anew that the judges "ought to have the dignity of life tenure."[46] At which point, a committee member reminded Rivers that "you have not given [USCMA] the dignity, because the President himself can remove them, and he cannot remove Federal Judges. . . . If we have a right to go this far, we have a right to go and say the removal should be on the same basis as any other Federal [judge]."[47] As he had attempted numerous times before during the other hearings, Blandford sought to explain why it was not that simple.

"We are attempting," he noted, "to exercise the authority of the Congress to establish a legislative court. This gets into a great realm of constitutional law. . . . [W]e are trying desperately to avoid using the same language, which would then be construed as clothing this court with all of the aspects of a constitutional court, where then we lose our jurisdiction. . . . We had to bend over backwards, otherwise we wouldn't even have jurisdiction over this bill to make it a legislative court."[48] Again, without even an informal vote, let alone a roll call, Chairman Carl Vinson noted that the "bill is unanimously reported."[49] Within three weeks, it reached the House floor.

In his report accompanying referral of the bill to the entire House, for a third time Mendel Rivers explained what the measure entailed. Drawing heavily on material furnished the Committee by the Court, he cited the need to "free the judges from the danger of political and other pressures," also to assimilate the USCMA bench "to that of a U.S. court of appeals, thereby bringing the administration of military criminal law closer to complete accord with that obtaining in Federal civilian courts." Finally, life tenure would

[44] Ibid., 3249–51. USCMA is "for practical purposes the supreme court of the military. And this bill will give them the dignity and prestige that ought to go with a court of that nature."

[45] Ibid., 3252. The entire hearing apparently took less than one hour.

[46] Full Committee Consideration of . . . H.R. 3179 . . . Armed Services Committee, June 18, 1963. 88th Cong., 1st sess., 3418. "I always wanted to do it. They should have it. This is one of the most important courts we have in America."

[47] Ibid.

[48] Ibid., 3418–19. In other words, the committee sought to give judicial tenure without involving the Senate Committee on the Judiciary. A year earlier, Rivers had been a little more candid, when he observed that "I do not want to get mixed up with the Judiciary Committee. That is why I want to stay clear, as far as possible, of the jurisdiction of the Judiciary Committee." 1962 Hearings, 3194. As was discussed in AMJ, the decision in 1949 to entrust the UCMJ—and USCMA—to the Armed Services Committees rather than the Judiciary Committees turned out to be an extremely important event. In 1950, the Senate barely defeated a move to give the Judiciary Committee jurisdiction over the bill. For additional discussion concerning the relationship between the Armed Services Committees and USCMA, see below.

[49] 1963 Full Committee Hearings, 3420.

"assure for the future personnel equal in professional capacity and standing to those recruited as judges of other Federal courts."[50] Rivers also extolled the accomplishments of USCMA to date. "Its insistence upon high professional performance by all legal personnel involved in trials by courts-martial, and upon strict compliance with the provisions of the [UCMJ], has resulted in the elimination of many of the justified grounds for the complaints lodged against the earlier procedures."[51]

In discussing the bill before the House, Rivers raised his level of rhetoric. He claimed that since its inception, USCMA "has been on trial and the experience has been very good. They have earned this distinction and it gives them a dignity to which they are entitled." As to the three incumbents—Quinn, Ferguson, and Kilday—"there are no three finer men in the judiciary."[52] Congressman Harold Gross, Republican from Iowa, responded that "I am not aware that we are in the business of passing laws giving people jobs for the rest of their natural lives on the basis of their being nice fellows."[53]

Democrat John Fogarty offered some eloquent, historical perspective. Reminding his colleagues first of the fact that "the best method of keeping our courts independent is through a tenure basis," and also of plenary congressional authority to regulate the armed services, Fogarty called the UCMJ "the most revolutionary change in the court-martial system this country has ever contemplated." But, he added, "of what profit is confidence, of what worth is justice, of what use is judicial excellence if these attributes are purchased at the price of discipline. . . ." The necessary balance "we were sure, could be struck by dedicated, mature, judicious minds applying, interpreting and explaining the law."[54] USCMA has "established one of the best records of any Federal court in the country." Shrewdly emphasizing the fact that two of the three current judges were former Congressional colleagues, Fogarty singled out Quinn for special attention. "This pioneer of civilian supervision of military courts has established for [USCMA] its judicial tone, its orderly administration, the currency of its docket, and its faithful conformity to the spirit as well as the letter of the uniform code."[55]

[50] 88th Cong., 1st sess., House Report No. 413, June 18, 1963, 2. Rivers made no mention of the thorny issue concerning the need for the court's "dignity," on the one hand, and life tenure being terminated by presidential removal, on the other.

[51] Ibid.

[52] *Congressional Record*, 88th Cong., 1st sess., House, July 9, 1963, 11637.

[53] Ibid. Gross complained further about the excessive retirement benefits available to federal judges. Rivers could not resist the opening. "I might say to the gentleman from Iowa: I know some Federal judges who are not worth any portion of their salary." Nevertheless, "the decisions which this court has rendered are classics in military legal jurisprudence." Ibid., 11637.

[54] Ibid., 11637–38.

[55] Ibid. See 11639, where Fogarty compared Quinn's work in "the pioneering of equal justice under law for all members of the Armed Forces," with Chief Justice John Marshall's success in bringing "direction" and "a basic philosophy" to the United States Supreme Court.

Rhetoric notwithstanding, Congressman Gross was "still unable to understand why this bill is before the House." Regarding the claim that tenure was necessary in order to give the judges the dignity they deserved, Gross was blunt. "I am not aware that you can legislate dignity. If this is the excuse for this bill . . . that you are lending dignity by giving these three judges lifetime tenures, then you have not very much to stand on."[56] Vinson summarized the Court's history, and added the point that enactment of the statute would "eliminate once and for all the baseless contention that the court is an instrumentality of the Executive by confirming its identity as a legislative court established under Article I."[57] Noting that the bill had unanimous support from his committee, Vinson called for the vote. Final passage followed, by an overwhelming margin, 314 in favor, 82 opposed, 37 abstaining.[58]

With such a favorable House vote, USCMA Clerk Proulx was understandably optimistic about life tenure for his court. "We're half-way home," he wrote, "and a good start time-wise for passage during the 88th Congress. We have high hopes that this will come about."[59] But it was not to be. As early as June 26, Proulx had been warned that Senate action might be delayed, as it "has just received from President Kennedy his Civil Rights proposal package, which could tie up the Senate for the balance of the session."[60] Indeed it did, and when one adds to this Richard Russell's continued intransigence, plus the tragedy of Kennedy's assassination in Dallas a few months later—one can understand why the Senate failed to consider the House bill.

Thus, in spite of all that had gone before, life tenure for USCMA judges remained remote. Quinn had hoped that Senator Ervin's subcommittee might represent a viable detour around the Russell roadblock. Early in 1964, he

[56] Ibid., 11640. In reply, Carl Vinson claimed that the intention of the legislation was "to remove Executive influence." Gross asked, "What evidence is there that there has been executive interference with this Court?" Vinson responded, "Not one particle at all." Then, commented Gross, "that argument does not stand up very well, does it?" Vinson insisted that a court should not be "dependent upon reappointment, and that it "should be given the same prestige and the same standard, at least, as other Federal courts. . . ." Possibly aware that his opposition was futile, Gross persisted. "I see no similarity between a judge of [USCMA] and a Federal appeals court judge. I see no real comparison in the type of work they do. A judge in the court of appeals is confronted with every conceivable kind of case, whereas the gentlemen on this court are confronted with one type of case and one type of case only, if I understand their duties." Ibid.

[57] Ibid., 11641.

[58] Ibid., 11642.

[59] 13 CF, July 31, 1963. Proulx and the USCMA judges had been previously informed that H.R. 3179 was slated for easy passage in the House. Even before the favorable vote on July 9, however, they were involved in planning strategy for action by the Senate. On June 26, Proulx noted that "Judge Kilday will contact Senator Russell directly and advise Vice President Johnson to the end of having Senator Russell report the bill out favorably for Senate action." Ibid., June 26, 1963.

[60] Ibid.

observed that Senator Pastore was "collaborating with Senator Ervin . . . in our behalf."[61] But Ervin was unwilling to break with his Southern colleague. A year later, Proulx conceded that Ervin "would not be disposed to introduce the life tenure bill in the Senate if it did not meet with prior approval of Senator Russell—being aware of the latter's opposition to life tenure for any court, we cannot look to Senator Ervin for assistance at this juncture."[62] In the meantime, Quinn's term was drawing to a close, and if he could not attain life tenure, he would have to seek reappointment, something that had not yet occurred in USCMA history.

QUINN'S QUEST

As Quinn considered his options, he could only have been well aware of Latimer's fate. Yet the former Rhode Island Governor hoped to capitalize first on his many congressional friends and contacts, as well as the fact that Lyndon Johnson had been elected by a landslide. Indeed, Senator Pastore suggested that the entire Rhode Island delegation (all four of them) join in a letter to Johnson requesting reappointment, and solicited a memorandum from Quinn's office to help him in its preparation. Proulx promptly complied.

The memorandum listed a number of reasons for Quinn's reappointment. They included the point that this would not be a new nomination. "Thus age [seventy-one] discounted." His record as the first and only Chief Judge in the Court's history warranted retention. Proulx quoted various encomiums from military personnel, as well as Senator Sam Ervin. He added that Quinn had resigned from a lifetime judicial appointment in Rhode Island to accept his current position. Finally, he noted of his Chief Judge: "Health excellent and capacity for work undiminished—mentally and physically sound."[63]

A few weeks later, the secretary to former Rhode Island Senator Theodore F. Green wrote President Johnson that "the Senator is definitely interested in having you consider [Quinn] for reappointment."[64] Apparently Green's stature warranted more than the usual acknowledgment from a presidential as-

[61] 14 CF, February 6, 1964.

[62] 15 CF, March 25, 1965. Ervin's decision not to oppose Russell—thus again leaving the Senate as an unmovable barrier to the measure—seemed even more unfortunate because there had appeared to be clear sailing for the proposal in the lower chamber. Fogarty assured Proulx that "there would be no difficulty in getting the bill through the House." Ibid.

[63] Undated "Memorandum for Senator Pastore," in Quinn Papers. Sent to the White House on December 13, 1965, the letter from the Rhode Island delegation made virtually no mention of these points, including Quinn's age. Lauding the accomplishments of "our fellow Rhode Islander" as "lawyer, judge, Governor, humanitarian and friend," the statement requested "an appointment with you so that we may personally present our support of this outstanding jurist . . . if you deemed this necessary." Ibid., December 13, 1965, 1–2.

[64] Ibid., January 4, 1966.

sistant. Instead, Cyrus Vance, the Deputy Secretary of Defense, drafted a proposed reply for "Special Presidential Assistant" Jack Valenti. Noncommittal at best, the letter merely stated that "the President appreciates Judge Quinn's outstanding career both prior to and after appointment to the Court . . . and recognizes the distinction with which he is serving. . . ."[65]

Upon learning from House Speaker John McCormack, another Quinn booster, that Valenti would be dealing with the Quinn matter, Pastore addressed a personal letter to him. He reminded "Jack" that Quinn had long been a symbol among Democrats in Rhode Island, and that as "Fighting Bob," he had been minority leader in the State Senate, "when you could count Democrats on the fingers of both hands." On a "very personal note," added Pastore—himself a former Governor of Rhode Island—"when I was a young boy . . . working as an errand boy in a tailoring establishment which made Bob Quinn's clothes, it was there that I was so impressed by his vigor and progressiveness in the Democratic cause that, I can humbly say, gave me the inspiration to follow a public career in the Democratic Party."[66]

Even before receiving Pastore's letter, Valenti had asked the White House Personnel Director, John Macy, for a "reading" on Quinn's status.[67] On February 25, Valenti heard from Macy's office that the Director would recommend two or three persons for the Court position, but not Quinn, "mainly because he is 72 years old." Valenti was further informed that "the President is fairly firm on such appointments over the age of 60," and "even in view of the strong desires of the R.I. delegation, they are still not going to recommend reappointment."[68] Whereupon Valenti sent a short note to the President, enclosing Pastore's letter, and reporting on the negative recommendation from Macy's office. "For all that I can determine, Judge Quinn's advanced age is the only reason that Macy is not recommending him." Should, he asked, "[w]e go forward with the nomination anyway?" Johnson replied with a notation scrawled on the bottom of the letter, "[s]ee me[.] Get Pastore in to see me[.]"[69]

[65] LBJ, White House Central Files, File Group 545A, Box 360, January 14, 1966. In his covering letter to Valenti, Vance had stated, "I think it is significant to note that Judge Quinn will shortly be 72 years old and the term of a Judge of [USCMA] is 15 years." Ibid., January 13, 1966.

[66] Quinn Papers, February 9, 1966, 1–2. Pastore concluded with an observation that "I feel, and very strongly so, that any attitude of indifference on this reappointment would be rather tragic in Rhode Island."

[67] LBJ, FG 545 A, WHCF, Box 360, January 24, 1966. In his former capacity as chairman of the Civil Service Commission, John Macy had already become acquainted with Quinn. The two men had exchanged courteous if not congenial correspondence on the subject of whether USCMA employees were covered by Civil Service—an issue that had concerned USCMA since 1951.

[68] Ibid., February 25, 1966.

[69] Ibid.

In the meantime, Macy's office submitted its own memorandum to Johnson, noting that Quinn would be "87 at the termination of a second term if reappointed." Macy urged that "a younger man be appointed" to USCMA, and "that Quinn be named to the existing vacancy on the American Battle Monuments Commission."[70] Pending Johnson's decision, Macy's office also continued lining up potential USCMA candidates for the President's consideration. Two of them warrant brief discussion because they reveal the way Macy's office went about locating candidates for such a position, as well as a concern for expertise in the appropriate field.[71]

In March, Macy's assistant James Marsh contacted Phil C. Neal, Dean of the University of Chicago Law School. Neal responded with a letter proposing several names. One was Frederick Bernays Wiener. A former Army JAG officer as well as an able legal historian, Wiener had presented testimony at both House and Senate hearings in 1949 on the proposed UCMJ and USCMA, and currently practiced law in Washington, D.C., where he argued extensively in the federal appellate courts, including USCMA. Apparently, Wiener's potential candidacy went no further. In the margin of Neal's letter appears the comment "Brilliant but lacks temperament."[72] Marsh had also discussed a nomination with Russell Fairbanks, at the time a professor of law at Columbia University Law School—and soon to become the first Dean of the new Rutgers Law School at Camden. Although retired from the regular Army, Fairbanks felt a possible position on USCMA so important that "I would be prepared to resign my commission."[73]

As is not unusual with presidential options, in the Quinn case Johnson found himself getting conflicting signals from some of his staunchest Democratic supporters, and his own personnel office. Macy's notes of a meeting with the President on April 4 well reveal his ambivalence. "The President is torn on this one. He would like to please Pastore[,] but he is clearly opposed

[70] LBJ, John Macy Papers (JMP), March 4, 1966. In a very real sense, the Battle Monuments Commission might have been a graveyard for Quinn, if only because it was responsible for the operation and maintenance of some thirty-seven overseas military cemeteries and memorials. Its eleven members "serve at the pleasure of the President, without compensation except travel expenses and a $20 per diem when engaged in Commission business." Ibid. In short, the commission was a "do nothing, dead-end" type job.

[71] The availability of the Macy files at the Johnson Library offers a good opportunity to study some of the actual options offered to a President in appointing USCMA Judges. Neither in Eisenhower's nor Kennedy's administration were USCMA candidates screened as thoroughly as Marsh and Macy appear to have done for Johnson. Besides having to respond to the usual potential office seekers, Macy's office also actively sought them out. Had he wished to do so, in other words, Johnson could have appointed very distinguished legal scholars and/or practitioners to USCMA positions.

[72] JMP, Box 753, USCMA File, March 25, 1966.

[73] Ibid., March 29, 1966. Macy—as will be seen—went forward with a positive recommendation for Fairbanks.

to reappointing a man who is 72 years old to a 15-year term. When I left him, he had a call in to [Judge] Kilday to ask what the burdens of this particular Court might be."[74] Macy mentioned several potential replacements to Johnson, including Russell Fairbanks (erroneously referred to in Macy's notes as Fairchild). Johnson apparently "did not know any of them, [and] requested that we run our usual checks on them and others and give him our best thinking as to a successor."[75]

Later on the same day, Valenti reported to Johnson that he had talked with Pastore. "He understands your position . . . but he finds himself in a bind." Pastore wanted to discuss the matter with John Fogarty, a Rhode Island Congressman and a dear friend of Quinn. Pastore "was sympathetic to the President's dilemma, but he kept saying 'what can I tell Quinn?' "[76] On the next day, Valenti again talked with Pastore who had discussed the matter with the former Governor. The Chief Judge was concerned about the fact that "he will not be eligible for federal retirement for a little under three years from now." According to Valenti, Pastore "is hopeful of getting a resignation from Quinn that would go into effect the moment that he becomes eligible for federal retirement. I remonstrated against the President's difficulty in the appointment for even a restrictive period of time."[77]

For a third day in a row, Valenti and Pastore wrestled with the Quinn quandary. Pastore observed that if Quinn could remain on the bench until the spring of 1968, he would apparently be entitled to a federal pension $4,000 greater than if he were to be retired in May 1966. Valenti then paraphrased some of Pastore's comments. "Look, I am with my President. He can always count on me. . . . Whatever the President does in the Quinn matter will make no difference to my loyalty. I am the President's man. . . . But it would be so heartwarming to me if in this difficult moment, the President would reappoint Quinn—and get from Quinn a resignation dated" on the appropriate day his pension is secured. Even if Johnson refused him, "it will not make one iota of difference in my continued support all the way for the President—but, God, it would be so good for me to say the President had a difficult decision, but he resolved it in favor of Pastore."[78]

[74] Ibid., Box 753, USCMA File, April 4, 1966.

[75] Ibid.

[76] LBJ, WHCF, FG 545A, April 4, 1966.

[77] Ibid., April 5, 1966.

[78] Ibid., April 6, 1966. Upon receiving Valenti's third memorandum in as many days, apparently Johnson agreed to see Pastore, and with the desired results. Although dealing with a potent politician, Pastore was no amateur either. Emphasizing his loyalty to the President even as the Vietnam quagmire deepened could not have hurt his cause. For the atmosphere of crisis concerning Vietnam that affected the White House from the spring of 1966 on, see Stanley Karnow, *Vietnam: A History* (1991), 493. Karnow quotes Jack Valenti. "No matter what we turned our hands and minds to, there was Vietnam, its contagion infecting everything that it touched, and it seemed to touch everything." Thus the Quinn matter was simply not a primary object of con-

Whether or not Macy was aware of Pastore's actions is not clear. He continued to gather names for submission to Johnson, and what stands out is the apparent candor with which he evaluated them. He described one USCMA candidate who enjoyed the support of "most of the Democratic leadership in Maryland" as a man who "would probably do [the job] acceptably, but his career has not been at a sufficiently high level to effectively compete with other candidates."[79] Five days later, Macy submitted his first three choices for Quinn's seat to the President. His leading contender was Fairbanks, whom Macy described as "the best candidate I have found." He characterized another of his choices as a man "who would make a good, but not outstanding judge."[80] But when Macy discussed his candidates with the President on April 23, Johnson told Macy that Quinn would be reappointed "with the understanding that he will only serve until the spring of 1968. The details [with] respect to this condition will be worked out by Mr. Valenti through Senator Pastore."[81]

With Quinn's term expiring on May 1, Macy urged that we "proceed as rapidly as possible, because USCMA judges *do not* continue to serve after the expiration of their terms."[82] The resignation letter from Quinn was drafted in the White House on April 25. Its key provision stated that "I hereby submit to you my resignation from the Court to become effective at such time as you may see fit to accept the resignation."[83] Two days later, the formal notice to the Senate of Quinn's reappointment had been prepared, but Valenti recommended to Johnson that "you allow me to call Senator Pastore and ask him to forward the undated resignation letter from Judge Quinn to you."[84] On April 28, Valenti's office received Quinn's handwritten resignation, dated June 20, 1968. Whereupon the nomination went forward to the Senate.[85]

---

cern. One week later, Pastore wrote to Valenti to "thank you for your cooperation in the Quinn matter. Frankly, this could have had a very disappointing result without your understanding and help, and I want you to know I appreciate it very, very much. I hope that someday you will grant me the opportunity to do something for you." Ibid., April 13, 1966.

[79] JMP, Box 753, USCMA File, April 15, 1966.

[80] Ibid., April 20, 1966.

[81] Ibid., Box 471, April 23, 1966.

[82] Ibid., April 25, 1966, emphasis in the original. Thus, in the interval between the end of Latimer's term and the confirmation and inauguration of Kilday, USCMA had functioned as a two-member court.

[83] LBJ, WHCF, FG 545A, Box 360, April 25, 1966.

[84] Ibid. Johnson's assistant Jake Jacobsen reported to the President that Pastore "told me that Judge Quinn would deliver the letter of resignation to him tomorrow and that he assures us that he will have it here. . . . he gave me his word that the letter of resignation would be forthcoming." Ibid., April 27, 1966.

[85] LBJ, WHCF, Executive FG 58, Folder 17, April 28, 1966. Apparently the fact that Quinn had dated his letter caused some concern, since one of Johnson's aides had assumed that the letter would be undated—as was the usual practice with "blanket resignations." However, Val-

Although the Armed Services Committee had not bothered to invite either Ferguson or Kilday to appear at their confirmation hearings, the Panel insisted on a formal session with Quinn present, because, as Russell put it, "we have had some additions to the Committee since Judge Quinn's original appointment."[86] Ordinarily, he added, "we do not hear those who are up for reappointment."[87] During the very brief hearing, Quinn gave no indication of the previous events concerning renomination. In a response to a question from Massachusetts Republican Leverett Saltonstall—and like the nominee a former Governor of his state—Quinn did remark, however, that he would "be glad" to continue, "if the committee would like to have me . . . I would be glad to serve at least for a few years, as long as the law will let me."[88] After superficial questioning, Quinn's nomination went forward to the full Senate, where he was confirmed on May 16, 1966.[89] On the same day, Johnson again designated Quinn as Chief Judge.

The President had assumed that with Quinn's resignation in hand, he would have a new USCMA appointment in 1968. Ultimately he did, but it would not be to replace Quinn. Moreover, Johnson probably did not anticipate that the tragedy of Vietnam would overtake both him and his adminis-

enti's office made it clear that "June 20, 1968, is the date to which, under the present understanding, Judge Quinn will serve, and that on that basis the nomination . . . can go forward to the Senate."

[86] According to Proulx, the reason for the need for a formal hearing was due to the sudden opposition of Senator Stephen Young to Quinn's reappointment, because one of Young's own judicial candidates had been turned down on the grounds of age, the candidate being over sixty years old. Young, it might be noted, was almost eighty. If Senator Pastore "is not able to persuade Senator Young to withdraw his objection, then Judge Quinn would have to probably appear and . . . they would see for themselves that he is healthy and vigorous." USCMAP, file "Reappointment of Chief Judge Robert E. Quinn," May 5, 1966. Young insisted on a hearing, although Pastore had indeed interceded with him on Quinn's behalf. See below.

[87] Nomination of Judge Robert E. Quinn, May 12, 1966—Committee on Armed Services, U.S. Senate, 89th Cong., 2nd sess.

[88] Ibid., 2. Quinn had dated his letter June 20, 1968, thus making his resignation impossible prior to that date. But he resigned "at such time as you see fit to accept it." Therefore, unless Johnson moved to activate the resignation, theoretically Quinn could continue in office until his term expired, in 1981. It might also be noted that the letter was addressed "to the President," not to Lyndon Johnson.

[89] Indeed, the rest of the session focused more on the type of airy persiflage that so often characterizes a pro forma type of congressional hearing. Saltonstall, for example, noted that "Judge Quinn is another Harvard man." Quinn: "Don't hold that against me." Russell: "We will see if we can find any mitigating circumstances, Judge." Ibid. Although he ultimately supported the reappointment, Senator Young seemed concerned more about Quinn's age than his ability. Referring to the White House proclivity to frown on appointing candidates beyond the age of sixty, Young related a conversation he had with Johnson's Attorney General concerning the appointment of District Judge Sarah Hughes, who was sixty-six. Attorney General Katzenbach allegedly responded, "Well, she was from Texas." Ibid., 6.

tration. Disappointed and defeated, LBJ left the presidency while Quinn remained on the bench. Richard Nixon would have to deal with the next segment of the Quinn saga which, it turned out, was far from over. Indeed, for disgraceful conduct Nixon would also leave the presidency in defeat and disappointment—and when he did, Quinn *still* sat as an USCMA judge.

CHAPTER 8

Litigation, Legislation, and Longevity for Quinn, 1965–1968

ROBERT QUINN has been the only USCMA judge appointed to a second full term. President Johnson, however, did not intend that the Chief Judge should serve out his fifteen-year renewal, an understanding that apparently had been accepted by Quinn. In the meantime, Ferguson, Kilday, and Quinn continued to function as The Court, and the various machinations concerning reappointment of the Chief Judge must be seen in the light of other developments between 1965 and 1968. While the three judges appear to have had mutual respect and regard for each other as colleagues, they strongly disagreed among themselves concerning several new developments in military justice. Not surprisingly, these divided opinions reflected the vigorous reactions among lawyers and judges triggered by the Warren Court's "revolution" in criminal law—a process well under way even as Quinn gained reappointment.[1]

DOCTRINAL DEBATES AND DIVERGENT DECISIONS

In 1964, by a vote of 5–4 the Supreme Court held that an incriminating statement made by a defendant during police interrogation "was inadmissable because the defendant had been denied the right to consult counsel."[2] Whether or not the Warren Court "Revolution" started with this famous decision, *Escobedo v. Illinois*, is less important than the fact that USCMA had grappled with its issues on a number of previous occasions. In 1957, for example, Quinn and Ferguson concluded that while "an accused is not entitled to appointed military counsel prior to the filing of charges . . . he is not thereby precluded from obtaining necessary legal advice."[3] One year later, the same two judges sought to clarify the important distinction between "no

[1] An excellent overview of Warren's distinguished career as Chief Justice, as well as the developments in criminal law during his tenure is in G. Edward White, *Warren: A Public Life* (1982). See in particular 263–78.

[2] *United States v. Wimberley*, 16 USCMA 3, 10 (1966), quoting *Escobedo v. Illinois*, 378 U.S. 478 (1964).

[3] *United States v. Gunnels*, 8 USCMA 130, 133 (1957). Over the strong objection of Latimer, his brethren added that "a suspect has no right to the appointment of military counsel, but he most assuredly has a right to consult with a lawyer of his own choice or with the Staff Judge Advocate." Ibid., 134.

right to appointed counsel as distinguished from no right to consult counsel."[4] These cases involved interrogation of a suspect, later formally accused.

Two years before the *Escobedo* decision, over a dissent by Ferguson, USCMA held that "an accused is not denied the assistance of counsel unless he requests and is refused the right to consult counsel during the interrogation, or is misinformed as to his right to counsel."[5] Two years after *Escobedo*, a unanimous Court declined to extend the right of counsel "to include the investigative processes." Indeed, according to Chief Judge Quinn, "nothing in the [UCMJ,] or in the decisions of this Court, and nothing in our experience with military methods of interrogation, indicate that the only feasible way to give maximum effect to the constitutional right to the assistance of counsel is that the accused have counsel beside him during police questioning."[6]

During the interval between *Petty* and *Wimberley*, Paul Kilday wrote a letter to his brethren expressing "my concern about the number of divided opinions in this Court." A surprising number of persons, he noted, have "expressed to me the hope that we could do something about the high incidence of divided opinions." Indeed, "other than the diehards who want no civilian court, this constitutes the major criticism that I have ever heard" concerning it.[7] The newest USCMA member probably agreed with this viewpoint, all the more because his brethren were the cause for such a condition.

I believe, he wrote, that "divided opinions militate against the prestige of any court." Moreover, "I believe it to be a very serious matter to any court and, especially, a three-judge court."[8] Worst of all, "divided opinions are most confusing in the field. Persons charged with the administration of military justice are left in a quandary as to the statement of the law and what should be followed." Particularly because USCMA normally acted only after a case had already been considered both by a JAG and a court of review—any judicial split "arms our critics with powerful ammunition."[9]

Coming from a perspective of more than twenty years as a Congressman, one who had repeatedly sought to fashion consensus whenever possible, Kilday's views were understandable, although somewhat naive. He held that, "there are not basic differences between the Judges. Our divisions . . . are on

[4] *United States v. Wheaton*, 9 USCMA 257, 259 (1958). Over a dissent by Latimer, the majority affirmed a Board of Review opinion that "the accused was misinformed as to his right to the benefit of counsel."

[5] *United States v. Petty*, 13 USCMA 398, 400–401 (1962).

[6] *United States v. Wimberley*, 16 USCMA 3, 10 (1966).

[7] FP, August 15, 1963. Kilday added that this objection had been expressed to him "in jocular terms," leading him to conclude that "this means that people are not likely to express criticism to members of a court. It does not mean that there is no strong criticism rampant." Ibid., 1–2.

[8] Ibid, 2.

[9] Ibid.

the facts or the application of the law in a particular case."[10] Nevertheless, he concluded, "our divisions have increased rather than diminished." Indeed they had, and the minimal role Kilday played in this trend is very clear.

An examination of several USCMA volumes during the seven years Kilday served on its bench confirms the paucity of his major dissents. In two sample periods, Quinn dissented at least 26 and 16 times, Ferguson 14 and 21 times, while Kilday did not dissent at all![11] In the vast majority of controversial cases, Kilday appears to have been the pivotal swing vote. The 1967 case in which USCMA adopted the Miranda rules for criminal interrogation is an excellent example of this trend.[12] Moreover, the decision also reflects the location of USCMA as an agent of judicial federalism, a key source for the harmonization of military justice with changing constitutional law.

Speaking for himself and Judge Kilday, Judge Ferguson noted that in this case, involving an accused who had requested counsel, the JAG for the Navy had filed an amicus brief in which it urged that "military law is in nowise affected by constitutional limitations." Thus, the principles in *Miranda v. Arizona* were both irrelevant and inapplicable.[13] The Air Force JAG, under whose jurisdiction the case arose, conceded the primacy of the Constitution to military justice. He argued, however, that the Supreme Court "has no supervisory power over military tribunals." Therefore, it was neither necessary nor desirable that USCMA follow its lead. Ferguson did not find any merit in the Navy's position. "The time," he wrote, "is long since past . . . when this Court will lend an attentive ear to the argument that members of the armed services are, by reason of their status, *ipso facto* deprived of all protections of the Bill of Rights."[14]

To be sure, military justice had evolved as a field of jurisprudence somewhat separate from its civilian counterpart.[15] While the extent of such separation remained controversial, by 1967 both USCMA and the High Court were

[10] Ibid, 3. Where, it might be asked, could there be more fundamental areas of juridical disagreement than over facts and law?

[11] The USCMA volumes that justify these conclusions are 13 (October term 1961 and 1962,) and 17 (October term 1966 and 1967). I also examined three other volumes with very similar results. For a rare example of a major Kilday dissent, see *United States v. Ortiz*, 16 USCMA 127 (1966).

[12] *Miranda* established that an individual held for custodial interrogation must be informed *a*) of the right to counsel, *b*) of the fact that in the case of indigency, one will be provided through the Court, and *c*) of the right to remain silent, having been advised that anything stated thereafter could be used in evidence. 384 U.S. 436 (1965).

[13] *United States v. Tempia*, 16 USCMA 629 (1967).

[14] 16 USCMA 629, 633 (1967).

[15] See, for example, *Orloff v. Willoughby*, 345 U.S. 83 (1953); *Burns v. Wilson*, 346 U.S. 137 (1953); *Parker v. Levy*, 417 U.S. 733 (1974); *Schlesinger v. Councilman*, 420 U.S. 738 (1975); *Brown v. Glines*, 444 U.S. 348 (1980); *Frontiero v. Richardson*, 411 U.S. 677 (1973); *Rostker v. Goldberg*, 453 U.S. 57 (1981); and *Chappell v. Wallace*, 462 U.S. 296 (1983).

"satisfied as to the applicability of constitutional safeguards to military trials, except insofar as they are made inapplicable either expressly or by necessary implication."[16] Nor was there validity to the contention that *Miranda* represented a supervisory function rather than one of constitutional adjudication. Calling the Air Force JAG's position an "ingenious argument," Ferguson reiterated the assumption that United States Supreme Court views on constitutional issues "are binding on us."[17] Because the defendant in this case had been informed "that no counsel would be appointed for him, [contrary to the Miranda rule] it follows that the statement thereafter taken from him was inadmissable in evidence."[18]

Although Kilday agreed with Ferguson that "this Court is bound by the Supreme Court on questions of constitutional import," Quinn insisted that the Supreme Court had not intended to apply *Miranda* "to the military legal system."[19] He pointed to the well-established doctrine set forth in the UCMJ against self-incrimination, arguing that its provisions in Article 31 "satisfy all constitutional requirements."[20] Quinn further claimed that although not specifically required by the code, the actual military practice of "according the individual faced with in-custody interrogation the right to consult the staff legal officer . . . is fully as effective a safeguard" as what is set forth in *Miranda*.[21] To demand more, as did his brethren "is to legislate, not adjudicate."[22] While in this case Quinn had found himself in dissent, on numerous

[16] Tempia, 634. Ferguson's prose concealed the real and lasting controversy in back of his statement. As will be seen in the final chapters of this volume, during the tenure of Albert Fletcher, Jr., as Chief Judge from 1975–80, the issue of "civilizing the military justice system" was of great concern. As will also be seen, Ferguson's rhetoric tends to differ from the reality of military justice.

[17] Ibid., 634–35. To make his point even clearer, Ferguson included a summary excerpt from *Miranda* in the introduction to his opinion, adding that "we commend a reading of [the decision] to all involved in the administration of military criminal law as well as the undertaking of educative measures to see that its precepts are not violated in pre-trial interrogations." Ibid., 636.

[18] Ibid., 638.

[19] Ibid., 643.

[20] Ibid., 643–44.

[21] Although with the benefit of hindsight, greatly utilized by historians, Ferguson was correct. In 1966 no less a constitutional scholar than Senator Samuel Ervin, Jr., had raised points that supported Quinn. "I am not sure," Ervin wrote, "that [the] decision in [Miranda] can be applied directly to the military situation. For a start, the constitutional foundation for the [UCMJ] is quite different from that underlying the Court's decision. Secondly, the code . . . under which the military operates is quite different from that pertaining to the civilian community. Thirdly, the social fabric of the military and the relationships between authority and the individual servicemen are so different that the problems of law, order, and military discipline create a distinctly different balance between accused and authority. Because of these circumstances, the precise rules ordained by the Supreme Court may be quite inappropriate in the military circumstances." Samuel J. Ervin, Jr., Papers, hereafter cited as ERV, September 8, 1966, Box 159, Folder 500.

[22] Ibid., 644–65. Ferguson had already referred to Quinn's forthcoming dissent in his majority

occasions he joined with Kilday, leaving Fèrguson as the dissenter.[23] On the other hand, the combination of Quinn and Ferguson, with Kilday in dissent, was very rare.

THE TENUOUSNESS OF TENURE

It will be recalled that in 1963, the House of Representatives had passed the bill granting USCMA judges life tenure, only to see it stalled in the Senate—a victim both of Richard Russell's unyielding opposition, and the legislative logjam of statutes proposed in the wake of President Kennedy's assassination. It will further be recalled that during 1965–66 Quinn's concern had shifted to the question of his reappointment. With that goal attained, USCMA sought yet again to gain equal tenure status with other federal appellate judges. Indeed, Court efforts toward this goal had been ongoing even before Quinn began his campaign to retain his seat.

Thus, Judge Kilday had visited with his friend Lyndon Johnson on October 23, 1963. He also urged Quinn to ask Senator Pastore to see both Johnson and Russell. By the time Quinn talked with Pastore in January 1964, Johnson had become President, and Russell had made it clear to House Speaker John McCormack [a close friend of Quinn] that he "is definitely opposed to the bill—to life tenure for any court."[24] Kilday also believed that

---

opinion, noting that "we are not persuaded by our brother's views that we have anticipated the Supreme Court in this area, or that the military justice picture is as rosy as he paints it." Ibid., 640.

[23] For a few examples of Quinn's disagreements with Ferguson and Kilday, see *United States v. Murray*, 15 USCMA 183 (1964); *United States v. Garlich*, 15 USCMA 362, 373 (1965). "The principal opinion starts with the wrong premise and ends with the wrong conclusion." *United States v. O'Such*, 16 USCMA 537, 548, 551 (1967). "Many undisputed facts and important procedural matters are disregarded by the majority. . . . Emotion-laden words are not substitutes for facts." For a representative sampling of Ferguson's doctrinal disputes wth Quinn and Kilday, see *United States v. Albert*, 16 USCMA, 111, 115–16, 118 (1966). "With cases such as this, the Court sounds a death knell for the [UCMJ provision dealing with command influence]. . . . Holdings such as this will only weaken public confidence in military justice, and rightly so. Nor may the armed services derive any comfort from them, for they will surely lead an aroused Congress to more restrictive and detailed legislation. . . ." *United States v. Crawford*, 15 USCMA, 31, 49 (1964.) "This case presents issues of the gravest concern to the administration of military justice. . . . I regret that my brothers have reached a different conclusion . . . because of the incalculable damage done to our system of military justice."

[24] USCMAP, Life Tenure File January 23, 24, 1964. Quinn reminded Proulx that "we're the only *Federal Court of Appeals* [emphasis in original] without life tenure, and that the only Court in the jurisdiction of the Armed Services Committee remains a kind of orphan." Ibid., January 29, 1964. As the first volume of this study noted—the decision to link the enactment of the UCMJ and thus of USCMA to the Armed Services Committee rather than the Judiciary had been based not only on the fact that the nature of the code was military rather than civilian, but also on the fear that the powerful Judiciary Committee chair, Patrick McCarran, would be less cooperative than would his Armed Services counterpart. In 1964, by an interesting twist of

Maine Republican Senator Margaret Chase Smith "has great influence with Senator Russell." In other words, as Quinn observed to Rhode Island Congressman John Fogarty, "there is work to be done."[25] By April, however, Kilday and Quinn had conceded that "any further effort to get Senator Russell to buy life tenure would be useless."[26]

Being no novices to political behavior, the next question may well have occurred both to Quinn and Kilday simultaneously. Since Russell "would not budge, would he buy the bill without life tenure[?]" The recalcitrant Senator agreed. His House counterpart, Carl Vinson, immediately indicated that the House bill would be revised, cutting out life tenure but retaining the fifteen-year terms, plus other pension benefits in the original measure. Thus by April 13, instead of gaining ratification for life tenure, in reality Quinn and Kilday faced its requiem.[27]

Within ten days, Proulx met with William Darden, a staff member of Russell's committee and longtime aide to its chair. Shortly thereafter, he prepared a summary of the benefits included in the house bill, albeit without life tenure. The measure would "confirm the Court of Military Appeals as a legislative court established under Article I of the Constitution." Moreover, "it would make explicit what is now implicit," that its judges "are entitled to the salary, allowances and perquisites of judges of the U.S. Courts of appeals." It would give USCMA judges the same retirement rights as their Article III counterparts. Finally, "It will enhance the standing and prestige of the court by providing security for those serving as judges thereof. . . . Currently, a federal district judge of proven ability would not aspire to membership on [USCMA] because of the diminished security and lesser retirement rights."[28]

Even though this measure was apparently acceptable to Russell, no efforts appear to have been undertaken to enact it until 1967. The delay was due in part to the vicissitudes of political action in Washington, including the lengthy debate and three-month-long Senate filibuster over the 1964 Civil Rights bill. In September 1967, Senator Pastore wrote to Quinn, reminding him once again of Russell's "antipathy to life tenure. Right or wrong, that's the way he feels not only to the military court, [but] I suppose to all courts."[29]

---

irony, the exact opposite situation took place. The rigid opposition of Armed Services Committee Chairman Richard Russell to life tenure doomed the measure, while the Judiciary Committee was much more sympathetic to the proposal.

[25] Ibid., February 6, 1964.

[26] Ibid., April 13, 1964.

[27] Ibid.

[28] Ibid., Undated statement on the "effects of changes to HR 3179, with removal of the life tenure provision." Rhetoric aside, while fixed terms were desirable, the question can be raised as to what judicial security could mean to USCMA judges without its most basic component—life tenure. Moreover, there is validity to the conclusion that by its refusal to grant USCMA judges equal standing with other federal appellate judges, Congress denigrates its own creation.

[29] QPPC, September 20, 1967. "This is a feeling," added Pastore, "quite prevalent among the southern senators and here again I suppose it stems from the Civil Rights issue."

The next day, Darden sent Pastore a draft of a statute based on the old 1963 House bill but stripped of its life tenure provision. He also provided an additional reason why USCMA may not have urged that the 1963–64 "compromise" bill be adopted. Darden noted that although "in 1964 this version of the bill was acceptable to Senator Russell, I think, . . . it produces so little change that the Judges of the Court apparently were in disagreement over whether such a bill was worth enactment."[30] For reasons that are unclear, by November 1967 Quinn and his colleagues may well have decided to accept what they could get, even though it was much less than had originally been sought. After satisfying himself that both Quinn and Russell would support it, Pastore introduced the new proposal—which cleared Russell's committee in less than three weeks.[31] No further hearings were held on the bill, possibly because there was so little of substance that remained in it.

Similarly, in reporting the bill favorably to the Senate, Russell could not point to any major legislative innovation contained in the measure. His statement emphasized "the congressional intent . . . that the Court of Military Appeals be a court in every significant respect." But "despite this clear intent, there have been contentions that the court is not a court at all but is an instrumentality of the executive branch or an administrative agency within the Department of Defense."[32] By redesignating the Court of Military Appeals as the U.S. Court of Military Appeals, and affirming its creation under Article I of the Constitution, the legislation would "reaffirm the congressional intent that the court be the civilian supervisor of the administration of military justice and the final interpreter of the requirements of military law."[33]

As if to leave the matter beyond all doubt, Russell added that "the bill proposes no change either in the term of offices or the retirement benefits of the judges." It did provide, however, for the possibility that an USCMA retired judge might be recalled to active status if needed, and could occupy offices in a federal building. In making the change in name official, the Senate merely ratified what had long since been the informal rule at USCMA, to refer to itself as the United States Court of Military Appeals.[34] Without

[30] Ibid., November 21, 1967.

[31] 17 CF, November 2, 20, 21, 22, 1967.

[32] 90th Cong., 1st sess., Senate Report #806 "Establishing the Court of Military Appeals as the U.S. Court of Military Appeals," November 27, 1967, 2. The report further noted that while USCMA is "located for administrative purposes in the Department of Defense," this phrase referred only to its function of furnishing the court with "such things as telephone services, transportation facilities, and to purchase supplies. The court justifies its own budget and funds are appropriated for its operations with no control exercised by the Department of Defense." For about the first twenty-five years of its history, this statement was apparently true. But during the controversial tenure of Albert Fletcher, Jr., as Chief Judge between 1975 and 1980, the Department actively interfered in the Court's budgetary procedures. See below, chapters 10–11.

[33] Ibid.

[34] The Court, however, had been calling itself the "United States" Court of Military Appeals since 1951. See 1 USCMA, xxiii.

formal discussion or recorded vote, the Senate passed the bill the next day.[35] Almost seven months later, and without serious debate or a recorded vote, the House concurred.[36] Thus far, the current congressional action concerning USCMA had been of such limited significance that earlier considerations within the Court about not even bothering to endorse such a bill become understandable.[37] But there remained substantial congressional interest in military justice, and immediately after passing the innocuous measure just described, the House turned to an additional piece of legislation that ultimately would be called the Military Justice Act of 1968. Its legislative history deserves some attention.

THE EXTENDED EFFORTS OF SENATOR ERVIN

After the 1962 Senate hearings, Ervin had introduced a number of bills to reform military justice.[38] The bills never left the Senate Committee to which they had been referred, and in 1965, Ervin submitted them again, reintroducing the measures with virtually the same comments he had used before.[39] In 1966, a special subcommittee drawn from both the Senate Armed Services and Judiciary Committees held hearings on the proposals. Many witnesses who had appeared previously came forward again to reiterate their views. But the 1966 hearings differed from the 1962 sessions in two important ways.

In the first place, all parties concerned were well aware that there was now a much greater public interest in military matters, even as the Vietnam War

[35] 90th Cong., 1st sess., *Cong. Record*, Senate, vol. 113, November 28, 1967, 33910.

[36] 90th Cong., 2d sess., *House Report #1480*, "U.S. Court of Military Appeals," May 27, 1968; *Congressional Record*, 90th Cong., vol. 113, part 11, June 3, 1968, 15804.

[37] To this day, the Court has not received life tenure.

[38] See above, chapter 7. Ervin, who served in the U.S. Senate from 1954–74, represented an intriguing amalgam of liberal and conservative views. Thus he was very supportive of due process protection for members of the military. Upon hearing that a Navy petty officer had lost his confidential security clearance because he criticized American policy in Vietnam, Ervin wrote a strong protest to Secretary of Defense Robert McNamara. "That a citizen should suffer any penalty because he dared express views contrary to official policy, is an affront to the most basic principles that we as free individuals and American citizens hold supreme." ERV, Box 180, Folder 622, October 7, 1967. On the other hand, Ervin denounced civil rights legislation with equal vigor. He did not believe that "the Federal government may constitutionally preempt the criminal jurisdiction of the States to punish private acts of discrimination. . . ." The Civil Rights Bill of 1968 was "another futile exercise in attempting to solve racial problems by the coercive power of the law instead of through increased understanding and cooperation of the races." Ibid., Box 201, Folder 560, April 17, 1968.

[39] "Military Justice—" *Joint Hearings Before the Subcommittee on Constitutional Rights of the Committee on the Judiciary and a Special Subcommittee of the Committee on Armed Services, U.S. Senate*, 89th Cong., 2nd sess., 1966; hereafter cited as Hearings2, followed by appropriate page number.

intensified. Moreover, the 1966 hearings revealed a well-orchestrated effort by the military to transform certain of Ervin's bills into a format acceptable to them. Ultimately, as is so often the case, neither the objects of the intended legislation nor its sponsor obtained all they wanted. But, in retrospect one is impressed with the way in which the military, in particular the Army, employed compromise rather than confrontation.[40]

Among Ervin's bills were several which would have made changes in USCMA jurisdiction within military justice. Based upon his 1963 proposals, they sought to: (*a*) strengthen the means for penalizing unlawful command influence; (*b*) provide a pretrial conference in certain court-martials; (*c*) provide military judges for special courts-martial; (*d*) give USCMA the authority to review administrative discharges and dismissals from the services; (*e*) prohibit a senior board of review member from evaluating another member; (*f*) set up a civilian board to correct military records; (*g*) increase the authority of the law officer, now to be called the military judge; and finally (*h*) replace the existing boards of review with new tribunals—to be called courts of military review, to be appointed by the service secretary instead of TJAG, and to have a civilian as chief judge. Taken as a whole, again these changes would have made major alterations in the operating procedures for military justice—although Ervin emphasized that it was not his purpose "to do anything whatever which would impair in any way the capacity of the Armed Forces to maintain discipline." Rather, he hoped to "ascertain whether or not we can bring that necessary function and the administration of military justice into harmony with each other."[41]

Although not directly addressed in any of Ervin's measures, the issue of

[40] Indeed, when compared to the antagonistic "stonewalling" with which the Army JAG Corps had blocked the Ansell reforms in 1919–20, the flexibility demonstrated during 1966–68 is striking. See AMJ, 112–18, and infra. Attention should also be called to the way in which Ervin sought to lessen, if not eliminate, possible jurisdictional friction between the Senate Armed Services and Judiciary Committees. The solution was to hold hearings under a special joint subcommittee, drawn from both bodies. In fact, however, the "decision-making power"—as a former legal staff member recalled—rested in the Armed Services Committee. Interview, February 13, 1995, Lawrence Baskir, Deputy General Counsel, Dept. of the Army. Although Ervin was a member of both panels, and although he chaired the special joint subcommittee, in fact the links between senior Senate members of the Armed Services Committee and the Defense Department insured that certain of his proposals would not survive.

[41] Hearings2, 14. Ervin was genuinely concerned with this goal. He sought, through his proposals, that the military justice system "attain, insofar as human wisdom can, the closest approximation to true justice." There was no intention to interfere with the "prerequisites of the national safety. Rather, it has been to maintain the integrity and prestige of the military judicial system, while at the same time incorporating the essential legal safeguards which have been nurtured and severed through centuries of our history. It is of the utmost importance that the arm of our society which is entrusted with the defense of our liberties and our freedom not be found lacking in one of the most valuable aspects of our civilization, judicial protections of individual rights." ERV, February 24, 1966, Box 158, Folder 483.

life tenure for USCMA could not be ignored. The well-known opposition of Richard Russell notwithstanding, one of Ervin's proposals involved life tenure, but not for that court. Supporting the measure that the new Court of Military Review must have a civilian as a tenured chief Judge, Quinn noted that in providing life tenure for this civilian appointment, the bill gave an intermediate court judge greater security than the highest appellate tribunal in military justice. Moreover, although he declined to push the proposal, Ervin remained troubled by the disinclination of the Senate to consider USCMA tenure. "I think it is a great mistake. I certainly think the other Federal courts rather look down their noses at the Court of Military Appeals, and are inclined to think that it is not a court in every sense of the word."[42]

All three USCMA judges appeared before the subcommittee, and all endorsed legislative efforts to deal effectively with command influence. But they insisted that Congress, not the judges, had to solve this problem. Quinn urged prosecution for "deliberate attempts to exercise command control," stating that "just because a general or admiral commits the offense should not make him any less amenable to prosecution than a private."[43] Ferguson pointed to the inherent impropriety of a staff JAG officer retaliating "against counsel's efforts to serve his client by giving him a totally unsatisfactory efficiency report."[44] Such a scenario, one that he claimed had actually occurred, represented a serious threat to military justice.

"If the defense counsel, in the best traditions of our bar, ignores the efforts to influence him and stands up and fights for his client, he gets a bad efficiency report which can absolutely ruin his military career." If the influence is ineffective, the court can do nothing, because "the accused has had his day in court and there is no basis for reversal. . . . If, on the other hand, counsel is in fact fearful for his career, we will hear nothing about it, for the record will be totally silent in the matter.[45] The dice, therefore, are loaded in favor of the sycophant, and something should and must be done by the Congress."[46]

[42] Hearings2, 282. "I think our court should have equal standing with other federal courts of the United States." It is interesting to note that Ervin strongly endorsed Quinn's quest for life tenure, even though he had already signaled his refusal to push for such a step given the implacable opposition of Richard Russell. Ervin claimed that he has "always been under the opinion" that life tenure was mandated for those exercising a federal judicial function. "I think the Constitution meant that, and I am an advocate of making that provision . . . effective in military appeals as well as in other courts. I trust we will get the Senate to go along with the House in that matter." Ibid., 290.

[43] Ibid., 287.

[44] Ibid., 302.

[45] It might be noted that Ferguson's logic could also be applied to military trial and intermediate appellate judges. But see *Weiss and Hernandez v. United States*, 510 U.S. 163 (1994).

[46] Ibid. Such comments contributed to Ferguson's reputation as "the scourge of the military justice system." See 90th Cong., 2nd sess., *Cong. Record*, Senate, vol. 113, part 23, November

While the view that USCMA was fundamentally unnecessary and undesirable may still have had some adherents within the JAG Corps, to say nothing of the military services themselves—by 1965 the armed services had long since abandoned doctrinaire opposition to its existence.[47] Further, its leaders—especially representatives of the Army JAG Corps—recognized that in 1966 blanket opposition to Ervin's bills might well be counterproductive. Major General Kenneth Hodson, who represented the Defense Department before the Ervin subcommittee and who shortly thereafter became *The* JAG of the Army, was candid in his recollections. The goal, he recalled, was "to come up with one package which we thought would be acceptable to the Army staff and might be somewhat acceptable to Senator Ervin as a substitute to his many proposals." It was necessary "to come up with a counterproposal . . . rather than merely take a negative approach, because a negative approach eventually will be worn down in the halls of Congress[,] but a counterproposal sometimes will be acceptable. . . ."[48]

On the other hand, the military had real difficulties with several of Ervin's measures just noted. More amenable to change if undertaken within the existing system, it remained hostile to any idea of increased civilian participation or jurisdiction in military justice. The bill to create a single civilian Board to review and correct military records could be seen as such an attempt to intrude civilian oversight into the military justice system. Thus Air Force Secretary Eugene Zuckert—who in 1948–49 had served as a member of the

---

1, 1967, 30718–19. Ferguson noted further that the specific deterrent of a punitive article in the UCMJ, as well as a mandatory dismissal from the service of an officer convicted of such conduct might be effective, "providing one can ever get a man who has violated the code in this manner brought to trial." But the jurist believed that "there have been no such prosecutions. Thus, I suggest you may also wish to provide for civilian prosecution of this violation." In point of fact, there appears to have been at least one instance of such a military prosecution. See AMJ, 199 n. 18. But one or two examples in almost half a century of military justice under the UCMJ is an unimpressive statistic. Indeed, the continued inability if not disinclination of the military to prosecute for improper command influence bedevils its justice system. Judicial rhetoric against the practice is impressive, but judicial retribution against its perpetrators as contrasted with its victims is virtually nonexistent. It may be unfair to criticize USCMA, as the court cannot reach beyond the specific case before it toward the individuals guilty of such an offense, yet the judges have failed to insist that the military must resolve the problem. In short, it can be argued that the Court has failed to make effective use of the admittedly limited weapons it possesses against unlawful command influence.

[47] An exception to this generalization was the first Air Force TJAG, Reginald Harmon, who in 1987 recalled of USCMA that "I don't think we needed it, and I don't think we need it now." AMJ, 181.

[48] USCMAP, Senior Officers Debriefing Program, Conversations between Kenneth Hodson and Robert Boyer, 1971–1972, U.S. Army Military History Institute, V, 2–4. It may be that Ervin, himself no stranger to the legislative process, realized from the outset that gaining passage of some twenty bills dealing with military justice would be an impossibility. If the military appeared ready to pick and choose with an eye toward compromise, so was he. The end result, as will be seen, embodied the Military Justice Act of 1968.

Committee that created both UCMJ and USCMA—criticized this proposal as an unwarranted introduction of appellate procedure in an area where administrative oversight was logical, appropriate, and indeed, ongoing.[49]

For similar reasons, the military as well as the Defense Department objected to the possibility that USCMA should review administrative discharges. "We feel," General Hodson emphasized, "that [USCMA] should not be burdened with matters that are not concerned with the administration of military justice. . . . It is unnecessary in the first place." Moreover, it would raise "unusual manpower requirements" within the JAG corps, resulting in expenses which could not be justified.[50] Although unarticulated, the military also held the view that permitting USCMA to review such discharges would further involve the civilian court in what had always been conceived as primarily a military responsibility.

Zuckert expressed even greater opposition to Ervin's idea that existing boards of review become courts of military review—with at least one of a three-member panel to be a civilian, designated as the chief judge, and tenured as well. The Defense Department, he wrote, "is not persuaded that the administration of military justice . . . would be improved if senior military officers who have devoted their entire adult lives to the practice of military law were replaced by civilian employees."[51] Moreover, such a change would have an "erosive effect on the prestige of military lawyers. By its terms, it tells all [JAGs] . . . that they will never be qualified to reach the top of their profession—that is[,] to preside over an appellate court appointed by a service secretary," a proposition which, according to General Hodson, "is simply not true."[52]

The military position on the subject of command influence, especially as it concerned improper evaluation of the lower appellate court judges, generally consisted of outright denial that such incidents occurred, let alone that they

[49] Hearings2, 490. Zuckert further noted that "the determination of whether a conviction should be set aside or modified for legal reasons is essentially the exercise of a judicial function. It is therefore believed that the authority to make such a determination should be given to the [JAG,] rather than to an administrative board operating apart from the established system of military justice." Ibid., 491. In testimony before Ervin's subcommittee, General Hodson made the same point, using the exact same words. Ibid., 20.

[50] Ibid., 99.

[51] Ibid., 504. From its inception, the UCMJ had authorized the use of civilians on the military boards [courts] of review, at the option of TJAG. Apparently only the Navy and the Coast Guard have in fact employed civilians—and on a very limited basis—as court members.

[52] Ibid., 22, 504. Hodson believed that "enactment of this bill, with its implication of lack of confidence in the ability of military lawyers to fill important positions in the administration of military justice, will make it even more difficult to attract qualified lawyers for service in the Armed Forces." He reiterated the point later during the hearings. "If we do not have jobs of challenge back here in the United States to assign these people to when they arrive at senior rank, then it means that the 30-year career is going to be spent in the boondocks in Korea because there will be no jobs back here for them." Ibid., 44.

were inappropriate. It simply was not true that the chairmen of the various judicial panels were unable to rate fairly and objectively. To say otherwise, as the legal officer to the Marine Corps Commandant noted, "misjudges the caliber and devotion of our people to the point almost of being slanderous. . . ."[53] As to the extent of command influence, while the military now conceded that the practice "is not legal[,] . . . our problem with [it] is really a question of the exercise of judgment, and we cannot legislate good judgment."[54]

Civilians who testified before Ervin's committee found the idea of a court member submitting efficiency reports on other court members unacceptable. Frederick Wiener, a retired Army JAG colonel and an astute observer of military justice, was both blunt and accurate. "You can't have judicial independence. What kind of court would the highest court of any jurisdiction be if the chief justice could write efficiency reports on the other members? You would have a one-man court. . . ."[55] Similarly, Wiener endorsed strengthening the UCMJ against command influence, although again he struck right at a potentially fatal weakness in such a reform. "I have an uncomfortable suspicion that the process of forbidding command influence in a hierarchial [*sic*] body is a little bit like the development of weapons and counterweapons: No matter how good a particular weapon, there will ultimately be developed an effective defense thereto, and no matter how effective any defense, there will ultimately be found a new weapon to overcome it."[56]

Ervin's joint subcommittee concluded its hearings in March 1966, but it

[53] Ibid., 47. No officer sitting as a judge, he added, "who has devoted his entire adult lifetime to the service of the law is likely to put an accused in and out of jail just to please his boss. . . ." Ervin could not resist pointing to "a human element which I admit I succumb to. I am always inclined to think that the wisest members of the Senate are those who share my sound views on questions." Ibid.

[54] Ibid., 59. Earlier, Ervin had scoffed at the idea of a total absence of command influence in any court-martial, saying that such a claim reminded him of the story about a lawyer "summoned down to the jail to see his client. The lawyer asked him, 'What have they got you here for?' And the client told him. The lawyer said, 'Well, they can't put a man in jail for that.' And his client said, 'Well, I am here.'" Ibid., 57.

[55] Ibid., 322. "Now somewhere I read that the services feel that this impugns the military honor of board chairmen. Well, I say with all deference, or not much deference, that is nonsense." Wiener had appeared before congressional committees dealing with military justice on many occasions. By 1966, he concluded that while "I would be the last to expound the infallibility of the [UCMJ], the services will have to live with it, the Navy along with the other three. The sooner the code is cheerfully accepted by all whom it governs, the sooner it is likely to be improved." Thus Wiener had found that the Navy's stubborn resistance to a separate JAG corps for its service "certainly casts doubts on the good faith of the consistent opposition to this proposal over the years." Ibid.

[56] Ibid., 314. "After all, the purpose of discipline in the Army is different from the civilian community. We are legislating for a different kind of social organism, if that isn't too sociological a bit of jargon. There is always going to be a certain degree of command influence." Ibid., 326.

was not until June 1967 that he reintroduced the "Military Justice Act of 1967" in the Senate. Recognizing the corrosive effect of the lengthening Vietnam conflict, Ervin reminded his colleagues that "more and more private citizens are being called to service in an ugly war. . . . We cannot wait, as we did a generation ago, until these men return to civilian life with their stories of injustice."[57] He claimed that, with few exceptions, the new proposals incorporated the provisions introduced earlier. The exceptions however, reflected legislative realities—and they were more significant than Ervin acknowledged.

Thus Ervin had sought to abolish the summary court-martial. The unanimous opposition of all the armed services, joined by the Defense Department—which, unlike the 1948–49 period, appeared increasingly inclined to speak for the military rather than to it—doomed this provision. Ervin was able to retain a stipulation giving a service member an option to decline a summary court, thus insuring that "no citizen would be forced to stand trial against his will in an American court . . . where the same man is judge and jury, prosecutor and defense counsel." Nevertheless, although the summary court "is an inferior court in concept, procedure, and in the quality of justice it dispenses[,]" it remained part of the UCMJ.[58]

Moreover, while Ervin's bill retained the intermediate appellate courts, and while he placed responsibility for selection of their judges in the hands of the service secretaries rather than the JAGs, he deleted the earlier stipulation that the chief judge must be both tenured and a civilian.[59] Now "the Secretary . . . shall from time to time designate one of the judges . . . as chief judge[,] . . . on the basis of seniority of service . . . and his judicial and administrative abilities."[60] Taken as a whole, however, Ervin's proposed Military Justice Act of 1967 represented a significant and far reaching transformation of the UCMJ. Promptly referred to the Senate Armed Services Committee, for reasons which remain unclear the omnibus bill never reached the Senate floor.[61] Further impetus for changes in the UCMJ shifted to the House.

[57] *Congressional Record*, vol. 113, part 13, 90th Cong., 1st Sess., June 26, 1967, 17323. See 17323–24 for a good summary of Ervin's efforts from 1962 to 1967 concerning this legislation.

[58] Ibid., 17324. It still does. See Eugene R. Fidell, "The Summary Court-Martial: A Proposal," *Harvard Journal on Legislation* 8, (1971), 571.

[59] Ibid., 17334. A civilian could, however, still be appointed to the CMR, but such selections have been extremely rare.

[60] Ibid.

[61] Ibid., 17325. On November 1, with no indication that immediate action on his bill was forthcoming, Ervin reminded his colleagues that "the importance of subjecting military law to public scrutiny cannot be overstated. . . . [P]ublic concern has not touched the military system. Where once it was truly a model for the civilian law, now it has been left behind in many respects. Much must be done by Congress and the military itself to restore military justice to the honored place it once held." Ibid., November 1, 1967, 30713.

Aware of the significant changes desired by Ervin, the military—aided by a special ABA committee—drafted an alternative measure. Submitted to the House Armed Services Committee in April 1967, it had the unanimous backing of all the services as well as the Defense Department. Compared to what Ervin had sought, one can easily understand why.

The bill focused primarily on increased participation of law officers on courts-martial. On the other hand, it made no changes in the courts of military review, provided no increase in USCMA authority, and barred trial before a military judge alone without the consent of the convening authority.[62] Moreover, it made no mention of any civilian board to correct and/or review military records. While the legislation blocked a special court-martial from awarding a bad conduct discharge unless the accused was represented by legally qualified counsel, this safeguard was waived in time of war. Representative Philbin was not guilty of exaggeration when he later claimed that the bill was merely "an attempt to make a few changes that are noncontroversial."[63] Even so, its supporters worried that any modification of its provisions might block ultimate enactment. Thus, Congressman Bennett warned his colleagues against tampering with it.

"There are a lot of things here that are greatly needed. . . . There are a lot of people that would like to improve on various aspects of it, but once you start improving . . . you get into a controversial area which in my opinion would absolutely doom this legislation in 1968. . . . We have been working on it for years. We finally got it down to something that nobody objects to." In response to a committee member troubled by the wartime exemption just noted, Bennett replied, "You have concern that it doesn't go further than it goes, but you don't have concern about how far it goes."[64]

Representative Price reassured Bennett that he favored the bill. He observed, correctly, that "when you give a man a bad conduct discharge you are putting a stigma on him for life, and I think he should have adequate protection." As written, the exception in time of war would give the military the "opportunity for people in the field to say, 'well, we just couldn't find a legal counsel.' They will find a way of justifying the reason they couldn't

[62] Ervin strongly opposed this provision, arguing—correctly—that it gave the commander the potential for improper influence over a court-martial proceeding.

[63] 90th Cong., 2nd sess., House Report #1481, May 27, 1968, 2; included in USCMAP, *Legislative History of the Military Justice Act of 1968*, 11; hereafter cited as LH, followed by appropriate pagination.

[64] LH, 76–77. Bennett added that he would have no objection to changing this exemption, "but you will find when you do so there are an unreasonable number of worms that will come out of the woodwork, to object to it. . . . I want to make the improvement. . . . I would like to make it, but if you insist on putting it in here, this law will never be enacted in 1968, in my opinion." 79. As was seen in 1949–50 during debate over the UCMJ, a favorite tactic of legislators was to argue that changing the proposed legislation in *any* way would be detrimental, possibly leading to its rejection.

find it, even if they could have gotten one by going a hundred miles down the road."[65] The Committee decided not to make any changes, but to add "a very strong statement in the report" that counsel should be readily available, before sending the measure to the full House.

Within a few weeks, however, the committee reconsidered the issue. Representative Philbin reported that he had been in touch with General Hodson, who "was able to get agreement within the Department of Defense to eliminate the exception completely."[66] As amended, the proposed bill cleared the House on June 3, 1968, without change, debate, or recorded vote.[67] Promptly introduced into the Senate, the enactment was duly referred to the Armed Services Committee where Senator Ervin was ready and waiting.

Although Ervin later submitted a committee report of more than thirty pages, endorsing a heavily amended version of the House bill, he insisted that his revisions were only "an attempt to make a few changes that can be agreed upon by the Congress and the armed services," trying "to improve some of the procedures and increase the substantive safeguards in courts-martial."[68] Ervin can be pardoned for his disingenuousness. But one need only compare the bill as originally passed by the House, with the alterations adopted by the Senate and later concurred in by the lower chamber, to see that the revisions incorporated many of the "reform" measures of concern to him for more than six years. In both his written correspondence and his later remarks to the Senate, as that body prepared to vote on the amendments, the North Carolina Senator was more candid.

Writing to TJAG Hodson only a few weeks after passage of HR 15971, Ervin claimed that the measure did not contain "the minimum reforms of the [UCMJ] necessary to return the military system of criminal justice to the leading position it so recently occupied in American Law." Therefore, he concluded that "a number of amendments are necessary . . . and I shall offer

[65] Ibid., 80. Earlier, Price had observed, "In my experience, the most unfortunate cases arise in time of war[,] and where the most damage and harm and lack of consideration is given is in time of war. This is where they need protection the greatest." Ibid., 77.

[66] Ibid., 121. It may well be that once Philbin made it clear to Hodson that there might be attempts—with the potential for success—at altering key provisions of the bill, Hodson convinced his colleagues that what they had in the bill was ultimately better than what they might receive. Elimination of the offending exception was not, apparently, too great a price to pay. Moreover, Hodson was well aware that the Senate might well restore it.

[67] Ibid., 205. Philbin described the bill as "the first of many revisions that will now be made in the [UCMJ]. I feel it is a good first step." Ibid., 204.

[68] Ibid., 39. Ervin's "few changes" would "redesignate the law officer of a court-martial as military judge to give him functions and powers more closely allied to those of Federal district judges, increase the availability of legally qualified counsel to represent the accused in courts-martial, redesignate appellate boards of review as 'courts of military review,' . . . increase the independence of military judges and members and other officials of courts-martial from unlawful influence by convening authorities and other commanding officers, and increase the post-conviction safeguards and remedies available to the accused."

them when the bill is considered by the Senate Armed Services Committee."[69] In a letter to his fellow southerner, and chairman of the Armed Services Committee Richard Russell, Ervin described the eight changes he desired in the legislation. Among the most important were:

1) redesignation of the "law officer" as the "military Judge"; 2) creating an independent field judiciary; 3) requirement of legally qualified military counsel in all special courts-martial; 4) facilitating the option by a serviceman for trial by a summary court-martial; 5) strengthening the ban against command influence; 6) providing that a military judge must preside at all special courts-martial empowered to adjudge a bad conduct discharge; and 7) redesignation of the boards of military review as courts of military review.[70]

In justifying these amendments, Ervin reminded Russell that his original Senate bill "is the product of eight years of study . . . and two series of hearings. . . . The record of those hearings ran to over 2,000 pages, and included the testimony and view of some 100 expert witnesses."[71] Rather than revive this measure, Ervin wanted to amend the House version. "I am hopeful that you will agree with me that all of the amendments are meritorious, and that, in view of the extensive hearings . . . no further hearings are necessary."[72] But Ervin realized that if more hearings were to be avoided, controversy over the bill had to be minimal; as his Subcommittee Chief Counsel and Staff Director explained to Robinson Everett.

Conceding that the House bill was a "far cry" from Ervin's measure, Ervin had to consider the warning from his House counterpart that the entire chamber "would not accept much more than the reforms" contained in its version." Rather than find out how true this assertion was, Ervin determined to "beef up the House bill" as previously noted. Several of the committee staff "had extensive discussions" with Army representatives from the JAG Corps, with a resulting agreement that the military would not oppose six out of the eight Ervin changes.[73] The military balked, however, at Ervin's insistence that legally qualified military counsel be available at all special courts-martial. Apparently, Ervin had agreed to meet with Army TJAG Hodson, to see if "some of these differences can be worked out. . . ." If not, "Senator Ervin intends to push them and I feel sure the Committee will accept them."[74]

[69] ERV, June 28, 1968, Box 201, Folder 564.

[70] Ibid., July 10, 1968.

[71] Ibid.

[72] Ibid. In a letter to Robinson Everett, a former committee staff member and a future chief judge of USCMA, Ervin explained that his decision to go with amendments rather than with his omnibus military justice bill "was based primarily on the short time remaining in the session during which agreement must be reached on some military justice bill if it is to be enacted by this Congress." Ibid., July 17, 1968, Box 201, Folder 565.

[73] Ibid., Box 201, Folder 570, September 12, 1968.

[74] Ibid. "If the House then will not go along, perhaps some of the amendments can be salvaged in conference."

The meetings between Ervin and Hodson did indeed take place, and as Ervin later wrote to all the members of the Senate Armed Services Committee, "I have modified some of the amendments . . . and have withdrawn others."[75] The result was Defense Department acceptance, if not enthusiastic endorsement, of Ervin's revised revisions, apparently a *sine qua non* for House approval. The Senator from North Carolina could now assert that his colleagues need have no fear that "acceptance of my amendments will jeopardize enactment of the bill this year." Ervin was fully aware that if the House endorsed the Senate Amendments without change, "no conference will be necessary"; hence his concern that the changes be acceptable to the military, prior to reconsideration by the House.[76] Following pro forma approval from the Senate Committee, Ervin described some of the key changes to his fellow legislators.

He emphasized that his proposed alterations had been accepted—some with marked reluctance—by the military.[77] One such provision—one of the very few deletions from the House bill—eliminated the need for the commanding officer to approve courts-martial before a military judge alone. Ervin explained that "the command structure in the military presents a possibility of undue prejudicial influence over the Court that is not present in civilian life. . . . [T]he military judge, having heard arguments from both trial and defense counsel concerning the appropriateness of trial by a military judge alone, will be in the best position to protect the interests of both the Government and the accused."[78] Another change preserved the right of a defendant to decline a summary court-martial, a forum "which affords literally no safeguards to the defendant."[79]

A third revision sought to strengthen the existing UCMJ ban against command influence by insuring that the performance of a court-martial partici-

[75] Ibid., Box 201, Folder 571, September 25, 1968. For his part, and with some difficulty, Hodson persuaded Air Force and Navy representatives to acquiesce in the Army's position. Opposition within the services focused on the projected manpower costs of providing counsel in special courts-martial. Hodson later recalled that the Air Force, composed of volunteers, had provided such counsel for a number of years. "It was my view that the Army could not in good conscience deny draftees the right to lawyer counsel when volunteers in another service were being provided with lawyer counsel in similar cases." Hodson, Oral History Interview, V, 10.

[76] ERV, Box 201, Folder 571.

[77] Ibid. Because Ervin shrewdly had retained virtually the entire House bill, adding rather than altering—he placed the military in the unpleasant position of either accepting his changes or seeing the entire measure, replete with all they had sought, face probable defeat. Ultimately, the Defense Department accepted Hodson's recommendation "that there were so many good aspects in the legislation that we really shouldn't turn it down" due to military opposition to certain of Ervin's additions, especially this one. Hodson, 11.

[78] LH, 219.

[79] Ibid., 220. Ervin added that this compromise, instead of outright abolition for the summary court-martial, "was no expression of confidence" in what he considered "to be an inferior court in concept, procedure and in the quality of justice it dispenses."

pant either as member, trial, and/or defense counsel "could not be evaluated in preparing an effectiveness, fitness, or efficiency report . . . nor could he be given a less favorable rating because of his zeal in acting as defense counsel in a court-martial."[80] Nevertheless, just as Ervin had to concede the impossibility of abolishing the summary court, so here he had to accept an exemption to this amendment which permitted "general instructional or informational courses in military justice if such courses are designed solely for the purpose of instructing members of a command in the substantive and procedural aspects of courts-martial."[81]

The Ervin Amendments retained the expanded functions for the military judge. They did not include, however, either an increase in USCMA authority or establishment of any civilian Board to correct military justice records, or to review administrative discharges. Apparently these changes fell victim to the editing sessions between Ervin and Hodson. Ervin was accurate when he claimed that the amended measure "includes many, but not all, of the proposals I have sponsored for many years. . . ."[82] With no discussion or recorded vote, on October 3, 1968, the Senate accepted Ervin's amendments.

The next day, Ervin wrote to key House Armed Services Committee members. "[T]he amended bill has been approved by the Department of Defense. I have taken care to assure that none of the provisions will impose responsibilities upon any of the services that cannot be discharged by them with proper attention and effort."[83] Expressing the hope that the changes would be acceptable to the Committee and House, "so that this vital measure can be enacted this year," Ervin emphasized the obvious. "I have sought enactment of many of [its provisions] for almost a decade. I believe very strongly that this Act will prove to be one of the most lastingly significant pieces of legislation considered by this Congress."[84]

When properly greased, the legislative process can be remarkably swift. One week after Senate action, the House concurred in a similar manner.[85] Thus the most important changes to the UCMJ since its adoption in 1950 were enacted by Congress without any sort of floor debate, let alone a formal roll call. Two weeks later, President Johnson signed the measure into law. The thoroughness of congressional consideration was conspicuous by its absence.[86]

[80] Ibid., 38.

[81] Ibid., 4. Judge Homer Ferguson had long railed against such lectures. See, for example, *United States v. Albert*, 16 USCMA 111 (1966), and other cases cited therein.

[82] LH, 220.

[83] ERV, Box 201, Folder 572, October 4, 1968.

[84] Ibid.

[85] LH, 224, 209.

[86] LH, 1–9. For a good summary of the provisions, see Kenneth Hodson, "The Military Justice Act," in *Judge Advocate Journal* 47 (1970) 31–38. For a more critical commentary, see

One suspects that the paucity of legislative attention was due to external circumstances, as well as a traditional—although unfortunate—lack of sustained congressional interest in military justice. The bill passed as Congress rushed toward adjournment, in the midst of a contentious presidential campaign that followed the disastrous (and bloody) Democratic Convention in Chicago. With Johnson's administration mired in the miasma of the Vietnam tragedy, and with the election one month away, the lawmakers had little interest in debating the nuances of court-martial procedures. Even as Johnson signed the bill however, his attention had been called once again to the question of Chief Judge Quinn's continued presence on the USCMA bench.

THE QUINN SAGA CONTINUES

It will be recalled that in 1965 as a condition of reappointment, Quinn had submitted a post-dated letter of resignation to Johnson. He would step down in June 1968, when he became eligible for federal retirement. As this time drew nigh, however, it became clear that the Chief Judge did not wish to leave office. At his request, Senator Pastore again wrote to Johnson, seeking an extension of Quinn's tenure. "If it doesn't happen," he later noted to Quinn, "it certainly won't be because I didn't try for one of the greatest men I know."[87]

On May 9, Johnson's aide Jack Valenti reminded Pastore's office of the agreement for Quinn to resign. He also stated that "the President had made a commitment to a longtime friend for the Court."[88] His assertion probably referred to Johnson's old friend and former congressional colleague Paul Kilday. Kilday had been an USCMA judge since 1961, and while Johnson could have designated any of the three sitting jurists as "Chief," he had made no change. Quinn had continued to hold the center seat on the bench. Even though he had Quinn's resignation in hand, for reasons that remain unclear but that might be related to Pastore's concerns, Johnson hesitated to activate Quinn's retirement.

Another of Johnson's aides, Larry Temple, informed the President that he had specifically asked Kilday if "there would be any problem—legal or practical—with permitting Judge Quinn to continue to serve as a member of

---

Edward Sherman, "Revised Military Code: A Qualified Assent." *Trial Magazine*, December–January, 1968–69, 44–45, excerpt in USCMAP. Sherman concluded that the "1968 Act unfortunately does not, as President Johnson stated in signing the bill, give our servicemen 'first-class legal service,' but it is an important step." He further stated, correctly, that "Command influence has been *and will remain* a constant threat to fairness in a court-martial." (Emphasis in original.)

[87] QPPC, February 18, 1968.

[88] LBJ, FG 545A, Box 360, May 9, 1968. Johnson had already announced that he would not seek reelection.

the Court and naming Judge Kilday as Chief Judge. Judge Kilday knew of no legal prohibition of this."[89] But he was concerned that "this might prove embarrassing both to himself and the President—and might cause some conflict on the Court. He did not want to cause any problems [and] had indicated his interest in being Chief Judge only because he understands Judge Quinn was resigning." According to Temple, Kilday indicated that "if Judge Quinn is to continue on the Court . . . it would be a preferable working situation for Quinn to remain as Chief Judge and Kilday to retain his present status." Temple summarized Kilday's attitude as "whatever the President wants to do is fine with him."[90]

Johnson's hesitation may signify that the President had not yet decided what he wanted to do, if only because an additional USCMA candidate now surfaced. Early in June, William Darden, the Chief of Staff for Senator Russell's Armed Services Committee, indicated his interest in succeeding Quinn. Indeed, as early as 1965 Darden had expressed similar sentiments, anticipating Quinn's exit at the end of his first term.[91] After Darden made known his latest aspirations to join the Court, John Macy received information indicating that Darden was "very able, and very close to Senator Russell."[92] His interest, according to Macy, "is in response to the Intelligence that Judge Quinn . . . will in fact retire some time this summer. In all likelihood, there will be a number of voluntary candidates for this post. It pays well. It has a long term. The work is not very demanding. This is low priority."[93]

[89] Ibid., May 18, 1968.

[90] Ibid. Prior to speaking with Temple, Kilday had written to Johnson, indicating that Quinn had told him that "he is resigning as a Judge of this Court." Kilday requested that he be named his successor. While such a move "will not increase my salary[,] [i]t would be an increase in prestige. More important, however, the Chief Judge controls the administrative procedures of the Court. . . . I believe I can increase its efficiency and effectiveness in that field." Ibid., May 8, 1968.

[91] Harry McPherson Papers, Box 3, October 27, 1965; LBJ Library.

[92] JMP, Box 132, June 7, 1968.

[93] Ibid. One can appreciate Macy's candor, while deprecating his conclusions. His views regarding the low priority of this appointment reflected a perception widely held in Administration circles about USCMA since its inception. Truman, if not his staff, may have been the exception, because he placed great emphasis on the appointment process. As far as can be determined, no other president since Truman has troubled to interview any potential USCMA members. At the bottom of Macy's comments is a handwritten notation referring to the anticipated USCMA vacancy: "Justice Department has no interest. Leaves it to us and to DOD." It is noteworthy that in December 1966, when the Justice Department issued a four-page press release extolling the record-breaking number of federal judges selected by Johnson since assuming office, seventy in all, no mention was made of Quinn's reappointment. McPherson Papers, Box 3, December 1966. While it is true that Macy had sought outstanding candidates for USCMA appointments, and would do so again—overall his attitude appears to have been all too typical, and cannot have been helpful to the continued development of USCMA as a judicial institution of distinction. One perspective on this point is not how good USCMA judges might have been, but that some have been as good as they were.

Late in June, Quinn's impending resignation received wide coverage in the Rhode Island press. The *Evening Bulletin* reported that Quinn had submitted a resignation "about a week ago, but that he has heard nothing from the President."[94] According to a White House staff member, however, "there is a possibility that [Quinn] may retire this year. . . . If the President does not act to give him an extension, he must leave the bench."[95] During the summer months the matter remained unresolved, as the Senate grappled with a related issue—that of a replacement for Chief Justice Earl Warren, who had retired. At least one newspaper writer commented that Johnson "has decided not to act on Judge Quinn's resignation because of Senate opposition to Justice [Abe] Fortas," Johnson's choice to succeed Warren.[96]

By September, with the issue of the USCMA Chief Judge's position still unresolved, Kilday and his supporters were becoming restive. His former colleague on the House Armed Services Committee, Representative Philip Philbin, wrote to Johnson extolling Kilday's qualifications.[97] Johnson's assistant acknowledged the letter, adding that "as far as I can determine, the present Chief Judge has not submitted a resignation."[98] Two days later, Johnson's assistant was informed that "Kilday had called again to urge that we accept or get Quinn's resignation so that he, Judge Kilday, can be named [USCMA] Chief Judge before court convenes for its fall session."[99]

On October 3, Johnson received a memorandum concerning what now might be called the Quinn caper.[100] First, the President was informed that the White House had "received no letter of resignation from . . . Chief Judge Quinn." Moreover, "Kilday called to say that the Court will open its fall

[94] USCMAP, file "Reappointment of Chief Judge Robert E. Quinn," clipping from the *Warwick-Pawtucket Valley Evening Bulletin.* According to the article, Quinn showed some pride in his accomplishments as an USCMA judge. "I really initiated the court and built it up."

[95] LBJ Papers, File 2, Box 11, June 27, 1968. The staff member appears to have been mistaken. While Quinn had indeed submitted a letter dated June 20, 1968, in order for the resignation to go into effect, the President would have to act on it. Put another way, for Quinn to stay where he was, required only that the President do nothing, which is exactly what happened.

[96] Supra, n. 94, clipping dated September 30, 1968. There is no evidence to justify such a conclusion. Indeed, it is based on the dubious assumption that Senate interest in the USCMA Chief Judge was in the same league as appointing the Chief Justice of the United States. A Senate filibuster blocked Fortas's confirmation, as Quinn's resignation lay pending. When both courts opened their fall terms, Warren and Quinn presided as usual.

[97] JMP, Box 753, September 5, 1968.

[98] Ibid., Box 753, September 12, 1968. The assistant, Barefoot Sanders, was wrong. More accurate was Macy's reply to a writer supporting a candidate for USCMA. "There is a widely held impression that a vacancy on this Court exists. . . . However, no vacancy exists and, at this point, it does not appear probable that one will occur in the near future." Ibid., September 26, 1968. It is reasonable to conclude that by this date, Johnson may have decided to leave the Quinn matter alone.

[99] LBJ Papers, File K, Box 126, September 28, 1968.

[100] Ibid., October 3, 1968.

term on October 8. He said that Quinn apparently thought he had submitted a resignation which would be accepted."[101] One can only wonder what Johnson concluded upon receiving this missive.

There are at least two copies of Quinn's resignation letter in the Johnson Papers. Also, as was noted in the previous chapter, correspondence related to the agreement reached on Quinn's reappointment clearly indicates the parties' knowledge of the resignation. Finally, Quinn's resignation had been announced, confirmed by Quinn himself, and indeed had been *the* sine qua non for renomination by the President two years before! Perhaps the confusion on this issue arose due to internal communication problems within the administration, as it grappled with a number of critical matters in its last months, including Vietnam and the 1968 presidential election campaign.[102] Whatever the reason, Quinn sat as Chief Judge when the USCMA fall term began. Four days later, Paul Kilday died of a massive heart attack.

Shocked by the tragedy, Johnson telegraphed Mrs. Kilday that he had "lost a friend and colleague. America has lost an outstanding public servant. Our men and women in uniform have lost a champion."[103] The administration, however, wasted no time in searching for a replacement. One day after Kilday's burial, Johnson's assistant Mike Manatos reported to the President that Richard Russell was in line to become Chairman of the Senate Appro-

[101] Ibid.

[102] The *Washington Examiner* stated that "some thought [Quinn] had actually written a letter to the White House about [resigning], but five offices in the White House which handle such matters report they never saw the letter and the President knew nothing about it." To make matters even more confusing, if possible, Quinn was quoted as saying that "I considered resigning but actually I had not resigned." USCMAP, clippings in Personnel File, Robert Quinn.

[103] Ibid. Kilday's widow asked that her husband be buried in Arlington National Cemetery. A newly adopted rule, however, restricted burials therein to "Medal of Honor winners, active duty and retired members of the armed forces, and honorably discharged veterans who have also served in high positions in the federal government." Kilday fit none of these criteria. Nevertheless and with Johnson's approval, his assistant Joseph Califano instructed the Pentagon to "find a way to bury Judge Kilday in Arlington." LBJ, Name File K, Box 126, October 16, 1968. As Commander in Chief, Johnson could have ordered the burial, "but this would be an unwise departure from practice." Ibid. Instead, the Army authorized the interment, "based on the unique role which judges of [USCMA] play as the ultimate tribunal in the military justice system." Ibid., clipping from the *Washington Evening Star*, October 15, 1968. On the day the ceremony was to take place, Califano was informed that a veteran's group "was so incensed over the burial . . . that it threatened to file suit in the District Court to require the disinterment of Kilday." A White House operative "immediately got in touch with the National Committee of the VFW and told them to stop acting like children. . . ." The end result was that the VFW National Headquarters "called the local office here and told them to immediately stop all harassment and to [f]orget the entire matter." White House Press Secretary George Christian emphasized that "there had been no pressure from the White House." Ibid., October 16, 1968. When Paul Kilday was laid to rest not far from the President who had named him to the Court, Lyndon Johnson attended the graveside service.

priations Committee. "This means that Bill Darden will be left hanging since there is no room for him on the Appropriations Committee[,] and chances are Senator [John] Stennis would want his own Chief of Staff on the Armed Services Committee."[104] Perhaps, "Darden might be considered as a replacement for Kilday." I suppose, concluded Manatos, that "Bill Darden has qualifications equal to or better than any one else in this area. When both Bob Quinn and Homer Ferguson are pushing the high 70s perhaps an infusion of young blood could be worked out for the Court."[105]

In the meantime, John Macy went about preparing his own recommendations for Johnson. He submitted four names to him—two judges and two law professors. All of these individuals had been considered during the 1966 search for a nominee who Macy had assumed would replace Quinn. Again, Russell Fairbanks headed the list.[106] He was "the best qualified candidate I know of at this date."[107] But Johnson probably gave little—if any—consideration to Macy's choices. Scrawled on the memorandum, although not in Johnson's hand, is a notation that "I would like to name Bill Darden. . . ."[108]

Macy's assistant checked with the Defense Department concerning Darden, since some doubt had been expressed that a "Senate staff man would measure up to the quality" of other individuals previously mentioned either by Defense Secretary Clark Clifford or Macy as potential court nominees in the event of a vacancy. Macy's informant "couldn't recall such unanimous enthusiasm for any candidate for any office in the past. Everyone, from the Secretary on down, has the highest regard for Darden."[109] Promptly informed of the Defense Department's positive recommendation, Johnson formally nominated Darden on November 5. In a typical example of the famed Johnson "style," the President personally called Darden to congratulate him on his selection.[110]

With Darden on the court, and with Richard Nixon elected as President,

[104] Ibid.

[105] Ibid.

[106] See above, chapter 7; JMP, Box 750, October 24, 1968.

[107] Ibid. Fairbanks "has all the qualities of a good judge; he is even tempered, fair minded, reflective, thoughtful, yet decisive."

[108] Ibid.

[109] Ibid., Box 132, November 4, 1968. Another of Macy's correspondents, perhaps inadvertently, offered an accurate assessment of Johnson's choice. Compared with some other candidates, Darden might be "no great brain," but there were other factors to consider. "[H]e has some 20 years' experience with Defense legislation, and as Dick Russell's boy all these years, he is sure to be confirmed." Ibid. Having just lost a bruising and bitter battle with the Senate over the ill-fated Fortas nomination to replace Earl Warren, one can understand why Johnson was drawn to Darden as a nominee, since he apparently was a "sure thing" for confirmation.

[110] LBJ, WHCF Name File "D," Box 32, November 5, 1968. Darden responded with a handwritten note referring to "the consummate graciousness with which you gave me the good news. The conversation with you was the most rewarding thing that has happened to me." Ibid.

the Quinn matter remained unresolved. On December 4, a member of Johnson's staff wrote a fitting epilogue for a fascinating and still unfinished episode:

> This is a screwed-up case. . . . Quinn was reappointed in 1966 on the condition that he resign in 1968. [The letter of resignation] is in the White House files. . . . but it has never been acted upon. Part of the problem, I am told, was that it was misfiled for a long time and nobody could find it. It is now found . . . but there is no plan to accept it. The matter is complicated by news stories this year indicating Judge Quinn has submitted his resignation. No one is too sure of the source of the stories. If you want to be judge of the Court of Military Appeals, Quinn's resignation is in the files.[111]

When Richard Nixon left the Presidency in 1974, the resignation was still in the files, and Robert Quinn was still on the USCMA bench.

[111] LBJ, WHCF, File Group 545, Box 380, December 4, 1968.

CHAPTER 9

Disagreements, Departures, and Decisions, 1969–1975

PRESIDENT Richard Nixon took office in January 1969, inheriting both the Vietnam problem and Judge Quinn's continued presence on the Court. It may well be that Johnson's preoccupation with the former crisis had prevented resolution of the latter problem. Within a matter of months, Nixon's new administration took up the issue of USCMA appointments even though, as Nixon aide Bryce Harlow wrote to Republican Senator Everett McKinley Dirksen, "there will not be another vacancy until May 1, 1971."[1] Unless, of course, Robert Quinn resigned. Now it was Nixon's turn to cope with the ongoing Quinn caper.

THE CASE OF THE DISAPPEARING RESIGNATION

By June 1969, it had been ascertained that "apparently . . . Quinn submitted his resignation during the Johnson administration, but it was not acted upon. He, therefore, resolved it." A staff member would try to "see if the resignation is still kicking around somewhere."[2] The new administration's interest in an USCMA opening had to do not so much with age or quality of the incumbents, as with the fact that such a vacancy "would greatly assist in carrying out the President's desire to give a highly visible job to a VFW type. . . ."[3] In addition, the Republican members of the House Armed Services Committee informed Nixon that they "strongly recommend" the appointment of their Committee Counsel, William Cook, to the Court. "We consider him eminently qualified for this appointment and offer our unqualified recommendation of him."[4] The problem for Nixon was the lack of a position, rather than politically suitable candidates to fill it.

The White House staff ascertained that Johnson had reappointed Quinn to a full fifteen-year term "on the understanding that an undated resignation

[1] Nixon Papers, WHCF, File Group 58, Folder 20, April 14, 1969. Hereafter cited as NP, followed by appropriate date. The date mentioned by Bryce Harlow referred to the expiration of Ferguson's appointment.

[2] Ibid., Folder 17, June 30, 1969.

[3] Ibid., July 1, 1969.

[4] Ibid., July 9, 1969.

would be offered by Quinn," when he had served sufficient years to qualify for a federal pension. A search of the White House files turned up "no evidence of an undated resignation," but Quinn's letter of June 20, 1968, had been located.[5] Whether the effective date for retirement benefits was June 20, 1968, or August 1, 1969, "it would appear that on any theory [Quinn] soon will have fulfilled his service requirement for the full pension. Is there any way we can pursue this matter with [Senator John] Pastore, so as to open up Quinn's job? Otherwise, we apparently will have him with us until 1981, at which time he will have achieved the ripe old age of 97."[6]

Asked by Harlow to contact Pastore, another staffer responded later in July that according to Pastore, "Johnson had agreed to leave [Quinn] on the Court and that Quinn's letter of resignation had been withdrawn and was no longer in effect."[7] Furthermore, Pastore stated that "Quinn was very important to him in his State . . . and that he, Pastore, would vigorously oppose any change. Pastore made his position very clear." Harlow was also informed that Congressman Les Arends, the Republican whip, and a senior member of the House Armed Services Committee, "asked me to tell you that the members of [this Committee] would stand behind their recommendation that [William] Cook be given the next vacancy on the Court."[8] On July 28, Harlow wrote to Arends that "your emphatic views in behalf of Bill are rightly and fully known and, of course, will not be overlooked." A staff memorandum stated that "when we finally get an opening on [USCMA] it will have to go to Cook, minority counsel, as Les Arends has made it clear this is one of the things he's really strong on."[9]

In the meantime, USCMA had other problems to confront. Even as replacements were proposed, and Quinn's resignation was pushed, the United States Supreme Court handed down one of its most far reaching and controversial decisions concerning military justice. It resulted in major contention

[5] Ibid., July 1, 1969. Quinn's letter, although clearly dated July 20, 1968, stated that "I hereby submit to you my resignation from the Court to become effective at such time as you see fit to accept it." As the letter had been written to "Mr. President," and not President Johnson, and as it had never been formally accepted by Johnson, nor—apparently—withdrawn by Quinn, the question arises whether Nixon could have acted to accept the resignation during 1969, or thereafter. As will be seen, however, he did not.

[6] Ibid.

[7] Ibid., July 18, 1969. Again, it should be noted that a diligent search through both the available Johnson and Quinn papers has turned up no evidence whatsoever of any such withdrawal. On the other hand, as pointed out in the previous chapter, Johnson's inaction was the only action necessary for Quinn to remain where he was.

[8] Ibid. Indeed, Arends had written a note to "Mr. President" on the July 9 memorandum endorsing Cook: "This I would like to see done very much." Ibid., July 9, 1969. Arends believed that Quinn's resignation was imminent, all the more reason why some twelve members of the committee "insist on Cook."

[9] Ibid., August 16, 1969. As will be seen, Cook ultimately would be named to USCMA, but not by Nixon.

between the High Court and the military, with USCMA caught in the middle. This case and its aftermath deserve some discussion.

THE ODD ODYSSEY OF O'CALLAHAN

On its surface, the case of Sergeant James O'Callahan was similar to many incidents in military justice. During the evening of July 20, 1956, while on leave from his post at a base near Honolulu, O'Callahan allegedly entered a hotel room and tried to rape its occupant, a fourteen-year-old girl. Arrested as he sought to flee the area, he was turned over to the military police, confessed to the attempt, faced court-martial for a number of offenses, and was convicted on all of them.[10] Along with other penalties including a dishonorable discharge, O'Callahan was sentenced to ten years' imprisonment at hard labor. For almost his entire prison term, military justice heard nothing from this defendant.

Toward the end of his incarceration, O'Callahan sought a writ from USCMA on the grounds that he had been denied certain constitutional rights at his court-martial.[11] The court required only two paragraphs to deny his plea.[12] Even as it did so, however, O'Callahan awaited response from a petition for habeas corpus that had been filed earlier on his behalf in federal court. Rejected by both district and appellate courts, he appealed to the United States Supreme Court. That tribunal agreed to consider the issue of court-martial jurisdiction to try a member of the armed forces for "a crime . . . having no military significance, alleged to have been committed off post and while on leave." In June 1969, a bare majority of the Court decided this question in favor of O'Callahan.

Speaking for the Court, Justice Douglas criticized military justice, noting that the court-martial judge was not one "whose objectivity and independence are protected by tenure and undiminishable salary and nurtured by the judicial tradition."[13] Quite aside from the potential for real abuse through command influence, "courts-martial as an institution are singularly inept in dealing with the nice subtleties of constitutional law."[14] Finally, he empha-

[10] At this time, Hawaii was not yet a state.

[11] He did not argue, however, the claim that would later make his case so notorious—namely, that the court-martial "had lacked jurisdiction to try him for nonmilitary offenses committed off post, while not on duty." Robinson O. Everett, "O'Callahan v. Parker—Milestone or Millstone in Military Justice?" *Duke Law Journal* 69 (1969), 853–96, 855—hereafter cited as *Everett.*

[12] *United States v. James O'Callahan*, 16 USCMA 568, (1967).

[13] *O'Callahan v. Parker*, 395 U.S. 258 (1969), 264.

[14] Ibid., 265 It should be noted that Douglas drew heavily on a 1955 case, *Toth v. Quarles*, 350 U.S. 11, in which the Court denied courts-martial jurisdiction when at the time of trial, the accused was no longer in the armed services. However, to use this conclusion as justification for

sized the "unusual" factors in this case. Defendant was "properly absent" from his installation. There "was no connection—not even the remotest one—between his military duties and the crimes in question. The crimes were not committed on a military post or enclave; nor was the person whom he attacked performing any duties relating to the military." Hawaii, he added, was not the occupied zone of a foreign country, but was under civil authority, with functioning civil courts. In short, "the offenses did not involve any question of the flouting of military authority, the security of a military post, or the integrity of military property."[15]

What then, was a "service connected" offense? The decision gave the military virtually no guidance.[16] Moreover, Douglas failed to mention, let alone resolve, the issue of retroactivity. Aware, if only from Justice Harlan's dissent, that the *O'Callahan* decision could create a strong sense of uncertainty in military justice, within two years the Court agreed to consider the issue again. In the meantime a great deal of commentary about the decision, much of it negative, appeared, sparing neither Douglas nor his opinion.[17] For

---

the release of O'Callahan, conceded by all to be an active member of the Army, went far beyond the 1955 holding.

[15] Ibid., 274; Everett, 858. Disturbed that the High Court would even agree to consider the question raised by *O'Callahan*, Army TJAG Hodson later recalled that the Government's attorney had been less than outstanding. "In effect, he gave our case away that day, because he was asked . . . for example, by Justice Marshall, 'have you ever been in a barracks?' And he answered, 'No.'" Hodson, Oral History, V, 30–31. In response to a statement that "more lenient penalties are given out by the court-martial," Justice Marshall asked: "Have you ever been to an Army court-martial?" When the lawyer answered "no," Marshall responded, "Then I can see why you say that." FP, Box 22, clipping from *The Evening Star*, January 24, 1969. Hodson felt that by such statements "of course, [the government attorney] lost his credibility almost instantly. . . ." Moreover, when the Army JAG office tried to show that there were numerous American precedents for trial of civilians by military tribunals, the lawyer declined to so argue, claiming instead that "well, there might be certain cases where we wouldn't have jurisdiction over civilians . . . and once he admitted that, of course, he gave our case away." Hodson, Ibid.

[16] An USCMA internal memorandum drafted by Commissioner Cabell Cobbs cited the "manifest difficulties entailed by the vagueness of the *O'Callahan* opinion," but concluded that under it "military jurisdiction" simply did not extend "to a civil-type offense against a purely civilian victim, committed during peacetime within the United States by an accused who was both off post and off duty." *Memorandum for Chief Commissioner*, USCMAP, June 12, 1969, 6–7; copy in FP, Box 19. Implicit in Cobbs's reasoning, however, was the assumption that a civilian such as a "colonel's lady" who had been assaulted by a member of the Armed services would have sufficient military connection to warrant a court-martial. Ultimately, the United States Supreme Court agreed. See below.

[17] The comments of Congressman John Rarick, Democrat from Louisiana, about Douglas were typical of extremist views that included not only Douglas, but the Warren Court in general. Only a few days after *O'Callahan* was announced, Rarick described Douglas as "a clear and present danger" whose "demonstrated bias renders him incapable of a fair and impartial ruling involving the Armed Forces." He claimed that the justice's "senility and emotion have replaced

its part, USCMA confronted the implications of *O'Callahan* only four months after that case had been decided.

As had been true when USCMA applied the *Miranda* warnings to the military, USCMA split 2–1 concerning application of the *O'Callahan* doctrine. Again, Judge Ferguson, joined by Judge Darden, spoke for the Court, while Chief Judge Quinn wrote a lengthy dissent, marked by bitterness and frustration. Ferguson noted that the defendant lived off post, committed crimes against "civilian victims, unconnected to the military," and that "accused's horrid acts, like those of O'Callahan, did not flout military authority, breach military security, or affect military property."[18] Simply put, the *O'Callahan* holding "requires us to set aside the findings of guilty . . . and order the charges dismissed. . . ."[19]

Judge Quinn tried to reject the reasoning of the *O'Callahan* decision even as he conceded that "I am constrained to accept its premise and its conclusion, but I hope that the searching criticism of the bench and bar may . . . convince a new or future majority" of its error.[20] Seeking, apparently unsuccessfully, to minimize the decision's scope, Quinn emphasized that it "cannot be read with the literalness of a first-grade primer. . . . I read *O'Callahan*, therefore, not by rote, but in light of the experience and reason of nearly two hundred years of American Government."[21] He insisted that the Douglas list of service connection variables "was not, in my opinion, intended to be definitive or exclusive. Other circumstances can establish the military significance of the offense or demonstrate its service-connection."[22]

Quinn ended his lengthy dissent with an angry rejection of the Douglas "fossil-like canard that military justice is institutionalized injustice."[23] Here, responding to the markedly anti-military justice tone of *O'Callahan*, the Chief Judge emphasized the not insignificant contributions of his own court-

reason, tradition, and law, to the continued disgrace of the Court. . . . Not even a second grade education is needed to conclude that Douglas must resign or be removed from any position of trust from which he can inflict further injury on the Court and the People." *Congressional Record*, June 9, 1969, E4734, copy in FP, Box 19, and USCMAP. A good listing of the scholarly and legal commentary generated by *O'Callahan* is found in the text of its 1971 sequel, *Relford v. Commandant, U.S. Disciplinary Barracks*, 401 U.S. 355, 356–59.

[18] *United States v. Borys*, 18 USCMA 547, 549 (1969). In short, none of defendant's actions based upon "his vicious and depraved conduct" were "service connected under any test or standard set out by the Supreme Court." Ibid.

[19] Ibid., 549–50.

[20] Ibid., 550. As for Douglas, Quinn commented that "I have looked askance at what I regard, rightly or wrongly, as the incontinent disorder of some of the constitutional opinions of the justice who authored the *O'Callahan* opinion. . . ."

[21] Ibid.

[22] Ibid., 558.

[23] Ibid., 559.

since its creation.[24] Moreover, many on the USCMA staff shared his resentment. The Chief Commissioner had written to the three judges soon after the Supreme Court's holding was announced. "To suggest, as does the opinion, that this Court has rationed these rights in a niggardly fashion, or at all, does this Court a grave disservice. It wipes out with hardly more than a blot of printer's ink the dedicated hard work of every Judge who is serving, or has served on this Court."[25] Carney suggested that the case be "limited to civilian offenses committed in the civilian community involving civilian victims and committed by an accused who is on leave and not in uniform, at a time when this country is not at war."[26]

At the urgent request of Army TJAG Hodson, Solicitor General Erwin Griswold—the former Dean of Harvard Law School—argued the High Court sequel to *O'Callahan*, The decision may have sought to "clarify" the earlier holding, but in retrospect it seems that the 1971 holding represented the start of a retreat from *O'Callahan* that did not end until its complete abandonment in 1987. The 1971 opinion was authored by a recently appointed Justice Harry Blackmun, who spoke for a unanimous court. Blackmun, possibly with a sense of understatement, began his opinion in *Relford v. Commandant, U.S. Disciplinary Barracks*, with an observation that the 1969 holding "already has occasioned a substantial amount of scholarly comment." He also listed more than fifty-five USCMA cases citing *O'Callahan*, stating further that the Court would not reconsider that decision. "Our task here concerns only its application."[27]

[24] Dissenting in a 1962 case, Douglas had made unfavorable comparisons between federal judges appointed under Article III, such as himself, and federal judges appointed under Article I, such as USCMA jurists. "Men of highest quality chosen as Article I judges might never pass muster for Article III courts when tested by their record of tolerance for minorities and for their respect of the Bill of Rights—neither of which is as crucial to the performance of the duties of those who sit in Article I courts as it is to the duties of Article III judges. . . . Judges who sit on Article I courts are chosen for administrative or allied skills, not for their qualifications to sit in cases involving the vast interests of life, liberty or property. . . . Judges who might be confirmed for an Article I court, might never pass muster for the onerous and life-or-death duties of Article III judges." *Glidden Co., etc., v. Zdanok*, 370 U.S. 530, 605–6 (1962).

[25] "Memo to the Court, O'Callahan v. Parker," from Daniel F. Carney, Chief Commissioner, June 17, 1969, 2–3, FP, Box 19, copy in USCMAP. Carney feared that given Douglas's *ipse dixit* concerning the "manifest destiny of [military] retributive justice," USCMA might well "be reduced to reviewing AWOLs—hardly a calling to which Judges of a caliber normally recruited for Federal Courts of Appeal will be attracted." He urged "in order to preserve this Court's past record and to insure a useful future for it," that "the narrowest possible interpretation—consistent with good judgment—be given" to the Douglas opinion. "This approach is not intended to evidence a state of rebellion against 'the law of the land.'"

[26] Ibid.

[27] 401 U.S. 360 (1971). Possibly by coincidence, several bills reforming military justice in the wake of *O'Callahan* were pending in Congress, even as the Supreme Court considered *Relford*. None of them came to fruition. See the excellent analysis by Edward Sherman, "Congressional Proposals for Reform of Military Law," *American Criminal Law Review* 10 (1971), 25–49.

Relford involved a member of the military on active duty but in mufti, who was accused of raping two civilians. The offenses "took place on the military reservation consisting of Fort Dix and the contiguous McGuire Air Force Base."[28] One of the two victims was the sister of a serviceman on duty at the base, while the other was the wife of another serviceman, also stationed there. In other words, both were "properly at the base." Taking all these facts together, "we readily conclude that the crimes with which Relford was charged were triable by a military court."[29]

Blackmun added a somewhat cryptic comment that "*O'Callahan* marks an area, perhaps not the limit, for the concern of the civil courts and where the military may not enter. [*Relford*] marks an area, perhaps not the limit, where the court-martial is appropriate and permissible. What lies between is for decision at another time."[30] As to the issue of retroactivity, of particular concern to the military, this "issue is better resolved in other litigation where, perhaps, it would be solely dispositive of the case. We take some comfort in the hope that the present decision should eliminate at least some of the confusion that the parties and commentators say have emerged from *O'Callahan*."[31]

Despite Blackmun's "comfort," two years later the Court returned to the issue of retroactivity in the confusing case of *Gosa v. Mayden, Warden*.[32] By a bare majority, the justices declined to apply *O'Callahan* retroactively, but as Solicitor General Griswold put it, "you have [to] read rather closely to find that out." Justice Blackmun's plurality opinion was joined by three other justices. "But that was just four votes out of nine." The fifth vote came from Justice Rehnquist, who felt that *O'Callahan* "if it stood," should be applied retroactively. But he also believed that that case had been wrongly decided, and should be overruled. Thus, "we do not have a majority against the retroactive application of *O'Callahan*, but we do have a majority against *O'Callahan*, retroactively."[33]

In 1987, six justices overruled *O'Callahan* in an opinion authored by Chief Justice Rehnquist that seemed as critical of Douglas's 1969 opinion as Douglas had been of military justice.[34] During the interval between the two cases, it had been left to USCMA—with some difficulty—to explore the reaches of the service connection requirement.[35] For its part, during the same

[28] Ibid.

[29] Ibid., 367. "[W]hen a serviceman is charged with an offense committed within or at the geographical boundary of a military post and violative of the security of a person or property there, that offense may be tried by court-martial." Ibid., 369.

[30] Ibid., 369.

[31] Ibid., 370.

[32] 413 U.S. 665 (1973).

[33] Erwin N. Griswold, "Appellate Advocacy," *Army Lawyer* 3 (October 1973), 14.

[34] *Solorio v. United States*, 483 U.S. 435 (1987).

[35] A number of the USCMA decisions are cited in *Solorio*, 448–50.

period, the High Court had handed down a number of rulings that severely limited the reach of constitutional protection to members of the armed forces, and the decision overruling *O'Callahan* should be seen in this context.[36] This notable trend appeared to justify Justice Marshall's plaintive dissent in *Solorio*, that now "members of the Armed Forces may be subjected virtually without limit to the vagaries of military control."[37]

COURT CHANGES

The question of Quinn's resignation remained unresolved as the *O'Callhan* and *Relford* line of cases were litigated. But Nixon received word that an opening on USCMA would soon be available, as Homer Ferguson came to the end of his term. Almost eighty-two years old, in February 1971 the former Michigan Senator asked to see Nixon, in order to inform him "of his plan to resign." Nixon's aide advised the President that "there will be no press involvement." However, "you may want to give the Judge a set of Presidential cuff links."[38]

A leading candidate to replace Ferguson appeared to be Albert Watson. A conservative from South Carolina, a former member of Congress and strongly identified with southern segregation policies, he claimed support from Senator Strom Thurmond and Gerald Ford.[39] Nixon, however, received a warning from Senator Hugh Scott, the Minority Leader, that "a considerable head of steam is building up against" Watson's nomination. The situation, he wrote, "is tailor-made for Senator Birch Bayh and for some of those

[36] The cases are cited in *Solorio*, 447–48. So eager was the majority to overrule the Douglas decision, that in *Solorio* it acted without even a specific request from the United States that it do so. Indeed, *Solorio* was a case in which the High Court endorsed without actually saying so, the USCMA finding of a service connection—and went on to overrule *O'Callahan*—an action it considered far more important. Justice Stevens protested that "today's unnecessary overruling of precedent is most unwise." Because the Court did not disagree with USCMA, "it has no business reaching out to reexamine [*O'Callahan* and *Relford*]. . . . The fact that any five Members of the Court have the power to reconsider settled precedents at random, does not make that practice legitimate." *Solorio*, 451–52. While Stevens declined to agree with the opinion, concurring only in the judgment—three other justices dissented. The opinions in both *O'Callahan* and *Solorio* reflected the narrowest of margins, a bare majority of the Court.

[37] Ibid., 467. "The Court's action . . . reflects contempt, both for the members of our Armed Forces and for the constitutional safeguards intended to protect us all."

[38] NP, FG 58, Folder 18, February 10, 1971. Shortly thereafter, Nixon's assistant, John Ehrlichman, alerted another aide that "the President sees this upcoming vacancy on the Court of military justice [*sic*] as a good appointment for a black judicial prospect." Ibid., February 18, 1971. It may well be that Ferguson's frequently pronounced bias against military authorities in USCMA cases was not appreciated by the conservative "law and order" supporters of Nixon's administration. On the other hand, Nixon had been acquainted with Ferguson for many years.

[39] Nixon Aide Peter Flanigan informed Nixon assistants Robert Haldeman and Fred Malek that Ford had called "to express in the strongest possible terms his support of Watson." Indeed, added Flanigan, "I trust nothing will interfere with this appointment." Ibid., May 19, 1971.

in adversary positions on the Armed Services Committee," and the appointment would come at a time "when every effort would be made to link the nomination with My Lai and other military furores [*sic*]."[40] As if to confirm Scott's prediction, three days later Senator George McGovern (Democrat from South Dakota) publicly denounced the proposed appointment. The plan "again demonstrates the Administration attempt to shape the judicial system to its own purposes without a real regard for the needs of justice and for courts which should merit the respect of all Americans."[41] Nothing came of Watson's proposed nomination.

While the question of a successor to Ferguson—who had assumed the position of USCMA Senior Judge—remained unanswered, Nixon did solve the problem of Chief Judge Quinn. Judge William Darden later recalled that a Nixon aide, Fred Buzhardt, had asked Darden if Quinn would resign "if he [was] not Chief Judge?"[42] Darden does not recall his answer, but without any notice to Quinn, Nixon's staff prepared a presidential document naming Darden Chief Judge. Drafted on June 10, 1971, and hand delivered to Darden by a White House messenger on June 24, it fell to the new Chief Judge to inform the seventy-seven-year-old Quinn, who had served in that post for more than twenty years, of his sudden replacement.[43] "It was embarrassing to me to have to tell Judge Quinn that I had that letter." According to Darden, Quinn "was shaken" by the event. His immediate reaction was to ask Darden "whether I thought he should resign." Darden urged him not to take such a step, and Quinn remained on the USCMA bench.[44]

If "shaken" privately, publicly Quinn reacted to the announcement with typical aplomb. No stranger to politics, according to Fred Proulx who wrote

[40] Ibid., May 26, 1971. Scott assured Nixon that "this is an objective appraisal based on the evidence available." For more on USCMA treatment of the My Lai massacre and the resulting trial of Lieutenant William Calley, see below. For insights into Nixon's behavior during 1970–71, see Stanley Karnow's *Vietnam: A History* (1991), 625–27, 642–69.

[41] Ibid., May 28, 1971. "Instead of appointing a man who has a consistent record of racism, of supporting segregationist policies and legislation, the President should appoint a man who can understand the problems and frustrations of . . . all Americans."

[42] Darden, Interview, August 4, 1994.

[43] The free transferability of the Chief Judge's position was abolished by a recent amendment to the UCMJ. Now—as is the case with other federal appellate courts—it rotates, with a nonrenewable five-year term as Chief Judge going to the jurist with the most seniority. If, on the other hand, that judge has less than five years of the appointment remaining, the term as Chief Judge is similarly limited.

[44] Ibid. Darden declined to force Quinn from his rather ornate chambers, where he had been ensconced for almost twenty years. Nixon's sudden move can be described as underhanded, if not vicious. On the other hand, Quinn had agreed to resign in 1968, but later declined to do so; and Nixon—not unreasonably—was unwilling to have him continue as Chief Judge with the potential to remain in that post until Quinn's term ended in 1981. This step, of course, did not solve the matter of Quinn's continued occupancy of a seat on the Court. If Nixon's strategy aimed at somehow pushing Quinn into leaving, it failed. Nixon would leave Washington before Quinn left USCMA.

to a former USCMA commissioner shortly after Darden's elevation had been announced, "the passing of the baton to Judge Darden was his wish."[45] With a Republican president, Quinn was under no illusions concerning his continuance as Chief Judge. The timing and manner of the appointment, however, was another matter—and Quinn's supporters were critical of both. An editorial in the *Providence Sunday Journal* noted that "just why" Nixon elected to replace Quinn "is not at all clear."[46] Another writer commented that "it was with considerable dismay that I read the article . . . relative to such an uncalled-for move."[47]

Proulx also commented on the proposed Watson nomination, calling it a "trial balloon" which the President sent up "before he ran the risk of being involved in another Carswell situation, which he can ill afford."[48] More important, "We hear rumors from time to time tossed around, including a black colored Judge on the Supreme Court of Ohio by the name of Duncan." Indeed, "The consensus of opinion seems to be [that] it will be a black appointment in the light of the Watson flak and also as a promotion piece for an all volunteer Army, which you know, will have a higher percentage of blacks than that which obtains in the overall population."[49] As was often the case, Proulx was correct.

A young attorney from Columbus, Ohio, Robert Duncan, had come to the attention of William Saxbe, the state Attorney General, who later became a Senator and then from 1974 to 1975 the United States Attorney General. Duncan served as Saxbe's Chief Counsel in 1965. Three years later he was appointed to fill an unexpired term on the Ohio Supreme Court, to which he was reelected for a full term in 1970. At the behest of Senator Saxbe, Duncan was also named to the White House Fellows Commission. As a black member of a state Supreme Court, with the Nixon Administration "interested," as he later recalled, "in some black presence as it were," Duncan was in the right place at the right time.[50] Moreover, as the *Navy Times* put it, unlike prior USCMA selections Duncan "is neither a practicing politician,

[45] USCMAP, Personnel File of Zeigel Neff, July 8, 1971. One month later, Proulx emphasized that "of course we are very pleased with Judge Darden's designation. . . . We have gotten to know Chief Judge Darden in his policies and views, which are more in tune with those of the Governor. He was the Governor's [Quinn's] first choice so it has all worked out for the best." Ibid., August 24, 1971.

[46] Ibid., Personnel File of Robert Quinn, clipping, July 27, 1971.

[47] QPPC, June 29, 1971.

[48] Neff File, May 28, 1971. The reference to Carswell concerned Senate rejection of Nixon's nominee to the Supreme Court.

[49] Ibid., August 24, 1971.

[50] Robert Duncan, Interview, January 4, 1988, 8. One of Nixon's "talent scouts" informed me that Nixon had wanted "a black republican senior state judge," relatively young, to replace Ferguson. Interview, Frank Rocco, September 11, 1990. The President had expressed concern about race relations in the military.

4. Judges Quinn, Darden, and Duncan

nor a defeated one."[51] Unanimously confirmed by the Senate after a brief and superficial hearing before the Senate Armed Services Committee, on November 29, 1971, he took the oath of office from Supreme Court Justice Potter Stewart.

[51] USCMAP, Quinn File, clipping, October 6, 1971. The editorial stated that Duncan's candidacy "sounds promising," and this was even before his formal nomination had been announced. The editorial further stated that "we are not sorry to see Judge Ferguson leave." It described him as "a judicial nit-picker—one of those who interpret fairness as meaning perfection." On the other hand, the editorial writer went on to extol the first panel of judges—Quinn, Latimer, and Brosman—as "non-politicians." Given Quinn's very political background, to say

Duncan's appointment heralded a period characterized by rapidly changing personnel on USCMA. Indeed, he served the shortest term thus far in the Court's history, less than three years. During his tenure, however, the Court decided one of the most notorious cases in its history, the court-martial that resulted from the My Lai massacre, *United States v. Calley*.[52] The case was most unusual.[53]

The defendant, Lieutenant William Calley, had hired former USCMA Judge George Latimer to represent him. Quite vocal in his contention that the extensive publicity engendered by the massacre and its aftermath had rendered the Army incapable of providing his client with a fair trial, Latimer found himself criticizing the very system that he had defended for ten years—an irony not lost on Proulx, just completing his second decade as Clerk of the Court. "By the way," he wrote to a former USCMA commissioner, "how did you like Judge Latimer running down the system which he strongly defended for 10 years?" Do you have "any suggestion as to what I should do with the first ten volumes of our reports where all the statements he made were diametrically opposed?"[54]

Altogether, Latimer represented Calley three times—his original court-martial, his appeal before the Army Court of Military Review, and the final appeal before his old Court on which one of his original colleagues, Judge Quinn, still sat. Observers noted, however, that the seventy-year-old Latimer "seemed often to be out of his depth. . . . losing his place among papers or repeating himself. . . ."[55] For his appeal before USCMA, Latimer asked the

---

nothing of his poorly concealed senatorial ambitions while serving on the USCMA bench, one wonders how much accuracy should be attributed to the editorial writer. Duncan later stated that he was "almost oblivious to the early developmental stage of the Court's jurisprudence." Interview, 11.

[52] 22 USCMA 534 (1973).

[53] For background on the massacre which took place in 1968, see two books by Seymour Hersh: *My Lai 4: A Report on the Massacre and Its Aftermath*, 1970; and *Cover-Up: The Army's Secret Investigation of the Massacre at My Lai 4*, 1972.

[54] USCMAP, Personnel File of Zeigel Neff, April 9, May 28, 1971. The publicity cited by Latimer also affected the Court. Proulx noted that during early April 1971, the Calley case "has flooded our office with approximately 1,800 letters received during the last five days. A week ago . . . we had a demonstration at our front door." Ibid., April 9, 1971. The letters, many of which apparently came from Texas, all carried the same message; and two brief excerpts will indicate their general tone. "In regards to the disgusting trial of Lt. Wm. Calley—I think it stinks. Here is a man who killed the enemy in the act of defending his country, only to have the same country to put him on trial for it. The whole rotten mess makes me sick to my stomach. . . . I am *not* [emphasis in original] a radical of any sort only a betroden taxpayer who is fed up with all this nonsense. Turn him loose." USCMAP, Calley Files, Box 2, April 1, 1971. "If he is going to be punished why not arrest former President Truman who ordered the atom bombs dropped on Hiroshima and Nagasaki? They too, killed millions of innocent children, babies, women, old men, old women, young innocent boys and girls, etc., etc." Ibid., April 12, 1971.

[55] USCMAP, Calley Files, Box 2, clipping of article by Warren Rogers, reprinted in the Providence *Sunday Journal*, n.p. Another observer was even more harsh in his assessment of

Court to rule on thirty issues drawn from a transcript of more than twenty volumes. The initial memorandum to the judges from the central legal staff member charged with examining the case recommended that every one be rejected. The staff director concurred, but recognized that "the seriousness of the crimes" (Calley had been convicted of murdering at least twenty "oriental human beings") might "warrant something more than a simple order of 'Deny.'"[56] The judges agreed, and ordered argument on three issues, involving the question of excessive publicity, insufficient evidence, and prejudicial error concerning the way in which Calley's defense of superior orders had been submitted to the trial Court.

Writing for himself and Judge Duncan, Quinn rejected all three issues, and emphasized that the instructions of the military judge "on all issues were comprehensive and correct. Lieutenant Calley was given every consideration to which he was entitled and perhaps more." The court-martial findings, reached after more than eighty hours of deliberation, "represent the truth of the facts as they [the court members] determined them to be and there is substantial evidence to support those findings. No mistakes of procedure cast doubt upon them."[57] Duncan later recalled that "I didn't think the *Calley* case was very difficult, either factually or legally. It was not a difficult case at all in my judgment. . . . There were some issues in *Calley* which weren't before the Court that I think were extremely important but the record we had to deal with, I thought, wasn't difficult at all."[58]

Several months before the *Calley* decision was announced, Judge Darden had written to Nixon expressing his desire to resign from USCMA. He had served for five years of a term—originally Kilday's—to end in May 1976. More than two decades later, Darden recalled that he had become "a little weary with the Court's routine." He had found that the issues were not "really stimulating," nor was "dealing with them very satisfying."[59] Not until

Latimer's performance as counsel. Latimer had apparently represented Calley without fee, "a fact that led some wits to remark after it was over that Calley had gotten his money's worth. The defense was confusing and confused, rambling, directionless, contradictory, and totally ill-prepared." Ibid., clipping of a review of Richard Hammer's *The Court-Martial of Lieutenant Calley*, by Geoff Metcalfe, n.d., n.p.

[56] QP, Calley Case, Petition Memo, May 10, 1973, 23.

[57] 22 USCMA 544. Duncan concluded that the prosecution "was not entitled to a presumption of what [Calley] knew or did not know about the illegality of an order. It is a matter for the factfinders under proper instructions." Nevertheless, he added, "I do not believe the results in this case would have been different." Ibid., 544, 545. Darden who had originally voted to affirm the conviction, and indeed had begun drafting the opinion for a unanimous court, found himself troubled by what he saw as a serious flaw in the instructions concerning the defense of superior orders. Ultimately he dissented, and made some of his original draft available to Quinn who promptly had it incorporated into his opinion. Ibid., 547; Interview with William Darden, August 3, 1994.

[58] Interview with Robert Duncan, January 4, 1988, 74.

[59] Darden, interview, August 3, 1994. Darden's candor was not new. In 1971, he stated pub-

December 29, did Nixon's staff send Darden a graceful letter of acknowledgment. "For more than five years," Nixon wrote, "You have met the challenges of your office with great skill and dedication. . . ."[60] Within a few weeks, Nixon appointed Duncan as the new Chief Judge—possibly because of Quinn's continued resolve to remain, and Nixon's consistent refusal to restore him to the position he had held for twenty years. For his part, on February 17, 1974, Duncan utilized a legislative provision enacted in 1968, and again requested Ferguson to resume full-time judicial duties as a "senior judge" until further notice.[61] Thus, USCMA could function with a full bench, although Ferguson and Quinn were eighty-five and eighty years old, respectively.[62]

This judicial stability was short lived, however, for within six months Duncan resigned to accept appointment as a Federal District Judge in Ohio. Although he recalled that his old sponsor and mentor William Saxbe urged him to accept such an appointment, which unlike the USCMA seat included life tenure—Duncan had personal reasons for making such a move. Work on USCMA was not "the sort of challenge that I felt presented itself to me intellectually as a professional. . . . After all, you are talking criminal jurisprudence when you are talking [USCMA], and although I certainly don't want to minimize to any degree or make any comment which dilutes the importance of that Court[,] in my own view . . . if you examine the agenda of matters that come before a district court and what comes before [USCMA] then the restrictions [are] with the Court of Military Appeals."[63]

With two USCMA vacancies to fill, the Nixon White House turned to consideration of candidates. While even in normal times, such selections were not considered urgent, in Nixon's case they received even less attention than usual. As the selection process got under way, the Watergate crisis was in full flower. President Johnson, occupied by Vietnam, had failed to act on Quinn's resignation. President Nixon would resign his office before final action on the USCMA vacancies could be completed. Gerald Ford (and later

licly that "I can't honestly say I enjoy the job. I haven't felt that I was good enough at it yet. I don't really have the confidence yet that I'd like to have. I just hope I'm able to do a satisfactory job." QPGF, Margaret Shanon, "Trials and Tribulations of Military Justice," *The Atlanta Journal and Constitution Magazine*, April 8, 1971, 39.

[60] NP, White House Central Files, FG 58/A, Folder 23, December 29, 1973.

[61] 27 USCMA iii.

[62] Although Darden was also designated as an USCMA Senior Judge, he appears to have sat only once as a senior judge, in 1995. He recalled that when in 1980, newly appointed Chief Judge Robinson Everett reiterated the invitation, "my first reaction was to say yes, [but] I came to my senses fast." Darden, interview.

[63] Duncan, interview, 65–66. One intriguing conclusion that can be drawn from Duncan's comments is that limited terms in office might be more desirable for USCMA judges than tenure—if only because a regular turnover of judicial personnel would help contribute to a sense of newness and intellectual stimulation on their part.

George Bush) each would subsequently make three appointments to USCMA, more than any other president since Truman.

THE PROCLIVITY FOR PREFERENCES AND POLITICS

On March 14, 1974, Vice President Ford received an "eyes only" memorandum from a White House staff member, Jerry Jones. He reported that Defense Secretary James Schlesinger had proposed Kenneth Pye as Darden's replacement. Currently Dean of Duke University Law School and later to become President of Southern Methodist University, Pye's credentials remained as impressive as they had been when John Macy first called them to the attention of Lyndon Johnson in 1965. Indeed, Schlesinger "feels Pye is the most outstanding candidate he has seen." His background "will allow Pye to provide the necessary leadership to bring the Court back to a position of prominence and efficiency."[64] However, there were some problems "in proceeding with his nomination."

In the first place, Pye "is a self-admitted Kennedy/Johnson Democrat. . . . Senator Helms has indicated he will not clear him, [and] considers [Pye] a very hard-line anti-Nixon man and threatens to 'go off the reservation' if Pye is nominated."[65] Moreover, there were a number of other candidates for the position—"several are Pye's equal and all have strong Republican credentials and support. . . ." In "order to give Al Haig the best input possible," Jones asked Ford "whether or not we should go ahead."[66] Haig and Schlesinger discussed the nomination, and "while not wedded to Pye, the Secretary is very anxious to have him as a member of the Court, and to have him named Chief Judge." Without comment, Ford rejected Schlesinger's proposal.

Two months later, Ford received another "eyes only" memorandum from David Wimer, a White House staff member. This time, Schlesinger proposed the appointment of a current Colorado Supreme Court Justice, William Erickson, "an extremely skillful juridical administrator, well able to take charge, intellectually and managerially, of a Court badly in need of repair."[67] Again the availability of numerous other candidates came up, and Wimer noted that "we are faced with the traditional interrelated dilemma of (1) more candidates than opportunities, (2) the potential disappointment of

[64] GF, Vice Presidential Papers, Box 219, March 14, 1974.

[65] Ibid. "Schlesinger has been working on Helms, however, and believes he can bring him around."

[66] Ibid., 2. Al Haig was General Alexander Haig, Jr., a former member of Secretary of State Henry Kissinger's staff who had become White House Chief of Staff in May 1973.

[67] Ibid., Box 218, May 16, 1974. Wimer's memo was actually a proposed draft of a confidential report to Haig, for which he sought Ford's approval.

Members of Congress whose candidates are not selected, and (3) balancing substantive requirements against necessary political concerns."[68] Wimer attempted to solve this problem by recommending that Erickson replace Duncan as Chief Judge.[69] For the Darden vacancy, he revived the name of William Cook, still serving on the staff of the House Armed Services Committee, and still receiving "the highest regard" for his "abilities and loyalties" from the Republican members of that Committee.[70] Ford approved Wimer's recommendations possibly because he felt that these two choices balanced the need for expertise with political realities.

At this point, another major figure in the Nixon Administration provided differing input into the USCMA selection process. In May 1974, Air Force Major General Brent Scowcroft, serving as Kissinger's deputy on the National Security Council, was asked about Wimer's recommendations. Scowcroft's assistant drafted a response that endorsed Erickson, but rejected Cook—whose "experience and other qualifications are less than adequate for the Court of Military Appeals."[71] Scowcroft's aide, Jan Lodal, further explained his opposition to Cook. "Currently we have two specific problems with [USCMA]. First, the system is antiquated and needs modernization; Congress and the DOD have emphasized this fact. Second, the current Court needs to have its stature upgraded and reinforced; its rulings have been continually challenged by other courts. There is no indication that Mr. Cook has the background and wherewithal needed to resolve these problems."[72]

Lodal urged that Scowcroft "strongly pursue this matter. We cannot tolerate less than highly qualified individuals on the Court, particularly in this period of special morale and discipline problems, the transition to the all-volunteer force, and urgent needs of minority members of the Services." He assured Scowcroft that the Defense Department "would wholeheartedly agree with the nonconcurrence. . . . At a minimum, we owe it to Secretary Schlesinger to have his full views brought to the attention of General Haig and the President."[73]

Scowcroft sent a "revised" memorandum to Wimer. It endorsed Erickson's

[68] Ibid., 2.

[69] A "well-regarded attorney and jurist" and active in the ABA, Erickson's "legal abilities are so well recognized that he was informally approached by the ABA to see if he would consider being recommended as the Watergate Special Prosecutor. He responded that he had no interest in any such participation since he strongly supported the President."

[70] On the other hand, Wimer had to acknowledge that the Defense Department "is not in favor of Cook's appointment and consider him a 'hack.' At the same time, they have indicated that if they get Erickson, they can probably live with Cook." NP, WHCF, Confidential Files, Box 22; undated, but is almost identical to the memo submitted to Ford on May 14, 1974.

[71] NP, WHCF, Box 22, Folder 19, probably May 22, 1974.

[72] Ibid. For further indication of contemporary perception concerning USCMA's rulings, see the discussion in chapter 11 of the 1979 Defense Department proposed "Reform" of the Court.

[73] NP, WHCF, Box 22, May 22, 1974.

nomination as Chief Judge, calling him "clearly well qualified for that important position." He made no mention of Cook, but noted that "the success of the all-volunteer force is related to the perceptions held by those who are potential volunteers. The equity with which discipline is maintained is important in forming those views[,] and it is essential that military justice and those responsible for it be of the highest caliber." He recommended that "efforts be made to solicit additional recommendations from the Defense Department and elsewhere in the interest of selecting a nominee whose experience and qualifications are more in keeping with the high standards and difficult demands to be expected of [USCMA] judges in the years ahead."[74]

Shortly thereafter, the General Counsel of the Defense Department, Martin Hoffman, suggested two additional candidates to complete Darden's term, one of them a sitting judge from Minnesota—Judge Stephen Maxwell.[75] Unlike Scowcroft, Hoffman did not mince words concerning William Cook. "We do not agree that William Cook is an acceptable candidate. In our view the Court as presently constituted, and the necessity for revitalization of the military justice system require appointments in the spirit of excellence. In view of the age and disposition of Judge Quinn, the appointment of Cook would place an undue burden on Justice Erickson that would probably preclude his assumption of a full range of necessary activities the Chief Judge should undertake and pursue."[76]

On the same day that Hoffman prepared his statement, Wimer forwarded another "eyes only" memorandum to the Vice President. He stated that "several additional perspectives and candidates have been presented with sufficient impetus to warrant this second request for your views." Wimer added that since Quinn had given no indication that he would retire, the only vacancies to be filled were those of Darden and Duncan. Because a strong consensus had been attained as to Erickson's qualifications, in reality Wimer was concerned only with selecting a candidate to fill the remainder of Darden's term.[77] He reiterated the issue of minority representation on USCMA, and concluded that Stephen Maxwell appears "to be a most competent jurist, and he is certainly well able to make a serious contribution to the court." Maxwell had been "informally recommended" by the Defense Department.

[74] Ibid., May 28, 1974. The way in which Scowcroft worded his memorandum obviated the need either to mention Cook or his nomination.

[75] Ibid., June 5, 1974. "Maxwell, of course, has the additional attribute of being black and there is general agreement that a black on the Court is very highly desirable."

[76] Ibid. The other suggested nominee was Walter Kiechel, Jr., who at the time was serving as a Deputy Assistant Attorney General. A member of Phi Beta Kappa, and holder of two law degrees from Yale University, "while lacking judicial experience, he has the attribute of knowledge of the military justice system and excellent familiarity with litigation and the attendant writing skills."

[77] FP, Vice Presidential Papers, Box 218, June 5, 1974. It would be barely two years in length, as Darden had been appointed to complete Kilday's term which would end in 1976.

Wimer also evaluated Walter Kiechel, on whose behalf several senators including Barry Goldwater and Roman Hruska "have intensified their interest to the degree that I present his credentials to you for your review."[78] As between Cook and Kiechel, "The Defense Department regards Kiechel as the better choice in substantive terms, but this may remain an open question as DOD seems to possess a slight anti-Cook bias." What Wimer asked of Ford was "your evaluation of Cook versus Kiechel [in political terms] versus Maxwell [in substantive terms]."[79] Ford indicated that Cook remained his first choice with Kiechel in the second spot.[80]

In an effort to gain Scowcroft's views, Wimer sent him the same memo. Again Jan Lodal reminded the General that "we cannot tolerate less than highly qualified individuals on the Court." Lodal prepared a memo for Scowcroft recommending Maxwell and Kiechel in that order. The memo, he added, "makes no mention of Mr. William H. Cook, who has considerable political backing, but whose substantive qualifications appear less than adequate for the Court." Moreover, "DOD views coincide with mine on this matter."[81]

In the meantime, on June 21 the White House formally announced Nixon's intention to nominate Erickson as Duncan's successor, and to designate him as Chief Judge upon Senate confirmation.[82] Duncan resigned effective July 11, and in his formal letter to Nixon described USCMA as "a strong and healthy judicial installation."[83] Shortly thereafter, Wimer submitted Cook's nomination to Nixon for final approval, informing him that "all necessary checks have been completed."[84] Even as Wimer sent his memo, the House

[78] Ibid. Hruska had gained some notoriety when he defended Nixon's ill-fated nomination of G. Harrold Carswell to the Supreme Court. "There are lots of mediocre judges," Hruska said. "[Mediocre people] are entitled to a little representation, aren't they?" See William Chafe, *The Unfinished Journey: America Since World War II*, 2nd ed. (1991), 386.

[79] GF, Vice Presidential Papers, Box 218, June 5, 1974.

[80] Ibid. On June 11, Wimer's office sought to make sure that Ford's recommendations are "in order as to his preference of choice. In other words, is Cook his first choice and Kiechel his 2nd?" Again, Ford confirmed that such was the case.

[81] NP. WHCF, Box 22, June 10, 1974. This author could not ascertain whether or not Scowcroft transmitted the memo to Ford.

[82] NP, WHCF, FG 58A, Folder 23, June 21, 1974.

[83] Ibid., June 28, 1974. "I am also," Duncan added, "appreciative for your manifested faith in my ability to serve as District Judge. As I view it, that office is among the most demanding and important in all of government."

[84] Ibid., July 30, 1974. On August 2, the White House formally announced Nixon's intent to name Cook to the Court. After he retired from USCMA, Cook summarized his path to the Court. "I began thinking what job am I qualified for . . . and not many people agreed to want to go on the Court of Military Appeals. Well there were thousands when the Court was first created. . . . But now it doesn't lead anyplace. I mean truthfully it is kind of a last job. So I followed up, I thought I was fairly qualified to serve on that Court[,] so I began talking to

Committee on the Judiciary passed the third and final article of impeachment against Nixon for his obstruction of justice in seeking to cover up the Watergate incident. Nevertheless, it appeared that Nixon had filled the two existing USCMA vacancies, and that the Court would return to full strength, including of course Quinn—now in his twenty-fourth year of service.

Nixon began what would turn out to be his final week in the White House by receiving an unusual letter from Erickson. He had expected to maintain his residence and chambers in Denver, "devoting so much of my time to work in the District of Coumbia as the Court might require." Apparently the Defense Department officials with whom he spoke had accepted such a stipulation which, Erickson added, "was deemed to be proper and workable in the light of the history of the Court."[85] Moreover, "a substantial majority of the Chief Judges of the [U.S.] Courts of Appeal maintain chambers and perform a large part of their judicial work at a place other than that at which the Court sits." Nevertheless, Erickson had "become aware of the strong objections of some members of the Congress, and of others who were closely related to the Military Court. . . ."

The nominee was "forced to conclude that the objections to my maintenance of a Colorado residence were well founded. In my opinion, it is necessary for the [USCMA] Chief Judge . . . to maintain his residence . . . where the Court sits."[86] Therefore, it became necessary for Erickson "to determine whether I could give up my lifelong residence, friends and family ties in Colorado to move to Washington. . . ." He "concluded that I could not, and regretfully must request that you withdraw my name from further consideration."[87] On August 6, Wimer drafted the formal withdrawal for the President's signature. Three days later, Nixon resigned.

Having made his preference for Cook clear on several occasions as Vice President, the new Chief Executive saw no reason to change his mind. Indeed, even before Nixon resigned, Cook had informed the USCMA Clerk that the Senate Armed Services Committee had scheduled a hearing on his nomination for August 15.[88] The hearing went off as scheduled, and it pro-

---

various friends and I became a candidate out of the committee to go on the Court." William H. Cook, Interview, September 29, 1987, 8.

[85] Ibid., NP, August 1, 1974. Erickson was well aware of Quinn's pattern of "commuting" to the Court only for oral arguments and conferences—spending most of his time in Providence. As will be seen, he also understood the inconvenience, if not resentment, that such a practice apparently had engendered for more than twenty years.

[86] Ibid., 2. "The Chief Judge should be available at all times to the other members of the Court and to the Court's staff, so that his duties can be performed expeditiously when problems arise or when immediate action is required."

[87] Ibid. "This letter is written with deep personal regret, but with the certain knowledge that the public interest can only be served by the Chief Judge residing in the Washington, D.C. area."

[88] QPGF, August 6, 1994.

duced more than the usual superficial banter. The nominee submitted a brief statement, concluding with the comment that "there is something unique about military law in a disciplined society and, as I view the role as a Judge on [USCMA], it is to preserve and protect individual liberties while, at the same time, assuring that the military establishment is able to function in an orderly fashion. Obviously, this is a fine line which can only be determined on a case-by-case basis."[89]

The Committee Chair, Mississippi Senator John Stennis responded that "you will remember, I know, that justice is blind. But you don't have to be blind yourself, and you don't want to be blind. . . . I have a feeling that out among the services maybe we have too much law and too little discipline."[90] Cook replied that he had said much the same thing in his statement, but expanded his point in a later comment to Senator Strom Thurmond. "I do think that there has been a tendency in the immediate past to forget discipline and forget the establishment and to think of the individual. We must think of the individual, but I think probably in my opinion the Court has gone overboard."[91]

Stennis observed that "if I didn't believe you would do your duty . . . as you saw it I wouldn't vote to confirm you, but I think we are up against some practical realities of life. . . . In the military, I think we have leaned over backwards trying to decide these military discipline cases . . . too much as a civilian court would decide them."[92] Senator Thomas McIntyre told Cook that "I had come into the Army, and I believed very much in the civil authority that you are innocent until you are proved guilty. So I hope you will remember that part. I believe in discipline as the Chairman is talking about. But you must not consider those guys guilty the minute they are charged."[93] Unanimously confirmed by the Senate a day later, Cook joined Robert Quinn on the USCMA bench.[94] In an ironic twist to the Quinn saga,

[89] USCMAP, "Nominations of Cook and Potter," *Hearing Before the Committee on Armed Services*, U.S. Senate, 93rd Cong., 2nd sess., August 15, 1974, 5.

[90] Ibid., 6.

[91] Ibid. Thurmond then asked Cook, "Do you feel that all the benefits of our civil law are applicable to those serving in the military uniform?" Cook replied: "Insofar as we can do it within this discipline society of which I was just speaking."

[92] Ibid., 9.

[93] Ibid., 10. Responding to McIntyre, Senator Taft recalled his days in the Navy when serving as a recorder on a naval court. The captain "called me in . . . and said, 'Look, I think you are doing fine, but your sentences are a little light. You are interfering with my prerogative to reduce them.'" Cook made no reply, but McIntyre stated, "That is the military attitude in its worst form."

[94] The record of his opinions and dissents indicate that Cook seems to have taken the Stennis warning to heart. They reflect a notable tendency to support the military's position. Indeed, one Army JAG colonel described a Cook dissent as "one of many that rank him among the finest jurists to sit on the Court of Military Appeals, or perhaps any court." Col. Craig S. Schwender, "Who's Afraid of Command Influence; or Can the Court of Military Appeals Be This Wrong?"

as Nixon left office the man he had removed as Chief Judge resumed that position, until President Ford designated another judge to fill it.

By 1974, USCMA was showing signs that changes in its internal administration might be appropriate. Quinn continued coming to the Court only for conferences and arguments. Both the original Clerk, Alfred Proulx, and his first deputy had now retired after more than twenty years of service, and relations between the new clerk and the director of the central legal staff were not always harmonious. Moreover, as Cook soon learned, communication between the Court and the JAGs of the armed services was not what it could be. The new judge had been on the bench for barely one week when he received a candid letter from a veteran court commissioner, Cabell F. Cobbs.

Cobbs reminded the new Judge of Article 67(g) in the UCMJ that required the Judges and JAGs to meet annually, and to submit a comprehensive report to Congress on the state of appellate military justice. Calling itself the "Code Committee," it "initially met at the Army-Navy Club for a dinner meeting, and this tradition was continued for at least one [annual] meeting until 1970."[95] Cobbs added that "generally, there is no agenda for the meetings." This weakness, coupled with the lack of regular meetings prevent the committee "from being an effective vehicle to convey to [DOD] and to Congress needed changes."[96] The commissioner proposed a number of steps to strengthen the committee's functions. These included scheduled monthly meetings, a formal agenda prepared by the Chief Judge, and basing the recommendations to Congress on majority approval within the Committee.[97]

The Court, explained Cobbs, "has the valuable advantage of having read a great number of records of trial and thus obtaining an overall and generally unbiased view of the administration of military justice. In contrast, the [JAGs] are generally and properly representatives of the command structures of the several military departments. They tend, therefore, to represent a much narrower viewpoint and one which is frequently resistant to changes that may be needed." Indeed, "as a body which was created to lead in the field of military justice[,] and with its independence fully established . . . this Court can take the lead on the Code Committee by insisting on careful annual reviews of the Code. . . ."[98] Cobbs's observations were accurate, but a sense of reality indicated that any reinvigoration of the Code committee

The Army Lawyer, April 1992, 21. Of course, one's perspective determines how one perceives a given decision. Other USCMA observers took a less charitable view than Schwender, who was moved to write this article because of a case in which he himself had played a role.

[95] FP, "Memorandum for Judge Cook," Box 21, Folder 10, August 29, 1974.

[96] Ibid., 2. Cobbs also criticized the "belief that a consensus of opinion is necessary for the presentation of recommended changes in the Joint Report."

[97] Ibid., 3.

[98] Ibid., 4.

would have to wait until the arrival of a new Chief Judge. As 1974 waned, Ford's aides indicated that they had found one.

FORD FINDS FLETCHER

In 1974, Albert Fletcher, Jr., served as a state judge in Kansas, a position he had held for almost fourteen years. He had received a law degree from Washburn University, where one of his classmates and acquaintances was future United States Senator and presidential hopeful Robert Dole. Coauthor of two studies on state judicial administration, Fletcher later recalled that in 1974 he had been under consideration for selection as a federal district judge.[99] Instead of such an appointment, Fletcher received a phone call from Martin Hoffman, still General Counsel of DOD, but soon to be named Secretary of the Army. Hoffman asked if Fletcher would be interested in being considered for a seat on USCMA—a court about which Fletcher was frank to admit, he "knew nothing."

Fletcher's expression of interest resulted in two letters to Ford from Senator Dole strongly recommending not only Fletcher's appointment but also his immediate designation as Chief Judge.[100] For his part, Hoffman interviewed Fletcher. In considering his appointment, Hoffman later observed that he had wanted to see on the court judges with "some really high visibility, strong modern-type people that would have the empathy of the military justice system in them, but have—you know—the flexibility to build the Court and modernize the Code." Fletcher "was obviously a dedicated, hard working sort of guy."[101] On February 12, Ford's staff forwarded Fletcher's name to him for consideration, although the White House Counsel's Office observed that "there is no evidence of quality."[102] Ford responded with a handwritten note that "I have no objection *but* [emphasis in original] this seems like a very choice appointment to someone I don't know or seems to come out of nowhere. Talk with me."[103]

[99] Albert Fletcher, Jr., Interview, August 4, 1994.

[100] FP, WHCF, Name File December 18, 1974. Ford also received a letter from New Hampshire Senator Thomas McIntyre, urging the appointment of retired Major General Kenneth Hodson, a former Army JAG. Ibid., Presidential Personnel Office Papers, Box 59, January 27, 1975.

[101] Martin Hoffman, Interview, October 19, 1988, 2. Hoffman also recalled "a worry about the stature of the people that were going to go on the Court." He further recalled Fletcher as a person with "a terrific temperament." He "didn't appear to have much of an agenda." Indeed, "I never saw an agenda and we didn't have a specific agenda that said you have to civilianize this thing. The agenda was, it's got to be a military thing, and the more it gets kind of eccentric and crabbed and mechanistic and too conservative for the times[,] the Supreme Court is going to step in there and straighten the God damn thing out and thats not what we want." 10, 11. Again, this comment is of special interest in the wake of what happened to the Court between 1975 and 1980. See infra.

[102] GF, James E. Connor Files, Box 49, February 12, 1975.

[103] Ibid. Given this response, one wonders if Ford ever saw Dole's letters.

One week later, Ford's personnel director replied to the President. Fletcher's recommendation "is the result of an effort by Secretary Schlesinger and Marty Hoffman to substantially upgrade the calibre of personnel on this Court which, historically, has been composed of retired congressional staffers." Furthermore, "the prestige of the court is generally thought now to be at an all-time low at a time when there is increasing pressure on the military justice system. . . . Finally, the department wishes to improve the quality of decisions by the Court. Apparently there has never been an opinion conference among the three judges."[104] This memorandum warrants a few comments.

Thus far in USCMA history, of eight appointments to USCMA only two "congressional staffers" had been named, and one of them by Ford himself. It is true that two former members of Congress [Ferguson and Kilday] had also been USCMA members, but to state that the Court "historically has been composed of congressional staffers" was incorrect. Moreover, at the time of the memo, Quinn had suffered a severe stroke and was unable to communicate. While he would not resign until late April he never again sat on the bench. Further, the comment that "apparently there has never even been an opinion conference among the three judges" is a striking example of ignorance. If it referred to the past twenty-five-year history of the Court, the statement is utter nonsense. If however, it was based on the fact that in early 1975, with only one full-time Judge (Cook) and one senior Judge (Ferguson), with Quinn incommunicado in Providence—formal conferences were probably considered unnecessary if not impossible—the statement seems more reasonable. At any rate, the memo—replete with its reference to the fact that Fletcher and Dole were classmates—must have satisfied Ford, because shortly thereafter Fletcher's nomination went to the Senate.[105]

The April 10 confirmation hearing before the Senate Armed Services Committee may well have set a record for brevity. Senator John Stennis submitted a letter on Fletcher's behalf from Senator Dole. Dole observed that "the American people, for a variety of reasons, no longer repose an automatic trust and confidence in their institutions whose ability to inspire confidence, only a short time ago, was unquestioned." What was needed, he added, "is the appointment to responsible positions of men and women who are perceptive enough to appreciate the dimensions of this problem and innovative enough to deal with them." It "pleases me to assure this committee," Dole concluded, "that [Fletcher] is such a man."[106]

Stennis asked Fletcher why he would accept the appointment "that is to come." Fletcher replied that "this is the court wherein that fine line which the judiciary and the court have to walk in order to balance individual rights

[104] Ibid., February 19, 1975.

[105] GF, Presidential Personnel Files, Box 14, March 13, 1975.

[106] USCMAP, "Nomination of Albert B. Fletcher, Jr.," *Hearing Before the Committee on Armed Services of the United States Senate*, 94th Cong., 1st sess., April 10, 1975, 4.

against society's rights becomes particularly important. This is because in the Armed Forces you have a disciplined society to balance against the individual's rights. It is the court's purpose to protect both and to preserve both[,] and this particular area is a great challenge in the law."[107] No other senator beside Stennis even bothered to ask any questions of Fletcher, and the Committee unanimously approved his nomination. The entire hearing lasted fifteen minutes. Four days later the Senate confirmed him by voice vote.

With his designation as Chief Judge that followed very shortly, the Fletcher era began. No one knew it at the time, of course, but Fletcher's term as Chief Judge would generate more controversy among the military than any other period in USCMA history. Rancor, resentment, and recrimination would characterize his tenure. But all this was yet to come. In the meantime, a more pressing matter confronted both the Court and President Ford. The Quinn era was at last drawing to a close, and before 1975 ended the USCMA bench would consist entirely of new judges.

[107] Ibid.

CHAPTER 10

Confrontation and Culmination, 1975–1980

Part One

FAREWELL TO QUINN AND FERGUSON

Although Robert Quinn's resignation was submitted to President Ford in April 1975, in fact the Quinn era had come to an end that January when he suffered a stroke. While the letter bearing his resignation requested status as a senior judge, its subject lay comatose in a Rhode Island nursing home. Nevertheless, the first USCMA Chief Judge was honored during a Court ceremony on April 25, 1975. Rumors had already circulated as to the seriousness of his condition, lending an almost surreal atmosphere to the proceedings—a foreboding that accentuated the possible with acquiescence in the probable. The ceremony, according to Judge Cook, who presided, was "being videotaped and transcribed so that Judge Quinn will know the very high esteem that is held for him."[1]

Among the highlights of the brief ceremony were the comments of Senator John Pastore, who had first met Quinn more than fifty-five years before. As Rhode Island's senior senator, Pastore had aided Quinn on numerous occasions, not least of which was the campaign for Quinn's reappointment in 1966. Now Pastore emphasized that his former Governor "was a good man. He loved people, knew people and that is why he was successful as a judge. He knew people and knew how to serve people."[2] Another member of the Rhode Island Congressional delegation added that "there isn't a day that goes by that Robert Quinn does not do something for somebody."[3] Army JAG General George Prugh commented on Quinn's ability to interpret the new UCMJ so as to make "the Code come alive," and this in a context "that set the highest standards of professional performance."[4] Perhaps William Darden best captured Quinn's essence when he described Quinn's "historic prescription for making a great judge—he should be first a gentleman, and it helps if he knows a little bit of law."[5]

A few weeks later, on May 19, 1975, Quinn passed away. His twenty-

[1] "Robert E. Quinn Retirement Ceremony," 23 USCMA vii (1975).

[2] Ibid., x. "[M]y prayer is that Bob Quinn will fight his way out of his sickness like he has fought for people and may God bless him no matter what it is."

[3] Ibid., xi.

[4] Ibid., xii.

[5] Ibid., xiv. "Judge Quinn was and is a gentleman, and knows much more than a little bit of law."

three year tenure as Chief Judge will stand as the record since Congress later mandated a five-year term based on seniority.[6] More instinctual than intellectual in his judicial approach, he emphasized in his opinions what he had often articulated during his political career—that law be both practical and practicable. He was a man of great personal charm, and with the politician's gift for "people relationships" he had managed to remain on cordial terms with the JAGs even when rejecting the military position in specific cases. On the other hand, especially in his later years, his frequent absences from the Court had deprived it of effective administrative leadership. And when a new Chief Judge sought both to revitalize the Court and expand its role in military justice, the military would find the differences between the Quinn and Fletcher approach disturbing—as will be seen.

The tributes to Quinn had temporarily obscured the urgency for a third USCMA appointment, in that the incoming Fletcher along with Cook, and Ferguson temporarily sitting as a senior judge, could keep the Court operational. Even before Quinn's retirement ceremony, Senator Strom Thurmond urged that Ford offer an incumbent South Carolina Democratic Congressman "a position on a second- or third-level basis," if only because the South Carolina Republicans have—according to Thurmond—an "outstanding" candidate who "would have an outstanding chance of being elected" to fill the seat.[7] His candidate was a conservative South Carolina Democrat who had served in Congress for about eight years. James Mann had the advantage of "strong support" from Thurmond, the senior Republican on a committee where seniority remained and remains very important. Although Ford signed off on the appointment in early June, Mann's nomination never reached the Senate.[8]

By the middle of June, rumors concerning Mann's "imminent" elevation to USCMA had circulated among the local South Carolina newspapers. Again Thurmond wrote to the White House, urging that "since the news is out, I think it would be advisable for the announcement of the appointment to be made as soon as possible. . . . This would hold down speculation and enable us to get on with the job of determining who the successor is going to be."[9] Apparently, Mann and Thurmond had differing perceptions as to what

[6] See the 1992 amendment to the UCMMJ, 10 USC, 943; Pub L. 102–484, Section 1061A.

[7] GF, John Marsh Files, Box 103, April 8, 1975. It is interesting that Thurmond considered an USCMA seat as "a second or third level." In this, he was not alone. With the possible exception of Truman, virtually every President who has made USCMA appointments has considered them less important than other federal judicial positions. At this point, it seems that Thurmond was much more interested in the Republicans winning a local congressional campaign than in seeking a well-qualified candidate for USCMA. He is neither the first nor the last congressional figure to have considered USCMA appointments in terms of political preference and advantage rather than judicial qualifications.

[8] Ibid., WHCF, FG 58, Box 140, June 5, 1975.

[9] Ibid., White House Name Files, June 18, 1975.

"as soon as possible" implied. On July 23, Mann indicated that Ford had agreed "*not* to nominate him . . . until after the congressional recess," in part because of unfinished legislation and a pending congressional trip to the Far East. Ford's director of personnel joined Thurmond in urging again that the "nomination be made immediately."[10] Possibly resentful of the implication that he was manipulating the timing of the nomination for partisan purposes, on August 6 Mann abruptly asked that Ford withdraw his name.[11]

Strom Thurmond wasted no time in urging yet another nomination upon Ford. Less than a week after Mann's withdrawal, he wrote "personal attention" at the top of the letter to the President extolling the qualifications of Matthew Perry. A young but experienced trial attorney, and also a director of the NAACP, Perry had already come to the attention of local Democratic politicians in the possible context of the forthcoming congressional elections. From Thurmond's perspective, it becomes very clear why he might be so eager to see Perry removed from local politics to the safe haven of a federal court in Washington. Perry, he assured Ford, has "successfully represented defendants in many significant cases relating to civil rights."[12]

Reminding the President that there had been only one black jurist in the history of USCMA, Thurmond concluded that Ford would "have the opportunity to restore balance to the Court with a Black American who is eminently qualified and greatly respected by all who know him." South Carolina Governor James Edwards telegraphed Ford that Perry "would make an outstanding member of the Court."[13] Other individuals in Ford's administration joined in support for Perry, with newly appointed Army Secretary Martin Hoffman being "particularly impressed with Mr. Perry's reputation, stature and ability."[14] On December 10, Ford sent Perry's nomination to the Senate. Within a week, the Senate Armed Services Committee briefly considered four presidential nominations, one of them being that of Matthew Perry to USCMA.

Thurmond extolled Perry's qualifications, whereupon the Committee Chair,

[10] Ibid., WHCF, FG 58, Box 140, July 23, 1975, emphasis in original.

[11] Ibid., August 6, 1975. See also USCMAP, untitled newspaper clippings from Greenville County Library, Greenville, South Carolina, August 6, 7, 1975.

[12] Ibid., Presidential Personnel Files, Box 31, August 11, 1975. It may indeed be that part of the "understanding" reached by Perry and Thurmond included an assurance of later appointment to the Federal District Court in South Carolina. What better way to remove a potential candidate from effective political candidacy than by appointing him not only first to a federal judgeship, but later to a judgeship with life tenure as well! In fact, this is exactly what happened to Matthew Perry. When urging his appointment, Strom Thurmond had the happy opportunity to merge political expediency with aspirations toward racial harmony, and a "fairer" system of military justice.

[13] Ibid., September 30, 1975. The President of the Spartanburg County Bar Association added that Perry "has good judgment, is an able leader, and has his feet on the ground." Ibid., September 30, 1975.

[14] Ibid., WHCF, FG 58, October 19, 1975.

Mississippi Senator John Stennis, noted that "your endorsement will go a long way in helping Mr. Perry."[15] Indeed, it appeared that Perry might not be asked even one question until Senator Goldwater inquired if "moving from the state bar into the military bar is going to present . . . you with any problems?" Perry replied that "I do not perceive of a great deal of difference except to the extent that there is indeed some principal difference in the philosophy certainly of the military as distinct from the civilian sector."[16] Reiterating a theme raised in earlier hearings, Stennis noted that "I do not believe that we can have an effective, dependable, military service unless there has been some real discipline drilled into these men." Perry responded that "there are some basic differences in the philosophies in the civilian sector as against the military sector. . . . [T]here has to be some device by which the command authority can induce the obedience, the allegiance of those whose duty it is to carry out the military purpose."[17]

Apparently satisfied with this reply, the Committee unanimously approved Perry, as did the Senate shortly thereafter. As Perry prepared to take his seat in January 1976, Ford quietly authorized the reappointment of William Cook to a full fifteen-year term on the USCMA bench.[18] Thus Ford's final USCMA appointment was in fact a reappointment, and with it the President had completely reconstituted the Court—something no other chief executive has done since Truman. In 1976, none of its judges had served for even two years.[19]

[15] U.S. Senate Library, LC 76–600779. CIS 76-S201–11, Hearings on nominations. . . . December 16, 1975, 3.

[16] Ibid., 18.

[17] Ibid., 19. "Obviously," added Perry, "discipline is a necessary factor. I was once in the Armed Forces myself and I recognize the value of the concept of discipline throughout our military."

[18] Cook had originally been nominated to fill out the remainder of Kilday's unexpired term, to which Darden had previously been appointed for the same purpose! Ford also participated in an USCMA retirement ceremony for Homer Ferguson who had served for almost twenty years. Presented with a Presidential medal of Freedom, Ferguson also accepted a letter from his old Michigan congressional colleague and friend. Ford emphasized that "to honor your long and distinguished public service is to recognize the finest qualities of integrity and civic responsibility."

[19] GF, WHCF, FG 58A, Box 140, January 12, 1976. Ferguson's career as an USCMA judge deserves more attention than it can receive here. It should be noted, however, that based upon his decisions and dissents his concern for the constitutional rights of armed service personnel has never been exceeded—if indeed equalled—by other USCMA members, either past or present. For a small sampling of cases reflecting such concern, see *United States v. Wright*, 10 USCMA 110, 114 (1967); *United States v. Dodge*, 13 USCMA 525, 531 (1963); *United States v. Tempia*, 16 USCMA 629, 631 (1967); and *United States v. Ivory*, 9 USCMA 516 (1958). When the Court later paid tribute to Ferguson, who died on December 17, 1982, Judge Cook expressed the "hope that we succeed in emulating his courage, foresight . . . and, above all, the belief that, insofar as possible, every military person whose case is being heard in this room is entitled to 'Equal Justice Under Law.'" *Memorial Proceedings for Homer Ferguson*, January 11, 1983, 16 MJR, clx–clxi.

5. Judges Cook, Fletcher, and Perry

STORM CLOUDS GATHER

The growing antagonism between Fletcher and the military justice "establishment" from 1976 until his replacement as Chief Judge in 1980, sometimes resulted in the accusations that he possessed a hidden agenda for change concerning military justice; and that he had assumed his office with instructions from an unnamed civilian official within the Defense Department to transform it. One example of this viewpoint claimed in 1984 "that there is a plan which has been in existence since the 1950s and which has dictated the course of movement in military justice matters over the years. . . . [I]t closely parallels the British system in which limited power is held by command with significant offenses being handled in civilian courts by civilians."[20]

It matters less whether such claims had any basis in fact. As will be seen, they did—but nowhere near the extent assumed. On the other hand, what people believe to have happened may well affect their perception of what

[20] Memorandum from Marine Corps Colonel Charles Mitchell, September 19, 1984, in materials made available to the author by Brig. General D. Wayne Hansen, USA ret. Indeed, Mitchell prefaced his comments with the statement that for some time he "had felt that those who were pressing 'military justice reform' had a game plan supporting a specific objective." Even though Fletcher had not been Chief Judge for four years, Mitchell still believed that "we are apparently at war and don't know it. . . . The success of the 'plan' was viewed . . . as being inevitable (I think largely because of its backing and our being asleep)."

did ultimately occur. Thus in exploring Fletcher's relationship to the military justice system, it becomes important to ascertain what changes he proposed, when, and in what context.[21]

Fletcher had been in office for barely two months, when on July 15, 1975, he addressed an eight-page memorandum to the JAGs, stating that he had discussed a number of ideas with his fellow judges, and that they had "concluded that it would be desirable at this time to offer some of our thoughts for discussion purposes. The enclosed memorandum reflects these concepts in very general terms." Adding that the Joint Committee on Military Justice "already has done substantial work in this area, producing a series of recommendations which warrant careful consideration," Fletcher invited the JAGs to a meeting on July 21 to "discuss your proposals as well as to hear your views. . . ."[22] Examination of the memorandum reveals a number of proposals for change which should be noted, but with twenty years' hindsight seem more prophetic than provocative. Among ideas "warranting discussion," Fletcher proposed the following:

a) Statutory powers of the convening authority to overrule trial judges on certain matters of law should be abolished.

b) Power of the convening authority to appoint judges and counsel should be eliminated.

c) Staff Judge Advocates should be rated by someone other than the convening authority.

d) Codified offenses should be substituted for the famous "catch-all" articles in the UCMJ, 133–34.

e) There should be a truly independent judiciary at both the trial and appel-

[21] It should also be remembered that Fletcher had been only the fourth Chief Judge in the history of USCMA, and that two of his predecessors, Darden and Duncan, had held this office for very short periods. Neither had made any significant change in administrative policies which had evolved over a twenty-five year period, and which were largely based upon a frequently absent Chief Judge. The comments of the White House Staff member who explained to President Ford why Fletcher had been recommended, should be recalled. "It is the result of an effort . . . to substantially upgrade the calibre of personnel on this Court. . . . The prestige of the court is generally thought now to be at an all time low. . . . Finally, the [Defense] department wishes to improve the quality of decisions by the Court." See above, chapter 9. In other words, there can be no doubt that Fletcher had been given an indication that changes were needed, if not a specific mandate to undertake them.

[22] USCMAP, July 15, 1975. Martin Hoffman as "ex officio" was sent a copy. By that time, he had become Ford's Secretary of the Army. Giving the military one week to absorb a number of proposals which were controversial may well have been unwise. A conservative institution within an even more conservative environment, the military justice system over the years has developed an almost reflexive hostitility to proposed change, especially from a newly appointed civilian. See, Eugene R. Fidell "The Culture of Change in Military Law," *Military Law Review* 126 (1989) 125–32. On the other hand, to claim that Fletcher's conduct revealed a hidden agenda or some masterminded plot to promulgate major changes—ill-disguised to conceal their radical nature—is unwarranted.

late levels. One way might be to appoint military judges for a term of years "with removal by appropriate authority for good cause only."

f) Trial and appellate authority should be vested with continuing jurisdiction, replete with authority to exercise a contempt power comparable to that wielded by federal trial judges.

g) Authority of military tribunals to exercise extraordinary writ jurisdiction should be clearly mandated.

h) Trial judges should determine sentences, since sentencing "is, in essence, a judicial function."

i) Random selection of court members rather than appointment by the convening authority "should be considered as a means of enhancing the perception of fairness in the military system of justice."

j) All the services should have a separate defense counsel structure. (In 1975 only the Army followed this practice.)

k) Power to promulgate procedural rules to govern courts-martial ought to be vested in the judiciary rather than the Chief Executive.

l) Codification of the supervisory role for USCMA "over the entire system of military justice would insure uniformity and enhance control" over the entire system.

m) The United States Supreme Court should be able to review USCMA decisions based on the petition for certiorari. "This would enhance the prestige of [USCMA] and the system of military justice as a whole. . . ."

n) A judicial council should be created to undertake "a continuous study of the organization, practice, procedure, rules and methods of administration and operation of the military justice system."[23]

What unified most of these proposals was a marked emphasis on expansion of judicial authority both for USCMA, but—to an even greater extent—the military judge. Although Senator Ervin had sought to enlarge that official's powers, and the Military Justice Act of 1968 had done so to a limited extent, Fletcher's suggestions went much further. Even as they increased judicial responsibility, it would be at the expense of the convening authority's jurisdiction. Thus, military hostility to such changes is understandable.

Given the informal, irregular, and frequently inconclusive nature of Court and TJAG meetings that had previously prevailed—with very few exceptions—during the Quinn era, Army TJAG Wilton Persons probably did not expect to receive such a memorandum from any USCMA Chief Judge, let alone a jurist with very limited experience in military justice newly arrived from a state court. He responded with a diplomatic note to Fletcher, and sent

[23] Supra n. 22. Although Fletcher stated who should comprise such a group, the Judge Advocates General were conspicuously missing from the list. See below for some summary comments on the ultimate fate concerning most of Fletcher's proposals.

along reprints of articles dealing with the UCMJ.[24] Fletcher replied that "after you submitted to me articles concerning the Code, I thought it only fair that I read them since they could influence my thinking as to what my priorities should be. I believe that they have made me reconsider some of the suggestions initially made."[25] Essentially, however, they reiterated what Fletcher had already proposed. But Fletcher urged Persons to consider that "the military courts should be parallel to the courts in the federal court system." Some of his proposals "must be done by statutory enactment."[26] Others, he noted, "could be accomplished by court decision."[27]

The military reply took the form of a memo for all TJAGs from the Joint Service Committee on Military Justice. It well reflected the military viewpoint, and although more temperate in tone the reaction still brings to mind the Army's Kernan Committee Report concerning the old Ansell reforms proposed in 1918–19.[28] Fletcher had urged that military judges should be appointed for specified terms. The Committee while agreeing that such tenure "tends to create the impression of an impartial judiciary," insisted that it should not be required by statute "in view of the inherent limitations in the application of tenure to the judiciary of the various services." The services would be denied "a necessary flexibility in the personnel area."[29]

In calling for "extensive further consideration" concerning Fletcher's proposal for a trial court's continuing jurisdiction, the committee emphasized that "the role of the convening authority in such a change should not be affected." Such a role in the military "must be vested with the type of prosecutorial discretion that usually exists in a district attorney." Indeed, in the military "where the administration of military justice not only has a direct but an *immediate* [emphasis in original] effect upon good order and disci-

[24] At the July meeting, Persons noted that the services "would need a reasonable amount of time to consider an extensive change." Fletcher commented later that "he would like to believe that moves could be made toward an independent judiciary, not necessarily one outside of the service, but a judiciary that has no susceptibility to pressures from any part of the chain of command." FP, "Minutes of Code Committee Meeting, July 21, 1975," Box 21, Folder 11, 2.

[25] USCMAP, August 1, 1975.

[26] Fletcher's new priorities included among other provisions: appointment of judges for specific tenure; authority so that the trial judge could have continuing jurisdiction from arrest through appeal; and establishment of a single court of review for all services. Ibid.

[27] Although there is no evidence that Fletcher meant these words as any sort of threat to the military, they were in fact prophetic. Whatever its extent might be, the Fletcher Court's "revolution" was driven by judicial decision not congressional enactment. Indeed, the lawmakers' response to several parts of it is discussed in chapter 11.

[28] See AMJ, 112–18. Unlike the Code Committee, this group had no civilian members.

[29] Hansen materials, Memorandum from Working Group, JSCMJ, October 1975, 2. While refusing to endorse any change in JAG selection of judges, the working group implied that by permitting successive tours of "those senior JAG officers in the military justice program," Fletcher's goal might be realized. They ignored his emphasis that a military judge should be truly independent once appointed.

pline, there must be an initial evaluation of cases to include necessary discretion on the convening authority."[30]

Fletcher's suggestion that "a single court of military review might bring more uniformity to appellate decisions and be consistent with the notion that the military justice system is uniform" received short shrift from the committee. It was true that the several military appellate courts "may result in inconsistency but USCMA provides the needed uniformity of interpretation in military law." Indeed, "the desirability of uniformity is outweighed by the vitality and originality of ideas and concepts that these separate courts maintain."[31] Understandably, the Committee was similarly unexcited by Fletcher's call for a judicial council without any representation by the JAG. On the other hand, it supported a judicial council that "could include a wide spectrum of law professors, trial and appellate judges, both military and civilian, and administrators. The members could be selected by and would report to the Code Committee," where the JAGs were well represented.[32]

This recommendation was accompanied by a comment that might be called prophetic in the light of later events. The committee reminded Fletcher that the UCMJ specifically gives the JAGs responsibility for the administration of military justice.[33] Nowhere, it may be added, does the Code indicate that this responsibility is also to be exercised by USCMA. On the other hand, it was certainly not unreasonable for its judges to assume that the highest appellate tribunal in the military should indeed exercise some supervisory authority over military justice. Whether by accident or design, for the most part both judges and JAGs had avoided a clash over the issue of supervisory jurisdiction during the Quinn era. The potential for conflict remained, however, if only because both parties could legitimately claim similar responsibilities. Nevertheless, to the JAGs in 1976 and thereafter, Fletcher's statement that USCMA was similar to the United States Supreme Court for the military justice system went much further than what seemed warranted by existing law and practice.

The tone of the committee report while critical, was definitely not confrontational. Fletcher had only been on the bench for a few months. Yet, the new Chief Judge had made it clear that some of the changes he proposed could be made through judicial decision rather than congressional enactment—the latter frequently guided by military and JAG input. They might,

[30] Ibid., 4.

[31] Ibid., 4–5.

[32] Ibid., 7. The Committee also rejected Fletcher's call that the defense counsel be rated by a person other than the commander or Staff JAG. Administrative steps "have been taken to eliminate" this "appearance of evil" which has not taken place "except in very rare and publicized instances." Ibid., 9.

[33] Article 6, section (a) of the UCMJ states that "the Judge Advocate General or senior members of his staff shall make frequent inspection in the field in supervision of the administration of military justice."

in other words, be implemented by the judges themselves. If his initial proposals were indicative of his intended policies, Fletcher and the JAGs seemed to be on a collision course. Impact was not far off.

CASES AND CONFLICTS

Several decisions handed down by the Fletcher Court during its first year should be noted. As individual outcomes, they might not have been so important—but when taken together they portended dramatic changes in military justice. In August 1975, Fletcher spoke for a unanimous Court in striking down the voluntary enlistment of a dyslexic soldier who had been given "a list of numbers and letters" by a local recruiter to insure his eligibility for service. Holding that "a government agency must abide by its own rules and regulations where [their] underlying purpose . . . is the protection of personal liberties or interests," he concluded that the "recruiter's misconduct" rendered the enlistment void, thus nullifying any attempt by the Army to court-martial the defendant for alleged wrongdoing.[34]

Three weeks later, USCMA overruled a twenty-year precedent dealing with search and seizure. It restricted authorization for such a procedure when conducted on a foreign military base, in this case by local British authorities.[35] Fletcher pointed to the 1961 landmark ruling by the United States Supreme Court, *Mapp v. Ohio*.[36] He emphasized its holding that no evidence could be admitted that had not been "seized in compliance with the [Fourth] Amendment's conditions." The new Chief Judge concluded that "from the military standpoint, we see nothing burdensome in also requiring for American prosecutions that the military authorities comply with our constitutional standards."[37]

In what would later become a fairly frequent practice, Cook dissented. To say, he argued, "that the Constitution operates against a foreign government in its own country is . . . in my opinion, quite wrong." He claimed that the Fourth Amendment protected only against action by Federal or State authori-

[34] *United States v. Russo*, 23 USCMA 511 (1975). "The result we reach will have the salutary effect of encouraging recruiters to observe applicable recruiting regulations while also assisting the armed forces in their drive to eliminate fraudulent recruiting practices." Ibid., 512. This decision basically reaffirmed an earlier unanimous holding. See *United States v. Catlow*, 23 USCMA 142 (1974). As will be seen later, both the military and Congress would act to reverse USCMA's unanimous findings—in which six judges (Quinn, Darden, Duncan, Cook, Fletcher, and Ferguson) had concurred.

[35] See *United States v. DeLeo*, 5 USCMA 148 (1954).

[36] 367 U.S. 643 (1961).

[37] *United States v. Jordan*, 23 USCMA 525, 527 (1975). Although the American serviceman is serving overseas, "it is American judicial power that is being exerted against him and in such a case, it is by American constitutional standards that he should be judged."

ties. "A foreign government, like a private person, is just not subject to these provisions." Indeed, "the majority's repudiation" of "settled constitutional doctrine . . . is . . . unjustified and unsound."[38]

Early in February 1966, a unanimous Court forbade the convening authority to reverse a decision taken by a military judge, in this case to dismiss a charge on the basis of denial of a speedy trial.[39] In one of his last opinions for USCMA, Ferguson noted that the 1968 Military Justice Act had amended the UCMJ to create a military trial judiciary "independent of the line of command." In this context, to allow a "*lay* convening authority to *reverse* a ruling of *law* by the trial *judge*" seemed inherently inconsistent, and "we decline to do so."[40] The convening authority could indeed direct reconsideration, but "the judge to whom the record is returned is not to presume himself reversed thereby." On the contrary, he "is charged to reexamine his own ruling . . . and to rule thereupon once again, which ruling will be the product of his own, independent legal judgment."[41] Thus the Court struck down the section in the Manual for Courts-Martial that required the military judge to "accede to the view of the convening authority."[42]

Finally, in August 1976, another unanimous decision authored by Cook resoundingly reaffirmed USCMA authority to issue appropriate writs in aid of its jurisdiction. "Drawing on boastful passages from earlier opinions, relying on analogies in Supreme Court practice and raising anew its congressional mandate to insure fairness in military justice," Cook had no doubt about USCMA's role in such cases.[43] To deny USCMA power, he wrote, "to relieve a person subject to the [UCMJ] of the burdens of a judgment by an inferior court that has acted contrary to constitutional command and decisions of this Court is to destroy the 'integrated' nature of the military court system and to defeat the high purpose Congress intended this Court to serve."[44] Undoubt-

[38] Ibid., 528–29.

[39] *United States v. Ware*, 1 M.J. 282 (976).

[40] Ibid., 286–87, emphasis in original.

[41] Ibid., 287.

[42] Ibid., 284. This decision is an excellent example of the Fletcher Court's determination to enhance the authority of the military judge, even if it came at the expense of the convening authority.

[43] John T. Willis, "The United States Court of Military Appeals—'Born Again,'" *Indiana Law Journal* 52 (1976) 151, 161.

[44] *McPhail v. United States*, 1 M.J. 457, 462 (1976). Although later repudiated by Judge Cook, *McPhail* has never been overruled by his Court. See *Stewart v. Stevens*, 5 M.J. 220 (1978). For a delightful insight into the art of judicial recantation, see Eugene R. Fidell, "Judicial Recantation: Homage to Baron Bramwell," *Judicature* 71 (1989) 259–61. On the other hand, thus far the U.S. Supreme Court has declined to delineate the limitations of USCMA's All Writs jurisdiction. And although it remains good law in theory, *McPhail* has apparently not led to actual relief for a plaintiff seeking to invoke its holding. Rather the Court has tended to claim authority to intervene under the All Writs Act, and then declined to do so in the particular case. See, for example, *Unger v. Ziemniak*, 27 M.J. 349 (1989). Such an approach is not without its difficulties.

At some point, implied but not implemented jurisprudential power becomes tenuous. More-

edly, "there are limits to our authority. . . . Whatever those limits are," and Cook declined to discuss them in any way, "as to matters reasonably comprehended within the provisions of the [UCMJ] we have jurisdiction to require compliance with applicable law from all courts and persons purporting to act under its authority."[45]

For court watchers, accustomed to the slower pace of the Quinn era, cases like these (and many more could be cited) portended a sense of both USCMA activism and aggrandizement. A few statistics illustrate the new trend. In 1974, less than 6 percent of petitions for review were granted. By December 1975—eight months into Fletcher's term—almost 17 percent had been granted. In 1974, less than 49 percent of the decisions had favored the accused. By the end of 1975, that number had risen to almost 69 percent.[46]

Writing less than one year after Fletcher took his seat on the USCMA bench, a former JAG officer now a civilian lawyer—John Willis—concluded that the Court has "exhibited a rather free tendency to subordinate precedent to its perception of justice by expressly overruling prior decisions affecting search and seizure, command influence and court-martial jurisdiction. . . . Civilianization through and of the judiciary," he added, "should improve military justice particularly when led by the example of its highest appellate court."[47] But Willis also was aware that USCMA's new activism contrasted markedly with the Supreme Court's clear intent to "accept broadly stated claims of military necessity or difference."[48] Indeed, he concluded,

---

over, it is a serious matter for USCMA to issue stays in cases that do not appear to fall within its jurisdiction, and this fact may explain why *McPhail* seems more a paper tiger than sound legal doctrine. Finally, it may well be that in 1989 Congress in effect overruled USCMA. See Senate Report 101–81, 173 (101st Cong., 1st sess., 1989). Commenting that existing practice has "led the appellate courts to review cases under the All Writs Act, which under applicable law should be used only in extraordinary cases," the Senate Armed Services Committee concluded that military justice "would be better served if such review were conducted under a jurisdictional statute as opposed to the ad hoc procedures of the All Writs Act." The resulting legislative enactment is in P.L. 101–89, Section 1302 (1989). It authorizes military appellate courts to review "any court-martial which [A] is subject to action by the [JAG] under this section, and [B] is sent to the Court of Military Review by order of the [JAG]; and [2] any action taken by the [JAG] under this section in such case." See generally, Fidell, *Guide*, 12–24.

[45] McPhail, 463. When this author asked Judge Fletcher why he had assigned Cook rather than himself to write such an important decision, Fletcher replied that it would be all the more appropriate coming from Cook because "he was the darling of the JAGs." Interview with Albert Fletcher, Jr., August 4, 1994.

[46] Willis, 153. "The nation's largest criminal jurisdiction has once again become active and fertile with the prospect of improving the quality and likelihood of justice for" those subject to the UCMJ.

[47] Ibid., 155, 163.

[48] Ibid., 164, where Willis enumerates the various "pro" military High Court decisions." See Scott Silliman's perceptive analysis in "The Supreme Court and Its Impact on the Court of Military Appeals," *Air Force Law Review* 18 #2 (summer 1976), 81–93. See also supra, chapter 9. In 1977, Chief Judge Fletcher noted that "the simple utilization of the terms 'security' or

USCMA surely "has rejuvenated military justice. But how long can the court continue its energetic resurgence?" In fact, "implementation of its rules and suggestions will require the cooperative efforts of others," and when "cooperation ceases," the tribunal "may again find itself floating without direction. The positive contribution of the present court can be negated, and its enthusiasm dissipated."[49]

Possibly by inclination, the military establishment rarely responds favorably to sudden change. Moreover, its organizational structure is such that doctrinal changes in military justice procedures typically go unnoticed by much of the command. But the JAGs, especially those who unsuccessfully argued case after case before Fletcher's Court, realized by mid-1977 that a new era was upon them. The best explanation from their perspective came from a young JAG officer, Captain John Cooke.[50] In a lengthy exploration of USCMA decisions for 1975–77, the first two years of the Fletcher era, he discerned two precepts which in turn led to several basic trends.

In the first place, Cooke found that USCMA was "reevaluating the balance between 'justice' and 'discipline' in the military justice system."[51] Claiming in effect that military justice is too important to be left to the commanders, the Court "feels that considerations of justice must be given greater emphasis." Thus it has tended "to distinguish and separate functions exercised by the commander. . . . [He] is permitted to retain his disciplinary functions but his . . . judicial functions have been taken away from him."[52]

More important, Cooke sensed a determination by the Fletcher Court "to play a dynamic leadership role in the [military justice] system." Indeed, USCMA "sees itself as the only institution capable of bringing to the system the type of constant leadership it believes necessary." Absent regular congressional scrutiny—which was possible but very improbable—"only [USCMA]

'military necessity' cannot be the talisman in whose presence the protections of the Sixth Amendment . . . must vanish. . . . [T]his Court once again must state that analysis and rationale will be determinative of the propriety of given situations, and that the mere uniqueness of the military society or military necessity cannot be urged as the basis for sustaining that which reason and analysis indicate is untenable." *United States v. Grunden*, 2 M.J. 116, 121 (1977).

[49] Ibid., 166.

[50] This section draws heavily upon manuscript material donated to the Court by Cooke, now a Brigadier General in the Army JAG Corps. From 1976 to 1980, one of his major responsibilities was to analyze and interpret USCMA decisions—furnishing badly needed guidance to the military as it responded to them. He managed to do this with an objectivity that remains impressive. Eschewing emotional rhetoric, emphasizing instead reasoned analysis and interpretation—Cooke's summaries of USCMA trends between 1975 and 1980 have been of great value in understanding the military reaction to the Fletcher Court's changes.

[51] John S. Cooke, "The United States Court of Military Appeals, 1975–77: Judicializing the Military Justice System," *Military Law Review* 76 (1977) 43, 52. Hereafter cited as Cooke.

[52] Cooke, 52–53. "This tendency deserves close scrutiny, for it must be recognized that justice and discipline are properly but two sides of the same coin; to the extent that the court separates them unnecessarily, it risks devaluing the whole system."

is in a position to interpret the Constitution and the UCMJ for the entire military justice system and to supervise it on a constant basis."[53] Hence the Court "will exercise extensive authority over the entire system."[54]

These two assumptions formed the basis for three noteworthy trends demonstrated by the new Fletcher Court: 1) the role of the military judge must be expanded, even as the convening authority's influence over trial proceedings was to be restricted, with a restructuring of "the military justice system along lines closer to its civilian counterparts."[55] 2) USCMA will supervise the entire military justice system, not only for all personnel within it, but to the extent of making rules and establishing policies to be followed by its practitioners—especially the judges on the intermediate courts of military review appointed, it might be noted, by the JAGs.[56] 3) In a number of areas, such as search and seizure, jurisdiction, and self-incrimination, the Fletcher Court "will interpret broadly the rights of individuals."[57]

Cooke could not help but be aware of the strains that USCMA activism had placed on the military justice system. "It is often difficult," he observed, "for military members, including lawyers, who are trained to execute the commander's desires, not to give undue weight to the commander's needs, be they explicit or implicit." Yet Fletcher's Court now insisted that the commander's needs, like any other element which may affect the outcome of a case, must "be proven, not presumed." Now the burden of proof for showing that military conditions or necessity required a different rule than that prevailing in the civilian community was increasingly upon the military not the accused.[58]

Moreover, Cooke was troubled by the potential isolation of the com-

[53] Although written in 1977, Cooke's words are very relevant in a contemporary context. The continued disinclination of Congress to employ any meaningful and regular scrutiny over the military justice system, matched with a noticeable lack of judicial interest in rigorous inquiry, may raise serious questions as to the actual effectiveness of civilian oversight concerning military justice.

[54] Cooke, 53. On the other hand, according to Cooke, USCMA viewed the JAGs "as playing only a limited role in the supervision of military justice." One can see that this assumption, quite apart from the numerous cases which reflected it, was an early basis for the friction between Fletcher and the JAGs that characterized his tenure as Chief Judge.

[55] Cooke, 132.

[56] Cooke, 43. Cooke commented on the tendency—already evident in 1977—for the courts of military review to reject the analysis set out by USCMA in particular cases. He emphasized that such action "will not only lead to reversal by [USCMA] in many of such cases. More importantly, it is likely to reinforce [USCMA] distrust of military courts and may as well lead the court to impose more rigid rules in this and other areas to reduce the maneuvering space available to lower courts." Cooke, 130–31. See below for further discussion concerning the friction between USCMA and the intermediate military appeals courts.

[57] Cooke, 43–44.

[58] Ibid., 162. The case which confirmed this trend was authored not by Fletcher, but by Judge Perry. See *United States v. Ezell*, 6 M.J. 307 (1979).

mander from military justice. It was one thing to bar a commander from the exercise of judicial functions because of his disciplinary role. It was quite another "to say that [his] interest in discipline should play no part in judicial determinations." The system should indeed be insulated from command control, but it "should not, and cannot be insulated from the basic elements of the military society it serves without seriously distorting the results it produces."[59]

Finally, Cooke noted that "courts are not, ordinarily, the best mechanism through which to institute widespread revision of the law."[60] Trying to change attitudes as well as law involves "an educational function which the court has occasionally neglected in its desire to move quickly. This has, not surprisingly, generated much uncertainty and distrust." But Cooke's conclusion was very dissimilar to the knee-jerk military reaction to USCMA holdings of an earlier era. For practitioners of military justice, the Court's new direction "should generate reevaluation, not retrenchment. . . . It should now be clear that the status quo is an unavailable alternative."[61]

Other critics of USCMA's activism joined Cooke in urging reevaluation, but from the Court *not* the military—with an emphasis more on retraction than reevaluation. They criticized the premise from which Fletcher's tribunal had acted—the very basis for its claim to supervisory jurisdiction over the system. Thus, during a speech delivered in early 1977, Navy TJAG William Miller insisted that USCMA "is not a constitutional Supreme Court and is not an Article III court, and its proper relationship to the military justice system cannot be deduced from the model of the judicial relations in our constitutional system." Indeed, he added, the role of USCMA, "or even its very existence, is not *constitutionally* mandated."[62] Rather it came from the UCMJ which, Miller reminded USCMA, "specifically and purposefully" assigned supervision of the military justice system "to a military official, the Judge Advocate General."[63] Finally, Miller claimed that making changes in it "is the province of Congress, not of the Judge Advocates General, *and not* of the Court of Military Appeals."[64]

This presentation appears to have been a warm-up for a second speech, this one delivered to the annual Conference of the Judge Advocates Associa-

[59] Ibid.

[60] Ibid., 163. "Our innate suspicions of power are magnified when such power is wielded by 'a non-representative, and in large measure, insulated judicial branch.'" The quote is from Justice Powell, concurring in *United States v. Richardson*, 418 U.S. 166, 188 (1974).

[61] Ibid.

[62] MP, William Miller, Remarks to the ABA General Practice Section: Committee on Military Law, February 11, 1977, 5 (emphasis in original).

[63] Ibid., 6. "It seems clear to me, therefore, that in evaluating its role and its authority, the Court must do so in the context of the Code itself, and not by analogy to the far different role of the Supreme Court."

[64] Ibid., 10 (emphasis in original).

tion in August 1977 with Chief Judge Fletcher among the listeners. Miller argued that USCMA had been established to respond to the needs of the military—needs which it increasingly failed to address because of "the Court's redefinition of its constituency as the civilian society as a whole, rather than as the military society which the court was created to serve."[65] But Miller had more criticism to offer, including "the sluggish pace of decisions prevailing at [USCMA] itself," even as it held the military to a rigid time standard for preliminary action in military justice cases. Even worse, was "the judges' inability, in a number of significant substantive areas, to write opinions commanding the votes of at least two members of the Court." The result has been a challenge to extract "the applicable rule of law in a case," which will often be "the lowest common denominator resulting from a close analysis of three separate opinions."[66]

Miller made sure that his speech was widely disseminated to other senior JAG officials, and he received much praise—especially from Naval officers—for his efforts. One writer claimed that "we are now facing a time" when the new procedural requirements imposed by USCMA would either render commanders "unable to use the military justice system effectively to enforce discipline, or to bring the military justice system into such disrepute [that] it will lose both its legal and moral force." The changes mandated by Fletcher's court "strike me as the result of either extreme naivete as to the requirements of a mobile force[,] or indifference to these requirements and a stubborn determination to enforce abstract procedural standards whatever the cost. We must resist these changes with everything we've got."[67]

But not all JAG officers agreed with Miller's assessment of the Fletcher Court, and at least one member of the Navy appellate defense division took "strong exception [to] the substance of your remarks."[68] They reminded him "of what I perceive as the Navy's continuing refusal to accept the UCMJ."[69] As to Miller's negative reaction to the recruiting abuse decisions—discussed above—they were in fact "a most logical outcome of the recruiting abuses which the military has tolerated too long. . . . The result is, however, long overdue."[70] Finally, the claim of "great instability to which you refer results

[65] Miller focused on what he considered to be USCMA "excesses harmful to the military society which is regulated by the Court's decisions." MP, Remarks at the JAA Annual Conference, August 9, 1977, 2, 13.

[66] Ibid., 5. "This uncertainty is heightened by the frequency of radical shifts in the law, which produces a psychology akin to shell shock in the minds of many senior convening authorities."

[67] MP, September 26, 1977. Another writer took Miller to task because "if anything, I submit you were probably too kind in your remarks where [USCMA] is concerned." Ibid., September 14, 1977.

[68] MP, August 15, 1977. The writer, Carl Horst, did not "believe, however, that they can fairly be interpreted as attempting, in any way, to influence the performance of those judge advocates assigned as defense counsel."

[69] Ibid., 2.

[70] Ibid., 4.

as much from the intransigent reaction of the Navy and a Marine-like orientation, end justifies the means, Nixon-like attitude of damn the law, full speed ahead."[71]

Chief Judge Fletcher did not respond to Miller directly, and indeed, this author has been unable to locate any correspondence between Fletcher and the JAGs dealing with their critical reactions to the decisions of 1976–78.[72] On two occasions, however, the Chief Judge took note of the growing tensions between his Court and the JAGs. At a conference sponsored by the Federal Bar Association in September 1977 dealing with the USCMA "revolution," he listed several "areas of concern within the Court," regarding military justice practices, "in which it would like to see deficiencies corrected." According to one observer, he added that the JAGs should not "complain if we do them because of default on your part." The Chief Judge then engaged in a question and answer session involving the TJAGs of both the Army and Navy, in which the atmosphere, according to a witness, "was not what I would call cordial."[73]

In November 1977, the *Army Times* published an article based on an interview with Fletcher. If the Chief Judge was upset by the growing criticism of his Court, he gave no indication of it. Indeed, his comments bristled with a confident and aggressive tone that could only exacerbate the situation. Unlike his earlier statements at the bar association meeting, these remarks appeared in a series of newspapers devoted to the military and widely distributed within it. "Military persons," he warned, "should not expect [USCMA] to sit on its hands and wait for change. . . . We have been left by default as the actor to bring about change."[74]

Fletcher acknowledged that the Court was interested in "civilianizing" military justice. "I think the Court has only one standard to look toward for change and that is the civilian system." As a result, "the changes being made are probably those which result from similar concepts found in the civilian system."[75] This was important because "the military is only a second society, not the primary." Rather, it had to function under the larger civilian world, whether the JAGs liked it or not.

Fletcher emphasized that "We don't serve the military. The civilians created us. We have no responsibility to the military. Our responsibility is to the civilian community called Congress. We are guided by their electorate which

[71] Ibid., 6.

[72] During his second interview, Fletcher stated that "I don't ever remember . . . any JAG ever coming up and sitting down and talking with me in chambers about why these changes . . . were destroying the military capacity to carry out their function." Fletcher Interview, August 4, 1994.

[73] CM, Notes of Conference September 1977; Memo to CLD members, October 3, 1977.

[74] *Army Times*, November 28, 1977, 30.

[75] Ibid. But Fletcher immediately added that "always foremost in our minds are the unique necessities of the military system."

wanted civilian supervision of military justice after World War II." Possibly with Miller in mind, the Chief Judge observed that "you've got to talk about who is responsible to whom. And we're responsible to Congress and the civilian society, not to the Judge Advocates General."[76]

According to Fletcher, military enlistees "are a more exact mirror of the civilian community today, and they expect to have more of the rights they had out in the civilian community." The military "just has not reckoned with this pattern yet. I think the Court has." As to any agenda that he supposedly had upon assuming office, Fletcher was candid and confident. Those who interviewed me, he recalled, "expressed a desire to look at reorganization of the military justice system to see if it could be improved or enhanced[,] and attempt to raise the status of the system."[77]

Finally, Fletcher conceded that the Court was behind in its decisions, facing a backlog of several hundred cases. "We attempt to get our philosophies in line so at least we can put out a majority opinion. Lately, we haven't been even doing that very well. So it takes time to get three opinions out of the Court." He also contrasted the differing backgrounds of his fellow judges. Fletcher and Perry had "practical field experience. We were both trial lawyers, both in the arena." Referring to Cook's limited trial experience, Fletcher described it as "actual trial work versus non-field legislative experience. . . . I'm not saying one is better than the other, but I think that is why you find the JAGs in agreement with Judge Cook, because they both have the same background."[78]

Whether he intended to do so or not, by going public with comments about his court's conflict with the JAGs Fletcher had upped the stakes. It was one thing to issue decisions within the confines of an appellate tribunal. It was quite another to assert in the military press that USCMA did not serve the military, and indeed had no responsibility to the JAGs. For their part, in their continuing dispute with Fletcher the JAGs found new allies, and if Fletcher had upped the ante, the JAGs were increasingly inclined to call the hand. Almost twenty years after these events, Fletcher recalled his remarks and stated in retrospect that he had "lost a golden opportunity to keep quiet."[79]

[76] Ibid.

[77] Ibid. Fletcher's recollections tally with the documentation circulating within Ford's administration at the time of his appointment. See supra, chapter 9.

[78] Ibid. Here, again, Fletcher's choice of words may been extremely unfortunate, even if unintentional. To equate experienced trial JAGs with an appellate judge who had not tried cases for many years may well have irritated JAG officers, to say nothing of Judge Cook. By 1977, a quip had circulated within the JAG Corps that "Fletcher will judicialize the system, Perry will civilianize the system and Cook will eulogize the system." Possibly originating in one of John Cooke's numerous presentations on developments with USCMA, the statement caused Fletcher to state that "it has a tendency towards humor but it's absolutely true. I want to judicialize the system." Ibid.

[79] Fletcher, Interview, August 4, 1994. Historians sometimes over rely on hindsight, which is not always accurate. Given the developments about to take place, however, Fletcher's rueful words were very apt.

CHAPTER 11

Conflicts and Culmination Concluded, 1975–1980

Part Two

EVEN as the military's hostility to the Fletcher Court's activism in military justice intensified, the Chief Judge faced additional attack from two unexpected sources—the Court's own staff, and the Office of the General Counsel to the Defense Department. While the dispute concerning the staff resulted in a lawsuit against the judges, it was easily resolved. By 1979, however, tensions between Defense Department General Counsel Deanne C. Siemer and Fletcher had escalated to the point where her Office coordinated and encouraged JAG criticism of USCMA—an action without precedent. Both developments deserve attention.

JUDGING THE JUDGES

The litigation between the three USCMA judges and their staff originated from the jurists' long-standing desire to control the employment and discharge of their own employees. Since 1951, the USCMA staff had been under the jurisdiction of the Civil Service Commission (CSC). As was noted in earlier chapters, this policy had resulted from an assumption that the Court was part of the executive branch of government. While the Judges had consistently disagreed, claiming juridical independence identical to that exercised by any federal appellate tribunal, in actual practice for almost twenty-five years their USCMA staff had been under CSC administration.[1]

At Fletcher's request, the Commission had obtained an advisory opinion from the CSC to the effect that USCMA was "beyond a doubt" a "proper component of the judicial branch of government." Therefore, wrote CSC director Joseph Damico, "we now consider your agency outside the Commission's purview, subject only to your own personnel [*sic*] authority."[2] Upon receipt of this advice, Fletcher, Cook, and Perry signed two resolutions that all existing CSC schedules, life insurance, retirement and health programs, as well as other provisions and regulations "are hereby adopted as

[1] Employees of Article III federal Courts were *not* under CSC jurisdiction.

[2] USCMAP, Civil Service Litigation File, undated. Attached to Damico's letter, however, is the legal memorandum, dated July 6, 1977.

our own on an interim basis until such time as a contrary intent is expressed by resolution of the judges. . . ."[3] Whatever the intent of these resolutions may have been, they failed to assuage fears of USCMA staffers who suddenly had been informed that they were no longer under CSC jurisdiction and protection. As one observer noted, "They retain only temporary rights subject to the whim of the court."[4] The staff promptly filed suit against the judges.[5]

The suit was of short duration. The CSC assumed that the Military Justice Act of 1968 had somehow changed the status of USCMA employees, a position that the Justice Department rejected. It noted, correctly, that the legislative history of the 1968 statute contained "no express discussion of the civil service status" for USCMA employees. Indeed, "there is no indication whatsoever that the Congress either contemplated or intended in 1968" to change [such status]. There was absolutely no reason "to reopen the question now." In other words, as the U.S. Attorney for the District of Columbia informed the assistant Attorney General, "we do not believe the position now taken by the Civil Service Commission's staff can be successfully defended."[6] The solution was "that we be authorized to negotiate a settlement."[7]

[3] Ibid., July 28, 1975.

[4] Ibid., clipping from column by John Cramer in the *Washington Star*, August 6, 1977. Fletcher recalled in 1994 that the issue was simply "control of our people." The judges, he said, had no desire or intent to deprive the staff of any benefits. Rather, it was to insure that they would have some flexibility as to staffing their own chambers. Fletcher, Interview, August 4, 1994. On the other hand, Fletcher may not have sensed that an additional issue for the plaintiffs was the independence of the central legal staff—a group of lawyers who, unlike counsel in chambers, worked for the Court as a whole, and not for a specific judge. What appeared to be a unilateral alteration of the long-term relationship between the CLS and the judges troubled the staffers.

[5] It is not clear whether the staff had any basis in fact for their fears as to what the judges might do. On the other hand, the files contain a letter from Ward Mundy, a former Army JAG officer, who had been appointed from the USCMA central legal staff as "Court Executive" by Chief Judge Fletcher. Aware that the three judges—all relatively new to their positions—had no knowledge concerning the flow of cases into USCMA, and disturbed by some apparent friction between the central legal staff director and the court clerk, Fletcher had determined that Mundy should serve as a sort of buffer "between those two." The Court Executive was to handle court mechanics and operations, while supervision over docket and cases would remain with the clerk. Fletcher, Interview, August 4, 1994. On July 29, Mundy wrote to the Personnel Director of the Defense Department, enclosing the resolutions just described. He pledged "to limit our differences in terms of personnel administration to the bare bones minimum." But he reminded the director that "the Court is not just another executive agency and certain allowances must be made in order to maintain the independent and first-rate military justice system which I believe all of us desire for our country." USCMAP, July 29, 1977. It is not clear if any other staff members were aware of Mundy's letter. When Mundy resigned his post as Court Executive in 1981, the judges chose not to replace him. Thus he served as the first and only Court Executive in USCMA history.

[6] USCMAP, Memorandum re: *Miele v. Fletcher*, August 17, 1977, 7, 9.

[7] Ibid. The terms were virtually self-evident. The plaintiffs would have to dismiss the USCMA judges as defendants, while the Government would stipulate that "the Court's employees will retain their civil service status." Ibid., 11.

Within a week, the assistant U.S. attorney had gained the concurrence of all three judges concerning their dismissal from the litigation. Fletcher, however, "takes no position on whether the [CSC claim] is correct or whether . . . our memorandum is correct."[8] With the disinclination if not outright refusal of the Justice Department to defend the USCMA judges, in reality they had little choice but to agree to the proposed settlement. By August 29 all parties had so acquiesced. In thanking the three judges for their cooperation, Assistant U.S. Attorney Royce Lamberth observed that he could "no longer agree with the old adage that judges make the worst clients."[9] On the other hand, the JAGs may well have viewed published accounts of the internal strife within the Court as further evidence of Fletcher's apparent disregard for well-established practice, as well as his capacity for aggressive self-aggrandizement.[10]

Although from its beginning USCMA has been a part of the Defense Department for "administrative purposes only," until 1976–77 there had been little, if any, friction between the Court and civilian Pentagon officials, as opposed to occasional clashes between the Judges and the uniformed TJAGs. It seems accurate to state that since 1951, the Office of the General Counsel had demonstrated minimal interest in USCMA. Moreover, the annual appearances by Chief Judge Quinn before the Senate Appropriations Committee to justify the Court's budgetary requests reflected a similar lack

[8] USCMAP, Follow-up Memorandum—*Miele v. Fletcher*, August 24, 1977. Although all three judges agreed to the settlement, essentially as described above, Perry and Cook apparently were less than enthusiastic about the need to challenge the CSC status in the first place. Indeed, Perry later claimed that Fletcher had "lobbied" the CSC for its statement, while the assistant U.S. attorney (Royce C. Lamberth, now a Federal District Judge) recalled that he had sensed real "friction" between the judges as he sought their separate acceptances of the negotiated settlement. USCMAP, Notes attached to newspaper clipping, August 12, 1977; Interview, Royce C. Lamberth, February 28, 1996.

[9] USCMAP, Memorandum, August 29, 1977. A reporter for the *Washington Star*, while possibly less tactful than Lamberth, may have been as truthful. "You might say one moral of this tale is," he observed, "that wise judges know when not to go before a judge." Ibid., clipping, *Washington Star*, September 5, 1977. Today, the Court functions under a sort of compromise—its staff is still under CSC jurisdiction, but USCMA judges may appoint a part of their chambers personnel on a rotating basis. The arrangement thus insures both stability and change.

[10] Thus, in November 1977, the *Army Times* reported that USCMA, "already criticized by military officials for 'civilianizing' the military justice system, has proposed 50 major changes," some of which give the Court "more control over the system." According to Fletcher, "the military has seen fit to ignore all 50 aspects by making no comment." He thought "they would say, 'Yes, some of these are good ideas and we will go ahead with them.'" The Chief Judge further added that about half of the 50 recommendations "are being resolved by opinions in the Court." *Army Times*, November 28, 1977, 30. In retrospect, again Fletcher's comments could only have worsened the tensions between him and the service JAGs. In a widely distributed "service" publication he had 1) acknowledged a list of major changes desired by the Court, 2) denigrated the military response to them thus far, and 3) stated that many of the changes would be—if they had not already been—implemented by the judges themselves, with a clear implication that acceptance or rejection by the JAGs was irrelevant.

of external concern, with the very brief sessions characterized by a tone of conviviality between the former Governor and the few Senators in attendance. All this changed during the Fletcher era.

Deanne Siemer, the recently appointed General Counsel, was an articulate and aggressive Washington attorney with ties to Lloyd Cutler—himself a highly visible advisor to senior officials in the new administration of President Jimmy Carter. She took office just as the tensions between Fletcher and the JAGs became more evident. For a variety of reasons, including mutual animosity, relations between Fletcher and the General Counsel's Office soon became equally tense; and by 1978–79 the General Counsel was actively involved in efforts *a*) to monitor the USCMA budget, *b*) to coordinate JAG criticism of Fletcher, *c*) to gain Congressional rejection of certain of USCMA decisions, and *d*) to replace Fletcher as Chief Judge. With Fletcher on the one side and Siemer on the other, relations between the General Counsel's office and the Court reached a level of hostility never before experienced in its history.

In 1977, Fletcher had sought an additional $150,000 "to fund a neutral and independent study by leading consultants to assess the qualitative . . . impact resulting from dispersion of military justice roles and responsibilities among military commanders, trial and appellate judges and multiple service courts. . . ."[11] An assistant to Siemer, Manuel Briskin, advised her that "it is of dubious propriety and doubtful wisdom for the Court to exercise an administrator's function rather than a judicial one by contracting to study the operation of the military justice system below them. There is at best bare support for this expansion beyond the Court's judicial role."[12] Anticipating Fletcher's insistence that, like other Article III federal courts, USCMA's budget should be submitted intact to Congress without modification from the Pentagon, he informed the General Counsel that there was no such comparable statutory provision for this Court. Thus, there was no "legal impediment to the President submitting a reduced budget estimate for the Court."[13] But the memorandum warned that "if the [Defense Department] reductions to the Court's request becomes a public issue, . . . there is a likelihood [that] the issue would be perceived as another deficiency in the military justice system and an attempt by the Department to thwart the Court."[14]

Faced with the decision to delete these funds from its budget, the USCMA Court Executive Ward Mundy dispatched a protest to Harold Brown, Carter's new Secretary of Defense. Himself engaged in a different dispute with

[11] USCMAP, Memorandum re USCMA FY 1979 Budget Request, Defense Department, Office of General Counsel, November 21, 1977.

[12] Ibid., 3. ". . . it would appear that contracting with a 'beltway bandit' would be unnecessary and a waste of Government funds."

[13] Ibid., 4.

[14] Ibid., 5.

Siemer over a proposed promotion to higher rank within the CSC classification system, Mundy's tone was blunt.[15] As to the General Counsel, "with due respect, I fear that your office has been gravely misled by some of your subordinates who have virtually no experience in military justice, a system whose integrity demands independence from command pressure at all levels, I urge you to consult counsel outside your department before taking a move which will have the most serious consequences for your administration and the independence of the military justice system and this Court."[16]

By January 1978, Siemer's office had become actively involved in the dispute between Fletcher and the JAGs. A memo to her from an assistant General Counsel noted that the Army and Navy JAGs "are separately to attack" USCMA in speeches before appropriate ABA committees at the ABA February meeting. "These speeches were reviewed and approved in our office this week." They would criticize USCMA "as an activist court bent on mandating changes in military jurisprudence through judicial decisions which contravene the clearly expressed will of Congress. . . . As a result of these alleged judicial excesses[,] military discipline is said to be in the process of being undermined and the perception of military justice as an effective instrument of law is being eroded. Support of remedial legislation is to be urged."[17]

As far as this author has been able to ascertain, never before in the history of the civilian office of the General Counsel had that department allied itself with senior JAG officials in preparing public criticism of the United States Court of Military Appeals. Issues of propriety to one side, Siemer's conduct raises some troublesome questions concerning not only the perception of civilian control over the military, but also how the General Counsel's Office had evolved to the point where it could actively pressure a civilian court to render decisions more in conformity with the military's desires. In later months Siemer went even further in this direction.[18]

[15] It might be noted that Article III Courts of Appeal have long had Court Executives. Although unique to Fletcher's Court, employing such an individual was a well-established federal practice.

[16] USCMAP, December 8, 1977. No reply to Mundy has been located, but a memo to Siemer suggested that a proposed letter from Defense Secretary Brown should emphasize that "the reduction of $150,000 for a duplicative management and policy study of military justice roles and responsibilities within the military departments does not in any way interfere with the Court's ability to perform its judicial functions." SMR, December 16, 1977.

[17] Ibid., Staff Reports, Office of General Counsel, vol. 2, January 27, 1978, 2.

[18] The speeches by Navy JAG Admiral Miller and Army JAG Major General Persons, as well as a response by Fletcher were later published in *Army Lawyer* 65 (May 1978). Another public critic of USCMA, Rear Admiral Roy Hoffman, tried to place what he considered the unfortunate increase in authority of the military judge in some sort of historical perspective. "Today," he emphasized, "most judicial punishing is done by military judges who are products of academic institutions whose teaching of the virtues of military discipline and patriotism is reflected

The next round in the fulminations over the Fletcher Court came from another civilian source, a Federal District Judge. An admitted conservative Republican, appointed to the bench by Lyndon Johnson in part—as he recalled—"because I voted for Barry Goldwater and willingly admitted it," Oliver Gasch had been a JAG officer in World War II.[19] Active in the Judge Advocates Association, he was well acquainted with senior Army JAG officials. It was at their suggestion that he agreed to visit the Judge Advocate General's School of the Army in March 1978, and presented a lecture entitled "Who Is Out of Step?" Gasch had no doubt of the answer.

Critical of USCMA's activist course, Gasch claimed that Fletcher had "openly stated that the Court will continue to make changes until the services decide to get in step with it, at which point the judges will 'lay down their mantle of the stimuli and put on the robes of response.' "[20] As other Fletcher critics had noted, Gasch insisted that the object of the civilian community differed dramatically from that of the military, where discipline was indispensable. "In the disciplined military environment," he said, "there is only a very narrow margin, for there is *no* payoff in *placing* or *showing* in war. There is no substitute for victory."[21]

In failing to be sensitive to the special nuances of the military environment, Fletcher's Court had subjected military justice to "a series of dramatic mutations rather than gradual healthy growth." Indeed, "when the system of justice is founded upon a relatively stable statutory code [the UCMJ]," Gasch insisted that "activism must be restricted." Moreover, if USCMA chooses "to continue along its present course of judicial activism, and the civilianization of the military justice system, the result may well be the erosion of public confidence essential to it and the impairment of discipline and effectiveness essential to the military, and ultimately to the life of this nation."[22]

Gasch's comments seemed relatively mild when compared to the criticism leveled at some decisions of the Fletcher Court by judges serving on the Courts of Military Review, the intermediate level of military appellate justice.[23] Thus, Senior Judge John Dunbar described recent Fletcher findings as

---

in their graduates' conduct at the Chicago [1968 Democratic] Convention and at Kent State[,] and who are detached from the problems posed to the commanders by persons disruptive to good order and discipline." Hoffman echoed Miller in accusing Fletcher's Court of demonstrating "a noticeable disregard of the needs of the society it was created to serve." MP, clipping from the *Charleston Evening Post*, March 2, 1978.

[19] Interview, Judge Oliver C. Gasch, February 28, 1996.

[20] Oliver Gasch, "Who Is Out of Step?" in *Army Lawyer* 66 (June 1978) 2.

[21] Ibid., 3 (emphasis in original).

[22] Ibid., 6, 8.

[23] These judges are appointed by and serve at the pleasure of the Judge Advocate General, without established terms. This practice which to many—including this author—seemed of doubtful utility was upheld by the United States Supreme Court as constitutional. See *Weiss v.*

opinions that lacked "clarity and accuracy of expression . . . [and] logic and meaning."[24] One case, *United States v. Booker*, that raised the issue of a right to counsel for relatively minor military justice offenses, particularly irritated Dunbar.[25] He described it as "pseudo-rational manipulation" that "smacks of a sort of youthful, one side idealism . . . devoid of the slightest realization that the services might have a stake in the matter." Fletcher's "leaky logic" represented an instance where "we do have a duty to make discriminating, critical, and level-eyed analyses of questionable opinions and to register our objection to them. . . ." Indeed, Dunbar insisted, if *Booker* was accepted "as representative of communicable and credible legal reasoning, then, in my opinion, there can be no further honest thinking in military law."[26]

Such comments may have been instrumental in leading USCMA to reconsider and modify its *Booker* holding.[27] Dunbar remained unimpressed. He commented on USCMA's continued failure "to render its opinions in clear, accurate and communicable language."[28] In his opinion, the language in the second *Booker* case remained "elusive and, in areas, woefully unintelligible. . . ." This was due to USCMA's "continuing efforts to civilianize the military justice system," an approach "fashioned by persons lacking broad and balanced military backgrounds. . . ."[29] "Never before," he added, "has there been such a tremendous gap between the decisions of [USCMA] and their interpretation by the service appelllate courts. Previously, the guidance of the High Court, however objectionable, was respected and by common consent accepted." Now, "the present Court's irreverent rejection of many military values" has created tensions that were both unfortunate and unnecessary.[30]

Of course, this is not the way most intermediate tribunals write about decisions from their High Court. That they occurred is evidence that Fletcher's course, however laudable in intent, had produced very serious internal friction within the military justice system. If Fletcher felt intimidated by these

United States, 510 U.S. 163 (1994). The unanimous and seemingly superficial opinion gave little comfort to those who support a judicially secure and independent appellate bench for the military.

[24] *United States v. Nordstrom*, 5 M.J. 528, 532 (1978).

[25] *United States v. Booker*, 5 M.J. 238 (1977).

[26] *Nordstrom*, 531, 533. Another judge described Fletcher's opinion as "a flagrant departure from a Supreme Court decision," one where "lip-service deference has been given to the Supreme Court, while refusing, in fact, to conform to its decision." Ibid., 536.

[27] *United States v. Booker*, 5 M.J. 246 (1978).

[28] Cursory examination of Fletcher's written opinions indicates some justification for Dunbar's comment.

[29] *United States v. Rivera*, 6 M.J. 535, 536–37 (1978).

[30] Ibid., 538. "We are left," Dunbar concluded, "with delineations and requirements which are patently defective, logically, and which serve no purpose but to hinder and impede the efficient administration of military discipline." Ibid., 540.

new attacks on his Court from fellow judges, he gave no indication of it. In April, when he appeared before the Senate Appropriations Committee, he first turned to the still ongoing dispute with Siemer and Brown. Without mentioning either by name, the Chief Judge took the offensive.

Fletcher stated that "the budget request before you does not represent the Court's desires but rather those of the Secretary of Defense. For the first time in the history of the Court, the Secretary of Defense has tampered with the Court's budget as well as its statutory responsibilities, both in violation of congressional mandates."[31] Unlike other federal tribunals, Fletcher added, "the military justice system literally has no one to turn to for consulting work, particularly when the Secretary of Defense takes it upon himself to meddle in the Court's internal affairs."[32] Indeed, he asked the Senate Committee "to take whatever action it deems appropriate, to include consideration of future criminal sanctions, to restore the Court's budgetary independence from the Department of Defense. . . ."[33]

Next, Fletcher commented on the increase in cases coming before the Court. Again without mentioning any names, he turned to the system administered by commanders and assisted by the JAGs. The heavier caseload was largely "a natural by-product of the tremendous number of courts-martial which still are being tried in the Armed Forces as an easy substitute for good leadership. My review of literally thousands of trial transcripts suggests that some commanders still rely upon the military justice system as a motivational crutch not only for problem soldiers and sailors, but also as a leadership crutch for themselves." For Fletcher, "it is an attitudinal problem which warrants attention." Indeed, he concluded, "somehow the word must filter down that courts-martial and other disciplinary actions are poor tools to motivate young men and women . . . and are poor substitutes for the leadership which has made this country's Armed Forces strong."[34]

In response to questions from Senator John Stennis concerning why the JAGs had declined to participate in a judicial seminar proposed by the Chief Judge, Fletcher claimed that "military judges also need to be exposed to the outside world, more specifically to the civilian bench and civilian academicians." He "did not mean that disparagingly to the military JAG schools," but "there needs to be some interaction with the civilian community which has many years of experience in dealing with court problems. . . . This interaction will allow us to determine whether the civilian experience can be of benefit to our unique system."[35]

[31] U.S. Senate Library, *Senate Committee Hearings*, vol. 3390, 881 (1978).

[32] Ibid., 881–82.

[33] Ibid.

[34] Ibid., 882.

[35] Ibid., 807. Given Fletcher's assumptions about the role and functions of his Court, as discussed in the previous chapter, his comments made good sense. Given the JAGs' assump-

During his 1979 appearance before the Senate Committee, Fletcher noted that in spite of the Committee's statement that "the [Defense] Department has no authority or prerogative regarding the Court's budget or operations," the additional funds had not been authorized.[36] Moreover, he claimed that Siemer had issued several "coercive statements . . . regarding the Court's operation." She had also tried to interfere with a court initiated promotion for Ward Mundy. "This abnormal interest in and unwarranted control of the Court's internal operation by the General Counsel coupled with her prior tampering with the Court's attempts to request funding . . . suggests that something drastic is necessary to end this David and Goliath relationship."[37]

Siemer probably agreed with this comment. Her next proposals, although indeed drastic, were far from what Fletcher had in mind. Privately, she undertook to replace the controversial Chief Judge as soon as possible. Publicly, she had already initiated a widely disseminated proposal to abolish the Court of Military Appeals in its entirety.

SIEMER'S SOLUTION

On April 3, 1978, the *Army Times* reported that Siemer "has proposed abolishing [USCMA] and assigning the judges to other positions until their terms with the Court expire." She further suggested that the intermediate military appellate courts take over as the final source of appeal "for most military cases." Controversies raising constitutional questions "should be referred to the Fourth Circuit Court," sitting in Richmond, Virginia."[38] Siemer had previously warned Fletcher that "if the current [military justice] system is unsatisfactory in any respect, we may have to consider a legislative solution."[39] The General Counsel expanded on her scheme during an interview published in the *Navy Times*.

---

tions about their role and mandate under the UCMJ to supervise military justice, his comments appeared arrogant and unwarranted. They declined to have anything to do with his proposed judicial conference, possibly—as Fletcher himself conceded—because "their reaction to other court undertakings suggests that they believe such projects undermine their authority. . . ." Ibid., 808.

[36] Vol. 3568, *Senate Committee Hearings*, March 27, 1979, 132.

[37] Ibid., 133.

[38] USCMAP, clipping from *Army Times*, April 3, 1978. Siemer added that "until the court is abolished, it should not be permitted to propose legislation." Judges Cook and Perry were in the audience as Siemer outlined her plan. Cook later recalled that "when I recovered consciousness, my first thought was of the legendary rejoinder by General McAuliffe to the Germans at Bastogne during World War II when he was asked to surrender his beleaguered troops—(Nuts!)." MP, undated newspaper clipping, probably from either the *Army* or *Air Force Times*.

[39] July 25, 1977, quoted and cited by Fletcher in his remarks to the Senate Committee. See supra, n. 37.

Siemer observed that one major question is "whether the military justice system needs a court at the top or whether it can function as other justice systems do, feeding into the regular court system. We are looking at that."[40] She had picked the Fourth Circuit Court not because it was more conservative than its D.C. counterpart; but the D.C. Circuit "is just loaded down with extra duties. . . . Those poor folks are just over their heads." The reporter also asked Siemer: "Is this a plan to civilianize the military justice system?"[41] Her answer did not mince words.

"That is such a misnomer. [USCMA] is a civilian court. There is not a military person on it. It could not be more civilianized no matter what it was. [USCMA] is a civilian court just like the Fourth Circuit is a civilian court." As to whether or not the military justice system might get "lost in another court," Siemer claimed that appellate courts pick the cases they need to hear.[42] "The military cases would be treated like any other cases. The ones that raise a substantial issue would get decided."[43]

Again, Siemer questioned "whether the military justice system needs the protection of a special court. Military decisions on constitutional questions are as forthright and forthcoming for individual rights as are so-called civilian courts. The impression that is created by having a special court to deal with this is that somehow they are different. That's not true. You don't need to trust [treat?] military constitutional issues any differently." Finally, the General Counsel implied that USCMA was overinvolved in legislative and administrative matters. This Court, she said, "is a strange animal. . . . It may be that the judges can spend their time better at being judges than worrying about administrative matters." Every other court, she implied, "is run differently."[44]

Siemer later explained the tactic she employed. She claimed that an effective way to force the JAGs to "consider whether they really wanted this Court was to propose that we get rid of this Court."[45] In other words, her

[40] *Navy Times*, June 5, 1978, 4.

[41] Ibid.

[42] Here Siemer was slightly inaccurate. In fact, the Article III Courts of Appeals exercise a jurisdiction that is not considered discretionary.

[43] Ibid. Not surprisingly, Fletcher rejected the proposed participation of the Fourth Circuit in military justice. It would only add "another layer of appeal before a criminal conviction becomes final . . . with no appreciable benefit to the accused or the government." Moreover, "it is highly questionable whether a federal circuit court should wade into the military justice thicket to review 28 years of decisions interpreting the [UCMJ]." Instead, the embattled Chief Judge called first for the expansion of his court to five judges, and second, that either plaintiff or the government be able to "petition the Supreme Court . . . to review any [USCMA] decision . . . involving a constitutional question." *Navy Times*, August 28, 1978, 25. Ultimately, Fletcher's proposals became law; one in 1983, the other in 1991—both after he had been replaced as Chief Judge.

[44] Ibid.

[45] Deanne Siemer, Interview, April 13, 1988, 14. Siemer further recalled that the JAGs "did not like any of the [USCMA] judges. They didn't think any of them were qualified, they

plan was more a "trial balloon," than a serious suggestion intended to become law.[46] Reaction to it would indicate whether JAG concern was due more to the personality and philosophy of a particular judge, as opposed to a fundamental flaw in the structure of the military appeals system in general.[47] Of course, Siemer also realized that a change in personnel might be a more tenable and desirable solution. Its immediate implementation, however, was beyond Siemer's control—although she was aware of Perry's rumored future appointment to the District Court.

For his part, Fletcher concluded that by 1978–79, "it became a very popular thing to criticize the Court. It was like jumping on a bandwagon."[48] This did not prevent him from continuing to press for what he considered necessary changes in military justice. In November, he called for "more independence for military judges and less interference from commanders in the operation of . . . courts-martial." He claimed that the military justice system—even at the courts-martial level—"has become a very technical and sophisticated criminal justice system, which is better administered by lawyers and laymen."[49] He also urged that military judges be given some sort of tenure, if not specific terms, so that they are "truly independent from the command structure and the JAGs." Moreover, he questioned the continued tradition of commanders selecting court members, and asked instead that "jury selection should be as random as possible."[50]

---

thought they were not a credit to the military system." But Siemer hastened to add that this "is only the way I read, that certainly is not what they said. Those folks are very diplomatic in their descriptions." Ibid., 7. In response to this author's observation that Judge Cook had long worked for the House Armed Services Committee, and had consistently demonstrated sympathy for the military viewpoint—Siemer replied that "just because someone is favorable to you doesn't mean that you think they are a good lawyer or a good judge."

[46] Ibid., 15. Yet Siemer insisted that "if that was the only solution, I certainly would not have hesitated to do it." Ibid., 16. In spite of Siemer's comments, this author remains very skeptical that there was ever a *serious* intent from the General Counsel to abolish USCMA. On the other hand, as will be seen, her office generated a lengthy study on the workings of the Court. Her tactics forced the JAGs to consider whether the alternatives she proposed might be worse than what they had had for almost thirty years; and they may well have led USCMA in 1979–80 to modify some of the doctrinal positions that had generated such controversy. See below.

[47] Indeed, from her perspective, "putting out the alternative of abolishing the Court brought forth lots of proposals with respect to what else could be done[,] and it worked splendidly in my view." Ibid., 35. Siemer had noted that "an activist General Counsel is just as difficult for the JAGs as an activist court. They would prefer no action anywhere." Ibid., 28.

[48] Fletcher interview, 3.

[49] *Navy Times*, November 13, 1978, 37.

[50] Ibid. Fletcher's remarks should be compared with those of Captain [now Brigadier General] John Cooke, who wrote in the 1977–78 *Indiana Law Journal* that "human nature being what it is, the appearance of justice is critical to accomplishing justice. Essential to this goal is the diffusion of decision-making to preclude arbitrariness and the allocation of it to decision-makers with no direct personal stake in the result. The commander's role in military justice collides with these requirements. The following questions thus remain: (1) to what extent should military justice be responsive to the commander's needs, and (2) what procedures are necessary to

By the spring of 1979, Siemer's office had prepared a thorough and reasonably unbiased analysis of USCMA and its relation to military justice. Colloquially called the "rainbow book" because each of its sections was printed on a different color paper, the project—according to Siemer—"was written for the purpose of shaping the issues and providing the necessary background for decision making." As such it did not endorse or represent any "official point of view of the Department of Defense."[51] The report did, however, describe the origins and transformation of USCMA after almost thirty years of operation—and in language that reflected the General Counsel's earlier comments about the current state of the Court and its relationship to military justice.

The first section detailed the "need for reform." Noting, correctly, that USCMA's creation had represented a compromise between those in favor of civilian review of military justice, and those opposed to this practice—it stated that USCMA had emerged as a civilian court, but one "entirely within the Department of Defense with no direct access to the federal courts of appeal or to the Supreme Court." Its judges had limited terms instead of life tenure, insuring "the possibility of replacing judges who proved unsuited to the task of applying military principles within a judicial system."[52] By 1979, judicial review had become "the accepted mode in the military justice system."[53] Moreover, "because the military justice system has outgrown the compromise reached in 1951," critical examination of it was needed in order to assess what improvements might be appropriate.[54]

The report found two fundamental flaws in USCMA's current operation. First, was the fact that "the appellate process is shut off almost completely from the Supreme Court." The alternative use of collateral attack to obtain such review was in reality "a judicial trek that has been criticized as inefficient, costly, time-consuming, and redundant." Even worse was the un-

make it so?. . . . It seems fair to begin with the principle that whatever powers the commander retains he should have because they are essential to insure that the needs of the command will not be ignored[,] and he should have these powers only where there exists adequate assurance that the interests of the individual will be recognized and properly protected. Where such assurance does not exist, as where the commander's powers are nothing more than the vestigial remains of some ancestral limb, they should be amputated. The military justice system today is vastly different from the one of fifty, twenty-five, or even ten years ago, and has significantly changed in the last five years." John S. Cooke, Book Review of Luther West: "They call it Justice," *Indiana Law Journal* 53 (1977–78) 294–95. Cooke also referred to the "kind of careful, objective study necessary to the continuing of military justice." Ironically, Fletcher had sought the same goal.

[51] USCMAP, Memorandum from General Counsel of the Department of Defense, "Reform of the Court of Military Appeals," May 7, 1979.

[52] Ibid., 5–6.

[53] Ibid., 7.

[54] Ibid., 8.

availability of any other tribunal to which the Government could appeal an adverse ruling. Although not mentioning Fletcher by name, the report stated that the current tribunal "has ruled against the government on cases considered by the military . . . to be of direct importance to the maintenance of order and discipline in the armed forces," and cited a number of decisions as evidence. When USCMA "declines to follow Supreme Court precedent, the government has no recourse." And when it follows civilian precedent "despite unique military considerations, the government also has no recourse."[55]

Without federal appellate review, USCMA "is the final arbiter of its own powers. . . . and when the court expands its powers into areas where there is substantial disagreement that Congress ever intended it to be," such action "creates a tension that adversely affects all operations of the military justice system. Over the past five years the Court has steadily sought to expand its powers. . . . That result ultimately may be judged right or wrong, but the instability in the military justice system that it produces is unmistakable. There is always available the alternative of a legislative solution to correct the substantive errors . . . or to correct the results that the Congress finds inappropriate, but that is an unacceptable way to administer a justice system."[56]

The second major flaw in USCMA's current operation is its "considerable turnover. During the last ten years, eight different judges have held the court's three seats. Within a four-year period, there were seven judges who sat at various times in nine different combinations. Only two of the vacancies . . . resulted from illness or death, suggesting that there are fundamental problems with the court that are causing this turnover."[57] The results, however, have been "to introduce substantial instability and unpredictability into the military justice system . . . and the state of the law has become more uncertain." Such uncertainty not only makes the teaching of legal doctrine difficult. It also creates an impression "that the military justice system is arbitrary and capricious."[58]

The major cause for preparation of the rainbow book was the military

[55] Ibid., 11–12.

[56] Ibid., 13. Even as this report circulated, Congress moved to overrule USCMA in the area of recruiter misconduct. As will be seen, although Siemer supported such an effort to the extent of urging congressional intervention against the Court, the result indeed proved the point that such "is an unacceptable way to administer a judicial system." See below.

[57] The report made no effort to explain what "these fundamental problems" might be. However three come to mind. First is the relative insecurity of a judicial appointment that in this period frequently was made to complete a predecessor's unfinished term, a practice recently banned by Congress. Second is the relative boredom that inevitably sets in for judges who can only consider cases involving a highly specialized and limited field of criminal law. Third, is the unfortunate application of political considerations, such as with the cases of Judges Duncan and Perry, which resulted in the use of USCMA as a mere stepping-stone to a lifetime appointment as a federal district judge.

[58] Ibid., 17. "In a system where respect for the law is of such paramount importance, it is imperative that such a development be avoided."

reaction to the Fletcher Court. Also beyond doubt is that the report generated the wide interest and varied discussions that Siemer had sought in ordering its production. Some specific proposals that resulted from it will be noted in the epilogue of this study. In the meantime, however, Siemer turned her attention toward encouraging congressional rejection of several Fletcher Court holdings concerning recruiter misconduct. But even as some hearings were scheduled, more conflict erupted between USCMA and its military critics.

Indeed, two months before the hearings, Fletcher acknowledged that his Court had become somewhat beleaguered. In an address to the Pentagon Chapter of the Federal Bar Association, he lauded its accomplishments. "The present Court," he said, "has proceeded to bring and maintain the word justice into the court-martial system."[59] It "has provided a series of decisions that make the military justice system a criminal justice system second to none." But "we are too successful. Apparently our system cannot stand the light that has been allowed to come into military justice. . . . All of a sudden the closed shop was no longer closed."[60]

This had transpired because "the Court acted like a Court. The regulations promulgated by the services mainly for perception purposes but seldom followed were now being enforced. The light that blinds is that the Court by decision was making the individual services follow their own devised regulations." Have you, Fletcher asked in conclusion, "seen or read any critical review of the last four years' decisions of [USCMA] by any one other than a military person?"[61]

The *Army Times* commented on Fletcher's speech with an article entitled "Top [US]CMA Judge, Military at War." According to the author, "a bitter feud between the Chief Judge of [USCMA] and the services has escalated into an all-out confrontation with Congress in the middle."[62] Further, "relations between the services and the Court have grown more tense," with the Army Chief of Staff insisting that USCMA's "desire to protect the rights of the accused 'has become so overwhelming' that command responsibilities have been degraded." The article also noted Perry's imminent departure from the USCMA bench, and reported that General Counsel Deanne Siemer "will chair the presidential commission nominating the new judge."[63] It was in this context that congressional action to overturn some Fletcher Court holdings took place.

[59] USCMAP, April 10, 1979, 3. Fletcher described USCMA before he joined it as "at a standstill." After all, "a court that could not get its own act together could not look outside itself at a total justice system."

[60] Ibid., 6.

[61] Ibid., 6, 8.

[62] *Army Times*, April 30, 1979.

[63] Ibid.

CONGRESSIONAL INTERVENTION

Early in his tenure as Chief Judge, Fletcher had spoken for the Court in a unanimous opinion dealing with recruiter misconduct, one which essentially reaffirmed a prior holding—also unanimous—by three other USCMA judges.[64] These decisions held that "defects in the enlistment of a military member, including recruiter malpractice, could be raised by an accused after the commission of an offense and could defeat court-martial jurisdiction."[65] In another case, Judge Ferguson had observed that while presidential authority to make rules and regulations for the conduct of courts-martial was indeed lawful, the same might not be the case for such regulations governing pre- and post-trial matters.[66] To the JAGs, the Catlow-Russo holdings had created unreasonable and unworkable demands for monitoring of recruiter conduct. Ferguson's comment, even though it had no force of law, seemed to imply a questioning of a long held executive function based upon constitutional authority as commander in chief.[67]

Speaking before a House Subcommittee, Siemer emphasized that "courts tread on difficult and uncertain [terrain] when opinions are based on public policy grounds." She detailed three tests that could justify such action, all of which had been supposedly ignored by the Fletcher Court in reaching its conclusion concerning recruiter actions: *a*) A mistaken assumption of "little guiding legal precedent." *b*) "When there has been a careful weighing of the benefits and costs to the public of the proposed outcome, and when on balance the benefits so far outweigh the costs that there can be really little question about where the public intent lies. That is not the case here." *c*) "When the rights involved rise to the level of importance that justifies judicial intervention in the normal policy prerogatives of the Legislative Branch in declaring public policy and in the Executive Branch in [its implementation]. We believe that is also not the case here."[68] Echoing the JAGs who had denounced the Fletcher Court's holding in these cases for the last four years, Siemer insisted that the choices imposed by the findings resulted in "an undue strain on the procedures that are essential for the maintenance of military order and discipline."[69]

Following Siemer's brief presentation, all three TJAGs appeared, almost

[64] See supra, chapter 10.

[65] Hearings, Military Personnel Subcommittee, House of Representatives, 96th Cong., 1st sess., June 11, 12, 1979, 2; hereafter cited as Hearings.

[66] *United States v. Ware*, 1 M.J. 282, 285 n. 10 (1976).

[67] For additional examples where both Fletcher and Perry reiterated Ferguson's position, see *United States v. Heard*, 3 M.J. 14, 20, n. 12 (1977); *United States v. Larneard*, 3 M.J. 78, 80, 83 (1977); and additional cases cited therein.

[68] Hearings, 4.

[69] Ibid., 5.

as if in lockstep, all following the lead of the General Counsel in calling for congressional intervention against the Court. Army Major General Persons claimed that USCMA had focused to an excess on the "illegal actions of the recruiter and ignored the enlistment misconduct of the [defendant]."[70] The Navy JAG commented on a related "aberrant interpretation" by the Fletcher Court of well-established Presidential authority as commander in chief to establish rules of procedure for courts-martial. One way, he noted, to solve this difficulty might be "by transferring this authority to [USCMA]. This may be what two members of the court would desire, as this would coincide with the court's present activist posture."[71] But Rear Admiral Charles E. McDowell did not "believe, however, that [USCMA] has the experience, resources, or basic understanding of or appreciation of the military justice system, especially in the light of some of their recent decisions."[72]

Chief Judge Fletcher also appeared as a witness, although it seemed an exercise in futility. He emphasized that the "integrity of the military justice system and, yes, the military services cannot withstand the condonation in any way of . . . recruiter criminal acts."[73] Moreover, he questioned the need for urgency in congressional intervention, as reiterated by the JAGs. If recruitment tactics were having a substantial negative effect on military discipline, "reason dictates that if the problem is substantial, then fraudulent recruitment practices must be the rule rather than the exception." In fact, his Court had published eight decisions in four years on this topic. "We average about 2,000 petitions a year, so it seems reasonable to draw the conclusion that either few cases of this nature are reaching our Court or, if they are, we are denying the petitions. Thus, if there is a substantial problem, then it must be through some regulatory procedure promulgated by the services themselves or through misinterpretation of our decisions by other military judicial tribunals."[74]

Another witness at the hearings was Robinson O. Everett, a former USCMA Court Commissioner, and author of one of the first treatises dealing with the UCMJ. A professor of law at Duke University and at the time of

[70] Ibid., 16.

[71] Here, the Navy JAG was referring to Judges Fletcher and Perry.

[72] Ibid., 22. As to the recruitment cases, "allowing miscreant service members to violate the law with impunity . . . is, I submit, disruptive, not preservative of public policy." Ibid., 26.

[73] Ibid., 89. Fletcher also rebutted a point that had been made by Siemer, namely, that his Court had ignored a United States Supreme Court holding, *In re Grimley*, 137 U.S. 147 (1890). On the contrary, he argued, that opinion "expressly noted that [Grimley's] enlistment did not involve any misconduct by a Government agent in securing Grimley's service in the military." Ibid., 90. Siemer's call for a reaffirmation of the *Grimley* holding was actually a plea for its extension and/or expansion.

[74] Ibid., 90 As to the proposal to reaffirm presidential authority to issue rules for courts-martial, Fletcher viewed this step as evidence that "Congress is willing to wash its hands of military justice legislation and is turning the reins over to the Defense Department, [the agency that actually drafts the great majority of the regulations "imposed" by the President]. That is not unlike asking the fox to guard the chicken coop." Ibid., 92.

these hearings chairman of the ABA Committee on military law—within four months his name would be submitted to President Carter for appointment to USCMA and designation as Chief Judge. Everett stated simply that "if the enlistment contract is signed by someone who knows what it is, regardless of the inducement and regardless of the fraud and regardless of whether he participated in it, it would be my view that the military criminal jurisdiction should attach."[75] Moreover, as concerned what Fletcher had said in dicta, that Presidential authority to impose rules for courts-martial might not apply to pre-trial and post-trial procedures, Everett believed that "the statute is susceptible to this interpretation." Therefore, it should be amended, and "I concur with the thought by Chief Judge Fletcher that there should be a greater participation in the amendment—in the promulgation of the Manual for Courts-martial and the rules promulgated by the President."[76]

Besides Fletcher, only one other witness came forward to oppose congressional action. Eugene R. Fidell, a Washington attorney with a great deal of experience in military justice litigation, represented the American Civil Liberties Union. Fidell mentioned that recent USCMA decisions had already "narrowed the scope of [Fletcher's] *Russo* holding"; evidence that "the law has been growing, [and] is continuing to grow. . . . I would question the need for Congress to intervene on a spot basis now. . . . and I would say that the law should continue to go on its usual case-by-case basis, and further growth and evolution can be anticipated."[77] Moreover, unlike the JAGs Fidell believed that the recruiter misconduct cases "were properly decided."[78]

Resolved "after full briefing and oral argument," congressional overturning of such decisions from "any federal court by legislation is not something to be undertaken lightly."[79] The current instance was even more undesirable,

[75] Ibid., 109.

[76] Ibid., 111. Everett also echoed Fletcher's implication that "Congress when it enacted the [UCMJ] had the view that the Manual for Courts-Martial would be under the scrutiny of Congress." Indeed, he added, as the manual is updated "there should be input, particularly from the organized legal profession. It is frankly somewhat frustrating when you are confronted with a fait accompli, when something has been completed, and then you have to comment on it." Ibid., 112. The concerns raised in 1979 by Fletcher and Everett are just as valid today. Indeed, it would not be inaccurate to characterize the attitude of both Congress and the United States Supreme Court today toward critical oversight of military justice as one of simple disinterest. In 1990, for example, Congress quietly deleted the requirement that changes in military justice regulations had to be reported to that body. See P.L. 101–510, Sec. 1301, subsection 4. The implications of such disinterest for effective civilian oversight of military justice speak for themselves. It might be noted that in 1996, the ABA Standing Committee on Armed Forces Law strongly recommended that the UCMJ be amended to provide for *a*) a broadly constituted, predominantly civilian advisory committee on rules of procedure and evidence at courts-martial; *b*) a method of prescribing rules of procedure and evidence at courts-martial; and *c*) a reporting to Congress and waiting period requirement for rules of procedure and evidence at courts-martial.

[77] Ibid., 116; *Navy Times*, November 6, 1978, 12.

[78] "Military jurisdiction, being an exception to the general civilian criminal process (with its attendant protections) should be narrowly construed."

[79] Hearings, 121.

as the JAGs had sought to change the law by amendments incident to the authorizing process, rather than by extensive congressional hearings and investigation. Indeed, the suggested UCMJ amendments had not even received scrutiny from the Code Committee, a body established by the UCMJ as "a forum for the exchange of views. That purpose has not been served here."[80]

The outcome of the very short hearings, spread out over portions of only two days, was never really in doubt. The proposed UCMJ changes quickly and quietly became law. Judicial relief for alleged recruiter misconduct by members of the armed services was curtailed, and presidential authority to establish policies for virtually all aspects of military justice was reaffirmed. Even as the hearings took place, however, both Deanne Siemer and the Carter White House had become involved in the process of selecting a new USCMA member. The ultimate choice, Robinson Everett, is the only USCMA appointment ever recommended to the President by a nominating commission. Thus the process which insured not only his selection, but also the way in which it took place is noteworthy.

THE ASCENSION OF EVERETT

By September 1977, rumors of Judge Perry's "imminent" departure from USCMA were circulating in Washington—although he had only been on its bench for one and a half years. In fact Perry would not leave until September 1979. California Congressman Ronald Dellums wrote to President Carter, expressing his concern that "representation from the minority community be retained given the increasing number of minority military personnel[,] and the high proportion of appeals from minorities that reach this Court."[81] Another consideration focused on the presidential nominating commission "that is in the works to recommend judges."

Thus, David Addlestone, director of the ACLU Military Discharge Review Project, wrote to the Associate Counsel to the President that his "major concern is that appointees in the past, with few exceptions, have been selected on the basis of whom they knew on the Armed Services Committees."[82] Addlestone recommended a number of well-qualified individuals to serve on such a commission, none of whom were currently employed by the Defense Department.[83] Addlestone's fears that the nominating commission might be

[80] Ibid.

[81] CP, Box C-6–170; FG 57, September 21, 1977. In fact, no USCMA judge from a minority community has been selected since Perry, and no woman served on its bench until 1991, when President Bush appointed Susan Crawford—who had been the Inspector General for the Defense Department.

[82] Ibid., White House Counsel Papers, Box 36, October 17, 1977.

[83] Besides himself, they included among others, Eugene Fidell; Robinson Everett; Edward Sherman (a law professor who had written on the "Civilianization" of military law); Homer

too intimate with the Defense Department were shared by the White House. Carter's Counsel wrote to his assistant that while DOD "wants to have a major input, to which I have agreed, . . . I also think that we should have a great deal of interest in the selection . . . of this commission, so that it will not be completely dominated by the Department of Defense."[84]

The nominating commission was duly established by President Carter's Executive Order of June 5, 1978, and would consist of six members, including Deanne Siemer as the chair.[85] Not until April 26, 1979, however, did she move to select them, informing the White House that "I think we have covered all the bases."[86] Her choices consisted of two officials in the Defense Department, plus an attorney, a federal judge, and Kenneth Pye, who at that time was the Chancellor of Duke University, and would later assume the presidency of Southern Methodist University. Siemer explained that she had not selected any representatives from the JAGs, "and we made that decision after consultation with them." Her nominations included "one black and one woman in the group of five."[87] Although Siemer claimed to have provided for "representation from the academic community, from the private bar, [and] from the federal bench," in fact half of her proposed panel—including its chair—came from the Defense Department.

It turned out that both the Defense Department and the White House insisted that Siemer's slate be modified. Writing again to the White House Counsel's Office, David Addlestone claimed that her list "is totally unrepresentative of the practitioners in the field." Even worse, from his viewpoint, was that it "seems to contain a majority of persons who would, or have taken a public position against, the current philosophy of the Court." The net result would be akin to "having DOD in effect select the members of the Court," which "of course violates the intent of the [UCMJ]."[88] As finally constituted, the Commission consisted of six lawyers—including two representatives from DOD (both women), and one black attorney.[89]

Moyer (a former Navy JAG, and author of a major treatise on military law, *Justice and the Military*); and two former ACLU officials.

[84] Ibid., December 9, 1977.

[85] *Public Papers of the President* 1 (1978), 1039. Carter's executive order required the Commission to submit "the names of no more than five persons whom [it] considers well qualified to serve in the position." Although, the basic rationale for the Commission was to screen up to five suitable candidates so that Carter could choose among them for his ultimate selection, in fact the order failed to require a minimum number. As will be seen, this omission was of great significance.

[86] CP, Counsel's Papers, Box 36, April 26, 1979. The delay may have resulted from uncertainty as to when Perry could fill a vacant seat on the Federal District Court for South Carolina.

[87] Ibid., April 26, 1979.

[88] Ibid., June 14, 1979. Even before Addlestone wrote, an internal note within the Counsel's Office staff stated, "Let's come up w[ith] alternatives—then discuss." Ibid., May 15, 1979.

[89] Ibid., August 17, 1979. Carter instructed his Commission to "make special efforts to consider well-qualified women and members of minority groups as possible nominees." Besides Siemer, the group consisted of Antonia Chayes, a Boston lawyer, then serving as the Under

Within two months, the Commission was ready with its report. It examined thirty-nine applications and interviewed eleven candidates, including three blacks. Out of this number, however, the Commission suggested only one nominee for Carter's consideration, despite the wording of its mandate. In explaining this step to senior Administration officials, Siemer sought to place the proposed nomination of Robinson Everett in a very broad context. She was both forceful and candid.

"When I first came to office," she wrote, "there was such strong, consistent criticism of the Court . . . that I undertook a lengthy study of the situation. This was an attempt to quiet the criticism and lack of respect for the Court temporarily by demonstrating active interest in reform." Regardless of the "rainbow book" findings, "my private view is that this Court has such serious problems with basic scholarship, use of precedent, and written expression of decisions that very substantial changes are necessary to bring military justice at the appellate level up to rudimentary federal standards of acceptable performance."[90]

A number of factors had persuaded the Commission to put forth only one name. There were only fourteen months left of Perry's term, a limitation that "makes finding qualified, much less outstanding candidates very difficult." Moreover, in accordance with the statute the nominee had to be a Democrat, and the vacancy needed to be filled quickly. "The two incumbent judges [Fletcher and Cook] have widely differing views on most issues and there will be no majority until the new appointment is made. Military justice will be at a standstill at the appellate level."[91] Further, the short term made it "vitally important that the nominee be a recognized expert in military law. There is no time for the lengthy education process necessary for persons not familiar with the field."[92] Most important, how-

---

Secretary of the Air Force; Neal Arthur, a graduate of Howard Law School; Clinton Bamberger, a graduate of Georgetown Law School who had served for six years as Dean of the Catholic University School of Law; Stuart Pollak, a San Francisco lawyer, and former staff member on the Warren Commission; and Kenneth Pye. When told of some of the names submitted by Addlestone, including his own, Siemer responded that "any candidate who came out of a commission with either of them on it would have problems with the military." Ibid., June 28, 1979. Again, attention is called to the atmosphere within which the Commission undertook its work, the palpable tension between Chief Judge Fletcher and the service JAGs.

[90] SMR, Memorandum for Lloyd Cutler, undated, but probably written in the middle of October 1979. While a number of long-term "solutions" to "a very difficult problem with [USCMA]" were under consideration, "this appointment is a key to the short-term solution."

[91] Ibid., 2. Here, Siemer indicated the frequent conflicts between Cook and Fletcher, noting that they strongly disagreed on issues of interest to the military.

[92] Ibid. Here, Siemer may have had in mind the number of USCMA judges who had been appointed for political expediency rather than practical experience in military justice. Although they served with dedication if not distinction, they all had a much longer period in which to familiarize themselves with military justice, to say nothing of the role that their legal staff in chambers might have played in such an education.

ever, was the availability of a candidate who "was by far the best qualified."[93]

Siemer listed Everett's qualifications which were, and still remain, impressive. They satisfied all the needs just noted. An academician as well as a practicing advocate who had appeared before USCMA, Everett had published widely in the field of military justice. As a law student at Harvard, he had been taught evidence by Edmund Morgan, the professor who chaired the committee that drafted the UCMJ and proposed the very Court that his student would later join. An imposing figure with a sleepy smile that concealed a sharp legal intellect, Everett "knows both of the incumbent judges on the Court . . . and gets along well with them." But Everett possessed more than experience, and expertise. He had served as an Air Force JAG, and he "deals very successfully with the Judge Advocates General, even though he often takes positions contrary to theirs." Indeed, he enjoyed the enthusiastic endorsement of all the service JAGs, who were eager to see a nominee with a broad knowledge of military justice.[94]

Having justified her panel's decision to nominate only Everett to President Carter, Siemer further urged that he be designated Chief Judge as soon as possible. "Many of the Court's problems . . . can be solved from within. A new Chief could quiet the rhetoric against the [DOD] and the [JAGs] that has been pouring forth in the current Chief Judge's impromptu speeches[,] and could create an atmosphere more conducive to respect for the Court."[95] In a separate memo to Secretary of Defense Harold Brown, Siemer emphasized Everett's personality. "He is both strong and diplomatic. I am confident that both his appointment and his leadership will greatly increase the stature of this beleaguered Court."[96] You know, she added, "that in my view the current Chief Judge has been a major cause of the Court's problems."

Conceding that the Commission's mandate might not extend toward recommending in effect the replacement of the current Chief Judge, Siemer obtained unanimous agreement from her panel that it "is of the opinion that Mr. Everett would serve with distinction as Chief Judge of the Court."[97] True, his designation "might cause temporary problems with [Fletcher], but Everett has both the character and stature to meet that challenge well."[98]

[93] Ibid.

[94] Siemer also noted that Everett had not sought this appointment, and "indeed, it would be a hardship for him to take it. . . ."

[95] Ibid., 3.

[96] SMR, Memorandum for the Secretary of Defense, October 12, 1979.

[97] Ibid., 2. "I cannot stress too strongly how important I believe that step is. Only as Chief Judge could he make the changes the Court needs."

[98] Indeed, Everett and Fletcher served together for the remainder of Fletcher's time on the Court in an atmosphere utterly free from any personal rancor. Fletcher later stated that he had fully expected to be replaced as Chief Judge at the earliest opportunity, and was not surprised by Carter's actions. Fletcher, interview, August 4, 1994.

Finally, Siemer reminded Brown that DOD would be recommending "a number of reforms in the current Court," and in all probability the President "may have two new appointments to make to this bench."[99] Her draft of Brown's recommendation to Carter, one that essentially repeated what Siemer had reiterated, concluded that "if [USCMA] has stability, consistency of doctrine, and an appreciation of the special problems of the military, we should reap substantial benefits in areas of military discipline. It is my belief that appointment of your nominee as Chief Judge would help achieve those objectives."[100]

Formally nominated on February 15, 1980, all that remained was the traditional perfunctory hearing before the Senate Armed Services Committee. Considering seven other Carter nominations, it spent minimal time on Everett's. The nominee did, however, have a chance to offer several comments both on USCMA and military justice in general. Everett appears to have been the only judge in USCMA history who, during the confirmation hearing, criticized a line of cases that had come from the very Court he was about to join. He noted that while the Court has "some unique responsibilities" concerning military justice, "basically it is a court and should behave as a court." Everett further described the Catlow-Russo holdings as "a good example of a point at which legal doctrine had broken away from some of the needs of the military community[,] and therefore had to be corrected."[101]

The nominee added that "it certainly is unfortunate when there are three opinions by three judges going off in different directions."[102] He mentioned the need "to produce a more predictable result," a goal that could be reached in part by "self-restraint as well." Indeed, Everett emphasized that he would not view his confirmation "as an opportunity to implement in an opinion my personal predilections or things I have advocated over the years but which are

[99] Siemer was mistaken. Although DOD urged that USCMA be increased to five judges, that did not happen until 1990. Within fourteen months (the remainder of Perry's term), Carter had been defeated for reelection; and Everett was his only appointment to USCMA. Recognizing its importance, Congress by special statute designated a ten-year term for him. After 1990, on numerous occasions Everett has returned to USCMA temporarily as a Senior Judge. His successor as Chief Judge, Eugene Sullivan, became the last presidential selection to that office. During Sullivan's term, Congress established a five-year tenure for the Chief Judge based on seniority. Ultimately, George Bush made three new appointments to USCMA, one of them to replace Everett.

[100] Ibid., undated. Carter's designation of Everett as Chief Judge was drafted on February 25, 1980, ten days after his nomination had been sent to the Hill, "to be submitted upon his confirmation by the Senate." CP, WHCF, Box FG-170, Folder FG 57A.

[101] Ibid., excerpt from Hearing, Senate Armed Services Committee, 96th Cong., 2nd sess., March 7, 1980, 39–40.

[102] Ibid., 41. Everett referred to a Supreme Court case, which he could not identify, where supposedly "they had ten opinions with nine justices . . . which obviously introduces some elements of uncertainty." Senator Levin responded that "I know the clerks are powerful; I didn't know they were that powerful." Ibid., 42.

completely at odds with the precedent of the Court. I think that it is important to maintain continuity and to be aware of precedent in rendering decisions."[103]

Even before the formal hearing, rumors concerning Everett's appointment had already dampened JAG enthusiasm for any radical changes to USCMA. Thus the Navy JAG noted that abolition of the Court was "too drastic a measure to overcome the more easily remedied faults. . . ."[104] Moreover, added Admiral C. E. McDowell, Siemer's proposed change "could result in the judiciary committees of the Congress becoming involved in military justice matters."[105] Finally, McDowell was aware that Article III judges usually held their appointments for life. Replete with his deficiencies, at least Fletcher's term was finite. One can easily understand why the thought of such a judge remaining on USCMA with indefinite tenure might well persuade the JAGs that minor change rather than radical transformation would be appropriate.

Major General George Prugh, recently retired as Army JAG, had been even more critical of Siemer's proposals. All too often, he noted, motivation for change "stems from disenchantment with the people involved, rather than the procedure itself."[106] In fact, Siemer's draft memorandum "simply does not make out a convincing need for the various remedies it considers." Can it be fairly said "that the Court has not properly done its job as Congress intended it to do? Before such a charge can be made there has to be a lot better justification evident than the weak arguments advanced in the [Rainbow book]."[107]

Promptly confirmed by the Senate, and immediately designated Chief Judge, Robinson Everett took the oath of office on April 16, 1980, almost thirty years after Harry Truman had signed the statute creating both the UCMJ and USCMA. Under his leadership, the Court reached out to the JAGs, emphasizing a commonality of justice rather than a clash of jurisdictions. Thus, his appointment signaled both the end of an era, and the advent of a new chapter in the Court's history. At some future date, I hope to chronicle its later developments. In the meantime however, the Everett selection provides an appropriate occasion from which to offer a final overview of USCMA's history during its first thirty years. As this study concludes, what can be said of this tribunal when measured both by its potential and performance?

[103] Ibid.

[104] USCMAP, Excerpt from Navy JAG publication, "Off the Record," August 15, 1979, 3. "I think the approach of abolishing the Court is like buying a new car when the old one only needs a tune-up."

[105] Ibid.

[106] George Prugh to Deanne Siemer, July 12, 1979, 1–2. Although General Prugh sent a copy of his letter to Fletcher, it could not be located in any USCMA files. I am grateful to Prugh for making it available to me, and hence to the Court for its history archive.

[107] Ibid., 3.

Epilogue

In 1951, Felix Larkin observed that the highlight of the Uniform Code of Military Justice was its new appellate procedure. It was intended, he emphasized, to resemble a civilian system, replete with appropriate counsel and civilian judges—"men of high caliber and judicial experience."[1] In 1949, Representative Philip Philbin had stated that "this Court will be completely detached from the military in every way. It is entirely disconnected with [*sic*] the Department of Defense . . . completely removed from any outside influences."[2] Similarly, Larkin and Edmund Morgan expected this new federal tribunal to take its place as an independent appellate court, with the perquisites, procedures, and stature of its sister institutions. In fact USCMA's history has been unlike any other federal appellate bench, and for a number of reasons that have been explored in this study, the results have been impressive as far as they go, yet at the same time both disappointing and a source of concern for the future. What kind of picture emerges of this Court? What are students, observers, and practitioners of military justice to make of its history? A few conclusions based on the preceding chapters may be appropriate here.

The very nature of USCMA's purpose, to serve—with few exceptions—as the final interpretor of *military* law was undercut from the beginning by the repeated emphasis on the unique *military* environment within which the Court operated. No other federal appellate bench has functioned both in the shadow of the huge defense establishment, and the Senate Armed Services Committee. Indeed, by keeping this tribunal under the jurisdiction of the SASC rather than the Senate Judiciary Committee, Congress has ensured that USCMA's future rests with a body for whom qualifications of legal ability and judicial distinction are secondary to political considerations and expediency. It is in no way intended as disrespect to the Armed Services Committee to point out that whatever its considerable contributions to the American military mission may be, careful and judicious screening of potential federal appellate judges is not one of them. Moreover, unlike the Judiciary Committee this panel has consistently declined to seek outside evaluation, such as ABA input, concerning qualifications of USCMA nominees.

While it certainly is to be expected that members of the Senate Judiciary Committee might inquire of judicial nominees concerning their judicial and constitutional philosophy, the Armed Services Committee rarely does so.

[1] See above, chapter 1, n. 8.

[2] AMJ, 231.

Given its purview, this fact although understandable remains unfortunate. Typically, its chair warned the first new USCMA judges in 1951—even before they took office—that "any abuse of the powers of this court will be disastrous to this Nation." Richard Russell emphasized that "this will indeed be a court of military justice, [and not] an agency that will be damaging to the observance of discipline in the armed services."[3]

Moreover, no other federal appellate tribunal has had to deal with a group of military lawyers, JAG officers who had been the principal operatives of the military justice system for more than a century before the Court's creation, and who under the new Code retained supervisory responsibility for it. The first three decades of USCMA's existence from 1950 to 1980 were characterized by serious conflicts between the Judge Advocates General and the Judges. Each time the JAGs sought to curb the influence or authority of the Court, either by limiting its jurisdiction, altering its composition, or by seeking congressional and/or civilian support to force a change in its decisions. The tension between the JAGs and the Court is a dominant theme in this volume, and one that has not yet been played out. In fact, it may never be resolved.

Finally, no other federal appellate tribunal has sought for so long with so little success to attain what its members believed so essential to judicial independence—life tenure. It can be argued, as Senator Wayne Morse did in 1950, that insisting that the new court be on a par with the United States Courts of Appeals while at the same time refusing to give its judges that security and tenure common to their federal counterparts was inconsistent.[4] It can further be asserted that absence of life tenure has diminished the stature due this federal Court, resulted in frequent turnover of its judges, unfortunate congressional lobbying for judicial candidates, and possible unwillingness of outstanding candidates to seek or accept appointment to its bench. Here, again, while the exercise of congressional patronage is commonplace, the key issue is how good the objects of such favor have been as USCMA judges.[5]

Although the jurists changed over the years between 1951 and 1975, the Court itself did not. The procedures put in place by Chief Judge Quinn who did not resign from the bench until 1975, and his first clerk Alfred Proulx, who served for more than twenty years, remained essentially the same. Also,

[3] See above, chapter 1, n. 79. Richard Russell saw no choice betweeen the need for discipline and the demand for justice. He believed that insistence on the former had to guide administration of the latter. After almost half a century of USCMA decisions, it can be said that emphasis on justice makes military discipline more effective.

[4] AMJ, 253.

[5] During the years included in this study, in terms of judicial distinction the two USCMA appointments most supported by congressional elements, William Darden and William Cook, were among the weakest in USCMA history.

while there were a few significant changes to the UCMJ in the Military Justice Act of 1968, they did not directly affect the Court or USCMA's relationship to the system. It was not until 1975 that Chief Judge Fletcher proposed a number of significant alterations in the way military justice had been administered.

Encouraged by those most responsible for his appointment to reinvigorate his Court, Fletcher's course of action resulted in controversy that involved clashing personalities, antagonism between judges and JAGs, and vigorous disagreement over judicial doctrine. When the smoke cleared, he had been replaced as Chief Judge, and the opportunity for major reforms in military justice had been lost—an occasion that at this writing has not reoccurred. For what could have been, as well for the denouement that actually took place, the Fletcher years remain tragic in their long-term institutional results.

Given the level of bitterness that existed between Fletcher and the JAGs by 1979, it is ironic that any of his proposals for judicial reform came to pass. Seized upon by his severest critics, the controversies he engendered may well have been the catalyst for the changes he sought. The convening authority can no longer overrule trial judges. This official has also lost the power to select both the judge and counsel in a court-martial. Every service now has a separate appellate defense division. Certain USCMA decisions may now be appealed to the Supreme Court, and the number of its judges has been increased from three to five.

Yet, many of his suggestions failed to become law, with unfortunate results for military justice. "For administrative purposes only," USCMA is still linked to the Defense Department. The two "catch-all" articles in the UCMJ remain unchanged.[6] The quest for intermediate military appellate judges to have specific terms of office has gone unheeded, random selection of court members by lot rather than appointment by the convening authority still is rare, if practiced at all. Most important, the legitimacy and parameters of USCMA supervisory jurisdiction over military justice remains uncertain. Senior military justice officials continue to resist both civilian involvement and input in the field, and effective civilian oversight of military justice by both USCMA and Congress has diminished in the years since Fletcher's term as Chief Judge.

In retrospect, the fate of Albert Fletcher's proposals for reform stands as a stark testament to the limits of the judicial function. Wherein, one might ask, beyond the USCMJ does USCMA authority exist? How can it enforce its decisions? What moral force attaches to its pronouncements? When the Court speaks in several separate voices, as it often did between 1975 and 1980, how can it achieve the tone, eloquence, and insights so vital for judicial/moral authority? It may be that the net effect of the Fletcher era ulti-

[6] Ibid., 4, n. 3.

mately was to retard the process of reform and embolden the forces of reaction, a development aided by the election of three consecutive conservative administrations between 1980 and 1992.

There is no doubt that USCMA has made a real difference in military justice since 1951. As indicated in this volume, to a greater extent than ever before the Court linked the Bill of Rights to military justice, sought to insulate the courts-martial from improper influence, and worked to insure the independence of the military judge, albeit with limited success. In spite of these dramatic contributions, however, its ultimate performance has not matched its potential. Traditionally and unnecessarily clothed with a reputation for the arcane, contemporary appellate military justice still suffers from a lack of critical civilian scrutiny, constructive interplay with civilian jurisprudence, an effective and functioning bar, and finally from a jurisprudence that—in the post-Fletcher era—increasingly has tended to benefit the prosecution. While continuation of USCMA as a federal tribunal seems certain, its effectiveness cannot be taken for granted.

Ultimately, much will depend on how all parties—Congress, the military establishment, the judges, and the bar—perceive the Court and its high function. Homer Ferguson and Albert Fletcher saw their roles in very different terms than did George Latimer, William Darden, William Cook, or even Senator Richard Russell. Given both the legacy of Fletcher's years, and the selection since then of less aggressive jurists, to some extent USCMA has retreated. On the other hand, this more conservative tendency since 1980 is not necessarily permanent. Judicial holdings are not carved in stone, and what is dissent today may well become doctrine tomorrow. Perhaps the history of its Court since 1950 will embolden USCMA judges, to paraphrase George Bernard Shaw, to see military justice not as it is and ask "why?" but to see the process for what it can become, and ask "why not?"

Appendix

Judges of the U.S. Court of Military Appeals, 1951–1980

Name	*Party*	*State*	*Active Service*	*years*
Robert E. Quinn	D	RI	1951–1975	24
George W. Latimer	R	UT	1951–1961	10
Paul W. Brosman	D	LA	1951–1955	4
Homer Ferguson	R	MI	1956–1976	20
Paul J. Kilday	D	TX	1961–1968	7
William H. Darden	D	GA	1968–1973	5
Robert M. Duncan	R	OH	1971–1974	3
William H. Cook	R	IL	1974–1984	10
Albert Fletcher, Jr.	R	KS	1975–1985	10
Matthew J. Perry	D	SC	1976–1979	3
Robinson O. Everett	D	NC	1980–1992	12

Bibliography

(See also footnotes in this volume)

Unpublished Materials

American Legion Hearings, May 1956, typed transcript, USCMAP files
Annual Court Report Files, 1951–1980, USCMA Clerk's Office
Reva Beck Bosone Papers, University of Utah Library
Chronological Files, 1951–1969, USCMA Clerk's Office
Jimmy Carter Papers, Carter Presidential Library
John Cooke Materials, USCMAP Files
Dwight D. Eisenhower Papers, Eisenhower Presidential Library
Samuel Ervin, Jr., Papers, Southern Historical Collections, University of North Carolina
Homer Ferguson Papers, Bentley Library, University of Michigan
Gerald Ford Papers, Ford Presidential Library
Lyndon B. Johnson Papers, Johnson Presidential Library
Felix Larkin Materials, USCMAP Files
George Latimer Papers, USCMAP Files
Legislative History of the Military Justice Act of 1968, USCMAP Files
Life Tenure Files, USCMAP
William Miller Materials, USCMAP Files
Edmund Morgan Papers, Special Collections, Vanderbilt University
Richard Nixon Papers, Nixon Project, Washington, D.C.
Robert Quinn Papers, USCMAP Files
Robert Quinn, *Oral History*, 1972. Providence College Library, Special Collections
Deanne Siemer Materials, USCMAP Files
Speech File, USCMAP
Harry S. Truman Papers, Truman Presidential Library

Government Documents

Full Committee Consideration of H.R. 3179, Armed Services Committee, 88th Cong., 1st sess., 1963.
Hearing Before the Committee on Armed Services of the United States Senate: Nomination of Albert Fletcher, Jr., 94th Cong., 1st sess., 1975.
Hearings Before the Subcommittee of the Committee on Appropriations on H.R. 5969, part 1, 83rd Cong., 1st sess., 1953.
Hearings Before the Subcommittee of the Armed Services Committee on H.R. 6583, 84th Cong., 1st sess., 1956.
Hearings Before the Subcommittee on Constitutional Rights of the Committee on the Judiciary, U.S. Senate, 87th Cong., 2nd sess., 1962.
Hearings Before Subcommittee No. 1 of the Armed Services Committee on H.R. 3179, 88th Cong., 1st sess., 1963.

Joint Hearing Before the Subcommittee on Constitutional Rights of the Committee on the Judiciary and a Special Committee of the Committee on Armed Services, U.S. Senate, 89th Cong., 2nd sess., 1966.

Senate Armed Services Committee: *Nominations to the Court of Military Appeals, June 16, 1951*. SRrt-T. 34. (Typed transcript in Senate Library.)

Uniform Code of Military Justice, Text, References and Commentary, Washington, D.C., 1949.

United States Army, *Oral History Program. Interview, Major General Kenneth Hodson*, Military History Institute.

———, *Oral History Program, Interview, Major General George Prugh*, Military History Institute.

———, *Report to Honorable Wilber M. Brucker, Secretary of the Army*, by The Committee on the Uniform Code of Military Justice, Good Order and Discipline in the Army. Washington, D.C. 1960 (The Powell Report).

U.S. Congress, *Congressional Record*, v. 109, 1963.

———, v. 113, 1967.

Periodicals

Avins, Alfred. "New Light on the Legislative History of Desertion Through Fraudulent Enlistment: The Decline of the United States Court of Military Appeals." *Minnesota Law Review* 46 (1961), 69–116.

Benson, Daniel. "The United States Court of Military Appeals." *Texas Tech Law Review* 3 (1971), 1–21.

Cooke, John S. "Recent Developments in the Wake of United States v. Booker. *Army Lawyer* 71 (1978), 4–13.

——— "The United States Court of Military Appeals, 1975–77: Judicializing the Military Justice System." *Military Law Review* 76 (1977), 43–163.

——— "United States v. Ezell: Is the Commander a Magistrate? Maybe." *Army Lawyer* 80 (1979), 9–20.

Cooper, Norman. "The Military Judge." *Army Lawyer* 44 (1976), 1–5.

———, and Cooke, John. "Military Justice: Marching to a Different Drumbeat." *American Bar Association Journal* 64 (1978), 1363–65.

Cox, Walter T, III. "The Army, the Courts, and the Constitution: The Evolution of Military Justice." *Military Law Review* 118 (1987), 1–30.

Douglass, John. "The Judicialization of Military Courts." *Hastings Law Journal* 22 (1971), 213–35.

Droddy, J. D. "King Richard to Solorio: The Historical and Constitutional Bases for Court-Martial Jurisdiction in Criminal Cases." *Air Force Law Review* 30 (1989), 91–133.

Everett, Robinson O. "O'Callahan v. Parker—Milestone or Millstone in Military Justice?" *Duke Law review* 69 (1969), 853–96.

——— "Specified Issues in the United States Court of Military Appeals: A Rationale," *Military Law Review* 123 (1989), 1–7.

Fidell, Eugene R. "If a Tree Falls in the Forest . . . ; Publication and Digesting Policies and the Potential Contribution of Military Courts to American Law." *JAG Journal* 32 (1982), 1–29.

——— "Judicial Review of Presidential Rulemaking Under Article 36: The Sleeping Giant Stirs." *Military Law Reporter* 4 (1976), 6049–59.

——— "Judicial Tenure Under the Uniform Code of Military Justice." *Federal Bar News & Journal* 31 (1984), 327–32.

——— "Military Justice: The Bar's Concern." *American Bar Association Journal* 67 (1981), 1280–82.

——— "The Culture of Change in Military Law." *Military Law Review* 126 (1989), 125–32.

——— "The Specification of Appellate Issues by the United States Court of Military Appeals." *JAG Journal* 31 (1980), 99–120.

——— "The Summary Court-Martial: A Proposal." *Harvard Journal on Legislation* 8 (1971) 571–7.

Fidell, Eugene R., and Greenhouse, Linda. "A Roving Commission: Specified Issues and the Function of the United States Court of Military Appeals," *Military Law Review* 122 (1988), 117–48.

"Free Speech in the Military." *New York University Law Review* 53 (1978), 1102–23.

Gasch, Oliver. "Who Is Out of Step?" *Army Lawyer* 66 (1978), 1–9.

Griswold, Erwin. "Appellate Advocacy." *Army Lawyer* 3 (1973), 14.

Hansen, Donald W. "Judicial Functions of the Commander." *Military Law Review* 41 (1968), 1–54.

Hodson, Kenneth. "Courts-Martial and the Commander." *San Diego Law Review* 10 (1972), 51–71.

——— "The Military Justice Act." *Judge Advocate Journal* 47 (1970), 31–38.

Illinois State Journal-Register, October 27, 1990, 24.

Landman, Bernard Jr., "One Year of the Uniform Code of Military Justice: A Report of Progress." *Stanford Law Review* 4 (1952), 491–508.

Lurie, Jonathan. "Military Justice 50 Years After Nuremberg: Some Reflections on Appearance v. Reality." *Military Law Review* 149 (1996), 178–86.

———"Presidential Appointments and Aspiring Appointees: Selections to the U.S. Court of Military Appeals 1951–1958." *Wake Forest Law Review* 29 (1994), 521–56.

Miller, Joel. "Three is Not Enough: Some Tentative Thoughts on the Number of Judges on the United States Court of Military Appeals." *Army Lawyer* 45 (1976), 11–14.

Note. "Can Military Trials Be Fair? Command Influence over Courts-Martial." *Stanford Law Review* 2 (1950), 547–58.

Page, William Herbert. "Military Law—A Study in Comparative Law." *Harvard Law Review* 32 (1919), 349–73.

Providence Daily Journal, 1941, 1946, 1960.

Reader's Digest, 1951.

Schiesser, Charles, and Benson, Daniel. "A Proposal to Make Courts-Martial Courts: The Removal of Commanders From Military Justice." *Texas Tech Law Review* 7 (1976), 559–600.

Schleuter, David. "Personal Jurisdiction . . .Whither Russo, Catlow, and Brown?" *Army Lawyer* 84 (1979), 3–13.

Sherman, Edward. "Congressional Proposals for Reform of Military Law." *American Criminal law Review* 10 (1971), 25–49.

Sherman, Edward. "The Civilianization of Military Law." *Maine Law Review* 22 (1970), 3–103.

——— "The Military Court and Servicemen's First Amendment Rights." *Hastings Law Journal* 22 (1971), 325–73.

Silliman, Scott, "The Supreme Court and Its Impact on the Court of Military Appeals." *Air Force Law Review* 18 (1976), 81–93.

Smith, Matthew. "The Real McCoy in the Bloodless Revolution of 1935." *Rhode Island History* 32 (1973), 67–85.

Thorne, Gary. "The Court of Military Appeals and Its Supervisory Authority." *Army Lawyer* 49 (1977), 17–21.

Wacker, Daniel. "The 'Unreliable' Court-Martial Conviction: Supervisory Relief Under the All Writs Act from the United States Court of Military Appeals." *Military Law Review* 100 (1975), 609–59.

West, Luther C. "A History of Command Influence on the Military Judicial System." *UCLA Law Review* 18 (1970), 1–156.

Wiener, Frederic Bernays. "American Military Law in the Light of the First Mutiny Act's Tricentennial." *Military Law Review* 126 (1989), 1–88.

White, Robert J. "The Background and the Problem." *St. John's Law Review* (1961), 197–214.

Willis, John T. "The United States Court of Military Appeals—Born Again." *Indiana Law Journal* 52 (1976), 151–66.

Books

Army Lawyer: A History of the Judge Advocate General's Corps, 1775–1975. Washington, D.C.: Government Printing Office, 1975.

Chafee, Zechariah Jr. *State House versus Pent House*. Providence: The Booke Shop, 1937.

Clopton, Beverly. *Her Honor the Judge*. Ames: Iowa State University Press, 1980.

Feld, Benjamin R. *The United States Court of Military Appeals: A Study of the Origins and Early Development of the First Civilian Tribunal for Direct Review of Courts-Martial, 1951–1959*. Unpub. diss., Georgetown University, 1960.

Fidell, Eugene R. *Guide to the Rules of Practice and Procedure for the United States Court of Appeals for the Armed Forces*. 7th ed., Washington, D.C.: National Institute of Military Justice, 1996.

Gilligan Francis, and Lederer, Frederic. *Court-Martial Procedure*. Charlottesville: Michie Co., 1991 and 1995 Supp.

Hersh, Seymour. *Cover-Up: The Army's Secret Investigation of the Massacre at My Lai 4*. New York: Random House, 1972.

——— *My Lai 4: A Report on the Massacre and Its Aftermath*. New York: Vintage Books, 1970.

Hodgson, Godfrey. *The Colonel: The Life and Wars of Henry Stimson, 1867–1950*. New York: Alfred A. Knopf, 1990.

Hoopes, Townsend, and Brinkley, Douglas. *Driven Patriot*. New York: Alfred A. Knopf, 1992.

Hughes, Emmet John. *The Ordeal of Power*. New York: Atheneum, 1963.

Karnow, Stanley. *Vietnam: A History*. New York: Penguin Books, 1991.

Lurie, Jonathan. *Arming Military Justice: Vol. 1, The Origins of the United States Court of Military Appeals, 1775–1950*. Princeton: Princeton University Press, 1992.

Manchester, William. *American Ceasar*. Boston: Little, Brown and Co., 1978.

Meador, Daniel J. *Criminal Appeals: English Practices and American Reforms*. Charlottesville: University Press of Virginia, 1973.

Moyer, Homer F., Jr. *Justice and the Military*. Washington, D.C.: Public Law Education Institute, 1972.

White, G. Edward. *Warren: A Public Life*. New York: Oxford University Press, 1982.

Index

Note: Italicized page numbers refer to photographs.